The
Seven
Laws of
the Learner

Bruce Wilkinson

Multnomah Books®
Published in cooperation with Walk Thru the Bible Ministries, Inc.

THE 7 LAWS OF THE LEARNER
published by Multnomah Books

© 1992 by Bruce Wilkinson
in cooperation with Walk Thru the Bible Ministries, Inc.,
4201 N. Peachtree Road, Atlanta, GA 30341

International Standard Book Number: 978-1-59052-452-7

Cover image by David Muir/Masterfile
Interior design and typeset by Katherine Lloyd, The DESK

Italics in Scripture quotations are the author's emphasis.
Scripture quotations are from:
The Holy Bible, New King James Version
© 1984 by Thomas Nelson, Inc.

Published in the United States by WaterBrook Multnomah, an imprint of the
Crown Publishing Group, a division of Random House Inc., New York.

MULTNOMAH and its mountain colophon are registered trademarks
of Random House Inc.

Printed in the United States of America

For information:
MULTNOMAH BOOKS
12265 ORACLE BOULEVARD, SUITE 200
COLORADO SPRINGS, CO 80921

09 10—35 34 33 32 31

Contents

Introduction 5

Law One: The Law of the Learner

1. Learner Mindset, Model, and Maxims 13
2. Learner Method and Maximizers 44

Law Two: The Law of Expectation

3. Expectation Mindset, Model, and Maxims 79
4. Expectation Method and Maximizers 109

Law Three: The Law of Application

5. Application Mindset, Model, and Maxims 137
6. Application Method and Maximizers 165

Law Four: The Law of Retention

7. Retention Mindset, Model, and Maxims 205
8. Retention Method and Maximizers 234

Law Five: The Law of Need

9. Need Mindset, Model, and Maxims 269
10. Need Method and Maximizers 307

Law Six: The Law of Equipping

11. Equipping Mindset, Model, and Maxims 345
12. Equipping Method and Maximizers 380

Law Seven: The Law of Revival

13. Revival Mindset, Model, and Maxims 417
14. Revival Method and Maximizers 449

Epilogue 487
Notes 491

Introduction

T his may sound a bit unusual, but this book is the result of ten years of repentance. My repentance.

Though I had been teaching and preaching all my life, I found to my utter surprise and dismay that much of my philosophy and practice of communication had been wrong. Incredibly wrong. Tragically misdirected.

So through searching the Scriptures and studying master teachers and communicators, I began to repent and change. This book is a distillation of that personal pilgrimage and reveals the revolution that has occurred first in my thinking and eventually in my teaching.

To repent means to change one's mind. In modern terms, we call it a *paradigm shift*, which means a new frame of reference or pattern of thinking. Seven times I stumbled upon concepts in the Bible that were exactly the opposite of what I had thought.

Much has been written about teaching that is Christian, but even a brief survey of the material quickly shows that the literature focuses upon the *content* of what is taught rather than the *communication* of how it is taught. Certainly the basis of all life change is the truth which sets one free, but how that truth is communicated has a great deal to do with how much freedom is enjoyed.

Although this book frequently discusses the content, it primarily focuses upon what the teacher does to teach that content to the students. This book is full of content—but the teaching process doesn't actually begin until the teacher begins to teach the students this content. The teacher is the living link between the content and the class, and how he or she accomplishes that is the heart of teaching.

That process of successfully passing on to the next generation the desired content, character, and conduct is the key responsibility of the teacher. Students come to us needing "to know" or "to be" or "to do," and it is our responsibility to enable them.

Because you are reading this introduction, I know you care about that process and are searching for ways to become more effective as a teacher or preacher or even parent—for we all teach, all of the time.

It's been an amazing journey of discovery, traveling around the world and teaching leaders, pastors, businessmen, teachers, and parents. And one thing that I've seen everywhere: If a teacher is boring back home, he'll be even more boring halfway around the world. If a teacher is irrelevant on the home court, he'll be even more irrelevant on the away court.

But if a teacher has mastered the teaching-learning process, you can give her any subject in any country to any audience and, with a suitable amount of preparation, she can be incredibly effective.

Some people have been able—with years of practice—to master the skill of boredom. Almost without effort they can drive an audience to slumber. Others hit the nail on the head time after time. Wherever they are and whatever they teach, lasting life change takes place. They love teaching and they help others love learning.

How do they do it? They have mastered the universal laws of teaching. Principles as universal as gravity. Principles that work irrespective of subject, speaker, students, or society.

The universals of life are incredibly powerful. Once you discover them and know how to work in cooperation with them, you can use them to accomplish your goals. Every time. Every place. Every one.

Are you interested in the universals that govern teaching and learning? Then this book is for you.

You are about to discover seven universal laws, with examples on almost every page to picture how they actually work in your life. Like the tens of thousands who have learned these laws before you, you'll find they are immediately usable. I mean, right at the moment you read or hear them. So many people have told me they went home that very night and rewrote their lessons for the next day. And they didn't wonder what to do; they *knew* what to do. We taught them, they learned it, and then they did it.

We call it teaching for life change. Unless you are highly unusual, before you have finished this book, you're going to think differently about teaching in far-reaching ways.

I'll never forget the long letter I received from a lady who inspired her pastor to attend the *7 Laws of the Learner* conference because their church was dying from an overdose of boredom and irrelevancy. She said the very next sermon was like it came from a different man. It was practical, life changing, interesting, biblical—and so relevant that she felt he had all of a sudden come to understand the needs of the church.

Later I received another letter, this one from the pastor. He was so thankful that the Lord had enabled him to learn the truth about teaching and preaching. For the first time in his long ministry, the people were really changing. For good. So he wrote to thank me. Those kinds of letters I treasure forever.

Maybe someday, if you allow these universal principles to revolutionize your teaching, I may receive a note postmarked from your neighborhood.

But right now, let me explain how to get the most out of this book.

How the Book Is Organized

The seven laws are discussed in two chapters each. The first of the chapters aims at changing your beliefs about teaching, and the second aims at changing your behavior as a teacher. The first, your attitude; the second, your actions. The first, your philosophy; the second, your practice.

Ultimately what we all do is dependent upon what we think. The Bible states this simply: "For as he thinks in his heart, so is he." Therefore, if the way we think can be changed, the way we live will be changed.

The goal of the first chapter on each law is to create a powerful paradigm shift in your thinking—a repentance to the biblical way of thinking.

The goal of the second chapter on each law is to equip you with an effective method and approach to instantly use what you've learned the very next time you teach—a renewal in your teaching process.

The seven laws are independent of one another and are stand-alone units. They have been arranged, however, in the most logical order for maximum helpfulness. If you have a need or interest in a specific law, then you may desire to jump ahead to the one that suits you best at this time.

If you want to learn how to *speed-teach* your students twice the content in half the time, then the Law of Retention is for you. Turn to chapter 7 and shift into fourth gear as you discover the four levels of mastery teaching that God revealed to Moses.

If you want to learn how to *help your students blossom* into everything they should become, then the Law of Expectation is for you. Turn to chapter 3 and watch your students flourish like never before.

If you want to learn how to *teach for life change* so that your students actually become different people and experience lasting change, then the Law of Application is for you. Turn to chapter 5 and watch your students begin to experience real, positive change almost immediately.

If you want to learn how to *motivate your students* so that they will want to come to class and learn what you are teaching, then the Law of Need is for you. Turn to chapter 9 and discover the five steps Christ used to motivate His students. They'll work for you every time.

If you want to *rekindle your flame for teaching* so that you enjoy teaching the way that you used to, then the Law of the Learner is for you. Turn to chapter 1 and discover the shocking meaning behind the words *teach* and *learn* from the Bible's perspective.

If you want to learn how to *teach a skill* to your students, from public speaking to tennis to witnessing that really works, even for the slow learners, then the Law of Equipping is for you. Turn to chapter 11 and learn the five steps that every successful trainer uses, including Jesus Christ when He trained His top dozen leaders.

If you want to learn how to lead your students to *walk with God* and flourish spiritually, then the Law of Revival is for you. Turn to chapter 13 and learn the process that a teacher used on King David to bring him back to the Lord. Use them the next time your heart breaks over a wayward student.

ONE LAST WORD BEFORE YOU BEGIN

I don't think I'll ever forget him as long as I live. He was a retired teacher who attended a *7 Laws of the Learner* seminar just because he was bored—and his teaching career was over. He came up after the conference with tears in his eyes. He had undergone a wrenching three days of repentance in his own heart as he had seen how far from the biblical mark his own teaching had been.

A year later I returned to the same area for another *7 Laws of the Learner* seminar. The first person who came striding up was this retired teacher. But this time his step had purpose and his eyes had sparkle. He could hardly contain himself when he told me what had happened. Neither could I.

He told me that when he left the conference last year he had been so deeply moved that he wanted another chance to teach "the real way." But he couldn't think how that could ever happen, so he began to ask God to give him one more chance in the classroom. He wanted to find out for himself what these seven laws of the learner could really do.

Just a few short days passed when the principal from the school where he had taught called him. One of the teachers had become very sick, and the principal wondered if he would come out of retirement and teach for one more year!

And then he took out a folded blue piece of paper from his coat pocket. "This paper tells it all," he said with a smile. Every one of the high school classes he taught were listed and beneath them how many students were earning As, Bs, Cs, Ds, and Fs when he started. They weren't very good. Not many As or Bs and a lot grouped at the failing end. But then he unfolded the paper which showed the grades as they are now. They were almost exactly reversed! Instead of the bulk of the grades being Ds and Fs, they were As and Bs.

Dramatic.

His eyes brimmed with tears of joy as he shared story after story of students who had turned around as he caused them to learn, caused them to blossom into their fullest potential, applied the lessons where they lived, taught the facts through speed-teaching, motivated them when they became disinterested or apathetic, equipped them to competence, and even worked with these secular students inside and outside of the classroom to build character and values.

The announcements were almost over and the conference host was nodding at me. It was time to start the conference. But my heart was riveted by this incredible story from this retired teacher. He refolded that blue sheet of paper, placed it in my hands, and said, "Now go share these revolutionary principles with this group of teachers—and next year there will be hundreds of blue sheets just like mine!"

Take out your blue sheets, my friend, and hold on as we enjoy together this wonderful pilgrimage of learning we call *The 7 Laws of the Learner.*

LAW ONE

The Law
of the Learner

—

CHAPTER ONE

Learner

Mindset, Model, and Maxims

The first time I heard him teach, I said to myself, *I want to study under that man!* His name was Howard G. Hendricks, and I entered seminary to learn everything I could from this master teacher. I wanted to learn not only *what* he taught but also *how* he taught.

During my four years of graduate study, I listened to Dr. Hendricks for more than 350 hours and always left his class instructed, challenged, and a step closer to God. By the time I was a senior, I began to wonder if "Prof" even understood the word *boring*.

After studying how he taught for four years, I discovered he followed a basic style. About three minutes before class began, his right foot began to bounce underneath the old oak desk. At the precise moment the second hand swept past twelve he raised his right forefinger into the air, announced "Ladies and gentlemen…" and delivered an opening one-liner that was so stimulating all of us couldn't help but copy it down. After three to four minutes he told his first joke. Eight to ten minutes into the class he would inevitably rise from his desk and draw a graph or chart on the whiteboard. Always the blue pen first. Then the purple. And always with that unique squiggly underline for emphasis. His rhythm was unmistakable. And it worked—just ask any of the thousands who have studied under him.

During my last year of seminary I decided to give Dr. Hendricks a test. I wanted to see what this master teacher would do if one of his students would not—no matter what—pay attention in his class. I sat in the back right-hand corner of the room, next to the only window, and decided to gaze out that window the entire class session. Since there were only thirty students in the class, he was sure to notice. I took off my watch and started timing. What would he do if he couldn't get my attention?

As expected, he started off with a bang and delivered his usual one-liner. Although my hand began to tremble, I forced myself not to record the line. From the corner of my eye I could see that he noticed immediately I wasn't paying attention. He broke tradition and in the first minute told a joke—totally out of context. If I laughed he would immediately know I was listening, so I discreetly put my hand over my mouth and continued staring out that window.

As the two-minute mark passed, he got up from his chair and started drawing on the board—much too early. He again noticed that I wasn't taking notes, and he stopped right in the middle of his chart and didn't even finish it.

He put the pen down and walked to the corner of the room in order to look down the aisle at me, trying to make eye contact. Sweat beaded on my brow, but the seconds continued ticking by. I wasn't going to pay attention.

Finally, he broke. The master teacher almost leaped down the aisle and yelled, "Wilkinson, what on earth are you looking at outside that window?!"

With a sheepish glance, I turned around and said, "Nothing, Prof. Sorry." I looked down at my watch to determine his grade. Only three minutes and thirty-seven seconds had passed! Incredible. His tolerance for one student not paying attention was limited to 217 seconds.

With that remarkable experience freshly imprinted on my mind, I walked down the hall into the next class with a different professor. Talk about a contrast. One side of the room was filled by students who never paid attention but did their homework for another class. This teacher, however, didn't seem bothered; he just turned and lectured to the students sitting on the other side. His mindset was, *It's not my problem if you don't want to learn.*

What a difference. One teacher could tolerate for only a few seconds one student not learning what he was teaching, and the other didn't seem to care for the whole semester!

How would you have fared on that quiz with one of your students looking out the window? *Would* you have cared? Would the clock still be ticking?

Dr. Hendricks believed that, as the teacher, he was the one responsible for my learning. By contrast, the second teacher thought he was responsible only to cover the material, regardless of whether anyone learned.

LEARNER MINDSET

What an extraordinary example of the heart of the Law of the Learner. Dr. Hendricks believed that, as my teacher, he was the one responsible for my learning. He felt responsible, and if I wasn't learning he did whatever it took—changed his lesson plan, his style, told an irrelevant joke, even ran down the aisle and confronted me—to get my attention.

This foundational attitude lies at the very heart of *The 7 Laws of the Learner.* In a sense, all of the laws are like a row of dominoes—this first one ultimately controls all the dominoes that follow.

Every master teacher I know shares the mindset that it is his or her responsibility to cause the student to learn. But do you know what the prevailing mindset is in the preaching and teaching community today? A tragic divorce has occurred: Teachers have separated themselves from their students and redefined teaching as *what the teacher says* rather than *what the student learns.*

Teachers have redefined teaching as "the coherent speaking of an adult located at the head of the class to a passive gathering of students." They believe their primary responsibility is to cover the material in an organized manner.

They think about teaching as what they do—their focus is upon themselves. Many teachers cover their material and leave the room thinking they have taught. But if you gave their students a pop quiz, you would find out they hardly learned a thing. The divorce between teaching and learning is tragic and is at the root of many of our educational woes.

Dr. Hendricks modeled a revolutionary mindset. He saw teaching as not what *he* did but what *his students* did. His focus was not upon himself but was upon his students. Since that student looking out the window was not learning, Dr. Hendricks realized he was therefore unable to teach. That's why he stopped delivering his content and ran down the aisle!

Can you sense what difference it would make in your life and the lives of your students if you joined the ranks of Dr. Hendricks?

We've been asking people wherever we travel how they would define the responsibilities of a teacher. Over and over again they say, "To teach the facts," or "To cover the material," or "To complete the lesson plan." The focus of all these definitions is upon *anything but* the student's learning!

Somehow we think teaching is talking. If I come to the class and go through my notes and get you to laugh a couple of times, and you copy down my notes and maybe ask one or two questions, then I have taught you.

No, that's not teaching. True biblical teaching doesn't take place unless the students have learned. If they haven't learned, I haven't taught.

What does the Bible mean by "teach" and what does it mean by "learn"? Does God divorce teaching from learning? Let's look at a couple of verses out of Deuteronomy that are very similar but have a different focus. One focuses on teaching, the other on learning.

And Moses called all Israel, and said to them: "Hear, O Israel, the statutes and judgments which I speak in your hearing today, that you may *learn* them and be careful to observe them." (Deuteronomy 5:1)

What does it mean to *learn*?

"Now, O Israel, listen to the statutes and the judgments which I *teach* you to observe, that you may live, and go in and possess the land which the LORD God of your fathers is giving you." (Deuteronomy 4:1)

What does it mean to *teach*? How are these two concepts—learning and teaching—related? Are they as divorced from each other as we have come to believe?

In order to grasp the full meaning of these words, let's investigate the terms in the original Hebrew. The word *learn* in 5:1 is וּלְמַדְתֶּם, and *teach* in 4:1 is מְלַמֵּד. When the prefix and the suffix are taken off of *learn,* all that remains is the root Hebrew word לָמַד. When the prefix and the suffix are taken off of *teach,* all that remains is the Hebrew root לָמַד.

It's the same word! That's right, the *same* Hebrew word means to learn and to teach. Do you realize the significance of that? We can't separate teaching from learning. They are married; they are one. Somehow and in some way, what the teacher does and what the student does must be inextricably related.

There is further insight into this Hebrew word for *teach* and *learn*. The root means "learn," but when you alter it and put it into another stem called the Piel, it changes the meaning to "teach."

According to Hebrew grammar, the fundamental idea of the Piel is to "busy oneself eagerly with the action indicated by the stem." What's the stem? "To learn." To teach, therefore, means to busy oneself eagerly with the student's learning. It also means "to urge," "to cause others to do," and "an eager pursuit of an action."

Do you see how the Bible's mindset is the opposite of the common mindset of today's teacher? The Bible says that teaching means "causing learning." This is the heart of the Law of the Learner. No longer can you or I consider teaching merely as something the teacher does in the front of the class. Teaching is what the teacher does in the student. How do you know if you are a great teacher? *By what your students learn.* That's why Dr. Hendricks stopped what he was doing and ran down that aisle to challenge me. He knew that because I wasn't learning, he wasn't teaching.

Can you imagine what would happen in classrooms across the country if teachers returned to their rightful heritage? If they walked down the aisles, not with their outlines and notes, but with their students? If they vowed to be fully obedient to the biblical mandate of *causing* them to learn? It would start a revolution. Learning would once again soar, discipline would return, and students would start to love learning instead of hating school.

The Law of the Learner is illustrated by this diagram. The left box represents the "speaker" or "communicator." The center box is the "subject" or "content." And the right box represents the "student" or "class."

LEARNER MODEL

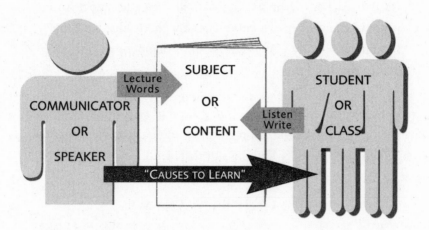

The two small arrows in this model represent the actions of the teacher or the student. Normally, the teacher focuses on the subject—"lectures" and speaks the "words," whereas the student "listens" and "writes" those words. Notice both of their points of attention: It's on the process of covering the material. And what often occurs is a thorough lack of learning. Students are free to move their minds into neutral with only their pencils in gear and all too often slide into the *pit of passivity*.

The preferred mindset requires the teacher to refocus attention from the subject to the student. This is represented by the lower arrow pointing from the teacher to the student with the words "causes to learn."

One of the most striking quotes I have ever read was from a frustrated inner-city father speaking of the school system's dramatic failure to cause his daughter to learn:

You people operate a monopoly like the telephone company. I got no choice where I send my child to school. I can only go where it's free. And she's not learning.

That's your responsibility. It's the principal's responsibility. It's the teacher's responsibility that she's not learning. And when you fail, when everybody fails my child, what happens? Nothing. Nobody gets fired. Nothing happens to nobody except my child.[1]

How tragic, but how true! *The 7 Laws of the Learner* is written to enable you to turn this situation around—to teach so effectively that no one would ever consider looking out that window.

LEARNER MAXIMS

This second section, introducing the *maxims*, continues to develop the main concept introduced in the *mindset* and *model*. In order to clarify and expand your understanding, the "big idea" under consideration is investigated from a number of different angles and perspectives. A maxim is a brief statement of a general principle or truth, and therefore each of the maxims that follow reflects a different facet of "cause to learn." By the end of this section, you should much more fully grasp the greater meaning and significance of what it really means to "cause to learn." The deeper and fuller your understanding, the easier it will be for you to use this truth in your own teaching.

Maxim 1: Teachers are responsible for causing students to learn.

It was a once-in-a-lifetime opportunity to conduct an experiment. It was my first class on my first day of my first year of teaching college. My slate was clean and my reputation as yet unformed. My students had no way to know what to expect.

Class started and I began teaching the way I had been taught by most of my teachers. You know, the traditional outline with main points and subpoints. The students dutifully took notes. After about twenty-five minutes, I said to my trusting class, "Please put away your papers. It's time for a test." You could almost hear their hearts stop in unison. They were freshmen, and this was their first class. When I announced a test—on the first day—their world almost came to an end.

Finally the deafening silence was broken by a courageous girl in the back row: "But sir, we haven't even had a chance to study this yet."

"I know, but let's see how you do," I said.

I offered no explanation. (It would have ruined my experiment.) There was a rattling of notebooks as they dug for paper. Then it got real quiet. I asked a few questions from the twenty-five minutes of "teaching" I had just completed.

All but a couple of students failed. Royally. Tension was heavy, and I could read the glances that shot across the room: *I'm transferring out of this guy's class!*

Then the girl in the back row raised her hand again. It was obvious she was used to getting As. "You can't count that!" she protested.

"Why not?"

"It's not fair. We didn't have a chance to learn it!"

"So how did you do on the test?"

She looked down and said, "Sixty percent."

"What am I?" I asked.

"The teacher."

"And what's the teacher supposed to do? Teach the class, right?" I paused and smiled. "If I'm the teacher and I'm the one who is supposed to teach you the material, then how did I do so far? What grade would you give me?"

Their faces said they were bursting to tell me.

"Young lady, if your test score revealed how effectively I taught you today, what grade would you give me?"

By now, no one was breathing. Everything in this young lady wanted to tell me, but she didn't know if she should. So I told her.

"Your grade is my grade," I said. "What you did or did not learn is dependent upon how I did as your teacher. So your grade of 60 percent designates me as a teacher who failed in his job. I failed to cause you to learn. Give me an F!"

The class was stunned.

I took off my coat, loosened my tie, and continued. "Now, why are you paying this college all this tuition and not expecting me to do my job? How come I can teach for thirty minutes and have the whole class not learn anything? I thought my job was to lead you to learn!"

They wanted to nod. Some wanted to cheer—this was starting to make sense. "From now on, when you come to this class, I'll take the responsibility for your learning. If you'll come with an open mind—and an open heart—then I'll do my part as your teacher to fill it."

For the next twenty minutes I taught them. I taught them until they knew the material. Then I tested them on the material and all but two got As. With a twinkle in my eye I told them we couldn't count the first test because I wouldn't want such incriminating evidence of my poor teaching recorded. Ah, the joys of college teaching!

How many times have you and I sat through an hour-long class, dutifully taken notes, and then met someone in the hall after class who asked us what we learned—and we couldn't remember one thing! Would the Bible say that we had learned? That "pit of passivity" can suck us into its mire if we're not careful.

Are you sensing the utter importance of this mindset, that the teacher is the one who is *responsible*? Obviously, the students are responsible to learn the material—but the teacher is responsible *to cause them to know* the material.

For the most part, the last few generations of teachers have been led to believe that they are not responsible; their students are. Any attempt to point out a connection between student performance and teacher effectiveness can quickly escalate into World War III.

Is our discussion really new or just forgotten? Have we not tragically abandoned what used to be clear? For instance, what do you think is the dictionary definition of *teach*? Want a shock? The dictionary defines *teach* as "to cause to know a subject"! Therefore, if the students have not been caused to know the subject, has the person who taught them been a good teacher? Wouldn't you say that a teacher is acting irresponsibly if she does not consider herself responsible for her students' learning?

At the very heart of *The 7 Laws of the Learner* is a total commitment to the full responsibility of the teacher to do everything in his or her power to cause the student to learn.

Years ago my son and I were talking about teaching, and I asked him if he ever had to learn anything over and over again—something that he was supposed to learn but didn't.

He laughed and said, "Yes! Language. You know how many times I've learned language, Dad? I still don't understand language."

I said, "Dave, you've never been *taught* language."

"What do you mean?"

"If you didn't learn it, your teacher didn't teach it to you."

"Sure she did. We were on language for weeks."

"Dave, did she keep teaching you until you learned it?"

"No, Dad, she said we had to move on."

"Were there other students in your class who also didn't learn it?"

He laughed, "Lots, Dad. Most of my friends didn't understand either. But we had to move on in the book."

You can see it now, can't you? My son's grammar school teacher thought she was supposed to cover the book instead of teach her students. This law says that the teacher really didn't teach because she didn't cause her students to learn.

While we unequivocally state that the teacher is responsible, we must quickly add that this responsibility is shouldered by others as well: the students, their parents, other related and interested individuals, and society in general. The teacher is not solely responsible for the students, but he is the one under consideration in this book.

When people begin to understand this law, they begin to reclaim their responsibility. It's happened many times as I've taught this course around the world. The light goes on and the teacher realizes, *It's my responsibility.* Then everything changes, because when you and I accept our rightful responsibility as God desires, learning soars.

One evening at dinner my son announced he wasn't going to get a good grade in math. When I questioned him further, he politely informed me, "Dad, those math grades are not my fault. My teacher is boring and class is terrible. He needs to come to the *7 Laws* course because he is not causing me to learn!"

My wife shot me a glance that said, "What on earth are you teaching our children?" and I realized this moment called for immediate innovation.

"Well, son, you are forgetting the Law of the Student," I said.

"What? You never talked about that at the conference!"

"I know. I'm making it up right now for you and for all who would attempt to follow in your creative footsteps. The Law of the Student states that the student is responsible to learn, regardless of the quality of the teacher. You see, Dave, when you are the teacher, teach like you are 100 percent responsible. When you are the student, *learn* like you are 100 percent responsible."

I could tell David didn't like this, but my wife sure did.

"But then who's responsible, Dad—me or my teacher?"

"Yes. You've got it, Dave! You're both 100 percent responsible. And by the way, son, I'm going to be holding you responsible for your 100 percent in this course!"

As Joseph Bayly has said, "Never let school interfere with your child's education!"

Former U.S. Secretary of Education Shirley M. Hufstedler was right on when she said, "The secret to being a successful teacher is...to accept in a very personal way the responsibility for each student's success or failure. Those teachers who do take personal responsibility for their students' successes and failure...produce higher-achieving students."[2]

My grandmother had it right years ago when, in a moment of frustration, she said to me, "I'm going to *learn* you, young man."

Maxim 2: Teachers will stand accountable to God for their influence.

The partner to full responsibility is *accountability*. When someone delegates responsibility to us for a given project, usually we must give an account for our performance.

God's Word clearly reveals that each of us is going to be held accountable to God for how we fulfilled His instructions:

> For we must all appear before the judgment seat of Christ, that each one may receive the things done in the body, according to what he has done, whether good or bad. (2 Corinthians 5:10)

There will be a future Day of Accountability. Not only will God hold us accountable for our motives, words, actions, and faithfulness; but He also has announced that He will hold some of us additionally accountable. Repeatedly the Bible admonishes leaders about the seriousness of their responsibilities and its accompanying accountability:

> My brethren, let not many of you become teachers, knowing that we shall receive a stricter judgment. (James 3:1)

James is clear: *Teachers will be more strictly judged by God* because of their greater responsibility. God will hold us accountable not only for how we live, but also for how we teach. We face a stricter judgment because of our role as teachers.

Obey those who rule over you, and be submissive, for they watch out for your souls, *as those who must give account*. Let them do so with joy and not with grief, for that would be unprofitable for you. (Hebrews 13:17)

The writer of Hebrews also notes that those who have positions of authority will give account. Because that is true, the author encourages the believers under those leaders to obey and submit to them, making it easier for them to fulfill their responsibility. It appears from this verse that not only will teachers be held accountable, but in some way so will the students.

There are several practical implications of this maxim. First, the only reason God can hold us accountable as teachers is because we are responsible!

Second, God views the role and responsibility of the teacher as extremely important. *Don't allow society's current lack of respect for the teaching community to lessen the honor you give it.*

Third, allow the emphasis of Hebrews 13:17 to impact you fully. Remember, teachers: Watch out for your souls, not just the test scores!

Finally, some classes and some students will be more inclined to cause you grief. Realize that such classes and individuals are part of the teaching territory. Even the Master Teacher Himself had students, such as the Sadducees and Pharisees, who attacked not only His content but His reputation and eventually His life. Don't allow yourself to retreat into the false conceit that when you teach for the right reasons and with all your heart, everything is automatically going to be wonderful. It may not! God never promised to give you a class that always responds joyfully to you and your subject.

So set your expectations clearly. Teach when you experience joy, and teach when you feel grief. Teach because God has divinely called and commissioned you. Teach for your students' grade on Friday's test, and teach for your grade on the Final Test.

Maxim 3: Teachers are responsible because they control subject, style, and speaker.

Although it may not always appear to be true, the teacher has incredible control in the teaching-learning process. It's because of that control that the Lord can hold us accountable. Consider for a moment what the teacher has control over.

Full control over the subject. The teacher can control every word he speaks. If he wants to change the subject at any time and for whatever reason, he can. If he wants to give an illustration, he can. If he wants to go in depth in one area and skim over another, he can. If he wants to tell a joke to relieve a bored class, he can.

Full control over the style. The teacher also can control his delivery and method. If he wants to whisper or shout, stand still or jump, clap hands or fold his arms, it's all in his control. Likewise, he can employ small groups or lecture or discussion or panel or debate or a film or a skit. Dr. Hendricks changed his style repeatedly during those three minutes and thirty-seven seconds in order to cause me to learn.

Full control over the speaker. The teacher also is in full control of himself. He can come dressed any way he wants, from formal to informal—even a costume. He can come early and stay late. He can talk with the students or remain distant from them. He can sit, stand, or walk around. The teacher has full control over the speaker.

Do you see how very much control the teacher has over almost everything in the teaching-learning process? It's amazing when you think about the incredible power and freedom of the teacher (within boundaries, of course).

The teacher has control over every major element in the teaching-learning process except one—the student! If the teacher is supposed to cause the student to learn, and yet cannot control him, how does this law work?

The teacher causes the student to learn by the correct and appropriate use of the *subject, style,* and *speaker.* Those three elements have the over-whelming power to cause the student to learn.

Do you know what an *effective* teacher does? Effective teachers control these three elements in the right way. Ineffective teachers don't.

Illustrations of this occur in classrooms across America every day. Just recently my daughter told me about one of her classes which is "just a disaster—people talk all the time, throw things, and don't learn anything." One week the usual teacher (and I use that word begrudgingly) was sick and a substitute teacher was brought in. Jennifer couldn't believe the difference. Within three minutes she didn't recognize the class. No one was talking—they were learning and even enjoying the subject for the first time that semester.

Then Jennifer said something I'll never forget: "Dad, I know this is not very kind, but I kind of hope my regular teacher doesn't get better very soon."

We can all identify with that, can't we? It's sad because it is so unnecessary.

I can almost guarantee, the regular teacher had long ago decided that the unruly class wasn't his fault; it was just that they were completely out of control. The truth was, *he* was out of control because he was misusing the subject, style, and speaker.

Do you know the only real difference between those two experiences of my daughter's class? Notice what was the same:

The same school.

The same subject.

The same day of the week.

The same students.

The same class objectives.

What, then, was the difference?

Must be the teacher, right? Yes, but what about the teacher?

Not the color of hair.

Not the height.

Not the width.

Not the type of clothes.

Not the personality.

What, then?

The only difference was that the effective teacher knew how to cause the students to learn by readjusting what she did, what she said, and how she said it.

Master teachers develop such an advanced understanding of the teaching-learning process that they immediately recognize the problem that is hindering learning and then implement the corresponding solution.

Too often teachers cast blame—"Something's wrong with my class"—when the problem really lies with the class's teacher! The first step in solving this almost universal problem is to clearly identify the problem. Once the problem is obvious, then identifying and implementing the correct solution becomes much easier. (The Learner Method, which will be presented in the next chapter, tells you how to determine the problem and implement the solution.)

Maxim 4: Teacher should judge their success by the success of their students.

Suppose you were a principal interviewing two candidates for the post of high school science teacher. Which of these two candidates would you select?

Candidate A. Female, forty-eight years of age, married with three grown children, master's degree in science, twenty years of teaching experience, published numerous articles in magazines and journals, served on various administrative committees, working on her doctorate, hobby of gardening and raising award-winning orchids.

Candidate B. Male, twenty-five years of age, single but has a cat named Whiskers, bachelor's degree in science, three years of teaching experience, no published articles or books, served on building-and-grounds committee, considering starting master's in the next couple of years, hobby of water-skiing, and volunteers at the nearby zoo.

It's decision time. Should you hire candidate A or B?

Believe it or not, you have no way of knowing. If the definition of *teach* is "cause to learn," then *none* of the above information gives me any real clues as to the teaching ability of either.

Not their gender.

Not their age.

Not their marital status.

Not their earned degrees.

Not the articles they've published.

Not the committees they've served on.

Not their hobbies.

Not even their years of teaching experience.

Of course, their credentials *are* relevant and important. But none of them tell us anything about how effective that person will be in the classroom because they all center around the teacher, not what the teacher can do in the lives of the students. Both of these candidates could be *dismal* teachers. Or they could be outstanding.

The only fact which indisputably proves what kind of teachers the candidates will make is how their previous students performed at the end of a school year compared to the start of class in the fall.

After I taught this Law of the Learner in a recent conference, a well-dressed businessman of about fifty came striding up to the platform. It was obvious he had something on his mind. "I decided after all these years in business to go back to graduate school and earn my MBA," he said. "But something recently happened that really upset me. I had to take a course on statistics, and the teacher was chairman of the entire MBA program. I couldn't wait to study under this great teacher. But do you know what she said on the first evening we met? She said that this course is so tough that more than 70 percent of us would fail! At first I was so impressed. I thought, *What a teacher this is!* But now I realize the opposite is true—she isn't that hot of a teacher. Only 30 percent of her class even passed!"

The businessman's conclusion was right. This professor may be a great leader, a smart woman, and an outstanding author, but her performance as a teacher earns her a dismal grade. Never forget this: *Teachers cause students to learn the material—and great teachers cause great numbers of students to learn great amounts of material.*

Not only do we hire people on the wrong basis; we also reward and promote on the wrong basis. Which of the two teachers listed below would get the higher recognition, promotion, and financial reward? These two high school teachers teach the same subject to the same age to the same type of students in the same school:

1. Teacher A is completing his second master's degree; Teacher B's students score 25 percent higher than Teacher A's students on the SAT exams for that subject.
2. Teacher A publishes three articles in a professional magazine; Teacher B's students win three blue ribbons in the subject at the statewide competition.
3. Teacher A serves on the education committee for the county; Teacher B's students average a full grade higher on their report cards.
4. Teacher A receives the majority of the teachers' votes for the Teacher of the Year award; Teacher B was fifteenth on the list. However, Teacher B receives the majority of the students' votes for the Teacher of the Year award, and Teacher A was fifteenth on the list.

The philosophy assumed in this book is that though the activities and committees and degrees are undeniably important, *the most important test of teacher effectiveness is student performance.*

Sometimes the very things we promote can lessen the effectiveness of the teaching process. It was an all-too-common joke among the students when I was in graduate school that the more degrees behind a teacher's name, the less effective the teacher probably was. More knowledge doesn't necessarily make a better teacher. This may sound untraditional, but it would be interesting to test student performance before and after a teacher receives his next degree.

Now, don't misunderstand me. I'm all for higher education and am constantly encouraging others to pursue further study. I attend courses, watch training videos, listen to audios, read books, and attend seminars. But the focus always must be upon the result of those educational activities, not the *accumulation* of them.

It's what the student does that counts, not what the teacher does. If the student has succeeded, then so has the teacher.

Maxim 5: Teachers impact more by their character and commitment than by their communication.

This maxim compares the impact of "who the teacher is" (character and commitment) with "what the teacher says" (communication). Character out-influences communication every time.

Consider your own career as a student. Pick out two or three of your favorite teachers. I'll bet your selection had more to do with what you thought of them than what you thought of their talk.

The timeless proverb "Actions speak louder than words" is true. When words and actions are in opposition, actions always overpower words.

Unfortunately, the world and the church often sing the tune that words are all that matter. Recently, a deacon of a local church told me the deacon board just voted six to three to keep the church's pastor, a man in the middle of divorcing his wife to marry another married woman in the same church! I asked him how his church could rebel so blatantly against the principles of Scripture. "Oh," he said, "our pastor is such a wonderful preacher, we don't want to let him go. Besides, a larger church in another state has offered him another senior pastor's position. We'll probably have to offer our pastor a large raise to keep him, but almost everybody wants him except for a few hard-nosed conservatives."

Is it possible for that pastor to openly sin, splitting his own family and another woman's, and still be a powerful preacher?

Yes, I believe it is.

Some of the world's "greatest" teachers and preachers are openly opposed to Christ. Many of the men who hold the most powerful pulpits in the land do not hold to the doctrines of the virgin birth, the inspiration of the Bible, the resurrection of Christ, or even the deity of Christ. Yet their powers of oratory and persuasion are remarkable. Their words can move us to tears. But being moved emotionally does not always equate with God's affirmation or bring about His blessing.

We err greatly when we think that just because a man or a woman can teach effectively or pastor graciously or preach powerfully that the hand of the Lord must be on that life. The hand of the Lord cannot be upon a person who rejects the deity of Christ—the Bible labels him an "enemy of the gospel."

When that church chose to retain its pastor, it took a public stand for sin and against the Savior. The unbelieving community will once again blaspheme the cause of Christ because even they know a moral outrage when they see one.

But what about that preacher's powerful preaching? Come back in five years and you'll see the fruits of what is now being planted. You can already glimpse the word *Ichabod* being etched over the entryway. I've seen it happen too many times without exception. God's principles for ministry have always been the same: first the character, then the communication. That's why 1 Timothy and Titus are so clear—the life of the communicator must first be in harmony with the message before he speaks the message.

In fact, *character will always control the content*—eventually. When the Spirit of God is quenched and sin is given free reign, not only will the Spirit not be present in the teaching, but soon neither will the Scriptures. The teacher or preacher will begin to shape the content to match his lifestyle. I shudder to think of that pastor, his new wife, and those six deacons when they stand accountable before another Court for the travesty they have wrought.

When I ask adults to select the teacher who most influenced them, it is always the one who had the most noble character and commitment. Those teachers usually were neither the easiest nor the hardest in the classroom, but something about them aroused genuine respect and admiration. We, their students, wished that someday we could be like them.

May *your* students desire to be like their teacher!

Maxim 6: Teachers exist to serve the students.

Everyone enjoys going out to a nice restaurant for a graciously served, delicious meal. How would you respond if the next time you visited your favorite restaurant and asked for some water, the waitress said, "Get it yourself! What are you, helpless? I'm not your slave, you know"? You'd quickly leave that place thinking the service was the worst you'd ever seen. You'd probably never return.

You view that waitress as your servant. Part of what you pay for is her willingness to serve you; that is her job. If, however, you were out on a picnic a couple of days later and saw that same waitress and asked her to get you some water, how do you think she would respond? The roles we play in certain situations influence the behavior we feel is appropriate.

Now consider the role of the teacher. Who in the classroom is supposed to serve the water and refill the plate and ask the people if there is anything else they would like? Unfortunately, many of us in the teaching-preaching profession have forgotten that we are servants. Most classes have a severe case of "role reversal"—by all appearances, the student has become the servant. Teachers have forgotten that they exist to meet the needs of their students, not their own needs.

Why is this problem so easy to recognize when it surfaces in the restaurant but so difficult to recognize in the classroom?

I remember the first time I had to speak in front of a large audience many years ago. My heart was racing, knees shaking, palms sweating, and I was frantically praying that maybe God could help me out by initiating the Second Coming right then. Sitting next to me on the platform was a well-known, seasoned speaker. While we were singing the hymn right before I had to speak, I turned to him and said, "I'm so nervous! I don't know if I can do this."

Without batting an eye, this great man said, "Bruce, don't be so proud and self-conscious."

That's not something you like to hear right before you speak. So I asked him, "What do you mean?"

"You are so concerned about yourself and how you will do and what the people will think about you—that's why you are nervous. If you'd get your eyes off yourself for a moment and on the people in front of you and start caring about meeting their needs, not your own, you'd stop being so nervous. You see, it's only when we are self-conscious rather than other-conscious that we become so very nervous. When we focus on serving our audience, then the Lord is free to use us."

Then he smiled and went back to singing the hymn as if nothing had happened. And I went back to the Lord for a moment of divine readjustment and purposefully stopped serving my needs and started attending to my audience's needs. Most of the butterflies headed south for the season, or at least they began flying in formation.

Serving students can be much like loving our children. Often we do things for our children that we think communicate love to them, but they don't receive it that way. Similarly, many times I think teachers strive to serve their students, but their students don't feel it. Perhaps it's because the teachers unconsciously do things that communicate the very opposite of their intentions.

Throughout this book I will present many ways to concretely serve your students—ways they will recognize and appreciate. In the Law of Expectation you'll learn practical ways to communicate love to your students. In the Law of Need you'll learn the secrets Christ used to motivate His students to want what He was going to teach. In the Law of Retention, you will be exposed to some revolutionary approaches that will enable you to speed-teach material.

All seven Laws of the Learner are focused on this very issue: How does the teacher truly serve the student in the classroom? As you begin to understand these laws and practice them, you will see frustration replaced by motivation. You'll have an incredible set of transferable skills that will work with any subject you are teaching to any age student. How can I make these claims? Because these principles are universal, like gravity, and when you and I practice them, our students feel served.

Learn them and join the small band of teachers who enter the classroom with clear resolve and unwavering purpose to serve your students with all of your heart, all of your mind, and all of your soul.

Maxim 7: Teachers who practice the Laws of the Learner and Teacher can become master teachers.

A number of people applied for an open teaching position at a junior high school in Dallas. After screening the candidates, the hiring committee narrowed the field to two finalists.

The first man had taught school for thirty-five years; the other candidate was in only her second year of teaching. The experienced teacher with all the credentials was sure he would get the job. But at the end of the week, the young woman was chosen.

The older man was livid. He stormed into the personnel committee meeting, demanding to know why he wasn't hired—after all, he was the one with thirty-five years of experience. The wise administrator paused for a moment and then answered, "Sir, it's true you have been teaching for thirty-five years, but I could not see any improvement over those years. The way I see it, you had one year of experience *repeated* thirty-five times!"

The popular notion is that great teachers are just born, but I believe master teachers are not born, not manufactured, but just improved! To believe that people are born great teachers is as illogical as believing that people are born great scientists. Of course, there are varying degrees of innate ability, but the majority of people who achieve in their fields do so with persistent effort over a long period of time.

Blot out of your thinking the other false concept that greatness comes through gigantic steps of improvement. Real effectiveness is developed through many years of improving just a few steps at a time.

Every year at the ministry of Walk Thru the Bible we saw concrete proof of this truth. We had a tradition of publicly recognizing the top ten Walk Thru the Bible instructors each year. Inevitably there was at least one surprise. One year, I had some intense discussions with our dean of faculty about one of our lowest-rated instructors. We held a high standard of excellence for our seminar faculty, and I kept encouraging the dean to dismiss this man. Finally he said, "Give this man one more year of opportunity to improve. If he doesn't, I'll be the first to vote to let him go."

I asked why he was so supportive of this marginal performer, and the dean said, "The man is working harder to improve himself than anyone else on the WTB faculty. He is watching the videos of the best teachers, having his wife and friends constantly evaluate him, always asking me for ways to improve. I believe he can do it, and he deeply wants to."

The next year, when evaluations were made to determine the top ten, guess who had achieved it? The same man I was ready to dismiss the year before. Did he have those rare abilities to make it naturally to the top ten? No, he didn't. The best rarely are the people who have the most natural talent, but rather those few who have a passion to fulfill their God-given talents and reach for their full potential.

MEANING

The essence of the Law of the Learner is these three words: "Cause to learn." The teacher should accept the responsibility of causing the student to learn.

CONCLUSION

As you have already sensed, this first Law of the Learner is the building block upon which every other law is built: *The teacher is responsible to cause the student to learn.*

For some teachers, this sense of commitment and responsibility has been with them for as long as they can remember—but they are the rare ones. To others, this commitment comes amidst difficulty and even trauma, but it alters their hearts and classrooms forever. And to still others, unfortunately, this commitment never finds entrance into their hearts or classrooms. Not only do these teachers suffer, but so do their students.

As a teacher of teachers, I have come to treasure those who have purposed to hold this commitment in their hearts, especially those who have had to pass through the fire to develop it. Of all the stories of such pilgrimages, my favorite is undoubtedly the Teddy Stallard story.

Teddy Stallard certainly qualified as "one of the least." Disinterested in school. Musty, wrinkled clothes. Hair never combed. One of those kids with a deadpan face, expressionless—sort of a glassy, unfocused stare. When Miss Thompson spoke to Teddy he always answered in monosyllables. Unattractive, unmotivated, and distant, he was just plain hard to like. Even though his teacher said she loved all in her class the same, she knew she wasn't being completely truthful.

Whenever she marked Teddy's papers, she got a certain perverse pleasure from putting Xs next to the wrong answers, and when she put Fs at the top of the papers, she always did it with a flair. She should have known better; she had Teddy's records and she knew more about him than she wanted to admit. The records read:

1st grade: Teddy shows promise with his work and attitude, but poor home situation.

2nd grade: Teddy could do better. Mother is seriously ill. He receives little help at home.

3rd grade: Teddy is a good boy but too serious. He is a slow learner. His mother died this year.

4th grade: Teddy is very slow, but well behaved. His father shows no interest.

Christmas came and the boys and girls in Miss Thompson's class brought her Christmas presents. They piled her presents on her desk and crowded around to watch her open them. Among the presents there was one from Teddy Stallard. She was surprised that he had brought her a gift. Teddy's gift was wrapped in brown paper and held together with Scotch tape. On the paper were written the simple words, "For Miss Thompson from Teddy." When she opened Teddy's present, out fell a gaudy rhinestone bracelet, with half the stones missing, and a bottle of cheap perfume.

The other boys and girls began to giggle and smirk over Teddy's gifts, but Miss Thompson at least had enough sense to silence them by immediately putting on the bracelet and putting some of the perfume on her wrist. Holding her wrist up for the other children to smell, she said, "Doesn't it smell lovely?" And the children, taking their cue from the teacher, readily agreed.

At the end of the day, when school was over and the other children had left, Teddy lingered behind. He slowly came over to her desk and said softly, "Miss Thompson...Miss Thompson, you smell just like my mother...and her bracelet looks real pretty on you, too. I'm glad you liked my presents." When Teddy left, Miss Thompson got down on her knees and asked God to forgive her.

The next day when the children came to school, they were welcomed by a new teacher. Miss Thompson had become a different person. She was no longer just a teacher; she had become an agent of God. She was now a person committed to loving her children and doing things for them that would live on after her. She helped all the children, but especially the slow ones, and especially Teddy Stallard.

By the end of that school year, Teddy showed dramatic improvement. He had caught up with most of the students and was even ahead of some.

She didn't hear from Teddy for a long time. Then one day, she received a note that read:

> *Dear Miss Thompson:*
>   *I wanted you to be the first to know. I will be graduating second in my class.*
>   *Love,*
>   *Teddy Stallard*

Four years later, another note came:

> *Dear Miss Thompson:*
>   *They just told me I will be graduating first in my class. I wanted you to be the first to know. The university has not been easy, but I like it.*

Love,
Teddy Stallard

And four years later:

Dear Miss Thompson:
    As of today I am Theodore Stallard, M.D. How about that? I wanted you to be the first to know. I am getting married next month, the 27th to be exact. I want you to come and sit where my mother would sit if she were alive. You are the only family I have now; Dad died last year.
    Love,
    Teddy Stallard

Miss Thompson went to that wedding and sat where Teddy's mother would have sat. She deserved to sit there—she had done something for Teddy that he could never forget.[3]

What can you give as a gift, my fellow teacher? Instead of giving something that money can buy, risk giving something that will live on long after you. Be extravagantly generous. Give the gift only you can give—yourself—to the members of your class. All of them. Give so much of yourself that they will learn so deeply and meaningfully that they'll invite you to their weddings, because it's the only reasonable thing to do.

DISCUSSION QUESTIONS

1. Who would you say was the best teacher you ever had? What three main characteristics made that person your favorite? How important was his commitment to "cause you to learn"? What do you think would have happened if he had lost that commitment?

2. How would you say the average teacher would define teaching today? If you flew in from outer space and were assigned to find out what happened in those buildings called "public schools" and invisibly visited a fifth, ninth, and eleventh grade classroom, what would you write to your supervisor? Remember, you've never seen a school before, so to develop a good answer, you will have to think outside the norm.

3. You have been asked by the president of the United States to develop a new model for hiring, training, and paying teachers. His only prerequisite is that he wants U.S. students to be back on top academically within the next three years. He has given you complete power and an unlimited budget; every decision is yours and will not be questioned except by the results. His only request is that your model be governed by no more than seven principles. What principles will you choose?

4. Consider yourself as a teacher for a moment. How much have you bought into this concept that it's your

responsibility to cause your students to learn? Let's say that I could wave a magic wand and instantly give you that attitude to the fullest. After one week of teaching, how would your students describe the difference between the "old you" and the "new you"? Which of the two would you prefer, and why?

CHAPTER TWO

Learner

Method and Maximizers

I had tried everything and my car still wouldn't run right. At the most unexpected moment it would start sputtering and missing. Finally I gave up and drove to my favorite gas station whose trusty mechanic had repaired my automobiles over the years.

After a few moments, he announced that he couldn't find anything wrong and would need to attach my car to a "diagnostic machine." I had never seen nor heard of a diagnostic machine, so I asked if I could watch.

He opened the hood, unhooked a couple of wires from the engine, and plugged them into his computer. When he flipped the switch the diagnostic machine started, the lights flashed, and before I knew it, he laughed and said, "Well, the reason you could never figure this out is because there's a short in one of your wires that creates the problem from time to time. But you can't see it with your eye."

He replaced the wire and I was soon on my way, my engine humming smoothly. Yet I couldn't get over how amazing that diagnostic machine was. Then the thought came to me—wouldn't it be great if there was a Teaching Diagnostic Machine! If class wasn't working, you would just grab some of your students, strap them to the machine, and know instantly what was wrong with the class.

Sometimes we can get the impression that the teaching-learning process is some unfathomable mystery. Once is a while your class runs like it's in the Indy 500, yet the next class can become so sluggish that you don't know if it will escape the garage. If you've ever wondered what's gone right or what's gone wrong, then be encouraged—a Teaching Diagnostic Machine (TDM) is now available. By the end of this chapter, you will be able to identify within only a few minutes what's causing the problem, and what to do about it.

In contrast to the numerous systems in an automobile, however, the teacher-learning process only has five primary systems that control its success or failure. Therefore, tracing the source of the problem in the classroom is much easier than in a car. With a little training, you can become skilled in not only discerning why something is not working, but also what to do to fix it.

So let's unwrap this mysterious Teaching Diagnostic Machine and see if you can't work it yourself. (No batteries required.)

LEARNER METHOD

Think for a moment about what must be present for there to be a teaching-learning experience within the Christian classroom. Listed below are the five major things that are in every classroom and Sunday school and sanctuary and home Bible study.

1. The Students—the individuals who are to learn the subject.
2. The Subject—the content or skill to be learned.

3. The Style—the manner or method in which the content is taught.
4. The Speaker—the instructor or teacher that causes learning.
5. The Spirit—the presence and influence of the Holy Spirit.

These are the ultimate *Causers of Learning*. The way you manage these Big Five will determine your success or failure in the classroom. If your class is working well—that is, you are causing your students to learn—it's because the Big Five are in harmony. If your class isn't working, one or more of the Big Five is out of kilter and needs adjustment.

Each one of the Big Five controls a distinct part of the teaching-learning process, and when it isn't working properly something predictable happens. When your car won't start because the engine won't turn over and the lights won't even go on, what system has the problem? Right, the electrical. And you can probably start it by jumping the battery.

This is an extremely important concept: Problems in the teaching system almost always look the same and have the same solutions.

The more you understand this principle, the more problems you will recognize and know exactly what to do to fix them. Teaching isn't some complicated and overwhelming skill that only the highly gifted should consider. Rather, teaching is a set of learned skills that are freely available to anyone who has the desire to acquire them. As we continue through these Seven Laws you are going to become exposed to revolutionary principles that are immediately usable right in your classroom. And then, when the class is not motivated or is disruptive or not learning, you'll know what to do to turn it around. The longer you teach, the more solutions you'll have up your sleeve. The more solutions you effectively use, the more your students will start calling you a master teacher. When that happens, my dream for this book will have been fulfilled!

The Learner Method:
Three Major Relationships

There are three primary relationships that directly impact the majority of all classroom situations. These relationships have to do with how you as the teacher relate to your subject, your students, and your style. Later in the book, we will further equip you in your relationship with the Holy Spirit and with yourself as the teacher.

People are always surprised that after only a few moments of observing them teach, I can give the reason their class is not working correctly and then prescribe what they need to do to fix it. You are about to learn some of the insights that make that possible.

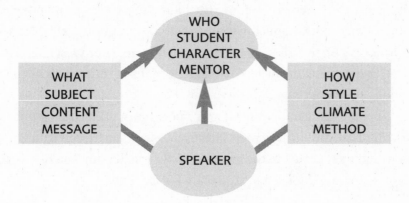

On the chart you can see that the "*Speaker*" or teacher is typed in the bottom oval. The "*Subject*" is on the left, the "*Student*" in the top middle, and the "*Style*" is on the right. Those three ever-present relationships govern the vast majority of the successes or failures in the classroom. Note that the arrows picturing this strategic relationship all start with the speaker/teacher and end with the student/learner.

The Learner Method focuses upon how these three relationships of subject, student, and style generally work with many more specifics in the following chapters. For example, in the Law of Retention you'll learn how to speed-teach the subject. In the Law of Need, you learn a powerful five-step method Jesus Christ used to motivate His students that you can likewise use every time you teach. The Law of Expectation trains you to blossom your students to reach their full potential. Each Law, therefore, builds upon these three primary relationships, enabling you to become an expert "Causer of Learning" to your students.

The Subject represents the "*What*" being taught, the Student the "*Who*" is being taught, and the Style the "*How*" it is being taught. Teaching, then, is How to teach the What to the Who! The Speaker must develop his Subject, which is his "*Message*," and disciple his Student as a "*Mentor*," and deliver his Subject with the appropriate "*Method*."

Each of us manages these relationships differently, but each of us manages one of those three relationships the best. Some of us are effective with the "content" side of teaching (subject-oriented), whereas others don't shine as much with the material but greatly influence the "character" of the class members (student-oriented). Other teachers excel at delivering the material so that the "climate" is interesting, motivating, and captivating (style-oriented).

Spend a moment and see if you can identify which of these three relationships you manage most effectively. Read the following descriptions and then put a 1 in the box next to the relationship you think best describes you, a 2 for the next, and a 3 for the least:

? Subject-oriented. "I love the content. I almost always have two or three times more material prepared than I need and frequently find myself hurrying at the end of class to finish on time. I enjoy explaining things and want my class to have a thorough understanding. I love lists of material, have a strong need to know the facts myself, and like to research in books and commentaries. Sometimes I have to watch that I don't let the material get too complex for the average student in my class."

? Student-oriented. "I love my students. I feel like they're more my friends than my students. I am interested in each of them and enjoy being with them in and out of class. I love to share stories from my own life and family and feel that my students are like my extended family. Sometimes I have to watch that our sharing and discussions don't stray from the subject too long, but I just want to be as much help to them as possible."

? Style-oriented. "I love what takes place during the process of teaching and learning. I love seeing the electricity of a class that is alive, with the students hanging on every word. I like to use my creativity in the classroom and always find myself trying new things to keep the class exciting and moving. The students enjoy what I do in class because it's never boring. Sometimes I might get a little carried away in my creative attempts to keep the material fresh and alive, but the students always seem to love the spontaneity and variety. I love to teach and can't wait for class to begin—the larger the class, the better I like it."

Have you uncovered your strongest relationship? If not, ask a friend because it's probably clear to everyone but you.

You can usually identify what kind of teacher a person is by what they do at the coffee break at the Walk Thru the Bible seminars.

If a person is subject-oriented, they'll head right for the book table and pick up a number of the resources that are always available. The advanced subject people will even pick up the new Bibles just to smell the leather!

If a person is student-oriented, they won't even get up from their seat initially at break but instead turn to you and ask about your spouse and your children and your work and your house and your favorite color and your favorite day of the week and your... By the end of the day, the advanced student person will often ask for your name and address and begin a lifetime pen-pal relationship with you.

If a person is style-oriented, at the very moment break is announced they will leap to their feet and with a clap, head off to the pop machine talking animatedly about how the teacher did the things he did including all those graphic four-color visuals (the subject-oriented person didn't even notice they were four-color and the student-oriented wanted more pictures of people and puppies). The advanced cases will be writing in their leather zip notebooks how they would have taught it and writing down the great one-liners and jokes for the next week's dynamic class.

See how it works? Each of us leans more toward one as our greatest strength. Let's flesh out these basic relationships to enlarge your perspective.

Relationship 1: The Speaker to the Subject

When the subject is your greatest strength, your students may call you a scholar or a "brain" or very cerebral. You like thinking about the material, and you warm to the world of ideas and thoughts even more than to your students (and certainly more than to all those creative methods, which seem like a waste of time). You love the original sources, and it has always bothered you that you haven't mastered Greek and Hebrew and Latin and German just to get to the real "deep" stuff.

Your students think you are very smart and know much about many things. They enjoy hearing you answer their questions about the subject because you always make sense—frequently more in the question-and-answer time than in the lecture. Your students probably think you expect too much from them and teach too many things that aren't necessary, but you always seem to think everything is important. No one ever feels that they aren't learning in your class, but some of the students have to run flat out just to keep up with you.

I studied under a classic scholar at graduate school. In our second class period of the semester, a student raised his hand and asked for further information about what seemed like a nitpicky piece of minutia. A couple of my buddies rolled their eyes when we heard the question, and none of us suspected that the professor could provide more than a sentence of further explanation.

What the professor did still amazes me many years later. He nodded, as if the question showed remarkable insight, looked up into the far right corner of the ceiling, wrapped his fingers around his thumb and placed them on the right part of his forehead. He proceeded to name a certain set of books that the answer was supposed to be in and then continued, "Volume 2, page 246, left page, right-hand column of type and down about 7 or 8 lines." He then closed his eyes and quoted about three or four paragraphs of material.

At first I thought it must have been a practical joke, so at the first break I raced over to the library and looked up volume 2 of the aforementioned book and found the page. I was shocked to discover he had quoted it word for word!

Except for his occasional excursions into the depths of theology, when he would slip into quoting the original German sources, we all found ourselves loving this professor and were stretched to new depths of scholarship. It was one of the most memorable learning experiences of my career.

But such strengths often have corresponding weaknesses. This same scholar told us about a time he spoke in Houston over a weekend, then flew back to Dallas and waited in the airport for his wife to pick him up. After waiting an hour he telephoned her to find out if she had forgotten. "Where are you?" she asked. "At the Dallas airport, of course," he replied, "but where are you?" "I'm home," she said, "waiting for you." Then there was a long, pregnant pause, followed by, "Sweetheart, did you forget—*you drove to Houston!*"

If you are weakest in the subject relationship you are probably insecure about your content and heavily depend upon your written notes. When someone raises a hand with a question, you die inside and say that you'll talk with him at break because you're sure you don't know the answer, but you don't want anyone else to know. Then you desperately pray he forgets the question by break. You probably find it easier to use other people's outlines as they seem so much better than yours, and you're never quite sure if you have enough good content anyway.

Relationship 2: The Speaker to the Student

When your relationship to your students is your main strength, they may call you a friend or an encourager or very "in touch" with them. You find it easy to relate to your students. You probably find your students far more interesting and important than the content or its delivery. After all, your students are the reason you teach. You love sharing with them about your life and its struggles and victories, and class feels more like one big happy family. You may find yourself spending your lunch hour in the student cafeteria rather than the faculty lounge. You want to get close to the students, not escape them!

Your students feel you are personable and practical. They feel you care for them and are a real and transparent person. They may find themselves coming to you when they have problems—many think you are the only teacher who understands them and can therefore help them.

I studied under a student-oriented teacher in my younger days. It seemed we spent more time discussing our life stories and hearing about his family than on the content. It used to be a challenge to see how long we could keep this teacher off the subject; many times we were able to keep him telling stories from his past for an entire class period. When he realized the semester was almost over and he'd only given a couple of pages' worth of notes, he dictated nonstop at a frantic pace for the last few class sessions, just so he'd have something to ask us on the final exam. But we didn't seem to care; we all thought he was incredible. Most of us would have done anything for him.

If you are weakest in the student relationship, then you're not very comfortable around students. You prefer to arrive just as class begins, and always seem to find important reasons to leave just as you hear the bell. You probably don't feel comfortable telling transparent stories about your personal life. Your students probably call you Mr. or Miss or Mrs. or Dr. or Professor; they would never dream of using your first name. You think that a solid amount of distance is healthy for effective teaching anyway. If you aren't careful, some students could consider you aloof or cold or even professorial, though you don't feel any of these are true for those who get to know you. Students may think your classes are too theoretical and not practical. They feel you probably care more about the content than about them. It bothers them that you haven't learned their names when the course is already half over.

Relationship 3: The Speaker to the Style

When style is your greatest strength, your students may call you a communicator or a powerful speaker or extremely motivating. You love communication and are thrilled to see the students respond to what you are teaching them. You love working and reworking your material so that it has good stories, nice visuals, and the outline is balanced and even alliterated. Not only must your material make sense, but it must look and sound good. You often spend as much time thinking of how to present your material as you do developing it. Usually you are "Mr. Spontaneity" and relish the challenge of the present moment and how to use it to the maximum. When you teach, you teach with everything that's within you and feel tired but exhilarated when you are through.

Your students think you are a great teacher and most of them enjoy your classes. They come filled with anticipation and the class hour always seems to fly by. They appreciate your intensity and ability to keep class interesting and motivating. They like the way you use variety and creativity. Many of them feel that your class is the high point of the day because they always leave feeling motivated and charged up.

Maybe you had a teacher who was "Miss Style" all the way. Not only did she teach with style, but she dressed with style as well. When you entered her class you felt an electric sense of anticipation. Her class walls were filled with posters and pictures and outstanding papers. She seemed to make the most complex concepts easy to understand. Unlike almost every other teacher, she deplored lecture. Drama, small groups, spontaneous debate, focus sessions, outside speakers, special films—all made their way into her wonderful climate of learning.

If your relationship to style is your weakest, then your middle name is probably "lecture" and the thought of using an overhead projector is as foreign to your thinking as it was to the apostle Paul's. You prefer standing behind the lectern and never feel quite dressed when you are out in the open. As far as drama, that's for Hollywood and the movies. As for small groups, that's for those who think the best way to discover truth is to share ignorance. Besides, the Sermon on the Mount was a lecture, wasn't it?

If this is your area of greatest weakness, your students probably feel class is too boring and everything is too predictable. As far as they are concerned, you seem to be more interested in the material than communicating that material. If it's too hot in class or too late in the afternoon, students may find their eyes closing and their heads nodding because there isn't enough excitement to hold their attention.

How to Identify the Problem in Your Class

Problems in the classroom are always demonstrated by the student's attitudes and actions. If a class is "broken," the students are the ones who tell you.

Listed below are several complaints from normal high school students about their teachers and the classes they attend. See if you are now able to identify the underlying problem—whether it's the Subject,

Student, or Style—before reading the answer. After identifying the problem I'll give some possible solutions. For the first two problems I've included more extensive answers. See if you can provide your own answers for the rest.

1. I can't stand my teacher. I don't think he even knows my name. Besides, he doesn't care if I live or die. I'm not going to study in his class!

Problem: Student Relationship—students feel their teacher is uncaring.

Solution: Concretely demonstrate through personal illustrations and public affirmation that you are a person who genuinely cares for them.

- Immediately memorize all the names of your students and use their names every time you speak with them.
- Start class for the next few sessions with a personal story, demonstrating that you are a real person who has experienced both victory and failure. For the next week, spend more time on stories of your failures than successes.
- At an appropriate moment, share the personal reasons you became a teacher and what you wish would happen in the lives of your students when you teach.
- Compliment students regularly through verbal comments in class and written comments on their papers. Affirm them individually and corporately and tell them how glad you are that they are in your class.
- Focus your attention and eye contact on those sitting farthest from you, because they are the ones probably feeling isolated and unattached.

- Give out an anonymous questionnaire with questions
  such as, "I wish my teacher would stop _____,"
  and "I feel most discouraged in this course because
  _____," and "If I taught this class starting tomor-
  row, the first thing I would do is _____."
  Implement at least three changes immediately and openly.

2. "Lecture, lecture, lecture; that's all my teacher does anymore."

Problem: Style—the only method the teacher is using to deliver content to the student is through lecture, which becomes monotonous and tiring to the student.

Solution: Vary your delivery regularly—even the best prime rib or Breyer's vanilla ice cream gets old after a while.

- Keep track of the percentage of lecture in the classroom. The younger the students are, the less tolerance
  they have for the lecture method.
- Vary your delivery by the three main methods of variety—
  what you do in class, what you have your students do in
  class, and what you do together in class.
- Lessen your content by at least 25 percent for a couple
  of weeks in order to have more time to use alternative
  teaching methods.
- Open class with a creative method and, even more
  important, close the last five minutes of class with a different creative approach. People remember the opening
  and closing more than everything in between. Scan a
  teaching method book for ideas.
- Build anticipation by announcing for the upcoming
  week a special film or guest speaker. Help your class see

that you are striving to serve them more effectively through these methods.

Now try your hand at the following problem. What solutions do you think would work?

3. "My teacher's head is in the clouds. I mean, none of us understand what she's talking about half the time."

Problem: Subject—teacher is presenting too complex or too much material for the students and the situation.

Solution: Stop covering the subject and start teaching the students. Simplify the material and ensure understanding before continuing. (See Law of Retention.)

4. "All we do is fill in the blanks on the notes all class long. He won't allow any discussion and we have to write our questions out on thee-by-five cards and he answers it next period. What a drag. I could have read the textbook—at least it had pictures."

Problem: Style—the teacher thinks the best and only method to effectively communicate the material is through the "fill in the blank" method.

Solution: Stop frustrating your students by using a method of delivering the material that they feel is beneath them as well as unnecessary. Initiate new methods of instruction.

5. "Class is so stupid. All we do is talk about simple stuff we had two years ago. We never learn anything new."

Problem: Subject—teacher is reviewing material that has already been learned by the majority of the class and is too thin on new material. Teacher is out of touch with level of student competence on the subject.

Solution: Reorganize the next three lessons to minimize review and maximize new learning. With enthusiasm highlight the new information you are going to teach them and how it will help their lives. Double the amount of information you have been normally presenting.

6. "I can't believe our teacher expects us to read these books— we're only in the tenth grade and my dad says he had to read them in college. I have to look up every other word in the dictionary."

Problem: Subject—teacher is out of touch with the ability of the students or may be trying to stretch them inappropriately.

Solution: Immediately announce a change in the reading assignments and give three levels of required reading: basic books, challenging books, and advanced books. Through a motivational speech, encourage the students to look at all three categories and select the ones that are just a tad beyond their abilities. In principle, never teach the whole class at the level of the top 10 percent, but always for the majority—and offer additional challenges for those who could excel.

7. "Class is a zoo—it's totally out of control. People are throwing things, talking back to the teacher and mocking her, and all the teacher does is yell at us all the time. And then when it gets to her, all she does is break down and cry."

Problem: Student—the teacher has abandoned her authority and leadership to mob rule.

Solution: Reestablish the rules for acceptable behavior in the class and through careful negotiation, hammer out a known and agreed-upon set of consequences. Type and post this agreement so all can see it as you consistently practice the positive and negative consequences.

Do these complaints sound familiar? Each of these comments is a verbal sign of teaching failure, of learning malfunction. Each of these is not only unnecessary, but is fully within the control of you, the teacher. As you've discovered through this process, the Teaching Diagnostic Machine is easy to use and immediately applicable.

LEARNER MAXIMIZERS

The purpose of the maximizers in each of the seven laws is to further equip you in the method just discussed by presenting seven additional tips on how to get the most out of the method. These seven suggestions will enable you to become more skilled as you undertake your calling to "cause your students to learn."

Maximizer 1: Love your students consistently and unconditionally.

Jesus gave us the most important maximizer of all when He said, "'You shall love the LORD your God with all your heart, with all your soul, and with all your mind.' This is the first and greatest commandment. And the second is like it: 'You shall love your neighbor as yourself.' On these two commandments hang all the Law and the Prophets" (Matthew 22:37–40).

Of the forty-nine maximizers presented in this textbook, this first is the unchallenged winner. Loving your students deeply and continuously will maximize your impact in their lives more than the other forty-eight combined.

In fact, if 1 Corinthians 13 is still true, then if you and I don't truly love our students, everything else we do in the classroom doesn't amount to much. How rare it is to sit in a class where the primary focus of the teacher's efforts and affections is the students. It appears that in most schools and churches, "loving your students" has gone out of vogue. Somehow the biblical admonition to love has been so watered down that few of us grasp the full depth of our calling— merely equating it to preparing our lesson, teaching with enthusiasm, and perhaps calling our students in an emergency or having a class social once a year.

We've also allowed our definition of love to become unemotional. Words such as *intense* or *ardent* or *zealous* or *fervent* don't seem to fit in the classroom. Should you be passionate? Isn't it sobering to consider that we can have incredible positive actions toward other people and yet not have love? For instance, 1 Corinthians 13 lists two actions beyond the imaginations of most of us—giving all our goods to feed the poor and giving ourselves up as martyrs—and says they can be done without love. Yet without love, they mean nothing.

Love acts, of course, because some of its actions are defined in 1 Corinthians 13:4: "Love suffers long and is kind; love does not envy; love does not parade itself, is not puffed up." But does biblical love include passion or fervency? First Peter 4:8 has a clear and specific answer: "*And above all things* [everything else in this book] *have fervent love for one another*, for 'love will cover a multitude of sins.'"

To have "fervent love" is to have intense and earnest feelings. Therefore, you and I must strive to become intensely and emotionally involved with our students, to fervently love them.

As surprising as it may seem, I think all teachers "love"—without exception. When you observe their behavior you can soon determine what it is that they love. Our behavior reflects our values and affections. The major "loves" of teachers seem to consistently fall into one of the following categories:

The love of content. These are the teachers who get so excited and motivated by the material that they lose sight of their class. The vast majority of teaching time is directed to the material. They become so enamored with what they are saying that they never have the time or energy to focus on who they are saying it to.

The love of communication. These are the teachers who get so excited and motivated by the thought of speaking to an audience that they lose sight of the audience! Their adrenaline surges as they walk up to the platform. They are stimulated by the response of the crowd. The meaningful pauses, the crescendos, the perfectly timed humor, the turn of the phrase, the powerful close, the crafted gesture—all combine to create the performance. The applause. The acclaim. It's the love of the event rather than the love of the student.

The love of the teacher's lifestyle. These are teachers who teach so that they are free to do what they really want during school vacations, especially summer. These individuals view teaching not as a calling but as a funding source. The students are something that must be endured.

Just how passionate, how fervent was Jesus about communicating with His class we call the world? Jesus left all of heaven's glory in order to sacrifice Himself for the good of His "class." He taught the truth with all of His heart and all of His soul and all of His mind—and ultimately with all of His life. *Christ died to teach us the truth!* That's the passionate love Christ has for His students.

When all is said and done, the greatest compliment you or I can ever receive as a teacher may well be, "See how he loved his students!"

Maximizer 2: Communicate the subject with the students' needs and interests in mind.

If you have heard Charles Swindoll preach, you probably have said to yourself, "That's exactly how I feel," or "That's what I really needed." He seems to have an uncanny knack of preaching exactly what you need at the time.

How does he do it? He is a master at expressing his content with his listeners' needs and interests in mind. He has one hand on your pulse and the other on the Bible. He disciplines himself never to change the truth but always clothes the truth with contemporary culture. It hits home because he always aims at your home.

Unfortunately, too many have both hands on the Bible and no hands on the pulse. Our lessons are biblical, to be sure, but as irrelevant as a raincoat in the deserts of Kuwait. Students leave our classes with notebooks full but hearts empty. They have come to feast at the banquet table but leave hungry, having discussed what was on those silver platters but never having eaten from them.

Always aim your content at your class. Make it hit home every time you teach. Because this is such an important law of teaching we will spend two entire chapters (the Law of Need) helping you become "people sensitive" when you teach.

Maximizer 3: Alter your style regularly according to each situation.

After speaking one evening at an outstanding Bible conference in the mountains of North Carolina, I became involved in back-to-back counseling situations that demanded two entirely different styles.

Slouched dejectedly over a chair in the corner, waiting until everyone else had left that night, was a young man who was obviously in deep distress. His tone of voice reflected brokenness and remorse, so immediately I had to transition my body language and tone of voice from platform teaching to personal counseling. I pulled up a nearby chair and lowered my voice, leaned forward and listened intently.

He was a young assistant pastor who was in severe conflict with his senior pastor. It was so serious that he intended to leave the ministry. After posing some strategic questions, I asked him how badly he wanted this problem solved. Would he do anything in order to find victory? His answer meshed with his body language—yes, he said through his tears, he was willing. With compassion I described the biblical answer to his problem and challenged him to obey the Lord fully and without compromise. As we stood, we shook hands, and he committed to telephone his senior pastor and make things right and recommit himself to following his leadership without a spirit of rebellion. My style? Quiet, personal, relaxed, intimate, soothing.

As we wrapped up our discussion, I noticed out of the corner of my eye that my wife, Darlene, was standing with a couple at the back of the auditorium. The woman had her hands on her hips and he had his arms folded. I couldn't understand their words, but their tone was belligerent and angry.

My wife was relieved when I finally joined this unhappy situation. Within seconds, the six-foot-four, 250-pound man was literally yelling at his wife, spewing furious comments seemingly without end or mercy. I started speaking to him in the same tone of voice I had with the young man—the same style—and was rolled over by this towering steamroller. I raised my voice to catch his attention, but he was already many decibels above me. I raised my voice further and he began shouting over me.

I realized that my style just wasn't cutting it. It was effective with the young minister, but if I wanted to serve the needs of this couple then I had no alternative but to turn up the steam. A lot.

I winked at Darlene to alert her that I was going to "put on an act" and started in on this guy. It was quickly apparent he hadn't listened to anyone for a long time. With a desperate prayer, I intensified my delivery.

Still I felt like a wimp under his attack. Finally, in a burst of emotion and intensity I hadn't experienced since my fistfight with Johnny Red in the eighth grade, I lit into this guy and began driving my finger into his chest. Every time he interrupted me I cut him off midsentence. Finally he began listening to me for the first time. His body language communicated that he had become a receptor rather than an attacker, and he became open to rebuke and counsel.

After the couple left an hour later, arm in arm, Darlene began to walk back to our cabin. I noticed that she was not saying anything and seemed upset. I asked her what the matter was and she said, "I've never seen you act like that ever in my life, and I hope you won't act that way with me!"

I was shocked! "Didn't you see my wink?" She had, but she didn't understand what it meant. She thought I had lost control. I assured her I was fully in control and had chosen an unusual and risky style to break open this hardened husband. I purposefully acted so strong because other styles were not having any impact.

Do you think I was comfortable in that situation? Not on your life! I was sweating, even trembling. So why was I doing that? Because my "student" had a severe case of "belligerentitis," and I sensed that unless I could break through, he or his wife might end their marriage that very night.

What do you do when your students' body language and silent response demonstrate they are bored and uninterested? Do you raise your intensity and unleash your creativity—or just tell them to pay attention and mundanely muddle on?

Do you know what the number one complaint is among all students? Eighty percent of the students I talk to openly confess they are bored the majority of the time in the majority of their classes.

I hope you now realize that boredom has nothing to do with the student component of teaching. And although you may debate me, neither is the subject component of teaching the primary culprit behind boredom. I once heard a speaker lecture for ten minutes on "the importance of the brown paper bag." As he finished, the whole crowd stood to its feet, cheering wildly. It was magnificent!

The tragic truth about boredom is that I have heard teacher after teacher bore their students to the point of tears while talking about the most important subject in all the world—the Bible! You see, boredom isn't what you talk about so much as how you talk about it.

Haven't you ever taken an elective class because it sounded interesting, only to begin dreading it after just two class sessions because the teacher put everyone to sleep? It seems that some of us have mastered the verbal equivalent of Sominex! In contrast, maybe you've dreaded taking a required course because you were sure it would be death warmed over—boredom with a capital B. Until the teacher got hold of you with her love for the subject, that is. Before long you were enthralled with the class and the teacher. It became your favorite class.

I saw the most remarkable illustration of this a number of years back on the top of Mount Carmel in Israel, where Elijah had his unforgettable battle with the prophets of Baal. There was a stunning sculpture of Elijah there, and everyone in our Walk Thru the Bible tour wanted to know what the lengthy inscription said. But for the life of me I couldn't read it—it wasn't English, Greek, or Hebrew. Then all of a sudden the youngest member of our group—a sixteen-year-old girl—began to translate this Latin inscription flawlessly and with emotion! I was so impressed and curious that I asked if I could sit next to her on the bus and hear her story.

She told me her tenth-grade teacher made Latin come alive with such intensity that it became not only her favorite class, but also that of many of her fellow students. This teacher made Latin live! I've had a number of teachers like her in my career. Somehow they never did understand the word *boring*.

And neither did their students.

Maximizer 4: Rest in your talents and gifts— be yourself.

Have you ever heard another speaker and wished you could speak like him? Most of us have found ourselves wishing we could teach or preach like someone else, as if power in the pulpit comes through imitation.

A great preacher spoke in chapel when I was a freshman in seminary and delivered one of the most inspiring sermons I had ever heard. I was so moved that I transcribed the entire tape. I couldn't wait to preach this man's masterpiece. Finally an unsuspecting little church asked the seminary for a pulpit supply, and I had my big moment.

I started preaching this sermon with everything in me. On the second page, however, I happened to look at the audience and was horrified to see that mass boredom had arrived in full force. I thought maybe I needed to use some of the great preacher's gestures, which I had also memorized—so I tried them. A couple of old ladies in the front row looked at each other and shrugged their shoulders. I waved my arms even more dramatically.

I turned to page three and started quoting from the Hebrew and Greek. *Wait until they hear this,* I thought. But some of them were already nodding off. In desperation, I glanced at my loving helpmeet for a smile of affirmation. When I located her in the third row, she had a bewildered look on her face, then started slowly shaking her head from side to side. I lost my place and my stomach announced its displeasure at this tension. And I had fourteen pages to go.

By the time we drove out of the parking lot, I had slid into dark despair. I announced to my wife that I'd had it—I was quitting seminary tomorrow. God had made a tragic mistake in calling me to preach.

Darlene was quiet at first. Finally she delivered her sermon of the morning, but it took one paragraph, not seventeen pages: "Sweetheart, the Lord has called you to preach, but He never called you to preach another man's sermon. And what were you doing with your arms? That wasn't you! God can't bless you if you try to be someone other than who He made you to be."

What a turning point in my ministry. If it hadn't been for my wife's kind counsel I might never have made it through seminary and into the ministry. I committed never again to preach another man's message or to copy another's style.

I fear that we often find ourselves desiring things of the flesh in order to attain things of the Spirit. We unwittingly seek for the right things in the wrong places. We wrongly conclude that if we just had the other person's gift, our teaching would be so much more powerful. That's dangerous and even unbiblical territory.

It's apparently a universal human tendency to envy another's gift and undervalue one's own. Scripture teaches that envy is a work of the flesh and not from God. When we desire something God has given to someone else and not to us, we secretly rebel against God's will for us. God is the One who made us, who directed the formation of our physical, mental, and emotional characteristics (Psalm 139:15–16).

When we desire another person's gifts, we are considering only the human side of ministry. We wish for another's talents only when we allow ourselves to forget the Lord's remarkable promise: "My grace is sufficient for you, for My strength is made perfect in weakness" (2 Corinthians 12:9). If we desire God's best in our lives, then we must realize His best for us includes both our strengths and our weaknesses.

Maximizer 5: Note constantly your students' attitudes, attention, and actions.

Effective teachers constantly read the "language of the learner," or body language. Master teachers are so adept at this that they almost develop an ongoing conversation between teacher and learner without the learner ever saying a word. As the teacher reads the physical, he responds with the verbal. Students sometimes describe such a teacher as "in touch."

When we have a personal conversation with another person who is effective at reading our nonverbal clues, we often describe that person as "discerning" or "insightful." Those twin terms are precise because such individuals have the ability to read between the lines of what we are saying and understand what we really mean.

Most of us have never given adequate attention to developing these skills of discernment. Our culture vastly overestimates the power of the verbal and vastly underestimates the power of the nonverbal. Whenever sociologists have sought to determine the relative power of each, the nonverbal has always out-communicated the verbal.

The more discerning you become at hearing what your students are saying through their nonverbal clues, the more you will know what you must adjust to better cause your students to learn. Teachers who are unskilled in this area have no idea what their students will achieve when given a test. But skilled teachers can predict almost precisely what the scores will be because their students have been unendingly communicating with them.

Maximizer 6: Excel by using your strengths to compensate for your weaknesses.

One of the secrets of all athletic champions is that they play to their strengths. If a tennis player's greatest strength is playing at the net, then he should always charge the net. Champions know how to focus. They consciously limit the areas they seek to excel in. They continuously say "no" to the many good in order to say "yes" to the few best.

By contrast, people who never fully achieve their potential have a different perspective. Instead of concentrating on their skills, they focus all their attention on strengthening their weaknesses. Many people I know are spending their entire lives trying to become "well-rounded" in all areas rather than excellent in those specific areas of greatest strength.

One of my lifelong hobbies is reading books about leaders. Common to all great men and women is this philosophy to focus their energies to excel in only a few, well-chosen areas.

If you desire to excel for Christ, you must narrow your choices. The apostle Paul practiced this priority as he exclaimed, "But one thing I do" (Philippians 3:13). Right before Paul died he reminded us that the person who is a good soldier of Jesus Christ does not entangle himself "with the affairs of this life, that he may please him who enlisted him as a soldier" (2 Timothy 2:4).

Therefore, if you desire to be excellent for Christ in the classroom, don't try to do everything equally well. Do fewer things better. Focus. Don't think that to excel you need to be well-rounded. You don't! When you begin to consistently choose to serve God through the areas in which He's gifted you the most, you will experience a growing flood of God's blessing.

As you focus on your strengths, remember two additional things about your weaknesses:

- Improve your weaknesses until they are not an irritant to your class and are within the "acceptable" range. Even though you may be superb rushing the net, to play tennis you must also be able to hit a strong forehand and backhand. You need to raise your failing grades to at least passing.
- Use your strengths to compensate for your weaknesses. "Rush your net" as much as possible.

Whether you are a subject, student, or style person, use that innate strength to shore up your innate weaknesses. I'll never forget how one subject-oriented teacher used his mind to compensate for his pronounced weakness in relating to his students. He had just joined the faculty and all of the students were full of curiosity about this scholar as we entered our first class period with him. About a third of the way into his first lecture, someone in the back of the room raised his hand and asked a question.

The professor responded, "That's a great question, Jim." You should have seen Jim's face—he had never met the professor. Then professor said, "George, what do you think?" and later, "Mary, that's a good point." We were amazed that a professor would care enough about us to memorize our names the first day of class. He had wisely used his strength (memory) to compensate for his weakness in relating to students.

So pursue your full potential by focusing your efforts to your greatest strengths, then use those strengths to compensate for your weaknesses.

Maximizer 7: Rely on the Holy Spirit for teaching that is supernatural.

This maximizer moves beyond the natural and introduces the supernatural. Although this vital subject is discussed more fully in the Law of Application, a few general comments are necessary.

The Spirit was described previously as one of the Big Five Causers of Learning. Except for those rare occasions when the Holy Spirit overrides the situation and accomplishes His divine work in spite of us, He almost always chooses to work in cooperation with the speaker, subject, and the students. The most powerful learning occurs when the human teacher consciously cooperates with the Divine Teacher, who is free to move in the hearts of the students. The Law of Application describes this key relationship more in depth.

There are three different levels of teaching, and all of us conduct classes at one of these distinct levels:

Selfish level. The teacher does what comes naturally to him and subtly uses the students to meet his own needs. He does not accept the responsibility of causing the students to learn but settles for covering the material.

Servant level. The teacher serves the student with all his heart, soul and mind. He concentrates on meeting his students' needs and uses his creativity and energy to cause the students to learn.

Spirit level. The teacher fully serves the student but additionally cooperates with the Spirit in preparation of the lesson, delivery of the lesson, and in his relationship with the student. When this regularly occurs, the students are taught not only by the external teacher but also by the internal One. As the Spirit anoints the teacher and convicts the student, learning is launched to the supernatural level.

May the Lord encourage us all to become servants of students, as well as of the Spirit.

CONCLUSION

During my first year of teaching college, I began to develop and deepen this philosophy about teaching and learning. A few weeks into the semester, I realized that three freshman students were failing one of my classes—and not by a little! Their grades began to bother me more and more. At the beginning of the semester I felt no compunction about giving such poor grades. After all, if they were failing, it was their own fault, right? But something kept gnawing at me. Perhaps I had better do something before it was too late.

I invited each of them to have lunch with me at a hamburger restaurant up the street. I chose not to tell any of the three young men that I was inviting the others, so they were all surprised to see each other. I bought them all hamburgers and shakes, but as you can imagine with three failing students and their professor, lunch didn't start out with a bang.

Finally I said to them, "You know, guys, there are four of us in this booth, and we all have one thing in common. We're all failing my class. You are failing, and therefore I'm failing. I know I hate failing and I have a hunch that you do, too. Is my class that bad?"

"No, it's all right," one of them said.

I sensed there was more so I asked, "How are you doing in your other classes?"

They all looked down at the table and chewed their all-beef patties on sesame seed buns.

I looked across the table and asked the first young man if there was anything bothering him. "Well," he said, "I'm a new Christian, and I'm the only one in my whole family who knows Christ. I tried to share the gospel with them before I came to college and they just laughed at me. They told me I was crazy to go to a Bible college. I figure if I flunk out, they'll never listen to me about Christ, and it's really getting me down."

Then I looked at the young man who was nodding as if he understood and asked him to tell us about himself. "Well," he stammered, "I was drunk a lot of my high school career, partying and in with the wrong crowd. Finally I rededicated my life to Christ in my last semester, but my grades were just terrible. I guess I never learned how to study. This college let me attend on probation and told me I had one semester to make it. I'm learning a lot and I'm improving, but I don't think I can put it all together in time." He blinked away tears. "And I just know God wants me to serve on the mission field, and I'm so afraid of failure I can hardly study at night."

By this time my hamburger was lying half-eaten on my plate. I looked at the last young man and noticed he had a sheepish look on his face. He looked off to the side and simply said, "I'm in love...and my sweetheart's back in Iowa. This is my first time away from home; I'm just really lonely."

So we talked about their lives, and finally I said, "You know, gentlemen, our next class is on the book of Joshua, and I have the feeling that Joshua has an answer for every one of your problems. I would like you men to come to our home on Friday night for the world's greatest homemade pepperoni pizza. Together we are going to find God's answer to each of your challenges. Then I want you to share your answers with the rest of the class next Tuesday."

Friday night they all showed up. We had an unbelievable time. Thankfully we were able to find answers for all of their problems, but I must admit that when we started, I wasn't sure if Joshua had all the answers!

The following Tuesday morning after I opened the class, the first young man came to the lectern and told the class his problem and fears, then Joshua's answer. Then the next young man strode up and described his love for his girlfriend and loneliness. He told about how Joshua felt with Moses gone and how loneliness can be faced through the power of the Lord. I noticed some of the girls were wiping away tears.

Finally the last young man quietly made his way to the front. I was most concerned about him because he had a great fear of public speaking. He started mumbling and looking at the floor, but he soon felt such acceptance from the class that he raised his head and began to look us in the eye. He told how Joshua learned to be courageous and face the giants of his life.

My heart was gripped, and as he made his way back to his seat, his fellow students began to clap. Class ended that day with all of us shouting and clapping and affirming our three friends. The students were never the same from then on—we had bonded together as one tight-knit family.

What do you think happened to those three men's grades? Not just in my class, but in all their classes that semester? You guessed it. They turned around! They now had a fire in their eyes, hope in their hearts, and courage to face their own giants and Jerichos in the mighty power of God's strength.

Such turnarounds warm our hearts as teachers. They make all the work worthwhile. What did it take to turn those precious lives around? Three hamburgers and a couple of pepperoni pizzas.

As we begin this wonderful adventure of learning how to teach the Lord's way, will you join with me in committing to "cause your students to learn"? Will you commit before Him that whatever it takes, you are going to rise up and serve the Lord through the power of the Spirit? Never again will you settle just to "cover the material." Never again will you look the other way when that student of yours stares out the window. You are going to teach your students with all your heart and all your soul and all your mind—all for the glory of God! Even if it takes *four* homemade pepperoni pizzas.

DISCUSSION QUESTIONS

1. Take a few moments and examine yourself as a teacher. On a scale of 1 to 10, rate how strong you are in each of the following areas: Scholar (subject-oriented), Friend (student-oriented), and Communicator (style-oriented). If you are to become a truly outstanding teacher, you are going to have to focus your efforts on your greatest strengths. Name at least three ways you can do that during the next twelve months.

2. What do you think is the biggest problem in your class—the way you deal with the subject, or students, or style? Reflect upon your major weakness which may have become an irritant or detriment to learning. How could you use your strengths to overcome that weakness? Make a list of two or three action points you could take immediately. Now, why not test your own advice?

3. The number one complaint of all students is that their classes are boring. Over 80 percent of the students we have surveyed across the nation say this is by far the major problem. Name the three things you think cause the majority of classes to be boring and offer a solution for each.

4. Take a blank sheet of paper to the next three classes or services you attend and rank the speaker with the 1 to 10 scale for Scholar, Friend, and Communicator. Write specific action points for each of the speakers that would help him double his effectiveness.

LAW TWO

The Law of
Expectation

Chapter Three

Expectation
Mindset, Model, and Maxims

I stood like a rock in a rushing stream of preoccupied Bible college students. It was fall registration. Organized chaos. I'd seen it all before many times, but this time instead of racing around the gymnasium signing up for classes, I watched as students signed up for my classes. It was my first year out of graduate school, and I was just hours away from my debut on the other side of the lectern.

Taking a closer look at several of the registration tables, I noticed that I had been assigned sections one, two, and three of the course called "Bible Study Methods." The remaining five sections were taught by others. After walking around for twenty minutes, I left the gym and headed across campus toward my office. A well-seasoned faculty member at the college caught up with me and said, "I just can't believe it!"

"You can't believe what?"

"They gave you section two, didn't they?"

"Well, yes, I guess they did."

He shook his head in seeming unbelief. "I just can't believe it. You're the new faculty member—first-year rookie—and they gave you section two."

He had me perplexed. "Why—what's so special about section two?"

"You mean they didn't tell you at faculty orientation?"

The truth was, I was the only new faculty member that year, so they didn't have a faculty orientation. I asked him to explain it to me.

"Section two has all the top high school seniors coming into the freshman class. The honors group. Cream of the crop. The most outstanding group of students in the whole college."

We stopped outside the faculty offices and he leveled his gaze at me. "Bruce, you are not going to believe the difference teaching section two."

"What do you mean?" I asked, not knowing whether to feel exhilarated or intimidated. Growing up, I had never been in a section two, I didn't think...

"Motivation! Like a team of wild horses straining at the reins. Those kids'll just pull it out of you. You're going to love every minute of it. Wow! First-year teacher. I can't believe the luck."

He walked down the sidewalk, shaking his head. I was intrigued, to say the least.

The next day, section one filed in and we had a good hour. Nothing outstanding, just a good give-and-take session with a solid group of young men and women.

After break, section two walked in. I couldn't believe it. He was absolutely right. I could feel the electricity in the air. From the ring of the bell, class just flew by as the teacher and students learned at almost warp speed. It was like stepping on a surfboard and riding the crest of the wave the entire hour.

At times the class's interest and desire to learn swept over me with such intensity that I had trouble staying on top of it. Everything seemed different—their questions, their eye contact, their facial expressions, even the way they sat in their chairs. It was incredible. My colleague was right: These students pulled the best right out of you.

Section three came in later that day, and I realized in only a few seconds they were just like section one. Good, but nowhere near the caliber of section two.

As the semester progressed, I found myself increasingly grateful to God for leading me into the ministry of teaching. I'd never felt so challenged and fulfilled. And though I enjoyed all of my classes, section two always made my day.

As we neared midterms, I found myself walking to a faculty meeting with the academic dean, Dr. Joseph Wong. "Well, Bruce," he said, "you're at the halfway point of your first year. The honeymoon is over by now. How do you enjoy teaching college?"

"It's absolutely terrific! It's better than I ever imagined."

He smiled. "That's great to hear. What's your favorite part of teaching?"

Without thinking I blurted out, "Section two!"

He raised his eyebrows and stopped walking in order to listen more intently, I thought. "You have section two? Tell me about it."

It was the first chance I had to express my delight and gratitude for the opportunity to teach thirty of the keenest students I had ever encountered. I must have sung their praise for a couple of minutes as I described the amazing difference between them and the rest of my classes.

The dean looked thoughtful as I went on and on about this gifted group of young men and women. When I had finished he said, "I'm glad you're having so much success, Bruce, but I need to tell you something that may surprise you—there is no honors class this year. We canceled it."

My mouth went dry. "Joe," I said, "you've got to be kidding!"

"No, I'm not kidding. Last year we decided it would be better if we spread the top students through all of the classes. We thought it would add a little more spark to each of the sections."

Dizzy with disbelief, I said, "Joe, I'll catch you in a few minutes. I need to go back to my office for a moment."

I raced into my office and dialed the registrar, sure that my colleague was trying to pull something over on this "rookie." "Joyce," I said, "I've got section two of Bible Study Methods, right?"

"That's right, Bruce."

I swallowed hard. "And Joyce, section two contains all the outstanding students—the top freshmen, right?"

"Well, no, Bruce. We canceled that program last year."

Groaning inwardly, I thanked her and hung up the phone. I couldn't seem to come to grips with what was happening. With reluctance, I reached for my grade book and opened it. I compared the grades of sections one and three with section two. The difference was staggering.

I pulled a stack of ungraded papers off my bookshelf. Stacking sections one and three on top of each other, I compared that pile with the stack from section two by itself. Section two had more pages than the other two sections combined!

I went through the papers, one by one, page by page, and the difference was dramatic. The section two students outshone their peers again and again.

That day proved to be one of the most dramatic learning experiences of my life. I've never quite gotten over it. For the first time, I realized that what I believed about my students made an incredible difference in what they learned in my class.

You see, there was no real difference between sections one, two, and three. It was the same content, same day of the week, same pool of eighteen- and nineteen-year-old students. Not one difference. In fact, never once did I say, "You're section two and your performance should reflect it."

Then how could I explain such a dramatic difference in what these students learned? The only difference was in the teacher's expectations. Because my expectations were much higher for section two, so was their behavior and learning. I'll never forget sitting back in my chair and saying to myself, "I wonder what would have happened if that faculty member had told me the outstanding students were in section three!"

That experience locked forever in my memory the reality of the Law of Expectation. My expectations undeniably have a tremendous impact on the lives of my students—both for good and not for good.

Since this book is written to help you maximize your ability to cause your students to learn, then obviously if you can master the power of expectations in your teaching, you can ensure that your students flourish as section two!

Before you complete this law then, you will know how to blossom your students, your children, your friends. This truth correctly implemented from a heart of love will have a beautiful impact upon everyone. Just remember that the Lord sees every student and every child as a "section two" person that He wants to blossom through you, the teacher.

EXPECTATION MINDSET

What is our normal mindset about our students? Do we usually expect great things of our children and students? Unfortunately, I don't believe most people do.

Actually, most of us think that our private thoughts about our class or individual student is no one else's business and won't make any difference anyway. Whether we think our class is full of exciting people or bores, we're convinced it makes no difference in the teaching-learning process. As long as we keep our thoughts quiet and don't let our true feelings show, everything will be fine.

The Law of Expectation categorically rejects this notion. It reveals that what you think has a powerful and undeniable impact on everyone you meet both in and out of the classroom.

Let's take this concept of "expectation" and place it into the biblical context and discover from two key passages the main concepts that surround it.

And let us *consider one another* in order to *stir up love and good works*, not forsaking the assembling of ourselves together, as is the manner of some, but *exhorting* one another, and so much the more as you see the Day approaching. (Hebrews 10:24–25)

Beware, brethren, lest there be in any of you an evil heart of unbelief in departing from the living God; but *exhort one another daily*, while it is called "Today," *lest any of you be hardened through the deceitfulness of sin.* (Hebrews 3:12–13)

"And let us consider one another..." Why should I consider you? Hebrews 10:24–25 says that I should consider you "in order to stir up love and good works" in you. The Greek word behind *consider* means to scrutinize, to evaluate, to constantly look at your audience and ask, "Where are they? Are they with me right now or not? What are their needs? How can I adjust my content and delivery to teach them more effectively?"

I must know what's going on in your life or I can't "stir you up" because I don't know where you need help. I have to know how you're feeling and what you're thinking. I have to discern whether you have a problem in order to help stir you up for love and good works.

Consider also means "to brood over." It means to quietly analyze the subtle messages you're sending me. Your body language sends all kinds of messages to those who have eyes and ears to see and hear. Too often, however, we who teach are so wrapped up in our content that we miss the messages from the people God has called us to "consider."

I'll never forget the day I met a true expert in "considering." In November of my second year of graduate school, Darlene and I were extremely pressed financially, so I decided to apply for a job at the largest department store in Dallas. I was given an extensive job application to fill out and joined forty or so others in a large, open area to wait for an interview. The personnel director sat in an office right in the waiting room; everyone could see what was happening the entire time.

While I waited, I enjoyed visiting with those around me. Quite a while passed between the time I finished the application and when I was called in for my interview. With typical nervousness, I finally entered that formidable door marked Personnel Director. As I sat down, the lady behind the desk smiled and said she had just the right job for me. She said they had been actively looking for the appropriate person for a number of weeks, and she was sure I'd be just perfect. As you can imagine, I was perplexed—she hadn't even looked at my application. How could she know my skills or interests?

And then she revealed the job: "I think you'd make a perfect Santa Claus."

"Santa Claus? What? How do you know I would make a good Santa Claus?" I blurted out. "I don't even believe in Santa Claus! And you've not yet looked at my job history or application!"

She just smiled. "I really don't need to, although we will do an extensive background check. But I don't think I will find anything to change my mind. After all, I already know a lot about you."

"I don't understand," I stammered. "We've never met, and you haven't even looked at my application yet. How can you know anything about me?"

She explained that she watched everyone in the waiting room and knew a lot about each person before they even walked through her door. Then she started listing off fact after fact about me—and every one was right. I couldn't believe it. Finally she explained that she'd been an active student of people for more than thirty years and knew how to read a person like a book.

Curious, I asked her to list some of the specifics she "read" in me that enabled her to know so much.

First, she had watched me make eye contact with the personnel clerk when I picked up the job application. I was friendly, direct, and courteous, even though I was probably anxious. Second, she saw me fill out the application with determination and diligence. I pressed hard on my pencil and bent over the desk—all showing intense commitment to overcome obstacles en route to my goal. Third, when a five-year-old in the seat in front of me began crying, I tried to entertain her by showing her my pen "and making some crazy faces." That said I cared for children enough to set aside my own interests.

During that amazing interview, she listed more than a dozen of my activities and their implications. Before she was finished, I was sure she knew the brand name of my underwear by the color of my socks! I left the store with a new and unexpected job as Santa Claus—but more important, with an unforgettable education on the power of personal observation.

It's been many years since those Santa Claus days, and since then I've developed a goal of becoming a careful observer of others in order to serve them more effectively. Do you brood over the people you're teaching? Are you constantly asking, "What are the needs of my students right now? Am I connecting or am I not connecting?" Consider your audience; brood over them.

If you're a parent, you must do this all the time. For instance, when our kids were younger, my wife and I noticed that sometimes they would act totally out of character. They would act annoyed, frustrated, irritated, they would stop making eye contact, and they would not respond well to us. Finally we realized their "emotional cup" had somehow become empty during the events of the day. They were emotionally insecure and needed to be filled up with our personal attention and love. Darlene and I would decide between us who had enough energy to work on filling that child's cup, and then either she or I would take our son or daughter to the den or bedroom and love him and hug her until eye contact was restored and emotional well-being had returned.

Sometimes I find I'm the one whose cup is empty. It's amazing over these years of a happy marriage how Darlene will sense that and take the initiative of meeting my needs. Sometimes she'll say, "Why don't you sit in the den, and I'll make you a cup of fresh coffee and keep the kids out of your way for a while." Then she'll sit next to me and ask, "How was your day? I sense you had a tough one."

The key to all these illustrations is "consider one another." Have you ever started talking with someone, sensed something was wrong, mentioned it to her, and heard her say, "How on earth did you know?" If you can read people like that, then you have taken this passage to heart, and you are ready to take the next step in becoming a wonderful people-blossomer.

Hebrews 10:25 begins, "Not forsaking the assembling of ourselves together, as is the manner of some, but exhorting one another." When I "consider" you in order to stir up love and good works, you probably aren't aware of what I'm doing. The "considering" happens inside of me while the "stirring up" goes on inside of you. But how does the Bible teach that we're to make that link from me to you? I am instructed to "exhort" you.

The word *exhort* is an encouraging word, not one of criticism. It involves mutual concern, coming alongside to nurture, to love, to care, to help.

These verses in Hebrews instruct us to first discern what's going on in your life so I can stir up love and good works in you. Do you exhort your students? Hebrews says we should exhort one another "daily." Have you exhorted somebody today?

Stir up your students to love and good works! That's the positive side. But there's another side, too. Let's look once again at how Hebrews 3:12–13 describes it:

Beware, brethren, lest there be in any of you an evil heart of unbelief in departing from the living God; but exhort one another daily, while it is called "Today," lest any of you be hardened through the deceitfulness of sin.

Exhortation, then, ranges from the positive to the negative. It's pleasant when somebody is sensitive to my needs, cares about me, notices I'm out of it, and gently redirects me back on track. But what happens when I'm not so pliable? We are to start slow and encourage, moving from positive, light affirmation all the way through some frank conversation down to rebuke and even strong rebuke. Sometimes, that's what it takes to get another person stirred up to choose to obey.

There's an amazing account of strong rebuke in the last chapter of Nehemiah. The people weren't obeying the Lord and wouldn't submit to what was right. So what did their teacher Nehemiah do? "I contended with them and cursed them, struck some of them and pulled out their hair" (Nehemiah 13:25). What a technique! Now, I don't recommend that you imitate Nehemiah's method, but why do you think he acted that strongly? He loved his God so much and was so concerned for his people that he jumped headfirst into a direct and forceful confrontation.

As a responsible parent, I must exhort or rebuke my children. When I begin to feel responsible for you and rebuke you when you need it, I risk your displeasure. But that's what love requires.

Are you committed to being an exhorter? Are you willing to obey the Scriptures and say to your class, "How can I help you grow spiritually, help you get out of sin, help you be more committed to God—whatever you need?" It's a commitment. And your class needs it every time you step up front.

That's what the Law of Expectation is all about. Expectations can be subconscious or conscious, positive or negative, edifying or destructive. We must grab hold of our expectations for our class, remold them by considering where our students are and what they need, and then exhort and rebuke them to draw near to God in full obedience. Let's summarize these observations in the Expectation Model.

THE EXPECTATION MODEL

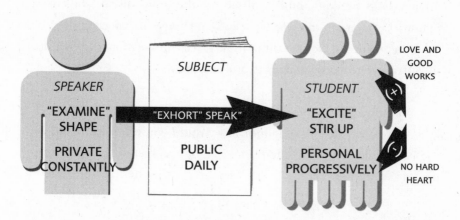

This chart pictures how these biblical concepts relate together. The box on the left stands for the "*Speaker*" or parent, and the box on the right represents the "*Student*" or child, and the box in the middle the "*Subject*," which is not under primary consideration in this law.

In the first box the speaker must "*Examine*" or consider the student to "*Shape*" the expectation, which is done in "*Private*" and should be done "*Constantly*" because the situation is always in flux.

In the student box, the goal of the teacher is to "*Excite*" the student for the positive, which is "*Love and Good Works*," as well as to stop the negative, "*No Hard Heart*." The process must "*Stir Up*" and is "*Personal*" and should be done "*Progressively*" according to the situation and development of your students.

The middle arrow reflects the process by which the teacher takes what has been privately considered regarding the needs of her students and "*Exhorts*" and "*Speaks*" to them in a "*Public*" manner on a "*Daily*" basis.

During the remainder of our discussion of this law, you will understand more fully how these three steps interact with each other, as well as become equipped through the Expectation Method to blossom your children and students.

The influence of our expectations is incredible, a gift from the Lord that should be consciously utilized for the good of our students and family. Listen in on this teacher's profound usage of expectations to blossom her students. Do you think these three short sentences would make a difference to your students if you said them?

"Johnny, I always teach better when you are in the class. When you come next Sunday morning, would you raise your hand so I can see you are in attendance? Then I will teach better."

EXPECTATION MAXIMS

In the musical *My Fair Lady*, British speech professor Henry Higgins makes a bet with a friend that he can transform a poor Cockney flower girl, Eliza Doolittle, into a refined blue blood, a society lady. To assure his success, the professor not only works with the girl on her manners, speech, and dress; he also spreads the word that he will escort a refined, beautiful princess to London's biggest ball of the year. He knew the power of expectations!

Weeks later, when the door to Higgins's gilded carriage opens, a gasp goes up as the crowds see what they expect to see: a dainty, elegant princess. Throughout the evening, Eliza's speech and actions are profoundly shaped by the city's expectations of her. At one point the professor asks the orchestra conductor his opinion of the "princess." The wizened old conductor, who has been to hundreds of balls all over Europe, opines that this young lady was clearly "brought up in the most refined of all palaces."

In the middle of the play Eliza makes a profound statement. She says the real issue isn't how she acts, but what people expect of her. And she says it was Professor Higgins's expectations that caused her to change the most. That is how a girl off the streets becomes a "fair lady."

A powerful force—for good or ill—lies within our expectations.

Let's consider through the seven Expectation Maxims how to direct this potent motivator into productive channels for the good of our students.

Maxim 1: Expectations exist in everyone about everything all the time.

The first step in blossoming your students is to realize that we all have expectations already. Even as you are reading this chapter you already have expectations about the next class you will teach, though you might not have formalized them consciously.

Expectations are as common as breathing. Tonight if someone were to ask you, "How did you enjoy your dinner?" you would answer according to what you anticipated (or expected). Let's suppose you had been thinking all afternoon, "I can't wait for dinner—it's going to be something really special." What happens if it's actually a poor meal? You'll be disappointed. Anytime you or I are disappointed, it's because reality didn't live up to our expectations. If, on the other hand, you find yourself enthused about your dinner, it's because reality matched or even exceeded your expectations.

We have expectations about everything. You have expectations about this book, about whether it will help you. If you expect this book to be great and it turns out to be only good, you will be disappointed. If you thought it'd be good and it turns out to be great, you'll be excited.

At Walk Thru the Bible, we faced this challenge every time we hired a new employee. Almost everyone who joined us came aboard with the unrealistic expectations that there would be no problems, no stress, no misunderstandings, no long hours. Some came expecting to find coworkers who were like angels and a work environment never marred by carnality.

But reality always hits! Numerous new hires experienced disappointment because Christian organizations are still staffed with regular people. Once we identified the problem, we were able to spend careful time adjusting those expectations realistically: The only perfect place is heaven.

If you realize that expectations exist in everyone all the time, you're light years ahead of the normal person. Realizing that will encourage you to think through how realistic your expectations are and adjust them if necessary.

Unrealistic expectations are why so many marriages are on the rocks today, including Christian marriages. The wife may expect the relationship to continue exactly like the last few months before the wedding—she will receive flowers every Thursday, be taken out to dinner weekly, have sweet nothings whispered in her ear, be invited often for tender walks by the lake, and frequently enjoy deep and meaningful discussions about life. In much the same way, a husband may expect his wife's hair to be perfect, for her to display a kind and gracious spirit at all times, to always be in a romantic mood, and to honor him above everyone and everything all of the time. After a few months of marriage, unless their expectations have settled down to some reality, this couple could be in for some rocky moments.

We go through a number of different stages if our expectations aren't adjusted. The first stage is *disappointment*. The further from reality your expectation, the greater your disappointment. "What a disappointing class we had today," you say. You had an expectation about how good that class session would be and reality didn't match it.

If the disappointment continues and neither your expectation nor reality changes, you enter the stage of *discouragement*. It's deeper than disappointment. You can be disappointed and not discouraged, but you cannot be discouraged without first being disappointed.

If discouragement continues, eventually you will move into the stage of *disillusionment*. When you become disillusioned, you no longer have a false sense of reality. For the first time you actually see reality for what it is, and usually you don't like it. You recognize that the chances of reality's living up to your expectations are nothing but lies, but since you haven't yet given up those unrealistic expectations, life doesn't look too pleasant.

If reality or your expectations don't change, you are headed down a rocky road. The last stage is *despair*, an utter lack of hope. You have no hope that reality will ever meet expectations.

Disappointment, discouragement, disillusionment, despair—all those are tied together and based upon our expectations. Since we all have expectations all of the time about everything, you can imagine the dramatic influence they have over how we interpret our lives and influence the lives of others in and out of the classroom.

Maxim 2: Expectations impact us and others.

As you saw in my story about "section two," our expectations have powerful influence. Without our even realizing it, they constantly impact us and others. Because of their dramatic impact and universal presence, we must learn to use expectations for good.

You probably know what a placebo is (it's a fake pill). Until 1890, 90 percent of all drugs prescribed were sugar pills. The sicker you were, the bigger the pill. If you were really ill and there wasn't any known drug to treat your illness, the doctor would prescribe a large, ugly pill and say, "Take one of these every four hours all through the night. Set your alarm and make sure you get up for the medicine to have its full effect." The doctor knew the placebo had nothing to do with the patient's getting better. But if the patient believed in its power enough to take it through the night, it was bound to have a positive effect.

I was explaining this at a 7 *Laws* conference once, and a man sitting about a third of the way back started to laugh. In fact, he was causing a scene! Finally I stopped and said, "Sir, what's the matter?"

"I'm a physician," he said, "and nothing has changed!"

He came up at the next break and told me what had just happened at his hospital. "Placebos—or expectations—are powerful. Unless you've seen it for yourself, you probably don't know the half of it. Yesterday, one of my patients became very ill and we had to put her in the hospital. Her sickness had only one drug that worked against it, so I asked if she was allergic to that medicine.

'Yes!' she said. 'I have a severe reaction to that medicine and break out in hives, experience heart palpitations, sweat terribly, have fainting spells, and become very nauseated.'

"I told her I was sorry that she had those reactions, but that was the only drug available. Because of the danger, I gave her a placebo but told her it was the real thing. Within an hour my name was called over the hospital loudspeaker, and I ran to her room to find she was having a severe reaction—her body had broken out in sores, she was short of breath, going in and out of consciousness, and was in severe distress."

The physician smiled and continued, "It is surprising that our expectations can have such a dramatic effect, but they can. Everything you have said about the power of expectations has been validated over and over again in the field of medicine. But I never thought my expectations could have a similar impact on my Sunday school class. I'm going to be more careful from now on!"

Not only can our expectations dramatically influence our body, they can also impact every part of our lives. A famous experiment from the past demonstrates this further. In 1900 the Census Bureau bought a new type of tabulating machine for its workers. It estimated that employees could type in 550 cards a day with the new machines. After a couple of weeks there was a great deal of emotional distress, and the director of the census was forced to conclude he couldn't require 550 a day. So workers began to average many fewer cards a day.

About a month later, the bureau found it needed more workers to do all the work that wasn't getting done. Due to the lack of room, however, the new employees were put in a different building. These workers were taught how to use the machines, but weren't told how many cards were expected of them. Guess how many cards that group processed each day? An average of 2,100 per person! They hadn't been told that a normal person could do only 550 a day, so they just whipped them out—without physical duress or headaches. Such is the incredible power of our expectations.

Maxim 3: Expectations are rooted in the past, influence the present, and impact the future.

We tend to build our expectations based on information—or misinformation—from the past. Once built, they influence our attitudes and actions in the present and impact ourselves and others in the future.

Imagine some teachers talking in the hallway about promotion Sunday. One says, "I hope you don't get Tony the Terror." You hear the horror stories about this seven-year-old and pray for months that Tony will be promoted to someone else's class. But on promotion day, guess who walks into your class? Tony the Terror! Does that kid have a chance? No way. The expectations you have already formed will control your attitudes and actions toward Tony. Your expectations will blossom the "terror" in Tony.

Our expectations come from one of four places. First, they can come by *recognition*—some right, some wrong. Imagine that I see you walking down the street and say, "I can tell by your hair and clothing that you use drugs." I've formed an expectation based on an external indicator. But that expectation may be totally incorrect.

Second, we build expectations through *reputation*. Somebody in the faculty lounge says, "I can't wait for the end of the year, because then I'll be rid of Johnny. He is always disrupting my class. You'll get him next year—and he'll be a terror for you, just watch."

The third way we build expectations is by *record*—looking in a file to see how a student has done in the past. A faculty member of a West Coast school once got a file which listed all the students' names and IQs.

The only problem was that a mistake had been made; one sheet listed each student's name and IQ, but the second sheet listed student names and their locker numbers. Nobody discovered the error. At the end of the semester, the students who had the higher IQs had outperformed those with lower IQs, as you'd expect. But those with higher locker numbers also outperformed those with lower locker numbers—simply because the teacher had mistaken locker numbers for IQs! The teacher's expectation radically influenced student behavior.

The fourth way we build expectations is by *relationship*. When we get to know someone, we come to expect certain behaviors. In time our relationship can correct the faulty expectations we had before we really knew the person.

Let's see how all these work together. Imagine a teacher who constructs an expectation, perhaps through reputation, regarding a particular student. The first day of the school year, the teacher notices the student walking across campus on the way to class. *Look at the way that kid walks,* the teacher thinks. *He sure looks cocky. He must be a real wise guy.* Before the very first class, the student is suspect in the teacher's eyes.

When classes begin, the student reacts to the expectation by responding to the hostile vibrations coming from behind the lectern. The teacher never says anything to the student, but he communicates suspicious expectations through his behavior, and the student senses something in the teacher's body language, eye contact, and tone of voice. Discouraged by the negative rapport with this new teacher, the student responds to the behavior. He begins slouching in his chair and demonstrating an "I don't care what you think" attitude. *Aha!* thinks the teacher. *I think I'm right about this fellow. Look at the way he's slouching. A problem for sure.*

The teacher has now confirmed his expectations. He moves past his initial, tentative judgment and becomes more overt in his expectation. The first stage was subtle; the second isn't. It comes through loud and clear in the way the teacher answers the student's questions, in the way he treats the student before and after class. The student feels stung by the seemingly undeserved hostility. *If that's the way you see me,* thinks the student, *maybe that's the way I'll respond. I'll show you just how rebellious I can be!*

So the student begins to reflect the expected behavior. He closely resembles his teacher's premature characterization. His expression looks more and more like a wise guy's, and his responses sound increasingly like a wise guy's. Now the student feels the cold glint in the teacher's eye that says, *I was right about you. You are a rebellious problem student. Now that I have you pegged, I'm going to ride your tail for the rest of the semester.*

With no hope of redeeming himself, the student gives up; he conforms to the power of his teacher's expectation. It ends up being an unpleasant, unprofitable semester for both of them. The teacher asks himself, *Why do I always get stuck with the wise guys?* And the student shakes his head and says, *Why do I always get stuck with such unfriendly, hard-nosed teachers?*

All of this can take place beneath the surface. The teacher may not even know he's communicating suspicion and hostility. The student may not realize he's responding as expected. But the learning experience has been spoiled for both of them. A potentially helpful relationship has been marred, perhaps beyond repair.

Now imagine flipping that process over, so that the teacher's initial expectation for the student is positive. Would the same steps hold true—only this time in the positive direction? Absolutely!

Maxim 4: Expectations are exposed through our attitudes and actions.

Expectations affect both our attitudes (internal) and our actions (external). If you were to watch a teacher relate to various students, before long you could determine her expectations of those students by watching her body language, eye contact, tone of voice, remarks made, and so on.

Various research has been undertaken over the years to discover how expectations impact teaching. Here are some of the findings.

When interacting in class, teachers with low expectations tend to:

- Wait less time for the student to answer a question.
- Call on the student less frequently to answer a question.
- Inappropriately reinforce an incorrect answer of the student.
- Prematurely give the student the answer or call on somebody else.
- Withhold helpful clues and fail to repeat or rephrase the question.
- Give briefer and less informative feedback to the student's questions.
- Interrupt more quickly when the student makes mistakes.

When setting the level of achievement, teachers with low expectations tend to:

- Criticize the student more often for failure.
- Praise the student less often for success.
- Write fewer explanatory notes on graded papers.
- Teach at a significantly slower and less intense pace.
- Fail to give the benefit of the doubt in borderline cases.
- Use fewer of the most effective but time-consuming instructional methods.
- Assign more busy work than meaningful projects.

When relating personally to the student, teachers with low expectations tend to:

- Fail to give specific or positive feedback concerning the student's public response.
- Pay less attention to and interact less frequently with the student.
- Interact with the student more privately than publicly.
- Engage in friendly interaction less often.
- Smile less and limit encouraging physical touch.
- Maintain eye contact less often.
- Limit positive nonverbal communication reflecting attentiveness and responsiveness, including leaning forward, positive head nodding, and general supportive body language.

These actions clearly demonstrate how students believed to be low achievers often fail to learn adequately or behave appropriately. They are not treated like students who are believed to be good students.

Teachers appear to "cause" their students to decline by providing them with fewer educational opportunities and by teaching them less material less skillfully.

Maxim 5: Expectations influence the future, whether stated or unstated.

The uncanny thing about expectations is that we can voice them or keep them private—even subconscious—and yet they still impact others.

I was picked up at the airport once by a pastor who for forty-five minutes spoke gloriously about how great the people in his church were. I found out later that he had also spent some time conveying positive expectations about me to his church. By the time I walked into the church and began to preach, I sensed I could do nothing wrong! The expectations were so positive and affirming that we pulled the best out of each other. While this pastor verbalized his expectations, don't forget that *you don't have to state your expectations to have a great influence on others.*

A psychology department at a major university decided to test whether students' expectations could influence animal behavior. Obviously, animals can't understand language, so they can't be influenced by stated expectations. Researchers picked seventy-two rats and seventy-two students. They brought together half of the students and rats and said to the students, "For generations, we have carefully been developing some 'maze-smart' rats. These rats are incredible. They can go through some of the most complex mazes in unbelievable times. We have devised some especially difficult mazes. Your job for the next thirty days is to see how fast you can train your rats to go through the maze. You cannot talk to the other thirty-six students. Now, let them loose."

Then they brought in the other thirty-six students, gave them their rats, and said, "These rats are 'maze-stupid' rats. They have parents who have been unable to complete even the simplest maze. We would like to challenge you to try to train these stupid rats to go through these mazes as fast as they can anyway."

The two groups used exactly the same mazes. At the end of thirty days, the "maze-smart" rats were getting through the mazes 200 percent faster than the "maze-stupid" rats—even though the rats had been chosen randomly! How did that happen? Researchers concluded that expectations don't have to be verbally communicated to influence behavior. Even of rats.

No one can explain fully how expectations work when they're unstated, but every test I've seen has validated that they do influence the behavior of others. We do know our expectations are expressed through body language. If I put my hands on my hips and cock my head, what am I showing? Exasperation. Disinterest. If I fold my arms across my chest, what does it convey? Defensiveness. "Prove it to me." Since your expectations control your body language, the only way to control and monitor your body language is by consciously shaping your expectations.

Maxim 6: Expectations impair others if set too low or too high for too long.

If expectations are unrealistic, the person may never be able to reach them and may always feel like a failure. Likewise if expectations are set too low or are negative, it is likely that the person will lose interest and become an underachiever.

Imagine a student coming home with a report card with five As and one B+. Mom responds, "What a lousy report card. How come the B+?" What does the student feel? "I can never live up to my mom's expectations."

How would a little soccer player feel if his father said, "The only thing that matters is that you score a goal. Nothing else is good enough"? The boy comes back from his game after making two assists and saving the game with a spectacular defensive play. Dad asks, "Did you score a goal?" The boy says, "No, but I was the star of the game! I—" Dad interrupts, "I don't want to hear it. When are you going to score a goal?" That kind of unrealistic expectation can crush a child.

In contrast, extremely negative expectations can be self-fulfilling. Parents must watch out for this all the time. Maybe you've walked into your thirteen-year-old daughter's bedroom and you can't even see the bed for the mess! You've had it. You've told that girl a hundred times to pick up her things. Without thinking, you say, "This room is a disaster! If someone from the health department should ever stumble in here, it would be condemned. You're going to grow up to be a slob. No man will ever live in the house you keep! You aren't going to amount to anything!"

Did you hear what you just said? You just formed the expectation. And guess who's going to start living up to it?

Or how about your son coming home with his fourth straight F in English? And last night you skipped your favorite TV show to tutor him! You can't believe it, and you hear yourself saying, "You're so stupid. Four

Fs? You have no brains in your head. You're never going to succeed in anything. You are a complete failure."

We've all done it at some point, haven't we? Parents have done it. Teachers have done it. Grandparents have done it. Somehow, instead of blossoming our children, our words rip them apart and breed a future of failure.

Be careful to set your expectations realistically and precisely. Avoid impairing your students by expecting too much of them—or too little.

Maxim 7: Expectations empower others when guided by love.

The ultimate reason for seeking to blossom another person must be love. We must desire to help everyone we can to become everything God wants them to become.

Such people-blossomers are rare, aren't they? If you were to look back over your life, you'd probably find only a few people who believed in you and encouraged you in a meaningful and life changing way. People like that help us stand taller and sprint faster and become what we didn't believe we could become. They love us when we don't love ourselves and share their biblical expectations because, as 1 Corinthians 13 teaches, love "hopes all things, believes all things…"

Like you, I know exactly who those people were in my life, and my life story would be much different were it not for the people-blossomers God sent my direction.

My godly parents were the first. Our home was filled with love and affection, and the belief that "you can do anything you really want to" filtered directly into our home. That can-do attitude rubbed off on us children and enabled us to achieve a great deal more than we would have ever dreamed possible.

I remember one day in high school when I told my parents that we were going to compete in physical fitness in a couple of months and would earn different color gym trunks according to our performance. The coach reminded us that we would have to wear those trunks as we daily ran around the track where the girls would be exercising (he knew the power of expectations too!). He told us the bottom group would wear yellow trunks, the top students would wear red satin trunks, and the very top student would wear "silver trunks." I remember thinking, "I hope I can get a black stripe."

My dad nodded in understanding and didn't say anything. The next day as I was cleaning out the stall of my 4-H bull, Dad stood next to the fence and asked, "When are you going to earn the silver trunks?" There was no question or doubt in his voice; he wanted to know when, not if.

"What? You really believe I could win the silver trunks?"

"Yup," he nodded, "no doubt about it. You just haven't decided you want to work hard enough to get them. But I have a feeling that it's about time. You're silver trunk material, son." Then he walked away. And just like that, because of my dad's expectations, I became silver trunk material.

And so did my brother a couple of years later. Last time I visited our old high school, I discovered the record still stood—we were the only two students from the same family to earn the coveted silver trunks. But if the truth were known, our parents really won those trunks.

I also remember Mrs. Rudin, my sixth-grade public school teacher who blossomed me so fully I can still remember how important I felt when I walked into her class.

And Pastor and Mrs. Richard Griffith of the church in Union, New Jersey, where I served as youth pastor for a couple of years while attending college nearby. Week after week they worked with this wavering and insecure young man, pouring their love and dreams into me. They kept telling me what God wanted to do through me and that God had His hand on me. I drank it up because I needed every word of affirmation I could find.

Then God provided Dr. and Mrs. Stephen E. Slocum as people-blossomers when we moved to Dallas for graduate school. Dr. Slocum would take me to lunch and say, "Tell me about your dreams." I didn't have a dream. "Tell me how you are going to change the world." I wasn't planning on changing the world. "I think your idea of Walk Thru the Bible can spread throughout the whole world! I think you're God's man for the job." There would never have been a Walk Thru the Bible without blossomers such as the Slocums.

Often our spouses are people-blossomers for us. I still have a letter from my wife that she wrote in 1978 and I reread it from time to time. In that letter Darlene expressed positive expectations about our relationship and the future of our marriage and family. That one letter has had tremendous impact on my life. Her convictions and dreams about me continue to blossom me as her husband.

Some time ago, the son of some friends of ours was having a difficult time after changing schools. His life seemed to be falling apart; he was failing in most subjects. His mother was frantic.

Then she happened to meet an old friend who always seemed to be on top of the world. She asked her friend, "How come you're always so positive and in control of everything?" Her friend replied, "There were six kids in our family, and my mom always kept a notebook on each of us. At the end of each month, Mom called us into our bedroom, took out our book and said, 'I'd like you to read this.' She did that for years."

Our friend decided to try it with her son. She bought a notebook and started to look for something good in her boy. For the first two weeks she couldn't find one good thing to write down. One night as she and her husband were discussing this problem, they realized that they'd been so down on their son they couldn't see even one good thing in him.

She confessed her blinders to the Lord and began to look harder and harder and finally found something to write in her book. One day she called him into her bedroom and said, "I have a notebook I want you to read." He was real quiet as he read it, then he said, "Do you really feel this way about me?" "Of course I do!" she replied. He began to cry and said, "I thought you and Dad were only down on me all the time. I didn't think you loved me anymore—that you thought I was a complete failure."

What a dramatic turning point in that young man's life and for that family. Within a few short weeks, that young man changed. His confidence was revived, his relationships with his parents and others were restored, he stopped fighting with his brothers and sisters, and his grades improved. What happened? His parents blossomed him! They found something good to build positive expectations upon for their son's future, and their son blossomed under those wonderful expectations for his good.

What are your expectations—about yourself, God, your family, and your students? Why not readjust them and use them to become a person who truly is a people-blossomer!

MEANING

The essence of the Law of Expectation is these three words: "Expect the best." The teacher should influence his students' learning and behavior by adjusting expectations.

CONCLUSION

When I think about what it means to expect the best, I remember my freshman year of graduate school. I had determined I was going to go to graduate school for my own priorities, not my teachers' priorities. So I set my goals before the semester started, instead of allowing my teachers to set my priorities by the amount of work they assigned. I had five courses, and I determined in which courses I was going to get an A, which courses I wanted to get a B, and which courses were less important and I should get a C.

Dr. Hendricks taught the course "How to Study Your Bible." I said to my wife, "Of all the courses this semester, that is the most important one for my future ministry. I want to know how to study the Bible. I'm going to excel in that class."

I calculated the time I had available for study each week and cut it down the middle, giving Dr. Hendricks's course half my study time and the other four classes the remainder. During the third week of class, we handed in a major paper that I had worked on hard and long. I worried about that paper all week because it was so important to me.

The day I finally got my paper back, my palms were sweaty and my heart was pounding. With trembling hands I took the paper out of the mailbox. There across the top, in red magic marker, Dr. Hendricks had written, "Dear Bruce, this is an absolutely outstanding paper. I believe you have the potential to be one of our country's greatest Bible teachers. It's an absolute pleasure to have you in my class. A+. —Prof."

I held that paper and read those words over and over again. I couldn't believe it! I carried that paper reading that written expectation by my favorite professor all the way down Swiss Avenue, all the way to our tiny corner apartment, where I called, "Sweetheart, come here! You've got to read what Dr. Hendricks wrote on my paper!"

I tacked that priceless paper above my study desk, and every time I was tempted to quit seminary and throw in the towel, I read and reread and reread again what Dr. Hendricks had said about me. I still have that precious paper.

Believe it or not, I had the audacity to believe what he wrote! Up to that point, I never thought that way about myself. I never had a dream like that hidden in the secret corners of my heart. I was just a lowly freshman, scared to death of flunking out.

What happens when a person you highly respect shares with you his high expectation for you? Don't you find yourself poking out new "blossoms" all over? Those people who love us enough to see something wonderful in us—and who care enough to tell us about it—help us become everything God wants us to become.

Your words can have a powerful influence on others. You can become the kind of person others will place on their list of those who believed in them. You can be a Dr. Hendricks to the people you meet—if you really want to. In the next chapter I'll give you an easy-to-use process that will help you blossom people everywhere you go.

DISCUSSION QUESTIONS

1. Who is the best people-considerer that you know? How has that person become so effective at reading others? List specific ways to "read" your audience in order to stir them up.

2. The apostle Paul was an extremely effective exhorter. Read through the book of 2 Corinthians and make a list of every emotion that he felt and employed as he exhorted the church to obey the will of the Lord. Write down the ones you usually use yourself and those you are not comfortable using as of yet. Which of these new ones do you think you can use in the near future?

3. Describe the expectations your parents had about you. Give a couple of examples (like my silver trunks) of either good or bad expectations. What lessons did you learn from your parents that will aid you in your parenting role?

4. Who blossomed you the most in your life? Describe a couple of incidents that had a real impact upon you and tell what difference they made. If you could blossom only three people in your life, who would they be and why? Next to their names, write at least one way you could blossom them during the next four weeks.

CHAPTER FOUR

Expectation
Method and Maximizers

G uy Dowd, a former National Teacher of the Year, once said, "No matter where you grow up, the people around you have a tremendous influence on you. They help shape and mold your life and your dreams. And when you grow up, you're going to be on someone's list as well."

How do you get on that list? How do you expect the best of your students? How do you verbalize that expectation?

EXPECTATION METHOD

Let me suggest five steps you can use with anyone at any place at any time. These five steps are universal—they work no matter who you are or who you want to blossom. They will allow you to take a normal moment in a normal day and use it to blossom the person you care about.

1. EXAMINE the person you want to blossom.

The first thing you must do is open your eyes. You must *"examine"* the people you want to blossom by always paying careful *"attention."* You must be alert for a situation you can use to share your positive expectations with them.

When you examine something, you study it, you pay close attention to it, and you consider what is going on. This requires your full attention. You have your antenna up. You're searching your students all the time, watching for an opportunity you can use. You don't create such opportunities; you just notice them when they appear. Once you become skilled at this, you'll recognize that opportunities exist almost everywhere.

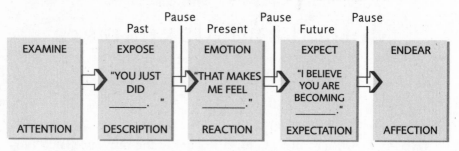

		Pause		Pause		Pause	
		Past		Present		Future		
EXAMINE	EXPOSE		EMOTION		EXPECT		ENDEAR
	"YOU JUST DID _____."		"THAT MAKES ME FEEL _____."		"I BELIEVE YOU ARE BECOMING _____."		
ATTENTION	DESCRIPTION		REACTION		EXPECTATION		AFFECTION

2. EXPOSE what the person did.

Once you see a person act in a way you can use for his good, let that person know you saw it. You have to *"expose"* it to him by giving him a verbal *"description."* Shine a bright light on his behavior and demonstrate that you have noticed him.

We do this verbally. We describe to the person, out loud, what we saw or heard. This forms the basis upon which we build an expectation. Often I begin this with, *"You just did _____"* and then reveal to the person what I observed.

Let's say your daughter Michelle has had a tough time with math. You've been on her case for what seems like fifty years. But you've noticed in the last few weeks that she's been studying without your even telling her to. Suddenly you recognize, *Here's an opportunity I can use to blossom my daughter!*

You walk up to her and say, "Michelle, I've noticed you're studying long hours lately. You've really been hitting the books hard, especially in math." Say it out loud. Tell her what you saw because she probably wasn't aware that you even noticed. Then let it sink in by pausing before going on to the next step (which I'll describe in a moment).

Johnny just received an A on a very difficult test. Your antenna is out and you think, *Here is a moment where I can really blossom my student.* So you say, "Johnny! You just earned an A in science!" Then pause. You let your statement settle down in Johnny's heart. Don't neglect this pause—it's very important.

By the end of this second stage, you both should have your full attention focused on the specific event that will be the basis of your expectation.

3. Describe your EMOTION about what the person did.

After you examine the person and expose his good behavior verbally, then proceed to tell him what you feel about what he just did. Describe to him your "*emotion*" and "*reaction*" to what has just happened.

Tell Johnny how you feel about that excellent paper. Use the formula, "*That makes me feel* _____." For instance, you could tell Johnny, "That makes me feel so proud of you, son!" Use whatever words Johnny can appreciate at his stage of maturity. Say, "That makes me feel jazzed!" if that's what it takes to communicate. Don't always use an adult phrase when you're dealing with a thirteen-year-old. Don't say, "That makes me feel really moved and touched." Get his attention with the very words you choose.

Then pause again. Let it hit home. Make sure your eye contact is clear and strong. Let him squirm a bit in a good way as he basks in your emotional approval. I guarantee that any child—even a teenager—will enjoy that moment!

4. Tell the person what you EXPECT of him in the future.

Up to this point you haven't blossomed anyone. All you've done is give a compliment. A compliment makes a person feel good about something he's done, but it doesn't change him because a compliment is based on something done in the past. It has no future dimension. The person is not sure if he can do it again. Johnny's glad about that first A in science, but he's thinking, *I'm not too sure I can get an A in science again tomorrow.*

That's where the power of expectations comes into play. Expectations take the past and thrust it into the future. This is the step where you tell the person what you "*expect*" from him and share your "*expectation*" by stating, "*I believe you are becoming* _____."

Expressing an expectation does far more than give a compliment. An expectation forces a person's attention off what she did and toward what she wants to become. It draws her out to the landscape where dreams take place.

When you tell someone what you expect of her, you're being a visionary. The media is constantly complaining that our country needs visionary leaders. What is a visionary leader? It's a person who can see what others don't yet see. A visionary leader can see out into the horizons beyond normal human sight and tell us the wonderful things only he can yet see.

God is calling you to be a visionary parent, a visionary teacher, a visionary boss. Not just about the goals or objectives of your family or school or company, but about the *people* in those families, schools, and companies. He is calling you to get out of the normal doldrums and into the soaring clouds of potential. Show your students that "silver lining" that is woven into their futures if they'll just go for it.

That's what Dr. Hendricks did for me in my first year of graduate school. He helped me envision a future I couldn't even begin to aspire to until he believed in me. I didn't see it at first because it was only in his mind's eye, but because I trusted him, I was able to believe that what he saw could actually take place. And because I saw it, I sought it, and whole new vistas opened.

When you expose something, you call attention to the *past* because the event already occurred. When you describe your emotion about that situation, you're in the *present*. But to shape the future, you have to move into the *future* and tell the person what you believe they can become by God's wonderful and enabling grace.

How often do you actually do this? In the last week, can you remember anyone talking to you about your future in such a way that made your heart beat a little faster? A way that made you say to yourself, *I like that picture of my future! I'd like to see it happen?* If you are like the rest of us, it's probably been a long time since someone stretched you and nurtured you and expected the best from you. Do you know what else is true? The person right around the corner is in the same situation—but that person has you. Why not sprinkle a little "faith and hope" in his direction?

Far too often, rather than painting golden pictures of the future, we complain about the past. But the Lord wants us to be people who envision what God can do in the future.

All effective expectations have a number of common characteristics:

First, express your *belief* in the person's potential. You can use words such as, "I believe you are becoming..." or "I can see that you are developing..." or "I sense that in time you will be the kind of person who..." or "I wouldn't be at all surprised if..." I tend to use *believe* a lot, because I don't know for sure what's in store for anyone, do I?

Second, use the *future* perspective—*becoming, growing into, starting to, developing, expanding.* These words signal something the person can grow into, something she can anticipate, something she can feel good about because it presents an open-ended opportunity.

Third, choose the *positive,* not the negative. Make sure that your description of the future is a golden dream, not a destructive nightmare. Avoid anything that even approaches fear; instead, always nourish faith in the heart.

Fourth, tailor your expectation to their *noblest aspirations*. The real issue isn't sharing *your* dream but finding *his* dream! The reason Dr. Hendricks's expectation had such a dramatic impact is that it touched deep aspirations within me. Those aspirations were mine—though perhaps I couldn't even admit them to myself at that point—and he discerned them and moved them into the realm of possibility.

Fifth, express your expectation in *inspiring*, not confining, terms. Don't be so specific that you don't leave room for the person to paint in her own details. Paint broad strokes of brightness and hope and put away the fine brushes. Never say, "I can see you getting straight As on your report card from now on." That could become a prison that hinders rather than wings that soar. Instead say, "I believe you are becoming a person who reaches for the stars and never settles for anything less than your best!"

Sixth, ensure that your expectations are within the realm of *possibility*. Never lie to the person you are trying to blossom. Never tell him something to make him feel good but which, down deep, you know he cannot achieve. Sometimes your expectation will push on his boundaries—but never cross over into clear impossibility.

If you've expressed an appropriate expectation, then you have touched a deep and wonderful chord in the heart of the person. And when it is played, it is sweet and precious. It enables and nourishes and empowers. You'll see it in her face, and sometimes a quiet hush will fall over her because she never thought another person could think such a wonderful thing about her. Allow her to savor the moment. Let it really sink in.

5. ENDEAR yourself to the person through appropriate touch.

"*Endear*" yourself to the one you're blossoming by becoming close and personal. Now it's time to cement your expectation in the person's heart. You've just said something incredibly precious to that person, and you should cement that moment with an appropriate touch. Move from anticipation to "*affection*."

If it's a young boy, you might give him one of those manly nudges. If it's a little girl, come down to her level and gently squeeze her hand. If it's a coworker, you could put your hand on the person's shoulder.

Sometimes when I'm doing this with a person of the opposite sex, I will not literally touch…but yet I will touch. I'll express the appropriate words, smile, and then affirm with my eyes and bow ever so slightly forward. In today's society, we must all be very careful how we exercise touch.

Now let's see the whole process together. Let's look at two situations—one in a typical home, the other in Sunday school.

Let's say it's Father's Day. You have had a hard week and you've been telling your wife that you are going to celebrate the day by sleeping in and getting caught up on the "rest" part of your life.

Saturday evening rolls around and you turn off the alarm clock and begin dreaming of sleeping in till 9:30. But in the middle of a deep sleep you hear some strange rattling. You don't know what it is, but you don't want to stir. Maybe it will go away. It's still dark outside.

Then the rattling noise hits the door. You turn over, wanting to put the pillow over your head, as your wife leaps out of bed and opens the door. "Oh, my goodness. Come in sweetheart."

Your youngest daughter. The little one. She's carrying this tray filled with plates and forks and napkins. You can barely see. This can't be true. Slowly she walks over to the bed with a sheepish, hopeful look on her face.

She made her dad breakfast in bed! It's so early you can't even see the sun. But she's beaming, holding this big tray in her little hands.

"Well, sweetheart," you mumble, "what's this?"

"Well, Daddy, today is Father's Day and I made breakfast in bed for you. Just like Mommy does!"

"You made breakfast in bed for me?" (EXPOSE) "And what are all these wonderful things you made for me?" (You don't know what they are because all kinds of unrecognizable things are floating around on your plate.)

"I made you scrambled eggs [*Oh, that's what that is*] and this is French toast [*This is going to be a challenge*]."

And then you see a large coffee cup with strange things floating around in it. "And what is this?"

"Oh, Daddy, this is my first time. That's your favorite coffee. I put some of that brown stuff in some hot water in the microwave. I hope you like it!"

Now, do you see how precious this moment is to your little girl? How about putting this Expectation Method into practice?

"Jenny, you just made me the most wonderful breakfast in bed that any daddy could ever want. Why, just look at the scrambled eggs, French toast, and even a special cup of homemade coffee! (EXPOSE) Do you know how that makes Daddy feel? Just wonderful! I feel so loved and so special. I think I'm the happiest Daddy in the whole wide world, and you did that for me!" (EMOTION)

Can you see her drinking in all that love and affirmation? But don't stop here; blossom her for the future. Remember what she said a moment ago? She revealed who she aspired to be like—"just like Mommy." So what's the vision of her future that she wishes she could grow into someday? Right, her mom.

"You are becoming a wonderful helper just like Mommy, and I believe you are going to grow up to be a wonderful mommy and make everybody in your home so happy! And a great cook, too!" (EXPECTATION)

Pull her up to your side and give her a huge hug and kiss. Physically demonstrate your love and affection by your closeness. (ENDEAR)

When she walks out of your bedroom she's going to be on cloud nine. Her daddy loved her first attempt at breakfast in bed—but more important than that, he said she was becoming like her mommy!

Why is that so vital? Because that little girl thinks the most wonderful person in the world is her mommy. All those traits of under-standing, caring, serving, loving, cooking, listening—she's starting to have!

Take this Expectation Method, friend, right out of these pages and right into the very moments of your day. It will work with everyone you meet if you will but care enough to use it for their good.

That's the process. First, you *examine* the person. You watch what's going on and find a moment that you think you can use to blossom someone. Second, you *expose* whatever it is that the person did. You describe the action taken, the thing accomplished, the goal achieved. Then pause. Third, you express how you feel about what the person just did. You tell what *emotion* the action triggered in you. Then pause again. Fourth, give the person a desirable picture of what her future could be like. Tell her what you *expect* of her in the coming days. Once more, pause. Last, to make sure the expectation hits the heart and stays there, move over and make appropriate physical contact with that person. *Endear.*

That's all there is to it. I guarantee it will work with anyone, in any place, at any time.

Let's do it one more time.

Imagine that it's Teacher Appreciation Day at your church. You've had a challenging Sunday school class, and one student in particular, Brandon, has been hard to motivate. On Sunday morning the class assembles, and after you've started the lesson, Brandon shows up late, carrying a small vase with some wilted flowers and a sample box of inexpensive candies.

"Come in, Brandon," you say. "And what are you carrying?"

"Uh, I brought these for you," he says sheepishly.

Now, you could tell Brandon he's late. And you know he has dis-rupted your class. Besides, not only are the flowers wilted; you can't stand that brand of candy. But you recognize that this is a special moment for him. You could give him a compliment and have him go sit down, but perhaps it's more important than that. Maybe it's worth delaying class for a "blossom moment."

"Brandon, you picked those flowers just for me? How beautiful! And you chose these candies for me? What a thoughtful thing to do. Do you know how that makes me feel? I feel wonderful. I think you've made me the happiest teacher in the whole wide world!"

Then pause. He may beam with your praise. Or he may squirm a little because he's not used to being praised like that.

"You know what? I believe you are going to grow up to be a very special person that *every* teacher is going to feel very lucky to have in her class!"

Pause again. Let him think about what that means. Then pat him on the shoulder or share a hug. This is a very special moment for Brandon.

That's what blossoming looks like. Not too difficult and ever so wonderful. Just think of all the good you could do in the lives of so many needy students and family members if you just changed your focus from the problems of the present to the dreams of the future. May you be known, my friend, as a person who has real blossoming power!

EXPECTATION MAXIMIZERS

"Both he who expects great things of others, and he who expects little, will receive what he expects." Because our expectations are so important to ourselves and those we teach, listed below are seven tips to enable you to get the most from your blossoming efforts.

Maximizer 1: Employ opportunities purposefully.

A pastor friend of mine is excellent at purposefully creating opportunities to blossom others. Every Wednesday night, after church and time with his family, he goes into his study and opens a little box on the corner of his desk. In that box are note cards, each with the name of one of the deacons and his wife, their children's names, the man's profession and employer, and any special prayer requests.

At about 9:45 P.M., he picks up the card at the top of the stack, reads through it, and then prays for everyone on that card. Then he rotates the card to the back of the stack and gets ready to use an opportunity purposefully.

He calls the deacon at home. "Hi, Bob, this is the pastor."

Typically he hears, "Ah…what's the matter, Pastor?"

"I wanted to let you know that I just finished praying for you and Susy and your kids, Tommy and Lisa, and the special prayer requests you gave me. But right now I wanted you to know what a pleasure it is to have you on the deacon board! Your contribution means so much to me. I feel so encouraged having men like you on the board, men who really care, who give their all, who are not merely 'yes' men. Thanks for participating, not just with your words, but also with your life and your action. It makes me feel really encouraged." Then he pauses.

"And Bob," he continues, "I sense that God's hand is on you. I believe that as you continue to mature and serve Him, God is going to use you in some mighty way in the future." Pause.

"It's a pleasure, a genuine pleasure being your pastor, Bob. Thanks for the privilege."

Then he says good-bye and hangs up.

Wow! What would you do if you received a call like that? What is that pastor doing? He is purposefully making an opportunity to blossom one of his co-laborers every Wednesday night.

This maximizer doesn't work only when good things happen; it can work just as well when bad things happen. We can train our family members and students through negative situations.

Years ago, our daughter Jenny brought home three Fs in a row in math and didn't tell me about it until what she thought was the most appropriate moment.

"Dad," she said, "I have something to tell you that you're probably not going to like."

"Yes, Jenny?"

"You have to sign these."

With that she handed me an envelope, which I opened. Three Fs stared me in the face. *Oh, boy,* I thought. But fortunately the Law of Expectation came to mind. I determined to try something different.

"Jenny, you got three Fs in a row in math. Do you know that makes Mom and me feel upset and frustrated with your lack of application in class? Jenny, I want you to get your coat on right now."

"My coat, Dad?"

"Yes. Get your coat."

Very quietly, she got her coat. She had no idea what was going to happen next, but it didn't sound too good.

"What are you doing?" whispered my wife.

"Why don't you come with me—it's time to blossom our daughter," I replied.

So all three of us got in the car, and I explained: "Jennifer, you received three Fs in a row. Mom and I are so glad you finally got that out of your system! Now we're going to get some ice cream and celebrate."

"Dad—are you kidding?"

"No, Jenny. Isn't it good to have those Fs behind you? I believe since you got that out of your system, you're ready to turn the corner and really apply yourself. I believe you are going to start living up to all the potential the Lord has given you. Mom and I feel you have the determination to rise to the task and conquer math."

"Really, Dad? And I'm getting an ice cream?"

"Yes, and it's a double-decker-dipper, Jenny. Mom and I love you, sweetheart, and it's going to be all right." Then we gave her a big hug.

The rest of the night was memorable. Jenny couldn't believe her good fortune, and we laughed and cut up together. She relished the attention and affection which demonstrated our unconditional love to her.

And she soon stopped getting Fs.

We have opportunities to express positive expectations even in the midst of negative situations. We need to recognize them and use them for the good.

Maximizer 2: Express expectations creatively.

Use your creativity to express your expectations. There are unlimited ways of doing this, but let me suggest five examples of things you might try.

Pray it.

Pray your expectations to God. Have you ever looked closely at Paul's epistles? He was forever praying to God about his expectations for people. He even wrote down his prayers!

> For this reason I bow my knees to the Father of our Lord Jesus Christ, from whom the whole family in heaven and earth is named, that He would grant you, according to the riches of His glory, to be strengthened with might through His Spirit in the inner man, that Christ may dwell in your hearts through faith; that you, being rooted and grounded in love, may be able to comprehend with all the saints what is the width and length and depth and height—to know the love of Christ which passes knowledge; that you may be filled with all the fullness of God.
>
> Now to Him who is able to do exceedingly abundantly above all that we ask or think, according to the power that works in us, to Him be glory in the church by Christ Jesus throughout all ages, world without end. Amen. (Ephesians 3:14–21)

What do you think this prayer meant to the people in Ephesus? Do you think it might have encouraged them to know that the great apostle was praying for them in this way?

Say it indirectly.

I learned this creative approach while working for Dr. Stephen Slocum, who was the executive vice president at the graduate school I attended. His office was right next to President John Walvoord's, and my desk was right outside their doors. One day Dr. Slocum and Dr. Walvoord walked by my desk. My boss turned to the president and said, "Dr. Walvoord, I want you to know what Bruce did the other day for the seminary." Then he reported some exciting achievements of the past few weeks. I was sitting right there, listening to the conversation. Neither man looked at me or spoke to me, but I couldn't help but overhear Dr. Slocum's compliments. "I just want you to know as president what kind of people we have working here, and I believe that even more exciting things are soon to come," Dr. Slocum said. Then they walked out. I floated for days, and I found myself redoubling my efforts in order to live up to those incredibly motivating expectations.

Consider this method the next time you are distributing the latest graded papers in your English composition class. Place the paper you want to use to blossom a particular person about halfway down in the stack, and when you get to it, stop and look around the room to gather everyone's attention.

"Now, class, do you see this paper? This paper is just outstanding. I couldn't help but give it an A+. As I read it I felt so great to have a student that puts forth such effort in my class. I believe this student is well on the way to becoming a person who can write articles we may read in our newspapers or even *Time* magazine. The student who wrote this paper is to be congratulated by all of us."

Then you walk over to the student and return her paper. "Well done, Jessica! I'm looking forward to reading your next paper." Reach over and touch her shoulder, if appropriate, and smile warmly.

Do you know what happens? Blossoms pop out all over Jessica—you can almost see them right before your eyes. Besides that, you can be sure that everyone is going to try a little harder on their next paper because they'd love to hear such things said about them as well.

So stir up one another. Directly and indirectly.

Write it.

It's amazing what a written note can accomplish. It's different from saying it out loud; it's permanent, tangible. I've discovered that many people will keep a note forever—such notes are so rare.

A little note on a piece of stationery or a card will work wonders. Place it on the person's desk, or insert it in the book she's reading, or send it in the mail.

My wife is very effective in her use of letter writing to blossom not only family members, but also many people all over the world that she quietly loves through letters. If you have a hard time telling someone in person, then express your expectations through your letters.

Use the telephone.

You have thirty eleven-year-olds in your class, and you decide to call one of them every Tuesday during the semester. Here's what you do: Wait until dinnertime. Everybody hates to be called at dinnertime, so that's when you call. You'll see why in a moment.

"Hello, may I speak with Timmy?" you say. Parents usually answer at dinnertime because they want to head off any calls from their children's friends. They don't like being bothered while eating.

"Who is this?" they ask.

"This is Mrs. Jones, Timmy's teacher. I need to speak with him, please."

The parent hands over the phone. "Timmy, it's Mrs. Jones, your teacher! What did you do wrong now? You're going to get it this time, young man!"

Poor Timmy doesn't know what to say, so he slowly walks to the phone and meekly ekes out "Hello?" Everyone has stopped eating by this time and the tension can be cut with a knife. The parents are looking at each other, thinking, *Trouble—big trouble.*

"Hello, Timmy? I was just in the middle of grading papers."

"Uh-huh?"

"I just finished grading yours, and Timmy, it was so good. It was excellent. You got an A+."

"I did?" His eyebrows are raised in disbelief, and his watching parents are waiting for the bomb to fall.

"Yes, and I wanted to call you and tell you how proud of you I am. I believe you are becoming one of my very special students, and I wanted to tell you I think you're just wonderful! Bye!" Then hang up. Never let him talk.

Timmy hangs up on his end, and his dad immediately barks, "What did she say? What did you do now?"

"Dad, she just called to say I got an A+ and how glad she was to have me in class. She told me I was becoming one of her special students!"

What a moment to go down in the family album! If you could have snapped a picture of the before and after, it would have been priceless. You've made that boy look good in front of his whole family. At *dinnertime*! What do you suppose Timmy's attitude will be in class tomorrow?

Use the phone to blossom someone each week from your class. That's what it's there for, you know—to "reach out and touch someone."

Send something unusual.

You can get really creative with this one. Suppose you're having trouble with a teenager in your class. You can't seem to get through to him and you don't know what to do. Here's one suggestion.

Go to a local pizza joint that delivers and say, "I would like to buy a pizza and have it sent to this address. But before you send it, I'd like to write something on the box." (Also be sure to have them pile on the pepperoni.)

Then get out your pen and write, "Just thinking about you. Sorry class has been tough on you lately. I wanted you to know I'm on your team, and I believe you are going to reach your dream! Thanks for allowing me to help you soar like an eagle in the midst of a world full of turkeys."

That kid won't have a chance tomorrow. You loved him in a way he understands. You really *can* cause him to learn…if you love him enough. Just send a pepperoni pizza with extra cheese, and redesign the cover with "blossom power."

Sometimes you don't need many words if you've selected the right thing to send. I'll never forget the time someone did this to me. Dr. Paul Kienel, former president of the Association of Christian Schools International (ACSI), had asked me a number of times to speak at their Southern California convention. I always told him my schedule was too full.

Then one day out of the blue, a large package with no return address was delivered to my office. When my secretary and I opened it, out unrolled a long red carpet with a little note pinned to the other end: "We're laying out the red carpet for you. We believe you are the perfect speaker for our convention."

Unbelievable. What an impact. I called Dr. Kienel immediately and signed on the dotted line. Since then we've become close friends and have ministered together all over the country in their great ACSI conventions. They have a way of always laying out the red carpet for their speakers and teachers.

Maximizer 3: Pick words precisely.

One big problem all communicators face is that people don't listen well. If you want to have a significant impact, you must choose your words carefully. Watch what you call people, or what you say about them. This includes nicknames:

"Hey, dummy, I want to tell you how well you did."

"Hey, princess, come here for a minute!"

"Hey, champ—you know what? I think you're going to be this generation's Billy Graham."

"Hey, fatty!"

One set of grandparents thought it was cute to call their grandson "Stinky." Do you think that boy thought it was cute? Pick your words with care. Think about them before you speak them.

Some of us have a greater problem with loose lips than others. Just remember: Nothing is harder to reel back in than harmful words you've let fly. So be careful. If you have a problem in this area, meditate on James 3. Think ahead of positive things to say.

Maximizer 4: Establish eye contact.

Eyes, not ears, are our primary receptors. Take advantage of this by communicating your expectations through your eyes. Direct eye contact validates your sincerity. It optimizes the impact of what you say.

Establishing direct eye contact gives power to your expression of expectations. Look right into the eyes of the person you want to blossom. Don't blink, and don't look away. This is a precious opportunity for you to build a treasure in someone. Don't just casually throw it in their direction. Wrap it up and give it to them. Without eye contact, your expectation may have little or no effect. Eye contact empowers your attempts to blossom people.

Frequently after a meeting at Walk Thru the Bible, as we all headed out the door, I would stop and turn around to face the person behind me. We would chat for a bit, and then I'd compliment the person on something he had done and link it to a future expectation. I would look right into that person's eyes and hold his gaze until the expectation had been thoroughly conveyed.

Maximizer 5: Communicate body language carefully.

Researchers have found people use more than a hundred nonverbal signals to communicate. Be careful, therefore, that the language of your body matches that of your lips. Take careful note of your students' body language. They're telling you whether they're with you or not!

Your body language is a powerful tool, so never express your expectations from behind the desk. Come around to the front. Don't allow anything between you and the other person. Look her in the eye, express affection appropriately, and she will know you mean what you say.

The proper way to express your expectations through body language is by leaning forward, relaxed, palms up, perhaps sitting on the edge of the desk or at eye level with the other person. If it's a child, you might even want to kneel. It's important to get close. And don't forget to make eye contact!

Maximizer 6: Touch others appropriately.

One Friday night years ago, I was working late at the office after a long and difficult week. I was scheduled to fly to a large conference in a few hours and speak five times over the weekend. Everything in me was screaming, "I don't want to go to this conference." I was exhausted. I was cranky. I was just plain out of emotional energy to minister to anyone.

I scooped up my briefcase and a box stuffed with other papers and was walking out the door into the lobby. My father, who also worked at Walk Thru, saw me stagger through the door. He was working late as well, and he instantly read me like a book.

"Just a minute, son," he called out. "Let me carry some of that for you."

"Dad, it's okay."

"No. Set them down."

I set them down. (You should always obey your dad.)

"Now, look at me for a minute." So I looked at him. He walked right over, looked me in the eye, and hugged me. Not a little hug. A bear hug—and he didn't let go.

"Mom and I know you're under a lot of pressure," he said, "but we're so proud of you, son. It's such a delight to be at Walk Thru the Bible with you. God's going to use you in a mighty way this weekend. It's going to be all right."

By the time he let go of me, the tears were streaming down my face. I still get choked up every time I tell the story. He picked up my briefcase and my box and started out the door. I was standing there kind of limply.

"Give me your keys," he said.

"Oh, Dad."

"No. The keys." I gave him the keys. He unlocked the car door and opened it for me. I sat down, and he shut the door and said, "It's going to be great."

As I drove around the little circle in front of WTB's international headquarters and headed toward the freeway, I found myself saying, "It's going to be a great weekend! The Lord is going to do a mighty work."

Dad's blossoming took my empty battery and recharged it. And he did most of it through touch.

Touch your students appropriately. But touch them.

Maximizer 7: Set expectations confidently.

Set your expectations for your students before class starts, and make sure they're positive. Transfer to your students your hope and belief in them so they can jump-start their own hope and belief from yours.

It may help to write out your expectations so they are specific and measurable. Set them confidently. Be bold and brave in expecting the best from your students. Never mumble. Never allow your tone to be anything but confident and assuring. After all, they are the ones questioning, not you!

CONCLUSION

In my last year as a Bible college professor, I taught a Bible Study Methods class to seniors. During the grading of the first set of papers that semester, I came across one that was only one page long, looked as if it had been wadded up into a ball and then smoothed out, and had ketchup smeared on the bottom right corner.

Immediately I looked at the name. "I don't even know who this Becky is," I said to myself. I wrote an F at the top. To be honest, I wanted to put a minus behind it, but I didn't.

The next time class met, I made an effort to learn more about Becky. She sat in the very back corner. Her hair was a mess. Her clothes looked like her paper. She was not in good shape. I tried to make eye contact with her throughout the hour, but didn't succeed very often.

When I collected the next set of papers, I immediately searched for Becky's. There was no ketchup this time and it didn't look like it needed to be ironed, but it was another F. I leaned back in my office chair and prayed, "Lord, maybe Becky is supposed to be our project this semester. Would You give me the creativity and unconditional love to blossom Becky?"

Then I wrote at the top of her paper, "Dear Becky, I believe that this paper does not truly reflect your true talents and abilities. I can't wait to see what you can really do. —Prof." And I didn't put a grade on her paper. After all, what would a second F do for her at this point?

Her next paper had improved to a D-. I wrote another note: "Dear Becky, thanks for cracking the door just a bit. I knew I was right about you. How about the privilege of seeing what you can really do when you apply yourself? I'm on your team. —Prof." No grade again.

The next time her paper was two pages long. A solid C. "Dear Becky, what a tremendous improvement! This paper is light-years ahead of your last and demonstrates incredible potential. I can't wait to see what your next paper's going to look like. —Prof." No grade.

The next paper doubled in size—four pages long. It was almost an A. "Dear Becky, your improvement is nothing less than astonishing. Your insights and the quality of your work are truly inspiring me. I believe you are ready to show me everything you can really do. —Prof." No grade.

The very next paper shot right through the roof. I wrote at the top of that paper, "Dear Becky, I'm now standing on the top of my desk cheering! I always knew you had it in you. I believe you're going to become one of our school's greatest Bible students, and it is a pleasure to watch you grow in my class. A+."

By the end of that semester, guess who was the uncontested leader of that class? Becky!

After that year God moved me away from that college to Atlanta, almost three thousand miles away. Years went by. I forgot all about my "project." One day I received a letter marked Personal.

My secretary never opens those kinds of letters because of the counseling I get involved in as I travel around the world. "Do you know who this is?" she asked, referring to the return address. I didn't recognize the name at all. I opened the letter and read the following:

Dear Dr. Wilkinson,

I just had to write you a letter after all these years. You don't recognize my name because I'm now married. I don't know how to thank you. You are the first person in my entire life to ever believe anything good about me. Your class totally changed my life. I'm now happily married and have two wonderful children. I honestly believe that had I not met you and been in your class, I probably wouldn't even be married today. I don't know how I can ever thank you enough for believing in me.

Love,
Becky.

I keep that letter in a special file at home as a reminder that blossoming can make a lifelong difference.

I think Christa McAuliffe, the teacher who flew on the ill-fated space shuttle Challenger, said it best: "I touch the future; I teach."

You teach. *You* touch the future. What kind of fingerprint will you leave?

Certain people in your life need your touch—right now. They are the Beckys that God has placed before your blossoming touch. Maybe you haven't quite seen them as such wonderful opportunities yet, but now you know, don't you?

Ask the Lord one question: "Lord, who is in my life that You would like me to blossom with Your help? Lord, who needs a new dream?"

Pause for a moment and ask the Lord to open your eyes. Thousands of people just like you have rediscovered someone right before their eyes—someone who desperately needs them. Would you ask the Lord right now to help you blossom that person in the next ninety days? Just say, "Dear God, would You help me to blossom _____?"

It's time, right now, to commit to touching the Beckys of your life. To expect the best of them. To blossom them.

And someday, years from now (or perhaps not even until heaven), you'll realize that because you loved your Becky enough to believe the best, you really did touch the future.

DISCUSSION QUESTIONS

1. Why do you suppose so many of us find it easier to believe the worst about someone rather than the best? Why is gossip always about bad news rather than good? What is it in each of us that wants to share the defeats of others rather than their victories, and to share our own victories but not our defeats? For there to be a change in this destructive pattern, we have to change our thinking in a deep and significant way. In your own words, describe what you think that change would look like for the average person.

2. Put your thinking cap on for a moment and move into the creative realm. Become the normal American adult Christian. What are at least three dreams or visions or hopes that every person, male or female, has hidden in his or her heart? What do all of us wish would come true about our futures? Try out a couple as you blossom some of your coworkers.

3. List at least a dozen words that you could use when you are expressing the emotion stage. Instead of "I feel so proud," how else could you say it?

4. Think of the people you know and have relationships with at the present. Which person would you like to blossom the most? Take a few moments and write a short paragraph about what you think this person's dreams and aspirations are. When the time is right, ask the person to share some of the most important

dreams he has about his future, then rewrite your paragraph. When you do, you'll be holding the "pollen" to sprinkle on this special person the next time an opportunity arises.

LAW THREE

The Law
of Application

CHAPTER FIVE

Application
Mindset, Model, and Maxims

W hen I was in high school, the second greatest thing on earth a guy could claim (next to a steady girlfriend) was his very own car. That was back in the days of tube socks and Brylcreem, when one's vocabulary consisted mostly of words like *cool* and *neat* and *wow*. In the early 1960s, the car that everyone would have given their right arm for was a vintage "woody" station wagon—the car of Beach Boys fame.

I was fortunate because my family's second car just happened to be a woody. For months I kept begging my folks to let me drive it to school to show it off. "Okay, keep your grades up, and we'll let you use it the last six weeks of your senior year."

Talk about motivation! I worked with everything in me to keep my grades up. Toward the end of my senior year, they finally turned over the car keys.

I almost didn't sleep that weekend as I lovingly prepared my woody for her debut at my school's "Senior Row." My parents must have been in shock when the same son who couldn't seem to find enough energy to mow the lawn worked far into the night, sanding the wood siding, tuning up the engine, rubbing in not one but two jars of Ever-Shine Car Wax, installing two rear speakers, replacing the muffler with a "cool" glass-packed muffler, and tacking down nine yards of remnant carpet. Sure, it was a lot of work, but worth every second. Because when I drove it to school, I felt as though the world belonged to me.

There I was, "Joe Cool," with the window down, my arm out, and the radio blasting into the next county. I drove into the school parking lot and cruised past everyone until I turned into the coveted "Senior Row." Then I did what every other high school senior did—I revved my engine. And revved it, and revved it. We affectionately called it the "Ritual of the Revving." All the other guys crowded around, opened the hood, stared inside, and made profound observations on what they saw. Then they all got in their cars, started their engines, and together we burned up gallons of gas, all without moving an inch. But what an incredible surge of power we all felt! It was inspiring and worth every drop of fuel.

Now, if you were to see me today in a church parking lot with my car hood up, revving the engine, music blaring, you'd probably wonder what on earth was going on. Such activities were normal for a seventeen-year-old, but for an adult?

As a seventeen-year-old, I considered that automobile an end in itself. I got excited about the noise from the engine rather than the transportation it could provide. By switching the means into an end, I displayed my immaturity. The purpose of an automobile is not to rev the engine but to transport from place to place. The real value of an automobile is the *application* of its engine, not in the engine itself.

Today, unfortunately, in the great majority of pulpits and classrooms, we rev the engine and get excited about the sound we make, while the people in the audience wonder, "When are you going to drive that thing somewhere?"We confuse the means with the end. *We get so tied up in our content that we forget the purpose of content is life change.*

We teachers love to rev our content—our three points, seven guidelines, fourteen keys. We proudly reveal our alliterated titles, outlines, subpoints, and illustrations as though they were rear speakers, glass mufflers, and carpeting. Seminaries, Bible schools, teaching seminars, and classes are turning out pastors and teachers who are better equipped than ever. But when you look within their classes and churches you see more and more problems. Drug and alcohol abuse. Immorality. Divorce. Rebellious children. Eating disorders. Misplaced priorities. The truth doesn't seem to get us anywhere!

Let's join together, shut the hood, put the woody into gear, and start driving to our destination. When we do, it may change forever the way we teach!

APPLICATION MINDSET

A *mindset* is a prevailing attitude or opinion. The standard mindset of the majority of teachers, whether sacred or secular, is that the purpose of teaching is to explain and "cover" the material. For teacher after teacher, the focus on what and how they teach is overwhelmingly about the content.

Almost every question on the tests given in our schools deals with knowledge. "Knowing" is the essence of being educated, according to the mindset of the average teacher. But is that the correct mindset? Does God desire us to teach so that we have covered the material, or does He have a far deeper and more significant goal for the Christian teacher?

I believe a biblical mindset for the Christian teacher is to teach not merely the content but the application of that content. Content relates to facts, information, and material. Application relates to wisdom, transformation, and maturity. Content is the "what" and application is the "so what." Content is typically what is discussed during class and application is primarily what is done as a result of class. Content centers around "knowing" and application around "being" and "doing."

A key verse in the Bible on this issue is one you're no doubt familiar with. Maybe you've memorized it, heard sermons on it, and even taught it. But perhaps you've never considered how it reveals God's heart for application.

> All Scripture is given by inspiration of God, and is profitable for doctrine, for reproof, for correction, for instruction in righteousness, that the man of God may be complete, thoroughly equipped for every good work. (2 Timothy 3:16–17)

Unfortunately, most of us think this verse says, "All Scripture is given by inspiration of God and is profitable for *doctrine*." We believe that God gave us the Bible primarily for the purpose of doctrine. Therefore, when you or I stand up to teach, we feel it is our job to explain the doctrine, to tell as best we can what the Bible means. The problem is that this passage doesn't teach that at all. It teaches something very different.

One way to uncover the main idea of a verse or passage is to cross out all adjectives, adverbs, prepositional phrases, and descriptive clauses. Many times this simple little exercise clears a lot of confusion. When we apply this method to the verses in 2 Timothy, the sentence simply reads:

> *Scripture is given*
> *and is profitable,*
> *that the man [of God]*
> *may be complete,*
> *equipped.*

Study those thirteen words for a moment. The Bible was given for what purpose? Does it say doctrine? No. Does it say the Bible was given for the purpose of correction or reproof? No. They are all merely descriptions of the central concept and even precede the word *that*, clearly proving they do not describe the purpose or goal.

What this verse says with unmistakable clarity is that the Word of God was given for two primary purposes:

1. That the Christian may become complete;
2. That the Christian may become equipped.

Do the words *complete* and *equipped* center around "knowing" or around "being and doing"? That's right—they both thoroughly target what happens in the life of the believer on the basis of content. *God's primary concern is not content but the application of that content to life.*

Therefore, the vast majority of teachers—whether Christian or non-Christian—are out of step with the purposes of God when they teach merely to "know." Unless they teach with the same purpose that the Bible was given, they may be tragically teaching at cross-purposes with God.

APPLICATION MODEL

So what are we as teachers supposed to do? We are charged by God with taking the Bible and applying it to the life of the believer so that he changes and becomes more complete and more equipped. That's the goal of our communication of Truth. Let's break this passage down a little further in the Application Model to uncover additional insights.

The Resource: God's Inspired Revelation for Believers

The Bible is the very Word of God. It was given by God and is inspired by Him. God, using the instrumentality of human authors, determined the Truth that He wanted to give His people in written form. The

Word of God is the standard by which we measure all of life and all of learning. It is the subject we teach.

The Scriptures are the primary *resource* for the Christian teacher to develop students who are complete and equipped. As Romans 12:1–2 teaches, transformation occurs through renewing our minds to agree with the Scriptures. The Bible is the basis for all life change!

The Methodology: How to Apply the Bible to the Believer

How do I teach the Word of God in order that the man of God may be changed, equipped, and made complete? Second Timothy 3:16–17 lists four primary methods of application we can use to accomplish God's goal of life change in the character and conduct of the believer. *Doctrine* and *correction* relate primarily to belief, whereas *instruction* and *reproof* relate primarily to behavior.

REGARDING BELIEF

- "Doctrine" (*didaskalian*) means teaching, instruction, that which is to be learned, kept pure, and defended against heresies. Doctrine occurs when the teacher explains the Word of God to the man of God, showing him the truths he should believe. This term is used also in Romans 15:4 of the Scripture written for our learning and in 1 Timothy 4:13, 16, where Paul encourages Timothy to attend to it and to heed it.
- "Correction" (*epanorthosin*) is made up of three Greek words meaning "to make straight again." Its goal is setting right, raising up those who fall, correcting those in error. This is the only place in the New Testament in which this word is used, and it means to correct false doctrines or beliefs that one may hold.

The purpose of doctrine is to explain the truth. It's the positive side: "This is the correct understanding of the truth." Correction is the opposite of doctrine: "What you believe is not in line with Scripture. Instead, the Bible teaches…" Both doctrine and correction relate primarily to the beliefs of the Christian.

REGARDING BEHAVIOR

○ "Instruction in righteousness" (*paideian*) refers to upbringing and means "child training." Its emphasis is on guiding believers in the way of God and includes chastening and discipline. According to a leading Greek dictionary, this term describes "the whole training and education of children which relates to the cultivation of mind and morals, commands and admonitions, reproof and punishment; whatever in adults also cultivates the soul, especially by the increase of virtue." Key uses of this word are found in Ephesians 6:4 and Hebrews 12:5, 8.

○ "Reproof" (*elegmos*) speaks of conviction or punishment of a sinner. It's a rebuke to those in sin or the convincing of a man of the error of his way and setting him on the right path. This is the only use of the word in the New Testament.

Instruction and reproof relate primarily to behavior. Instruction is positive; reproof is negative. *Instruction* is training the Christian how to live for Christ on a daily basis. *Reproof* stops the Christian from conducting himself in inappropriate ways and strives to bring the behavior back in line with Christ's commands.

These are the four main methods to produce life change in the man or woman of God. They include belief and behavior, positively encouraged and negatively corrected. When I understood this and began to use it, I got back on track about how to apply biblically.

Because the Bible was given for life change and because these four methods are universal, the books of the Bible fit into these four methods of application. For instance, where would you put 1 Corinthians? Reproof. It says, "Don't behave this way." Where would you put Romans, especially chapters 1–11? Doctrine—"here's what you ought to believe." What about Philippians? Yes, instruction in righteousness: "Here's how you should behave." And Galatians? That's correction—"stop believing that incorrect doctrine." You won't find any extended passage in the Scripture that doesn't fall within one of those four methods because that's how teaching for life change occurs—as a parent, as a teacher, as a preacher.

So what's the purpose of the Bible? Unfortunately, we miss it most of the time. Yes, the Word of God is profitable to memorize. But that's not the main point. Yes, the Word of God is profitable to study. But that's not the main point either. The Word of God was given and is profitable to do one major thing—to change the Christian's life so that he is more like Christ and does more for Christ.

Therefore, the next time we teach, if we want to use the Bible for the reason it was given we must aim for one thing: life change! The vast majority of all teachers, however, aim for understanding and wonder why that understanding doesn't result in life change. They think the purpose of the Bible is doctrine instead of application; they think that content will do it. Content rarely develops lasting life change without careful and biblical application wedded to it.

The Result: Mature and Equipped Christians

Paul says the goal is "that the man of God may be complete, thoroughly equipped for every good work." The Greek word behind "complete" is *artios*, which means fit, complete, sufficient; able to meet all demands. Generally this relates to one's character—who a person is. The student's character will be transformed over time into the image of Jesus Christ. That is God's primary goal.

The second goal is "thoroughly equipped" and comes from the Greek word *exertismenos*, which is related to the same root word as *artios*. It means completely outfitted, fully furnished, fully equipped, fully supplied. For what? For every good work. Thus, the believer's *conduct* is appropriate and active in serving the Lord.

God gave us the Bible to accomplish two goals—*change in character* (who I am) and *change in conduct* (what I do). If the learner is not becoming more Christlike, more a man of God in his character, and if he is not being equipped for more effective service, then we as teachers are not allowing the Scripture to fulfill its purpose in that believer's life.

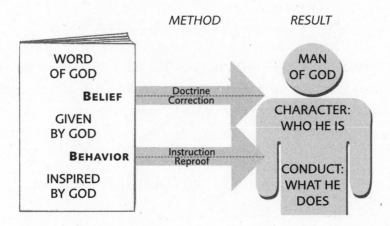

These insights are summarized on the Application Model. On the left the book represents the "*resource*," which is the "*Word of God*," "*given by God*," and "*inspired by God*."

The figure on the right represents the "*result*" of teaching the Bible for life change: the "*man of God*" is changed in both his "*character*" ("*who he is*") and his "*conduct*" ("*what he does*").

The "*method*" to accomplish this is through changing first his "*belief*" by affirming his correct "*doctrine*" and "*correcting*" his erroneous doctrine. On this basis, he will receive "*instruction in righteousness*" and "*reproof*" when he is living in sin.

When you teach, therefore, make sure your goals are always God's goals—that you are teaching for life change through powerful applications based upon the Scriptures. Don't ever say, "I'm going to explain this passage to you," and leave it at that. All you have done is rev your engine. The Bible wasn't given for our information but for our transformation.

This law has revolutionized my life and ministry. I used to teach and preach for information. Only since I have learned and implemented what I'm about to relate to you have I been able to experience the joy of seeing lasting life change in my students. It is my prayer as you read these next seven Application Maxims that the Lord will prepare you to learn the revolutionary Application Method of the next chapter.

APPLICATION MAXIMS

D. L. Moody had it right when he said, "The Bible wasn't given for our information but for our transformation." God did not give us the Bible to tell us what happened in the past but to equip us to live in the present in light of the future.

Maxim 1: Application is the central reason for God's revelation.

When you and I stand before the Lord for an accounting of our lives, do you think He is going to hand out a heavenly "blue book" with multiple-choice and true/false questions? Do you think He is going to ask us to list the books of the Bible in order, name the twelve apostles, or describe Ezekiel's wheels within a wheel? Of course not! Then why are so many of our classes concerned only with those facts that can be listed on true/false quizzes and not concerned for those matters that will be on the Final Exam?

I remember my children, Dave and Jenny, returning from Sunday school week after week with little interest and excitement. We'd ask, as I'm sure all parents do, "What did you learn in Sunday school today?"

"Nothing, Dad. We already knew the story." At first that made Darlene and I feel good because we were trying hard to train our kids. But as this conversation was repeated week after week, it caused us great concern. Their teachers had defined teaching as telling what was in the Bible. They were misusing the Bible because they took only the first step, telling the facts. The real reason God wanted those stories to be taught was to mature Dave and Jenny into godly Christians.

This may shock many Sunday school teachers, but I don't believe our children were being taught the Bible. They were being told Bible stories. There is an indescribable difference between teaching the facts and teaching lives to change on the basis of the facts. Knowing the stories doesn't change anyone—just visit a secular "Bible as Literature" college class and see for yourself.

According to 2 Timothy 3:16–17, "all Scripture" was given by God so that the "people of God" may become like the "Son of God." God gave the Bible not for content but for Christlikeness. To teach only to inform is to teach in direct defiance of the revealed purpose of God.

Don't misuse God's book for your purposes. Any time we alter the purposes of God, we are in danger. We must teach the Scriptures correctly, which means teaching the Bible for lasting life change.

Maxim 2: Application is the responsibility of the teacher.

Since the Bible was given by God for the purpose of application, the person who teaches it must honor and fulfill that same purpose. Yet I find that the vast majority of teachers don't think it's their responsibility to apply. Application must be the responsibility of someone else—some miraculous undercover agent who mysteriously makes application happen.

Until I understood this principle, I didn't see it as my responsibility either. I remembered a heated debate with an older man of God after he listened to me teach all content and no application and then end class with that wonderful Christian escape clause, "And now may the Holy Spirit apply this truth to your lives." With a faint smile on his lips he asked me if I ever wanted to see the answer to that prayer. "Of course," I said, "who wouldn't?"

"Hold on, because you are the very answer to your own prayer!" He explained that the Holy Spirit wanted to apply the truth, but His primary tool was the very teacher who taught it. I left that conversation distinctly aware that I must not expect God to do what He has given me to do in His power. The Holy Spirit works through the applying process of the teacher.

The difference between teaching for content and teaching for application is staggering. The content teacher thinks his responsibility is to cover and explain the facts. The application teacher thinks his responsibility is to apply the facts for lasting life change in his students.

The apostle Paul understood that application is the primary responsibility of the teacher: "Him we preach, warning every man and teaching every man in all wisdom, [Why?] *that we may present every man perfect in Christ Jesus.* To this end I also labor, striving according to His working which works in me mightily" (Colossians 1:28–29).

Maybe the reason we do not experience the supernatural release of God's power as we teach is because we have unknowingly misused God's Book and blocked His anointing. He doesn't need an informer; He desires a transformer.

Jesus Christ delegated to us this responsibility of application and teaching for life change in His famous Great Commission (Matthew 28:18–20). Do you remember how He directed us to teach? "Teaching them to observe [do, obey] all things that I have commanded you." Christ was clear. He wants His teachers to teach so our students "observe/do/obey" everything He said. When our students "observe," it means they apply the truth.

Not only did Paul teach for life change, but so did Peter, James, and

John. Disciples of the first century and disciples of the twentieth century follow in the footsteps of the Master—they teach for life change.

Maxim 3: Application and information should be balanced.

If teachers want to apply when they teach, then how much class time should be devoted to application?

Before giving the answer, let me ask you another question. What percentage of the average Sunday school class or sermon do you think is devoted to content (what the Bible means) compared to application (how I'm supposed to live)? Think about the last few classes you've attended and sermons you've heard. Which received more time: content or application?

I've asked that question of thousands of people around the world, and the answer has been surprisingly consistent—90 percent content, only 10 percent application. Oftentimes, the more a group believes the Bible is God's inspired Word, the higher the percentage of content—sometimes exceeding even 95 percent.

For many years I was a "99 percenter" and proud of it! I didn't want to take time away from "real teaching" in order to waste time on that practical stuff. But in the middle of this pilgrimage I stumbled on something that amazed me.

I remember the very day this discovery began to dawn. It shook me so deeply that I have never recovered. I asked my secretary to type out three recent sermons preached by Charles Swindoll, who I felt had one of the most effective preaching and teaching ministries in the nation. Then our editor at the time, Larry Libby, and I took those sermons and highlighted in orange those parts that were content and in yellow those that were application.

It turned out to be a fascinating afternoon. What do you think was the percentage of Swindoll's application? Over 50 percent! Surely something was wrong, so we checked some other well-known preachers such as Charles Stanley and Howard Hendricks. The results were similar. In fact, some of the best sermons contained more than 75 percent application!

I couldn't believe what I was finding. So I looked back over church history and came up with a list of those people who were used mightily by God in their generations. Preacher-teachers such as D. L. Moody, Jonathan Edwards, Charles Finney, Charles Spurgeon, John Wesley, and writers such as Dietrich Bonhoeffer, A. W. Tozer, and Oswald Chambers. What was their percentage? Surely, I reasoned, many of these men would join the ranks of those with 90 percent content!

I started with D. L. Moody, a favorite of mine. We made copies of a few of his sermons and went to work, markers in hand. What a shock! Moody—who many consider the most important Christian spokesman of the last century—averaged over 70 percent application! Without exception, there wasn't one with 90 percent content in the bunch. They all averaged between 45 and 75 percent application. In most cases, *significantly more application than content*.

Could this be a universal trait of communicators uniquely anointed by God throughout church history? If it was, then I was in bad shape—along with most of modern Christendom.

But they were just men, I contended. Where is the verse in the Bible that reveals the correct percentage? What was the will of God for teachers? Days went by as I sought the biblical answer to this crucial question. There weren't many sermons in the Bible to help. Finally I realized the epistles were, in reality, written sermons. Maybe the answer lay there.

Can you imagine what happened when the Ancient Express delivered one of Paul's scrolls in the mail? The church probably scrapped the order of service that week and read that written sermon out loud. I'm sure they liked Ephesians, but can you imagine how the nursery workers felt when the sixteen chapters of Romans arrived?

That was it—I had my answer! All I had to do was find out the content/application balance in those God-inspired written sermons.

Finally, I could prove my 90 percent theory. Little did I know I was in for the surprise of my life.

I started with Romans because it was the most doctrinal book in the Bible. Surely that's where content was king! With those same two markers, I attacked the sixteen chapters of Romans. It wasn't too hard to determine which chapters were primarily content and which were application:

Chapter 1—content
Chapter 2—content
Chapter 3—content
Chapter 4—content (I started getting excited—90 percent was on the way!)
Chapter 5—content
Chapter 6—application
Chapter 7—application
Chapter 8—application
Chapter 9—content
Chapter 10—content
Chapter 11—content
Chapter 12—application
Chapter 13—application
Chapter 14—application (What's going on here?)
Chapter 15—application
Chapter 16—application

Count them, my friend! The heaviest content book in the Bible contains eight chapters of content and eight chapters of application! Fifty-fifty!

Immediately Ephesians came to mind, the second most doctrinal book in the New Testament. Surely we content people would find solace there! But the first three chapters were content and the last three were application. Fifty-fifty. The Lord was beginning to get my attention.

I decided to check the book of James. I couldn't believe it when I discovered all five chapters overflowing with application after application after application. So let's just skip James, as it approaches 80 percent application.

I tried 1 Peter. Over 60 percent application. ·

They are all the same; each of the epistles of the New Testament has as much or more application than content. The truth was closing in on me fast. Conviction was falling upon me like a flood.

In a final act of desperation, I photocopied Christ's primary sermons. The Sermon on the Mount (Matthew 5–7) was well past 65 percent application. The Upper Room discourse (John 13–17) overwhelmed me with application. Passage after passage reflected the same percentage. *Christ was the application king!* Never do you discover Jesus merely explaining the Old Testament or even revealing New Testament information as an end in itself. His content always provided the basis for the application.

Until that moment, this search had been an academic exercise. I wanted to validate my practice. But the scales were falling from my eyes; everywhere I looked I saw the teaching heart of God, seemingly for the first time. Now I understood. God was convicting me. And the full force of what I had unwittingly been doing all these years pierced my heart. I found myself on the floor of my study in the middle of the night in tears, full of repentance.

Even as I write this, many years later, my heart is still stirred by that experience of stumbling over such a crucial truth. It has forever changed my life and ministry.

So where do you fit into all of this? If you find yourself under the conviction that the Lord would have you change the purpose and proportion of your teaching, then you are experiencing the same work of grace that I did.

Now let me ask you a very important question full of application: Will you commit to the Lord that from now on, you are going to teach and preach with an appropriate balance of content and application? Fifty-fifty, not ninety-ten. Such a commitment will change your teaching for the rest of your life!

Before we leave this maxim, however, please remember that this balance issue is a general and guiding principle, not a hard-and-fast rule. Sometimes your class may sound a lot like James with nearly 80 percent application; other times it may be closer to the technical passages of Hebrews with over 90 percent content. Relax. Don't allow yourself to fall into the trap of the Pharisees by making general principles into lists of rigid laws never commanded by the Lord. Just keep in mind that when you look back over the past few months of teaching, it should be evenly balanced.

But if you desire to teach like Jesus, then hold on, because your application will have to exceed 60 percent. Maybe that's too revolutionary. Unless, of course, you want to be included in the ranks of Moody, and Swindoll, and Stanley, and Hendricks, and Spurgeon, and Wesley, and Paul, and Peter, and James....

Maxim 4: Application focuses Scripture on the students' needs.

God gave the Bible for life change. Teachers are responsible to apply the Scriptures for life change. At least 50 percent of our presentations should be application-oriented. But how do you know where to focus your application? The fifth Law of the Learner, the Law of Need, presents the full treatment of this issue, but let's at least break some initial ground.

The most important characteristic of an application, in addition to its being biblical, is that it be appropriate for the audience. The applications a teacher would give from John 15 (the parable of the vine and branches) for a class of seven-year-olds would be different than those for a class of middle-aged married couples. Age guides our application. Purpose also guides our application. Consider how you would apply John 15 if you were speaking at a parent-teacher conference versus giving a devotional at a senior citizen's Bible study. The needs of your students are the most important ingredient to determine what your applications should be.

It's all related like an intricate spiderweb. When content is king, its needs are most important. The only problem is that content does not have a need. But when application is king, then the student's needs are most important because that's who must receive and act upon the application.

Applications that most influence eternal life change are the ones focused most precisely on the greatest point of need in the student's life. When you read the Law of Need in chapter 9, you will discover how Christ taught to the needs of people using five revolutionary steps that you can use the next time you teach.

Maxim 5: Application has maximum influence when the student sees its biblical basis.

One of the major reasons many good applications don't produce life change is because they don't have the authentic ring of "thus saith the Lord" behind them.

Somehow we have lost this most basic of all requirements of Christian teaching. We have strayed from the utter necessity of making sure our students see for themselves that we developed our application right from the Bible. How rare for students to depart from a class or sermon saying, "I must do this because the Lord said I must—right in this verse." In order for our applications to have maximum impact, they must have the authority of the Bible in, around, underneath, and behind them.

Recently I taught the 7 *Laws of the Learner* course in the Philippines to Christian leaders from over a hundred countries. On Sunday morning many of us worshiped at a local church in Manila. The pastor opened the Bible, read about eight verses, then closed it and put the Bible underneath the podium. His message was eloquent, yes. But life changing? No, because there was no authority behind his words.

His sermon was biblical. His sermon was orthodox. His sermon was well organized. But he never took us to the mountain. He never placed the will of God directly before our eyes. Hungry men and women and boys and girls didn't taste the manna from heaven. Instead of delivering the Word of God to us, he delivered his own word to us. We heard the voice of a man when we came to hear the voice of the Almighty.

So few speak for the Lord today. Instead many scratch and claw up the proverbial ladder in order to have a platform for their thoughts. We have decided we will be the Word. So we close God's Book, open our mouths, and wonder why there is no power.

Friends, unless our students come directly in contact with the biblical verses themselves and see what the Bible clearly commands, I fear we may have spoken our message and not God's. The Bible may remain open on our podium, yet His Word remains closed.

Are not you and I modern-day Moseses? Are we not called to gather all the people together and tell them what the Lord has commanded? I'm confident that the Israelites left Mount Sinai sure of one thing: They had heard a word from the Lord. Not from Moses, not from the angels, not from a teacher or preacher—they heard from the One who dwells in the holy mountain. But don't forget this—Moses spoke it!

Has not God beckoned you and me to His holy mountain, entrusted us with a message—not from two tablets but from sixty-six books—and commissioned us to teach "all things that I have commanded you"? When you walk into your classroom, make sure that you just walked down from that mountain—that your face is ablaze and your heart is afire.

Speak to them. They have come to hear what the Lord has to say…through you.

Maxim 6: Application that has impacted the teacher tends to impact the student.

This maxim is the flip side of the previous one. Applications are most effective not only when the student hears from the Lord, but also when he hears through a teacher who has already been impacted by the truth he teaches.

The teacher is the intermediary of the message. He stands between the Lord and the people. He is the delivery mechanism that the Lord gave to the church. *The teacher of God is the living link between the Word of God and the people of God.*

Teachers cannot improve upon the Scriptures but they can contaminate them. A Christian who is behaving carnally clogs the communication. It's clogged in both directions—not only from the Lord but also to the people. The more Christlike our character and conduct, the clearer our message.

The teacher can choke the communication of the Scriptures in one of four ways. First, the *character of the communicator* can subtly dull the impact of the application if the class doesn't sense the integrity of the teacher. Are you for real? Because if you aren't real, then your class won't feel the message is real either. A phony delivers a phony message. Phonies pollute the proclamation. "Who you are speaks so loudly that I cannot hear what you say."

Second, the *conduct of the communicator* can block the Bible if the teacher is guilty of carnal behavior. If the teacher is openly sinning, then the message preached often produces alienation from the Almighty. Not only does sinful conduct quench the Spirit of the Lord, but it also quenches the spirit of the Lord's people.

Third, the *communication of the teacher* can detract from the message. A poor delivery can greatly diminish a great message. Communication that is boring and delivered in a monotone can put any audience to sleep.

Fourth, the degree of *change in the communicator* due to his obedience to the Word also either limits or liberates the truth in the hearts of the hearers. If the truth has already transformed the teacher, then the truth has a far greater chance of transforming the students. That's why teaching other people's material often lacks power. Unless your presentation has your fingerprint on it, and has made a difference in your life, you can almost count on it not to compel your students to make changes in their lives.

When we teach, the people are constantly checking our integrity. They are asking, "Do you practice what you preach or do you just like to preach?" Do you just lecture about the truth, or do you live the truth and then lecture about the truth? Paul had a clear philosophy about this when he said, "For I will not dare to speak of any of those things which Christ has not accomplished through me, in word and deed" (Romans 15:18).

Tragically, a divorce has occurred between the conduct and communication of many teachers. We have separated what the Lord Himself has joined together. We have said the *character* is not directly related to the *content*.

What a travesty! What a mockery of the Lord. For proof of how God views this blight on His integrity, just read His requirements for church leadership in 1 Timothy 3 and Titus 2. Or read Jesus' scathing words in Matthew 23 to those who teach the truth while practicing the lie.

Character is God's major prerequisite for communicating His content! The teacher who follows the Master Teacher realizes that although the *what* and *how* of the lesson are important, the *who* presenting the lesson is of ultimate importance.

There are three practical steps teachers can follow to ensure they have obeyed the truth before they teach the truth. The truth is more frequently caught than taught because life communicates more powerfully than the lips. How, then, can you approach your life and lessons with that in mind?

1. Prepare your lessons during the whole week before you teach.

Since powerful applications are greatly influenced by how powerfully they have impacted you, you can forget the late Saturday night or early Sunday morning class preparation. God doesn't make truth miraculously real during our sleep Saturday night. We must give the Lord ample time to work in us and to work through us.

I attended the grand twentieth-anniversary celebration of ministry for the pastor of a large and thriving church. Thousands of us were packed into the Fox ballroom in downtown Atlanta. What a wonderful evening of mutual love and respect between congregation and pastor. While the pastor was thanking his congregation, I heard him say, "You know, friends, I'm not particularly smart. I'm not the world's greatest orator. But one thing I do every Monday morning when I crawl out of bed is fall to my knees and pray to the Lord, 'What are You going to teach me this week that I can share with Your people next Sunday?'"

I turned to my wife and said, "That's the secret of this man's powerful ministry." His secret wasn't what he did in the pulpit on Sunday morning before thousands; it was what he did on his knees on Monday morning before the Throne. Therefore, begin preparing for next week's class the moment your last class is over.

2. Ask the Lord to apply the specific truth you are going to teach to your own life during the week.

Ask God to make it real to you. You can count on that prayer being answered, because that request is right in the center of His will. The Lord wants nothing more than for His children to obey Him.

When we allow God to apply the truth we teach first to our own lives, we follow the example of the "life-teacher" Paul: "Brethren, join in following my example, and note those who so walk, as you have us for a pattern" (Philippians 3:17). Paul purposed that all of us be "life-teachers," not just "content-teachers," when he stated, "...in all things showing yourself to be a pattern of good works; in doctrine showing integrity, reverence, incorruptibility, sound speech that cannot be condemned, that one who is an opponent may be ashamed, having nothing evil to say of you" (Titus 2:7–8). Perhaps such integrity of lifestyle would enable us to have integrity of teaching.

Both the life and lips of the teacher communicate the truth. When they communicate the truth in harmony, the power of God is freely unleashed through the teacher of God.

3. Communicate with all of your mind, will, and emotion the applications the Lord has taught you from the Bible.

The content comes from the Scripture and the communication comes through your life. Make sure that you communicate with passion and fervency what you learned through the living process.

Teachers almost universally overestimate the power of their words and underestimate the power of emotion that flows behind their words. As will be discussed in the next chapter, life change occurs not only when a person thinks differently, but also when they are moved emotionally. Break free from the bondage of the "thinking only" approach to teaching. Involve all of your life to touch all of their lives. Laugh, weep, mourn, rejoice. Be fully human when you teach.

At the same time, watch that you don't become the star of your own show. You and I are servants, not superstars. We are tutors whose emphasis must not be on our abilities or lessons but rather our students and their progress toward maturity. In that context, guardedly and authentically disclose incidents from your own life, including both successes and failures.

Christ came to reach the whole man—not just the mind, not just the emotions, not just the will, not just the spirit. Christ came to provide a way for all men in all ways to be all things in Him. As His representatives, may we follow in His footsteps. May the Truth always touch our lives before it touches our students. May we communicate the whole gospel in a whole presentation to the whole man.

Maxim 7: Application must ultimately lead the student from studying the Bible to obeying the Lord.

This last maxim requires the teacher to lead his students through two major transitions. First, the teacher must lead the students from studying to obeying. Second, the teacher must change the focus of the student from the Bible to the Lord. Both of these are crucial to dynamic applications. The first transition concentrates upon what the student is doing—either studying or obeying; and the second, upon what the student is focusing—the Bible or God.

Christianity is not a set of facts. Christianity isn't a system of content or theology. Christianity isn't even the result of an understanding of our class notes. Christianity is a relationship with a living Person, Jesus Christ. Unfortunately, we frequently teach as if it were merely an understanding of information.

Lead your students beyond the truth to the One who is the Truth. All too frequently, students leave classrooms week after week having studied God's Word, but never having met God! I'm not talking about coming to Christ at the point of salvation. I'm talking about meeting the Lord as the result of, and even during the process of, studying what He has said. We study the Bible week after week, but we never meet the Lord anew and afresh.

One of my favorite Christian writers, A. W. Tozer, says we are like those who select perfect stones to construct an altar. We arrange twelve rocks in a nice pile, then cut down a tree and place the wood neatly on top of our altar. We kill the fatted calf and place it on our altar as a sacrifice to the Lord. Then we all stand around our nice altars and discuss the rocks, rearrange the wood, and reposition the sacrifice. We sing songs about our altar. We analyze every part of our altar. After an hour or so everyone leaves and goes back to their homes, somewhat satisfied about the experience but sensing that something was missing.

As Tozer prophetically points out, we have forgotten that the point of it all—the rocks, wood, altar, and gathering together—was for the "fire from heaven" to fall and devour our sacrifice, wood, and altar.

My friends, people don't come to hear us count the rocks. Our students don't arrive to analyze how best to cut the wood. They desperately wish to meet the Lord. We must build the altar, of course, but build the altar for the wonderful purpose of seeing the Lord! Somehow we have settled for dead sacrifices rather than the living Savior. Isn't that at least one reason why we have such masses of Christians who languish week after week hoping that somehow, someone will arise to call down fire from the heavens?

Welcome home, Elijah. Your altar awaits you.

MEANING

The essence of the Law of Application is these four words: "Apply for life change." The teacher should always teach for the purpose of life change.

CONCLUSION

My wish for you is that you will deeply desire to be a man or woman of God with whom and through whom the Lord can speak and work mightily as you teach His Word. You must desire deeply such a relationship with Him or you will not be able to carry the cross He will eventually ask of you. You must seek the Lord with all of your heart, and all of your soul, and all of your mind. You must hunger for the hand of the Lord when you speak.

What we need most is to have Elisha's desire for the mantle of Elijah. We need men and women who will not settle for anything less than the fullest blessing of the Lord in their lives and on their ministries.

Twice in my life I have asked the Lord God to bestow upon me the mantle of another. Many years ago in the midst of a seminary class, when the Spirit of God was overwhelmingly present, I bowed my head and asked for that teacher's mantle. Then a decade later, in the midst of a national conference where no one seemed to speak except with human power, the last speaker—crowned with white hair—carried us all to the very throne room of glory. Once again I found myself through tears begging our Lord for that old saint's mantle.

Teaching for the Lord is the highest calling in the universe. Someday, before you enter heaven's gate, may some young student petition God for your mantle. That may be your greatest day. But remember, bearers of the mantle have one thing in common—hearts committed to application.

DISCUSSION QUESTIONS

1. Two Bible-believing Sunday school teachers present the same lesson on the same Sunday to the same age group. One believes it is his responsibility to explain the Bible and the Holy Spirit's responsibility to apply it. The other believes it is his responsibility to rely on the Holy Spirit for the entire lesson, but feels responsible both to explain and apply it to his students. You conduct some market research and interview four people from each class. What differences would you find in their thinking and living?

2. What percentage of content versus application do you think is typical for the classes you attend? Why do you think so many teachers think that content is so much more important than application? What organizations do you think foster this attitude and what could be done to change it?

3. In an age when everyone is pushing for only one absolute in life—namely, that there aren't any absolutes—the Bible still contains numerous absolutes. The Book hasn't changed, but our society has...and we are reaping the fruit of our error. One reason so many Christians live defeated lives is that Bible teachers are waxing eloquent on their own ideas rather than the Lord's. Why is a teacher's normal tendency to push his or her own ideas rather than God's truths? Do you think more lives would move in the direction

of godliness if people wrestled with the very Word of God? By the way, was your class faced with "thus saith the Lord" from the Bible during your last lesson?

4. There is a price to be paid for having the Lord teach you the truth before you teach it to others. How would you describe that price? How would your teaching change if you made sure each lesson filtered through you first before you shared it with others?

CHAPTER SIX

Application
Method and Maximizers

I had just spoken at a pastors' conference on the importance of balancing our content and application. One pastor came up to me after the session, frustration written all over his face. "As soon as I get home," he said, "I'm going to have my secretary type out my last sermon and see what percentage was content and what percentage was application."

That would be great, I told him, but be prepared for a shock. Then I asked him to call me and tell me what he discovered.

On Tuesday morning he called. "I can't believe it, and I hate to admit it. My sermon was 92 percent content, only 8 percent application."

I could believe it because I've often heard those same revealing words.

"What do you think I should do?" he asked.

I told him to balance his preaching and teaching to try to average at least 50 percent application, starting the next time he preached. He told me he preached for forty minutes so I suggested he give content for the first twenty minutes and application the next twenty. I asked him to call me the next week and report how it worked.

On Monday he called again. "How did it go?" I asked.

"Interesting," he replied. His tone indicated not a good interesting. "The first twenty minutes went great, but I hate to admit it, I couldn't think of anything past five minutes of application. Church ended at 11:45. For the first time in the history of our church, we ended before noon!"

I challenged him. "In other words, Pastor, you couldn't think of any applications, any ways your content could be helpful to your congregation? Just think, then, how hard it must be for your congregation! If you can't think of an application, you can be sure they can't. And if they can't, how much life change do you think is taking place in your church week after week?"

It was quiet for a moment as the significance of the question sank in. "Not much, I guess. But Bruce, I don't really know how to apply the Bible. I wanted to apply it, but I didn't know where to start. Seminary was great at helping me figure out the content, but I must have missed the lectures on application. What should I do? I don't want to miss the main point ever again. I want my people to grow because of what I teach, not in spite of it."

Do you know what to do when it's time to apply? Do you know how to prepare your material so that it makes the Bible come alive in the lives of your students? Do you know how to cooperate with the Holy Spirit so that you regularly experience His presence and power?

If your heart is eager and your mind open, the insights on the next few pages may be life changing.

APPLICATION METHOD

Why is it that some teachers can bring us to the heavenlies and others cannot raise our heads off the desks? There are many reasons for this, but one lies at the heart of our faith. Most of us have stopped believing that such powerful teaching is possible. We know that God moved greatly through teachers of the past. We also know there are a few teachers today who seem to have the same unbelievable ability. But we think it's beyond the rest of us normal folks.

In the next few pages I'll be describing a powerful method for applying any truth to anyone for lasting life change. These principles are universal and transcultural. Although I will focus these five steps on teaching the Bible, they work for any subject, whether math or science or anthropology.

The flow between the five steps is dynamic and fluid. The steps overlap and build upon each other. Generally, the five steps begin with belief and conclude with behavior. The earlier steps are more obvious and widely practiced, whereas the later ones are more advanced and rarely practiced.

Part of the secret of using this method is to make sure you don't progress to the next step before completing the previous one. When these steps are regularly practiced, the difference in teaching is immediate and striking. If our heart is right, our content biblical, and our method effective, the Lord responds in ways that can leave us breathless—and our students Christlike.

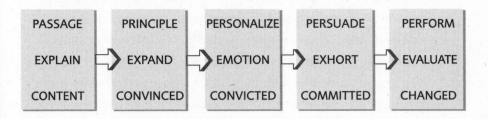

Step 1: Passage

The first step is to make sure your students know the truth. The teacher exposes the "*passage*" to the class and puts on the "*explain*" hat to discuss the "*content*."

Because the emphasis of this chapter is upon the application and not the content, suffice it to say that an effective teacher knows he has accomplished this step when his students demonstrate they understand the material. The time devoted to the explanation stage is controlled by the difficulty of the subject and the competence of the students.

Step 2: Principle

After the class understands the content, you must draw the life changing essence from it and help them understand it. That essence is called the "*principle*" and is normally the main idea of the passage. The teacher must then take this principle and "*expand*" upon it from other related passages in the Bible so that the class becomes thoroughly "*convinced*" it is biblical.

This step is a bridge between the original audience and the current audience and spans the wide gap between the time and setting of the first century and the twentieth century.

Just think of it. You start with a book that is thousands of years old and yet somehow the teacher is to enable modern audiences to readily grasp its relevance. That's always the basis for life change—truth presented so clearly and powerfully that the audience cannot help but apply it. When done effectively, people soon sense this truth is made for them; it becomes so real that they forget anyone else is in the room. Someone must have read their mail or even their mind.

The teacher must deal with three distinct time periods during this step. First, the *original time* of the passage. Last, the *present time* of the twentieth century. And in between is the timelessness of *universal time*, where the principle must dwell. The teacher must lift the universal truth from the ancient text and translate it to the category of universal truth.

Remember the classic "Where's the beef?" advertising campaign for Wendy's? In this step the teacher shows the class the "beef"—the meat of the passage. He pulls away the bun, scrapes off the ketchup, and sets aside the lettuce and tomato. All that remains on the plate is the beef.

The pity for most students is that their teacher never delivers the beef. Rather than sink their teeth into meat, they only nibble on limp lettuce and scattered sesame seeds. That's why so many people can come to church week after week and hear the Bible taught and yet never grow. Someone may say, "Well, they really didn't want to grow." Sometimes that's true, but it has been my experience that Christians everywhere are bloated with bread but starving for beef.

This "principle stage" is critical to powerful teaching and ultimately determines the amount of life change possible in a class. We must differentiate between the story and the essence, between the passage and the principle. Laymen know the difference; just ask them. But be prepared—many of them will say, "We're not being fed!" Teachers or preachers are often shocked when they hear that, because they thought all along they had been teaching the Bible. In one sense, they had. But in a deeper way, they had not. You can be served a caloric requirement of rice every meal, but in time you'll starve from malnutrition.

It's the difference between the history teacher who knows all the facts and another teacher who makes history come alive in such a way that it has an immediate and dramatic impact on you.

Power in teaching comes from the essence behind the events, the message behind the narrative, the precept behind the passage. Teachers who teach the "beef" never lack an audience. Students always leave taught, convicted, and changed.

There is one more difference between the first and second stage in application. The passage stage has many different points of explanation and emphasis. The principle stage has only a single point of emphasis. The idea is to leave all the specifics of the Bible text and weave the threads into one beautiful tapestry. Rearrange the parts and place them into a whole. From the many find the one. Sift and meditate until you can state the timeless truth in one sentence—truth that is beyond culture, beyond nationality. In other words, find the beef!

Here are a few brief insights on how to become a master of the principle:

Want to find the meat of the passage. Desire it. Seek it. Motivate yourself to continue wanting it.

Hold fast to the belief that every passage contains at least one key principle. There's no exception. When everything in you says there isn't a principle to be found—or "I can't do it, it's too hard"—go back to the bedrock: All passages have at least one principle. Don't give up!

Finding the essence of the content takes time and effort. One time I worked with another teacher on developing the principle from a passage. He kept asking what it was and grew impatient with both the process and with me when he sensed he should have been able to find it quickly and easily. It takes time and hard work for all of us, so anticipate the process and you won't be disappointed.

Pray for illumination from the Holy Spirit to see more of what already has been written. Don't ask Him for more revelation; ask for more illumination of what you hold in your hand. The more you pray as you prepare your principle, the more insight the Lord will grant you. Sometimes I find myself pounding the doors of heaven for insight because I'm just flat-out stumped. "Ask," Jesus said, "and you will find."

Think! Think a lot! Meditate over and over on the passage. Put down the book, turn off the TV, take a pad of paper, and just think. Record your thoughts on paper about the possible timeless truths. Spread your meditations throughout the week before you teach. Don't expect to have the greatest insights the first time. Plan at least three times during the week to meditate and you'll get more insight than the same amount of time focused at one sitting. Use your drive time. Use your downtime. Time your meditations so your mind can work for you in "background" mode. Review the issue right before going to sleep and right before going to work. Carry the key ideas of the passage with you on a note card and read them over and over. Discuss the concept with someone who has a fertile mind and enjoys brainstorming.

Don't hunt for the principle in the commentaries. It's been my experience that commentaries only deal with the first stage—the facts. The Lord wants the principle to come through your personality and experience. When you process it personally, you have forged the link in your mind between the passage and the principle. The stronger the link, the more powerful the proclamation.

Relax. Enjoy developing the principle through your personality. The Lord doesn't expect us all to come up with the same principle. Trust yourself and the Lord's work in you. Sometimes you'll know the principle through a burst of insight and the "aha!" will almost blind you. Often you'll laugh out loud because suddenly it is so obvious. Other times it will dawn slowly, like a sunrise. As you practice this stage you will develop a sense of whether you "have it." The Lord develops in all of us a sense of feel that is hard to describe. All the master teachers I have interviewed know what I'm talking about. Therefore, if you studied and prayed and meditated, relax!

State the principle in a simple and motivating sentence. Keep it simple. Think short. Be as direct as you can without being authoritarian. My principle from 2 Timothy 3:16–17 was simply "Teach for life change." Boil down your message to the essence and then package it.

Think like a poster or a billboard. Catch your audience's attention. Motivate them to do it. *Your principle should market the message.* I just completed a lesson on the power of thinking about eternity and how it makes a significant difference in our lives. My principle? "Think heaven—now!"

Somehow we think the principle must be some complicated and complex sentence that captures every part of what we are trying to say to everyone. Are you kidding? Most of those principles motivate no one. If you want to watch a master in action, read the Gospels and watch how Jesus summarizes His point in a catchy, motivating statement or phrase. "Come, follow Me!" or "If you love Me, keep My commandments" or "Abide in Me" or "My sheep hear My voice."

Make sure your principle is thoroughly biblical. During this stage, compare other key verses in the Bible on the same subject. Review with your class other "central passages" regarding your "big idea" to validate and illustrate.

It is as though you lead your class into a dark room and begin to turn on one light after another. As the room lightens, focus those beams of light on the one object you want to teach. Your role is to shine enough light on the principle so the class can see all its parts. Hold the principle up to the light and turn it every which way. Look at it from the bottom, the sides, the top. Crawl inside of it. Dissect it. Demonstrate how it fits together.

Lead your class to leap past your principle and "pre-discover" their own applications. The clearer the principle, the more the truth will hit your audience with power and conviction even without your comments. Well-crafted principles reveal their applications immediately. They are so clear that they are transparent to the students who intuitively realize what they should do in order to be obedient to the biblical principle.

Master teachers are highly skilled in this stage. Everything they speak in the passage step is aimed at providing the basis for their principle. Their students eat beef regularly. They are well fed. Their teachers ensure that.

Step 3: Personalize

By the time you come to this third step, your class should understand both the *passage* and the *principle*. During passage and principle, you focus on the content, but during the *"personalize"* step, you refocus on the class. During this stage the application really takes shape and touches the student's *"emotion"* so he becomes *"convicted"* by the Holy Spirit of his need to obey.

Until this point, the lesson has been objective; now it must become subjective. The students must move from understanding the "what" to the "so what." During this step the truth becomes incarnate. The facts put on flesh. The principle strives to become personal. This third step is the heart and essence of application. It is the turning point of the five steps, the pivot of the entire effort. The first two steps prepare the student for this step and the last two build upon the results of this step.

Personalize has two distinct yet interrelated parts. When successfully completed, the student should know what to do and feel convicted to do it. When these two conditions are met, the next major step, *persuade*, commences.

Personalize occurs when the general and timeless principle becomes a specific and timely application. During this step, the student should see how the passage in the Bible is to be lived out in his life. Mr. Theoretical moves out and Mr. Practical moves in. For this to develop correctly, a remarkable partnership must develop between the human teacher and the Divine Teacher. Each has his own role as the two work in tandem:

The role of the teacher is to clarify to the students what this principle would look like if they obeyed it either in their character (*"complete"*) or conduct (*"equipped"*).

The role of the Spirit is to convict the students of their responsibility to the Lord to obey that principle immediately and completely through the specific ways He is leading them.

Clarification occurs in the mind and conviction in the heart. Clarification occurs as the teacher pictures what the principle would look like in the student's life and circumstances. Conviction occurs as the Spirit pricks the student's heart, causing him to feel the need to obey the Lord and put the principle into practice.

The clearer we paint a picture of what the principle would look like in the imagination of the student, the quicker and more effectively the Spirit can penetrate the heart of the student. Furthermore, the stronger the conviction, the far greater the potential for genuine, lasting life change.

These interrelated activities greatly influence the degree of life change that occurs when you teach. How effectively you complete your role as a clarifier usually either quenches or liberates the Spirit to work in your students. Although the Holy Spirit is all-powerful, he almost always chooses to work in cooperation with the human teacher. That is why some teachers seem always to have the anointing of the Spirit and others (even with the very same content) do not.

How to Communicate the Principle with Clarity

Have you ever said, "I just can't picture myself doing that"? I bet you didn't do it, did you? Before we act, we must be able to see ourselves doing it. Your role as clarifier is to help your students "see" themselves doing the principle. You must picture the principle in action. One common reason so few people experience life change is that the teacher never helped them to see the life change occurring.

We call that *insight*, the ability to "see into" something. When you help your class see the principle in their lives, you have helped them "see into" a new area of action and have contributed insight to areas of blindness.

So provide pictures. Tear off the blinders. Broaden their horizons. Help them imagine themselves living out that principle. Here are a few pointers I have found helpful:

Picture the principle in action in different settings and circumstances. Introduce your class to the principle everywhere you can. Lead your students on a grand tour of this glorious land of the principle. Show the principle at work, at home, at the office, at the lake. Demonstrate that no matter where they live or work, the principle can make a difference.

Enlarge their perspective by introducing the principle's family. Show your class how the principle lives with men and women, boys and girls, marrieds and singles, old and young, rich and poor, sanguines and melancholics. Lead everyone in your class to the conclusion that the principle wants to live in them. Demonstrate that no matter who they are or how they live, the principle can make a difference.

Picture the principle having a wonderful impact everywhere it is invited. Reveal the wonder and awe and glory of the principle. Grip your students with the overpowering benefits bestowed upon those who embrace the principle. Shock your students with the tragic consequences to those who reject it.

Tell gripping stories that incarnate your principle. The best storytellers are able to draw their students right into their stories and help them live the reality of their principle. Tell stories that capture the essence of the good and the bad for those who employ or disregard the principle.

Whatever you do, capture the imaginations of your students. When you do, move over, because it's time for the Spirit to make His convicting presence known!

Reasons the Spirit Does Not Display His Power

There are four primary reasons Christian teachers are not experiencing the power and presence of the Holy Spirit when they minister. The first two have to do with the *personal life* of the teacher, the third with *principalities and powers*, and the fourth with *partnership with the Spirit*.

Presence of unconfessed sin. The first and primary reason the Holy Spirit does not move through the Christian teacher is sin. Known and undealt-with sin grieves and quenches the Spirit.

Stronghold of unbelief. The second most frequent reason the Holy Spirit does not display His power through Christian teachers is that they lack faith that God's Spirit desires to use them mightily. These teachers neither seek nor experience the Spirit's awesome power in their teaching because they have given up believing God will use them greatly by His Spirit.

Attack of principalities and powers. We don't struggle merely against people and circumstances and nature. We also wrestle with principalities and powers and rulers of the darkness of this age—spiritual hosts of wickedness in the heavenly places (Ephesians 6:12). Many teachers who have no known sin and believe that the Lord wants to use them mightily nevertheless are defeated regularly because they lack discernment in these matters. Many Christian teachers cannot identify when their teaching is under attack while others do not know how to defeat the enemy when they do recognize his opposition.

Lack of cooperation with the Spirit. For those teachers who are serious and growing in their walk with God, this is the primary hindrance to regularly experiencing the awesome movement of the Spirit. The Holy Spirit is not a presence, nor a ghost, nor a thing. The Holy Spirit is the third Person of the Trinity. He thinks, feels, responds, indwells, leads, fills, convicts, and is grieved. He teaches.

How to Cooperate with the Spirit as He Convicts

Cooperation with the Spirit is the climax of all teaching, causing the revolutionary difference between natural and supernatural teaching. Here are the main ways you can effectively cooperate with the Spirit if the first three hindrances have been handled and you are in fellowship with the Spirit, believe He wants to work through you, and are not under specific attack:

Depend upon the Spirit. Before you teach, pray for the Holy Spirit to use you mightily. Give Him your unconditional allegiance and tell Him you are willing and wanting Him to do His work. Consciously relax in His presence and power. Be at peace resting in His strength to speak through you and use you. Lean back on Him. Ask Him to use the material you have prepared—or if He so chooses, to communicate different material. You'll know that you are fully dependent upon Him when two distinguishable factors are present—your sense of deep inner peace and your sense of great anticipation.

Discern His movement. The Holy Spirit can and does move during all parts of the lesson, but He seems to focus most frequently and noticeably during this third personalize step. When the truth you have taught is attempting to plant itself in the heart of the student, the Spirit works the soil. You work to clarify the truth, and He works to implant the truth. It's for this movement of truth that the Spirit of Truth rises to the task.

When the Spirit moves either in the heart of a person or in a large congregation, He ripples the waters. And to those who are discerning, the ripples are unmistakable and consistent whenever and whoever you are. A hush sweeps across the audience and nary a man, woman, or child seems to breathe. No one moves. Faces reflect His presence either with marks of conviction or signs of deep peace and fellowship. These signs are physical and universal and are open to all who would seek to cooperate with the mighty wind of God. Watch and discern therefore as the Spirit of the living God works in the hearts of men.

When the Spirit moves you must do one thing and one thing alone: You must rest. You have taught for this moment and He has waited for this moment. Your role must now be fulfilled in His wonderful role. Up to this point you have been the "John the Baptist" to the Spirit and are called to "prepare the way" for Him.

When His presence is felt and His work noticed, then it's time for you to actively "decrease as He must increase." Get out of the way! Move over for His movement. How? Release your control of the class to the Spirit's tender, all-powerful hand by speaking more quietly, slowly, and with many pauses. Soothe the audience and let your voice become like gentle music in the background. Don't move suddenly or gesture noticeably. If possible, move around your pulpit or desk—get close physically to your audience. You need to be utterly sensitive to the Spirit by being completely sensitive to His work in them.

You'll know when His work of conviction has been accomplished. His movements are discernible when He begins and when He concludes. Your class will once again begin moving, people will cough and begin to look around, and their body language will change. Don't fight it! So many teachers mistake this moment and either tell their audience to "pay attention" or even make a joke because they have totally misread the work of God. Be careful. You haven't lost their attention, God has just given their attention back to you. They are undergoing a physical transition from the supernatural back to the natural. They are reentering your territory.

Direct your students. When this part of the Spirit's work has been completed, then you must immediately take active leadership again. Usually at this point the class will be a little out of control—they are between teachers—so change your delivery by raising your voice, intensifying your gestures, and increasing your pace. Now it's time to move your students to action. You must exercise leadership by directing your students to act on the basis of what the Spirit has done.

It's important that you recognize that although the movement of the Spirit is supernatural, it is not "spooky" or too difficult for you to understand. Indeed, my fellow Christian teacher, this Divine arrangement is a part of your calling, a part of your heritage. Deeply desire and seek teaching that is supernatural. Once you have tasted of this heavenly gift, you'll never want to teach again without Him. Neither will your students.

Step 4: Persuade

By the time you have reached this fourth step, your students will have understood the passage, been convinced of the principle, and seen clearly what they should do while feeling the convicting work of the Spirit. This fourth step occurs as the emphasis transitions from the emotion to the will. Now the stress is to "*persuade*" the student to apply the truth. Teachers must "*exhort*" so that the student becomes "*committed*" to obeying the Scriptures, not just feeling they should.

If the student never chooses to obey, he probably will not obey. Therefore, if you don't persuade the student to action, he will most likely not experience life change. The student must move from "I understand" to "I feel I should" to "I am going to do." This stage is the final link in the whole application process. Without it, life change occurs infrequently and lasting life change almost never.

Therefore, to ensure that your commitment to teach for life change actually becomes a reality, you are going to have to learn some of the secrets of persuasion. Unfortunately, most adults neither understand persuasion nor feel trained in the principles of persuasion.

To persuade someone is to convince them to do something. The word comes form the Latin *per,* which means "thoroughly," and *suadere,* which means "to advise." Therefore, persuasion has the concept of "thoroughly advising" a person to the point that they become convinced. When a person is thoroughly advised, he has seen everything from the beginning to the end of the matter.

When you persuade your students, you help them see all the issues thoroughly. The more thoroughly they see a matter, the more persuaded they become. To persuade your students means that you have taught the material so effectively that they saw the material clearly and were absolutely convinced. Think about that a moment. The whole point of the preceding three steps in application was to make the truth so utterly clear that your students could see it very clearly. Good teaching is clear teaching. *Good teaching is therefore persuasive teaching!*

To apply the Scriptures to your class to the point that they actually change, you are going to have to help them to "see clearly" the issue. If you have helped them see clearly, they will behave differently.

"Once I was blind but now I see" are the words of the student who is blessed by a teacher who is persuasive. The more effectively they see, the more effectively they will change. The more effective you are at guiding them to see, the more persuasive you are.

It is the will of God that your students "see thoroughly" to the point of utter and complete obedience to Him. It is therefore the will of God that you become proficient and committed at persuading your students.

The best teachers and preachers are the most persuasive.

But so many Christian teachers think they shouldn't try to persuade their students. Therefore, they've never pleaded with their students to do it God's way. They've never wept over their hardness of heart. These teachers think that teaching is merely talking about the content. They don't realize that if they aren't persuading, they have never really taught their content clearly.

Don't focus any longer on being a "good" teacher. Don't desire any further to be an "interesting" teacher. Desire to be a "persuasive" teacher, because then lives will be changed—and God will be pleased.

Now that you understand the importance of persuasion, what can you do to persuade your students to do what is right? We'll discuss this a great deal further in the Law of Need and the Law of Revival, but at present there are two areas you could use the next time you teach. Persuasive teaching is caused by two separate activities of the teacher: The first is *what you say*, the second is *how you speak*; the first is your *substance*, the second is your *style*; the first is your *content*, the second is your *communication*.

When a student is fully persuaded, it is usually because your information and your presentation convinced them. Depending upon your personality, you will lean more toward the one than the other. Either your content will be so compelling that the students will be persuaded or your delivery so commanding that the students will be convinced. The most compelling teachers effectively blend both.

How to Persuade Through Your Content

Consider the content part of that equation for a moment. What should you say to your class now that they understand but aren't convinced? Perhaps your customer likes your product (lesson) but doesn't know if he is going to purchase (apply) it. All your effort builds to this point because the real issue isn't just that he understands what he should do, but that he chooses to do it! Remember what the Lord commanded us in the Great Commission? "Teach them to observe/do."

Christ desires obedience, not merely consent.

Therefore, my friend, teach for obedience. Teach beyond mere assent. Don't ever permit yourself to think you have completed your job as Christ's spokesperson with only agreement from your students about what the Lord desires of them. As we all know, there is a world of difference between knowing the truth and doing the truth. Our task is to guide them to do what they know.

That vital transition beckons for persuasion. Help them to "see thoroughly" enough that they sense they must act. And act now.

Arrange your content to convince. Amass all the reasons you can for why a person should obey the truth. Share the positives and then share the negatives. Don't use paragraphs; use short, punchy sentences. Be direct. Tell them what the principle beckons them to do. Warn them of the dangers of disobedience. Exhort them. Carry them to the point that there is no logical step left except to obey the Lord, because, fellow teacher, there is no logical step except obedience to the Lord!

Don't try to convince them merely by what's in your mind; rather, share in such a way that they begin thinking their own thoughts in favor of the idea. Get them on the side of the idea. Get them on the side of the truth. Get them envisioning themselves wanting and then acting on the truth.

Appeal to the deepest part of the person. Appeal to what is good and right. Appeal to their conscience. Appeal to their spirit which desires to do the will of God. Appeal to their wisdom in such a way that their thoughts precede yours in thinking how to apply the principle.

If you want to see such persuasion in action, read Romans or James. And if you want to see such persuasion in the life of Jesus, just read His Sermon on the Mount (Matthew 5–7)—compelling, logical, thought-provoking, life changing.

Whatever you discern about Jesus as the Master Teacher, don't miss the fact that He was constantly presenting reasons to be persuaded, telling stories that beckoned for action. Jesus taught to persuade men and women to follow Him, and He told us to follow in His footsteps. Compel them to come.

How to Persuade Through Your Communication and Style

Second, persuade your students not only through *what* you say, but also through *how* you say it. Engender obedience through your tone of voice. Solicit action by your intensity. Raise your voice, shake your finger, pound the desk, overturn the temple tables, weep with the hurting, oppose the stubborn, rebuke the proud. See how the Lord did it? His delivery was powerful and compelling.

A particular sermon once had such a powerful impact on my life that I ordered a copy of the tape and wrote the entire sermon out long-hand. I wanted the content. But when I read the material, I couldn't understand why I had been so moved! The content didn't really move me; it was the sincerity and conviction with which it was communicated that did. Frequently, how you express yourself is more persuasive than what you say. Therefore, *never mumble your message!*

Boring teachers never persuade anyone to do anything except avoid their class. Boring teachers have let their fire burn out. They have joined the ranks of those who believe that if they cover the lesson for the day, then they have taught. They may have "covered the material" but not in a way pleasing to the Lord.

Teach beyond the head and reach down into the heart. Is not the Word of God so precious to you that you would die for it? Then decide that while you are yet alive, you'll live for it! Exert your entire being to communicate for life change.

Rip out the habit of delivering the truth in brown paper sacks and wrap the truth in the fabric of your personality and creativity. Carry your students across the threshold of reticence and disobedience. Let them grasp your confidence, let them hold onto your belief, let them find the joy of full obedience.

And when they resist the truth and won't obey it, express your concern to them. Read 2 Corinthians if you want to see a teacher express his feelings with fervor. Don't teach for less than complete obedience to the will of God—now, today. If they become hardened in their heart, then be direct and straightforward. They need to be confronted. Do not give in to the fear of their negative reaction. Be more concerned with the Lord's displeasure of you than their displeasure of you.

As Jesus sought the lost, seek the ones that don't desire to be found. Don't you recall Moses' thunderous denunciations? Don't you remember the stinging rebukes Jesus gave to those who would not obey the truth? Why do we "beat around the bush" until no one remembers why we are even gathered around the bush? Why do we mumble when the Lord shouted? Why are we so vague when He was so very pointed?

Only because, my friend, we are not burning within for the good of our students. Only because we don't love them as Christ wants us to love them. Only because of our selfishness do we not speak the truth in love.

Maybe that's why the Lord asked the teacher named Peter the same question three times—not to make sure he knew the content, but that he obeyed the content! "If you love Me, then feed My sheep." The deeper we love the Lord Jesus, the more we care about His sheep. They are not our sheep; they have been purchased with the blood of Christ.

Jesus wants His sheep fed, and well-fed sheep obey. Feed them so they will obey.

Reject the false notion that nicely-packaged content translates into well-fed sheep. God forbid that we think the essence of feeding the sheep is a wonderfully outlined sermon. Rise up against such thinking. It is unworthy of you. You have been called to "teach them *to observe* all that I have commanded you." Teach them to obey. Your goal is not a wonderful lesson but a transforming lesson.

Can't you become emotional about such things? Can't our desire for our students become so overwhelming that we find ourselves on occasion in tears of desperation for their good? Can't our burden for their obedience drive us to plead with them? Indeed it may, and indeed it must. To do any less may not fully persuade.

I once served as the chairman in a church discipline issue where one of the men of the fellowship was threatening to sue another brother. I asked both of them if they would allow a committee of elders to listen to their case and make a ruling that would be fully binding on both of them. They both agreed. The meeting began at 7:30 in the morning and we never left the room, even to eat, until 11:00 that night. It was intense and emotional. And when the elders prayed for consensus, we all agreed that the one who was sure he was in the right was indeed the one in error. He had a blind spot that all of us saw but him.

When we called the two men into the room and presented our judgment that the offending brother was to give $30,000 to the other man and stop harassing him, the offender jumped up from his chair and said we were all wrong and he wasn't going to do it.

I was struck by fear. I had seen too many times the divine judgment that comes on a person who rebels against church discipline conducted according to the clear teachings of the Bible. As chairman of the committee, I felt the whole weight of his rebellious spirit crushing me. We all tried to convince him to submit to the elder's decision, but he refused. In utter desperation, overwhelmed with grief and fear for my good friend, I fell to my knees and begged him not to say no.

He was shocked to see me in such agony. He was embarrassed to have me kneeling at his feet. I didn't care. I couldn't let him leave that room and walk into the discipline of the Lord. The Lord aided us greatly in our weakness because at that moment my friend chose to repent. He said if his obedience was that important to us, he guessed he had better do what we said.

I don't think I have ever been more exhausted than at the end of those sixteen hours. I am convinced, however, that had I not fallen on my knees and begged my friend, he would have walked out of that room and directly into the disciplining hands of his heavenly Father.

All the content in the world wasn't doing it. These godly men had spoken their mind all day long. The truth was effectively communicated. He understood the truth. He could have given us every major point of the issue. Only our passionate expression of our love for him kept that special sheep from leaving the fold.

Fellow teachers, how far will you go to keep your sheep in the fold?

Jesus went all the way to the cross for the sheep. The highest persuasion known in the universe was His willing death to convince us that "God so loved the world that He gave His only begotten Son, that whoever believes in Him should not perish but have everlasting life."

He died teaching the message. Jesus commissioned us to teach the message with all of our personality and passion. All of His message through all of our life for all of our students...until they are fully persuaded.

Step 5: Perform

This last step is the quality check of life changing teaching. The question you must now ask is the most challenging one for you as the teacher as well as for your students. Did they actually do it? Not did they understand the passage, not were they convinced of the principle, not were they convicted of what they should do, not were they persuaded so they committed to do it, but *did they do it?*

Unless the "doing it" actually occurred right in class, you must wait until the next class to ask this question. You want to know if they "*performed*" what they "*committed.*" You must "*evaluate*" whether or not they were "*changed.*"

We're at the bedrock now, aren't we? This is the only way to validate the true results of our teaching.

During this step you must move beyond what you do and discover what they have done. The only way you will know is by asking. So take a deep breath, hope for the best, and ask for the truth. Remember, ignorance may be bliss, but it does not please the Lord!

If you have done your job up to this point, all you are seeking to discover is whether your students' resolve was strong enough to overcome the normal hindrance to change—called *habit.*

Have you noticed that the older you become, the more difficult it is to initiate lasting change? Know why? Because the longer you have been alive, the longer you have been developing a way of doing something, a regular response to stimuli, a habit.

Change requires the breaking of a habit, and your students are going to need a great deal of resolve and encouragement to break their well-entrenched habits. Change can be thought of as breaking a habit by exchanging one kind of behavior for another. The person has to stop the undesired actions in order to start the desired ones.

Life change means the teacher aids the student to cooperate with the Holy Spirit in breaking an existing habit and practicing the new and desired habit. But remember, forming new habits is difficult and frequently takes more than thirty days.

Bringing your students to the point of genuine commitment does not equal lasting change. Commitment only means intention and desire and resolve. Commitment provides the foundation for change, but accountability actually ensures the change.

Remember, lasting life change involves changes that last for life. May your resolve be deep enough to teach to the point of lasting life change.

APPLICATION MAXIMIZERS

After reading the five steps in the Application Method, you may be feeling unsure of your ability to apply anything to anyone. Don't lose heart. Although these five steps may seem a lot to learn, they will quickly become second nature.

To further equip you in your question to become a Master Applier, consider carefully these seven Application Maximizers.

Maximizer 1: Ask God to develop in you an applier's heart.

How does it make you feel that the Lord has called you to apply the truth you teach? Do you sense you are adequate for the task? I sure didn't at first.

When this truth first dawned on me, I wrestled with strong feelings of inadequacy and insecurity. I felt I couldn't do it. Obviously, somebody else should do it. I thought of other teachers who must have this ability, this "gift of applying," because I didn't. I had the "gift of content."

In the corners of my heart crouched the unsettling suspicion that this transition from a 95 percent content teacher to a more balanced ministry was no easy journey. Many times I retreated to lessons laden with information but empty of meaningful application.

Along the way, however, one practice proved of great value to me. It may lie at the root of how my teaching was transformed. I began asking God to give me something I didn't have—an applier's heart. I sought a change in my heart so deep that I would be set free to apply the way He wanted me to apply.

The Lord is so gracious when we sincerely pray for something in the center of His will. On this subject He had made His will clear: "teach them to observe [apply] all things that I have commanded you." How could He not be pleased when we pray for His gift of an applier's heart?

Let me encourage you to join in this prayer. You may wish to write this in your Bible and date it today. Then as you prepare each lesson, begin your time with this prayer. Perhaps someday we can meet and encourage each other with the answers we've experienced.

PRAYER FOR AN APPLIER'S HEART

Lord, it is my deep desire always to teach others
"to observe all things that You have commanded," and
therefore I ask You to empower me through Your Holy Spirit
to teach for lasting life change. I invite You to work in any
way necessary to develop an applier's heart in my life.
Impart to me, therefore, Your heart for the world!

I can promise you one thing: Once the Lord begins His transforming work, you'll never return to the old way.

One last secret: Once you start cultivating this applier's heart, you will start recognizing it in others. They betray themselves because "out of the heart come all the issues of life," including such issues as application. It's one further proof that you have joined the ranks of the remnant who teach for eternity.

Maximizer 2: Prepare applications in relation to your students' needs.

Why do your students gather to listen to you? What do they hope will happen before class is over? Don't they hope you will teach them something that will help them?

Now consider yourself as the student instead of the teacher. Why do you attend a class at the office, college, or church? Is it not to seek help? And if you sought help but the teacher didn't offer it, how did you feel about the experience?

Teaching carries an unstated expectation that the student has a problem and the teacher has the solution. When that agreement is not fulfilled, disappointment inevitably occurs. Students feel betrayed by their teacher and teachers feel frustration toward their students.

Such need not be the case. Why do to your students what you hated teachers to do to you? You are now the teacher and it is fully within your power to help. Choose to help your students every time you teach!

Powerful applications touch your students' deepest needs. So many teachers have strayed so far from meeting the needs of students that frustrated students declare their classes are irrelevant and a waste of time. If you have the slightest question about this, just ask a college student how many of his required courses are a waste of time. But be prepared. Students often feel most of their classes offer little or no help.

Of course, we know the common retort: "Students don't know

what they need. Wait until they grow older and they'll change their minds." Well, I'm older and I haven't changed my mind. You're older, too. Would you have chosen the majority of required courses had you been given a choice? Do you remember walking out of class time after time saying that you didn't know what good this class would do? Looking back, were you right?

So change your mind now. Don't become trapped by the presumption that teaching isn't really to "help" the students. Commit to meet your students' needs and—as Dr. Howard Hendricks likes to say— "They'll rise up and call you blessed!"

Maximizer 3: Plan all parts of the lesson to contribute to the application.

Imagine an archery enthusiast who purchases the finest equipment and heads to the range for target shooting. He strings his bow and lets his arrow fly, only to realize that he has failed to set up his target. With a burst of speed and luck, he grabs the target, rushes ahead of the flying arrow, and in the nick of time positions the target so that the arrow pierces the bull's-eye! Then he pats himself on the back for his skill as an archer.

Absurd, isn't it? Yet teachers frequently conduct their classes in ways not much different from this. They teach for an hour, then step back and pronounce themselves successful for having conducted another class. Meanwhile, their students wander off wondering what class had to do with anything.

Your teaching has one primary target: life change! You have to know what parts of your students' lives need changing and then devise appropriate applications to meet those needs. You must structure all parts of your content to hit that life change target.

If you want to excel at applying, learn to employ all parts of the teaching-learning process. Once the target is established, all parts of the arrow—point, shaft, feathers, and notch—play an important part in hitting it. Likewise, all parts of the class session—introduction, content, transition, illustrations, and conclusion—play a crucial part in hitting the life change target.

Focus everything to maximize the application. Put the muscle where it matters. Don't use a shotgun. Instead aim a machine gun at the target and hit the bull's-eye over and over again. Hit it so many times that no one can miss the point.

Unfortunately, many teachers think that an application is not the point but rather something tacked on the end of their class—a few parting words, an obligatory moment of meditation.

How foreign from the teaching of Christ and His disciples! Christ did not consider application as a way to tidy His teaching, but instead the whole point of His teaching. His content served as the basis for the application. Never develop your content and then wonder what application you can add. Never present any part of your lesson unless it points to the final target.

Plan the end from the beginning so that you can strategically allocate every resource to empower every application. Never again be an arrow-chaser. Pick your target prayerfully and carefully. Prepare your arrows. And then with everything that's within you, let them fly! Hitting the target on purpose is a whole lot more satisfying than doing it accidentally—and you don't waste nearly as many arrows.

Maximizer 4: Lead your students beyond general applications to specific steps of obedience.

Life change never occurs in generalities but always in specifics. Therefore, teachers must lead their students to apply the truth in specific and identifiable ways.

The challenge is to lead students beyond abstract concepts such as "forgiveness" to concrete actions such as "forgiving that person for that act." Unless the student makes this all-important transition from something he thinks to something he does, life change will occur only in his imagination and not in his life. The teacher must lead the student to personalize the application. The lesson you presented in class must become the lesson he applies after class. Your truth must become incarnate in him.

I have found that students frequently want to take action but they need a plan, a track to run on. Second, teachers frequently quench the Holy Spirit's leading by making the plan too specific or too dogmatic so that all students start acting the same way, losing their God-given distinctiveness. Instead of telling them specifically what to do, lead them into an understanding of the relevant, guiding principle of Scripture. Then encourage them to seek what the Lord would have them do in light of that principle. If you teach the truth, trust the Lord to communicate how He wants that truth lived out in each student's life.

Although there is only one correct interpretation and a few guiding principles, there are innumerable applications. Our responsibility is to present the interpretation and principles and then help the students discover their personal and specific applications.

So resist the temptation to help so much that you overstep your ground as the teacher. Resist the temptation to pay God. We don't want to produce "cookie-cutter Christians."

Maximizer 5: Illustrate the application with Scripture, history, personal experience, and imagination.

Illustrations are pictures drawn with words. Illustrations visualize. Illustrations clarify. Illustrations motivate. Illustrations make the main point while allowing students to fill in the details. A good picture, whether drawn or spoken, is easily worth a thousand words of explanation.

Illustrations can be used effectively in four different parts of the lesson:

1. Illustrations that *introduce*: Captures interest and develops curiosity.
2. Illustrations that *explain*: Develops understanding of information and facts.
3. Illustrations that *apply*: Pictures the use of the application in real life.
4. Illustrations that *conclude*: Deepens commitment and moves to action.

Amazing as it may seem, the same illustration can be restructured and used effectively in all four parts. Illustrations that apply guide the learner to see how the application works in real life. Illustrations move the application off the page and into the person. Illustrations lead the learner to say "I want to do that" and "I will do that."

Does it bother you when the only comment people make about your lesson is how much they liked your great story? Or that all they can remember of past lessons are the stories? Do you feel they missed the point? How could they forget our five-point alliterated outline and remember that stupid story?

It doesn't only happen when *you* teach, it happens when *anyone* teaches. It happens everywhere, no matter what the subject, no matter what the age of the audience. *The power of illustrations is universal.* Why buck the system? If the system is universal, guess Who may be behind it?

Therefore, use illustrations—a lot. If you want a stimulating assignment, take thirty minutes and glance through the teachings of Christ. Try to get a sense of what percentage of His words were illustrations. We call them parables or allegories, and they are on almost every page of the Gospels. By the way, can you give me the outline of the Olivet Discourse in Matthew? But how about the Parable of the Good Samaritan? See how the story clarifies and is memorable?

Recently I asked my teenage son, Dave, what percentage of Christ's words he thought were illustrations. Without thinking he replied more than 80 percent. And then he added, "That's why Christ is so interesting."

Why do we continue to teach in opposition to the way of the Master Teacher Himself? He knew people would remember His truth more through stories than lectures. Perhaps that's why master teachers are also master storytellers.

Where do you find great illustrations? As far as I can find, there are four primary sources of illustrations:

1. Illustrations from *personal experience*: Use people, places, and events that you encountered.
2. Illustrations from *history*: Use secular or extrabiblical people, places, and events.
3. Illustrations from *Scripture*: Use Old or New Testament people, places, and events.
4. Illustrations from *imagination*: Use people, places, and events that you created through your imagination and creativity.

These four sources of illustrations are listed in the order of present-day use. More than 80 percent of the illustrations used by the vast majority of teachers are taken from personal experience, with the remaining 20 percent divided between history and Scripture. It is the rare teacher who uses imagination to construct an illustration.

If you want a real thought-provoker, consider Jesus Christ's use of illustrations. You'll find that His practice was exactly the opposite of ours. *The primary source of Jesus' illustrations was His imagination*—the parables were all fictional stories. Modern teachers use more personal examples than anything else—creating the real danger of using their own lives as the primary standards and examples for others. So use your imagination and tell stories your students can never forget. Then the next time one of your students can remember only your story, smile because you wrapped the story around your application!

Maximizer 6: Employ an appropriate style when calling for commitment.

The climax of teaching is not what the teacher says but what the student does. Will the student actually choose to apply the truth to his life?

Here we have arrived at the heart of the matter. You're now an applier, you've discovered your students' needs, all parts of the lesson have been carefully aimed at the application, you've led them to the steps of obedience and illustrated to them effectively. Your students are right there with you. You can see it in their faces. Now it's time to ask them to make a commitment to actually do it.

This is the moment of truth—for them and for you. In the business world, this step is called "closing the sale" or "asking for the order." Unfortunately, most teachers expect this moment to be easy and therefore shy away from it if they experience the slightest degree of internal tension. Through God's enabling grace, you can and you must overcome this normal fear and challenge your students to "choose for yourself whom you will serve."

So many times I listen to effective teachers and ministers bring their audience right to this point...and then close in prayer. Their audiences are prepared and willing but never asked. A great work in the lives of those students has been aborted. They were impregnated with the truth but the truth was never fully birthed. If you are committed to teach for life change, you must ask for commitment. Ultimately, change is a result of choice—so ask them to choose!

Moses asked for a choice: "Whoever is on the LORD's side—come to me!" (Exodus 32:26). Jesus asked for commitment all the time. "Leave your nets, leave your tax office, leave and follow Me." Joshua, Nehemiah, Ezra, Josiah—they all taught and then challenged. They so strongly believed that the truth is to be obeyed that sometimes they led their class to make great covenants to God, pledging their utmost commitment to do His will.

Do you know why so many Christians are so weak? No one challenges them to the depths of their soul. No one blows the trumpet and says, "Come and join the Lord's side."

Let me say it again and again. *Love them enough to ask.* Some will flee into the darkness. Others will cower at the thought of such complete and loyal commitment. But others will rise out of their passivity and walk with wonder and joy in the light of unbridled commitment. There is joy in following Jesus. But remember, even many of His students left Him when He called for commitment. They said it was too hard even when the Master Teacher challenged them.

But a few remained! With the Spirit strong in their midst and their commitment unwavering after Jesus' resurrection, they turned the world upside down.

Once you decide to ask, the next issue is how to ask appropriately. I wish there were a nice and simple answer to that question. There isn't. Sometimes we know we asked too hard while at other times we didn't ask directly enough. Like many areas of life, "appropriateness" is a question of balance.

Some who preach and teach use too much emotion or too much pressure when calling for commitment. Perhaps some have become so addicted to wanting and needing results that they have fallen prey to manipulation and deceit. Such excess falls into five categories:

1. Too emotional—haranguing, pleading, weeping.
2. Too extended—"Now for the fifteenth verse of our hymn..."
3. Too expansive—"All who have ever sinned need to come..."
4. Too manipulative—"If you want complete financial freedom..."
5. Too "Madison Avenue"—slick, polished, packaged, and hyped.

When challenging for commitment, make sure your words funnel through a heart of love. Remember it's for their good, not for your glory. Those sheep have been divinely appointed to be under your leadership. Be tender if they respond easily or be tough if they need it. Filter your challenges for commitment to ensure they are specific, reasonable, faith-stretching, and biblical.

Your call should be clear and concise and require a response. It should be solidly positioned upon the clear presentation of the truth and solidly linked to a specific passage in the Bible. Because you applied directly from the Bible, your students will recognize that your call for commitment is ultimately God's call and their response is not to you but to Him.

"As for me and my house, we will ask for commitment." Will you?

Maximizer 7: Strengthen applications with student accountability.

Accountability is the "ability to account" for something. In this final maximizer, five proven ways are presented to ensure that when your students "account" for their actions, they share good news!

Voluntary accountability greatly strengthens our resolve to do something. The more difficult the commitment, the more helpful and important the accountability. That's why people actually pay money to be held accountable—by groups like Weight Watchers. That's why people will give up many evenings of the week to be held accountable—in meetings such as Alcoholics Anonymous.

There are five key relationships of accountability available to you as the teacher:

1. *Accountability to self.* This is the most mature form of accountability, as it depends solely upon the self-discipline and inner resolve of the person. When the student behaves in this responsible manner, he is a mature individual and operates through internal motivation. The

remaining four relationships of accountability are all external, as the student is influenced by individuals outside of himself.

Those teachers who have called forth the best from us have often stirred our internal resolve. They helped us to desire so deeply that we put ourselves "under notice" that we were going to hold ourselves accountable to complete it. As a teacher, ask such questions as "How committed are you?" or "What's it going to take for you to decide to complete your goal no matter what?"

2. *Accountability to peers.* Depending upon the age and circumstances, the student's peers may be the most effective and simple relationships of accountability available to the teacher. Form teams to do an assignment or to compete for major achievements, or have each person tell the class what he or she is planning to do, or make the smarter students responsible to instruct the slower ones.

3. *Accountability to significant person(s).* Schools often use this type of accountability when they send home graded papers for parents to sign. With certain discipline issues, teachers call parents. Now that's heightening accountability!

Sometimes I will ask a student what other person cares the most about whether they achieve a stated goal. Who would most encourage them to keep running the race? Sometimes I have encouraged students to telephone their favorite grandparents and tell them of their commitment. Sometimes traveling businessmen call their best friend each night to hold them accountable not to watch pornography on in-room movies.

Every time I call my good friend Dennis Rainey from FamilyLife, we ask each other how we are doing in our relationship with our wife. Just knowing someone is going to ask the hard question deepens our resolve to be able to have the right answer!

4. *Accountability to teacher.* This is the most obvious source of external motivation in the teaching-learning process. When I taught college, sometimes I would conclude the opening session by telling students of

my commitment to them and then by asking them to write down their commitment to me as the teacher.

Sometimes you have to go to a student in trouble and bring him back to his commitment to you to stay on the right track. It sometimes can take hours for that struggling student to finally shake your hand in commitment. It may mean you go to a person in the midst of a secret affair and help him end it. Whatever your students' needs, be there for them and hold them accountable to do the right thing.

5. *Accountability to God.* When it's appropriate, consider leading your students to make a commitment to the Lord. Sometimes have them pray their commitment aloud, using your words. At other times have them pray it silently in their own words, or have them write their prayer of commitment and pray it daily as they carry it throughout the week.

The ultimate test of our success occurs in the life of our students when we are no longer present. Did we develop in them ample internal and external motivation sufficient to apply the Truth until it becomes a lasting part of their life?

Remember, the Lord holds those of us who teach more accountable. Therefore, in preparation for that day, let's spread around some of that accountability in the here and now. For our students and for us.

CONCLUSION

This issue of application always fills me with amazement and awe. Isn't it a wonder, my friend, that the Lord has sovereignly allowed us to share with Him in this miraculous thing we call life change? God used people not only in the writing of the Bible, but also in the teaching of the Bible. I hope that we never get beyond the wonder and privilege of teaching for the Master.

Effective, biblical applications have tremendous power to bring about lasting life change. A well-known verse often painted on a banner and hung in front of churches during a building program is "Without a vision the people perish." Sermons are preached across the land that unless we have a vision (a dream, a goal, a building program) then the people perish (lose motivation, slip into apathy, decline in attendance). The only problem is that Proverbs 29:18 has nothing to do with any of those things.

The word *vision* in the original Hebrew never means a plan or goal or project. Instead it has the very distinct meaning of "divine revelation." For instance, the book of Isaiah begins, "The *vision* of Isaiah," and refers to the supernatural revelation Isaiah received. Do you know what we would call the "vision" today? The Bible. So Proverbs 29:18 could begin, "Where there is no Bible…"

Second, the word *perish* in the original Hebrew never means to lose motivation, slip into apathy, or even perish or die. A clear example of its meaning is captured when Moses came down from Mt. Sinai after getting the Ten Commandments and discovered the blatant sins of the people. Some Bible translations describe their condition as running wild, or being naked, or widely participating in immorality and adultery. All those descriptions picture the meaning of *perish*. The word means to run without restraint into immorality. Therefore this verse would simply read, "The people run without restraint into immorality."

Put these two words together and you will know why you and I must apply the truth every time we teach: "Where there is no Bible [correctly taught], the people will run without restraint into immorality." Obviously, then, one of the main reasons Christians are living like the world is we are not teaching the Bible correctly.

I saw the profound truth of Proverbs 29:18 recently when I preached in a large church in the Midwest. After the service, a man walked up to me and said, "I need to talk to you. You're not from around here, so I can tell you. I have some very bad news. I'm in the midst of getting a divorce." I nodded in agreement that that was very bad news. "But I have some worse news than that—I'm a deacon in this church."

I told him that as far as God was concerned, he couldn't choose to do both. If he was going through a divorce, he must resign immediately from the deacon board—or get his marriage back together and continue serving as a deacon. I urged him to obey God's will and restore his marriage.

Then he continued, "There's even more bad news than that. I'm not the only deacon in this church who's getting a divorce. During the past three years, nine deacons have gotten divorces."

"*Nine deacons?*" After I recovered from my shock, I said, "May I ask you two questions?" (And if you are beginning to understand this law, you may be able to guess what they were—and also what the answers were.) "When's the last time your pastor preached on marriage and marital fidelity?"

"Never," he said.

I told him I already knew that. "Second, what's going on in your pastor's personal life and marriage that is sin?"

I'll never forget his face when I asked that question. He stepped back and stammered, "Who told you?"

I said, "You did."

"No I didn't! I promised I would tell no one. Who told you?"

I continued, "You just did. You told me that you are the ninth deacon to get a divorce. If people are running wild in this church to that degree, it's because the Word isn't being preached. And the only reason for that truth not being preached with such widespread sin so evident would have to be that the same sin exists in the life of the preacher or his immediate family."

That pastor couldn't speak the truth because he wasn't living the truth. I believe that pastor will have to answer not only for his own sin but also for withholding the truth from the lives and families who are now broken and suffering. Can you imagine the devastation that will continue for generations all through that church because this preacher-teacher did not apply the truth to the needs of his people?

As Proverbs 29:18 teaches, people run wild when the Word of God is not taught and applied. Therefore, apply the truth every time you teach. Commit to the Lord that starting now and forevermore, every place and every time you teach you will teach for lasting life change—by God's grace and for His glory.

DISCUSSION QUESTIONS

1. How can it be possible for a person to teach the Bible and yet not "feed the sheep"? What is missing when the sheep haven't been fed? Do you think the teacher or preacher is usually aware of this? When you teach, do you think your students feel fed?

2. What percentage of the time do you sense the Holy Spirit actually moves with power when you teach? Do you think the Spirit desires to move every time you teach or just some of the time? What do you think is the primary reason for the lack of our experiencing His presence in the classes of today?

3. Most teachers have never considered the fact they are to be persuasive teachers. Why? Do you think Jesus and Paul and Peter and James were persuasive? If you desired to follow their example, what would you have to do differently when you teach?

4. List as many differences as you can between an applier's heart and a content heart. Who has the greatest applier's heart you know? On a scale of 1 to 10, how would you rank your applier's heart? What could you do to move it closer to a 10?

5. Glance quickly through the words of Jesus in Luke and John and pick out three stories He made up to teach a point. After studying them, write out a step-by-step approach you could take to write your own "Stories with a Purpose." Then write one for your next class.

LAW FOUR

The Law
of Retention

CHAPTER SEVEN

Retention

Mindset, Model, and Maxims

I was sure I'd flunk my first semester of graduate school. I had heard all the war stories of impossible workloads in Hebrew, Greek, theology, and Bible. I was petrified. In just one of the courses, more than two thousand pages of reading was required. Seminary graduates took great relish in telling us how tough it was, how many people dropped like flies in the first few weeks, how freshmen lost their minds!

That's why my wife and I decided I'd better sign up for a nationally advertised speed-reading course. I was promised I could triple my reading speed and greatly increase my retention.

On the first day of class the instructor told us, "I want to show you how fast you'll be able to read by the end of this course." To her left was a table where three class graduates were seated. "Watch them read!" she said, as they each picked up a book they had never read—big, fat books—and began turning the pages so fast, I felt the breeze all the way to the back row!

I started to laugh and thought, *That's impossible! They're not really reading that fast—I'm being set up. I want my money back!* The teacher must have read my mind because she said, "If you follow our instructions and do all the assignments, you will be able to read just like they do—or I'll give you your money back." I was hooked.

Her assignments were often unique and unorthodox. We were told that in order to read one thousand, three thousand, or even five thousand words a minute, some radical procedures were required. The first week's assignment was structured to begin to retrain our eyes from reading words to reading whole pages. What a thought!

I walked into our nearby county library and asked where I could find the children's books.

"Do you have children?" the librarian asked.

"No, ma'am, I don't."

"You must be checking these out for some relatives or friends then?"

"Nope, just for me."

"Oh," she said. "And what kind of children's books do you have in mind?"

Trying to appear as nonchalant as my growing self-consciousness allowed, I answered, "Doesn't matter. Any of them will do just fine. I don't think the subject makes any difference."

The woman looked like a stereotypical librarian—gray hair tucked in a bun, reading glasses, tall and slender, a bit aloof. With a suspicious look on her face, she guided me to the children's books. Paying no attention to the type, size, or subject, I stacked ten to fifteen volumes under my arms and carried them to the nearest table. The librarian didn't move.

Then I began my assignment. I turned the books upside down and began turning the pages as fast as I could. I could hear the librarian breathing behind my left shoulder. "Young man, are you aware the books are upside down?"

"Yes," I said, "it's remarkable." And with as straight a face as I could muster, I added, "Have you ever tried it?"

Finally she walked around, looked me in the eyes, and with a concerned expression asked, "Are you really reading that?"

"No, ma'am, I have no idea what's on these pages. But my teacher said it didn't really matter."

Every day for several weeks I returned to that same library. For an hour I'd turn children's books upside down and turn the pages as fast as I could. As I walked out, I'd smile at my favorite librarian. By the end of the second week, she wouldn't even look at me. Eventually I graduated to more serious books—big reference works. I did the same thing with them for an hour every night. I didn't tell the poor woman what was going on until I finished the course, and then we enjoyed a good laugh together.

Our peculiar assignments were designed for a purpose. As children, we had been taught to read word by word. But to speed-read, you can't look at each word—you must learn to read a whole page. Turning the book upside down prevented us from reading individual words. We were retraining our eyes and minds to see words like we see a picture—all at once in a split second, without concentrating on the pieces.

Our class's average reading speed rose from 200 to 450 words per minute (wpm), to 1000, to 2000, to 3000, and a few to over 5000. Against all our preconceived notions, even our retention improved. Many completed the course reading 3000 to 5000 words a minute with 80 percent or better retention. Somehow, our instructor had uncovered a secret of speed-reading.

Just think of the tremendous difference the ability to speed-read would make in an average person's life. In recent weeks I have read seven books—a mix of Christian classics and leadership/management. They total approximately 445,000 words.

Compare the results if I had read these same books at the following wpm speeds:

445,000 words at 250 wpm = 1780 minutes, or 29.5 hours
445,000 words at 1000 wpm = 445 minutes, or 7.5 hours
445,000 words at 3000 wpm = 148.33 minutes, or 2.5 hours

Using that information, consider what would happen over the four years of an average college education. Let's say we only spend two hours a week reading for those four years. That totals 24,960 minutes of reading. Compare how many books you'd read in those four years at 250, 1000, and 3000 wpm, assuming each book contains 63,500 words or 200-plus pages.

At 250 wpm you would read a book in 254 minutes, or 98 books over four years. That's a stack of books five feet two inches high.

At 1000 wpm you'd read a book in 63.5 minutes, or 393 books over four years. That's a stack twenty feet seven inches high.

At 3000 wpm you'd read a book in 21.2 minutes, or 1177 books in four years. That's a stack sixty-two feet three inches high—about the height of a five-story building!

Now, before you start thinking this is an advertisement for a speed-reading course, let's transition to the real point of this chapter. Take that same student and replace the two-dimensional book with a three-dimensional person—you, the teacher! And instead of discussing speed-reading, how about speed-teaching? An even more exciting scenario.

If you ever attended a Walk Thru the Bible seminar, you experienced speed-teaching. The consistent feedback we received was, "I've learned more in one day than I have in years." Or "I've learned more in one day than I ever thought possible—and I enjoyed every minute of it!" Well, you're about to learn some of the revolutionary secrets we discovered using this speed-teaching method in nearly fifty countries to more than a million learners.

If you are to improve the speed at which you teach (and your students learn), there must be some way to measure how rapidly you are now teaching. Think back over your last presentation. How many facts did your students learn during the class you taught?

To determine how "fast" you taught last hour, simply count the specifics you just listed. If there were six specifics per class session, you were teaching at six "fpc's" (facts per class).

What's your current fpc? A good way to find out is to test your students immediately at the end of the next class period. Unannounced. Having tried that, I know the results are often depressing.

Before we teach you the secret of speed-teaching, let's experiment with the real-life implications of speed-teaching. What amount of knowledge can be gained in pursuit of a college degree through normal teaching? If a student takes sixteen hours of class each of her eight semesters and averages fourteen class periods of actual instruction for each credit hour, she'd be in class about eighteen hundred hours over four years.

Next, estimate how many facts the normal student learns each period, not including his own homework, reading, or outside assignments. Let's be generous and say an average teacher teaches an average pupil ten specific items each class session. Therefore, in earning the average college degree, a student could expect to learn eighteen thousand items (eighteen hundred hours times ten facts per hour). Relate that to the potential of teaching those same facts to the same students at a speed-learning rate similar to the ratios of speed-reading:

10 fpc (250 wpm rate) x 1800 = 18,000 facts
40 fpc (1000 wpm) x 1800 = 72,000 facts
120 fpc (3000 wpm) x 1800 = 216,000 facts

Look at the incredible difference—18,000 versus 216,000 facts! Does that seem impossible or unrealistic? No more unrealistic than improving your reading from 250 wpm to 1000 or even 3000 wpm. Unlike the normal American driver who has a problem not exceeding the maximum safe speed, the normal teacher's problem is teaching far below the safe minimum rate. If you normally spend sixty minutes covering ten facts (10 fpc) and could learn a way to do the same amount of teaching in fifteen minutes, just think of the extra time you would gain for other, more meaningful learning experiences.

Just as a person can learn to quadruple his reading speed, so a teacher can quadruple her teaching speed. Just think of the potential! But how? How do you take information and reformulate it so that a person remembers it without even trying? How do you speed-teach?

We might get some clues by watching God do it. For example, think of what He did after the Flood. Why did He put the rainbow in the sky? He didn't want us ever to forget His promise to never again destroy all life through a flood.

When God wanted to lock something in our memory, He used a picture. I doubt any of you find it necessary to sit down and concentrate; *I've got to remember that the next time I see a rainbow, God said, "No more flood." I'd better review that ten times.* Of course not. God used one of the universal principles of speed-teaching, and you and I learned His "content" instantly and forever! God's method of speed-teaching enabled our speed-learning. And our retention rate was lifelong.

I wonder what would happen if you and I copied God's method of speed-teaching and used pictures to teach content quickly and forever. As you'll discover later, your fpc's would immediately soar. Double, triple easily.

But that's just one of the methods God uses. Before we finish this Law of Retention, you will know the main methods God utilizes to speed-teach. You will apply those same methods the very next time you teach.

Please remember, though, that this law isn't for every time you teach. This is a specific tool in your teaching toolbox. When you want to teach some facts or chunks of content, pull this tool out and use it. You'll be amazed how well this law works, and I can promise you one thing from years of personal experience: Your students will love you for using it.

Retention Mindset

This law, then, focuses on the art and science of how to teach the student the most information in the shortest amount of time with the least effort (for the students, that is) and for the greatest retention. The law deals directly with two primary issues of the teaching-learning relationship:

Effectiveness—Is the teacher teaching the student the right material?

Efficiency—Is the teacher teaching the student in the right manner?

In order to lay the groundwork for increasing your effectiveness and efficiency, let's consider the four levels of teaching as outlined in Deuteronomy 6:4–9.

"Hear, O Israel: The LORD our God, the LORD is one! You shall love the LORD your God with all your heart, with all your soul, and with all your might.

"And these words which I command you today shall be in your heart; you shall teach them diligently to your children, and shall talk of them when you sit in your house, when you walk by the way, when you lie down, and when you rise up. You shall bind them as a sign on your hand, and they shall be as frontlets between your eyes. You shall write them on the doorposts of your house and on your gates."

Do you want to be a great teacher? Then love God. That's the starting place. It's the lead domino in a whole string of dominoes. Do you desire to be a really magnificent teacher? Then love God with all of your heart, all of your soul, and all of your might.

"And these words which I command you today shall be in your *notes*." Is that what the verse says? Hardly! The words or content aren't to be in our notes, but in our hearts. When we love the Lord, we cannot help but honor His content.

According to the Scriptures, all parenting and all great teaching have two foundations: loving God and knowing the subject. You can't be a great teacher and neglect either one. Love God! Know your subject! Then you'll be ready for the next step: Getting the material that's in your heart into your students'. Is not the goal of all Christian education to effectively transfer your love for the Lord and your wisdom to your students so they also love the Lord and know His Word? The good news is that in this text God reveals four ways to do just that.

1. *Teach.* "Teach them diligently to your children."

That's formal schooling—you sit down for a class session. This first level is what comes to our minds when we think of school and normal academics. The teacher is in charge. You have the agenda and control the teaching-learning process with your objectives and lesson plan.

We did this recently with our kids on the subject of money. We increased their allowance with the understanding that they must purchase all their personal things—shampoo, makeup, and other personal items. In order to do that effectively, they needed a budget. We showed them our own household budget so they could get an idea how it's done. Then we helped them set up a budget, with an envelope for each fund. That's an example of sit-down, formal teaching.

2. *Talk.* "[You] shall talk of them when you sit in your house, when you walk by the way, when you lie down, and when you rise up."

This second level of teaching is best characterized by "talking" in contrast to "teaching." In the teaching process, talking is more fluid, casual, and two-directional. Talking is often student-directed, while teaching is more teacher-directed.

Effective teachers stimulate student talking as it opens the window of the students' real questions and difficulties. Often the most effective teaching occurs "off the subject," or between classes, or at social functions over a Coke.

3. *Personal reminder.* "You shall bind them [the Content] as a sign on your hand, and as frontlets between your eyes."

One summer I was on a flight to Israel, and on board were a number of conservative Jewish men and women who were returning to their Land of Promise. As the sun was rising, at about four in the morning, several men from all over the plane got up out of their seats and went to the back corner, lifted the window shades to let the sun shine through, took out their black robes, and wrapped little boxes on their arms—the very same box this verse is talking about. Then they took out their Scriptures, began to read, and bowed in humility while praying toward Jerusalem.

I soon figured out what they were doing and joined them, although I didn't have an appropriate robe or a copy of their Torah. As I got in the midst of that group and began to pray, I watched how intense they were, how much they honored the Torah, the phylacteries, and frontlets. I was carried along with them and had a great time of worship, but as a Christian believer who worships through Christ.

This third level is the first *nonverbal* method of teaching whereby something we wear or something we do functions as a *sign* to others. Those Jewish worshipers placed something on themselves that immediately communicated a message—not by sound but by sight. And unlike "teaching or talking," which can occur only when the teacher is speaking, the frontlets speak all the time to everyone who sees the sign.

Inherent in the meaning of a sign is the concept of representation. One item represents or stands in the place of another. Often a sign can represent a great deal of meaning through just a small tangible item. Consider what you think when you see a wedding band on the finger of a person you just met. Recall what the minister said, "What token or sign of these vows...?" The moment you see that wedding ring on a person's finger, a whole host of meaning floods your mind.

Likewise, personal actions can also be used as signs for the watching public. I'll never forget the impact of a public action my daughter saw late one evening when our family stopped for a snack returning from a Florida vacation. Jenny and I went to order while the rest of the family waited in the car. All of a sudden she tapped my shoulder anxiously and said, "Dad, look!" As I turned my head, I saw a mother and her five children, all with their heads bowed, praying—and Jenny appeared almost in shock. Finally she revealed her thoughts: "That's the first time I ever saw anyone pray in public, except for us."

What a disappointing surprise! A Christian teenager never having seen others pray in public. Why don't we all bow our heads in public? Could it be that too many of us have forgotten that bowing and praying in public is a very effective sign to others?

We can also put on a tasteful piece of jewelry, such as a cross or fish symbol. These things reveal to others that we're believers. They're personal reminders.

One time a lady got on an elevator with a number of us. She was wearing a pin that said, "Ask me." I knew what it was about, but I asked her anyway. "Ask you what?" She said, "Well, ask my why I'm so happy." I said, "Ma'am, why are you so happy?" She replied "Because I met a Person who met all the needs of my life." I loved what she was doing so I continued asking the questions. I said, "Really, what's His name?" The whole elevator heard the Good News as I asked the leading questions and she gave the biblical answers.

4. *Public recognition.* "You shall write them on the doorposts of your house and on your gates."

The fourth approach to teaching that God revealed more than three thousand years ago is commonly called passive advertising. For instance, when you read a large billboard while driving on the freeway, you are in a sense seeing a creating expansion of "writing them on your gates."

Both of the third and fourth levels of teaching are nonverbal and this last method occurs in the absence of and independent from the actual presence of the teacher. You've heard of the "absentminded professor"; now you know about the "absent teacher."

Don't miss the rich gems of God's insights in this last directive for the teacher. First, we are instructed to "write" them—that is, take an active stance in ensuring that the content is legible, understandable, and visible.

Second, write "them." This whole passage is focused upon the effective transference of the "them" from your heart to their hearts. In this case, the content that is to be written is "these words which I teach you today" and is normally viewed as the Scriptures.

By application of this principle, you could "write" the truth of your lesson on your gates using the same guidelines. When content is publicly displayed, it continues as a reviewing factor for all who see or hear its message.

Third, these teaching inscriptions are to be specifically placed on your "house and on your gates." The Lord maximizes the transference of the message by placing it on the two most used locations of life—the home and the office (or the classroom, for the teacher).

Hang a plaque on your front door: "As for me and my house, we shall serve the Lord." Or put a fish symbol on your mailbox or business card, or a bumper sticker on your car. (If you do, be careful how you drive. Otherwise you may have to pick one that says, "I walk with God, but I drive like the devil!") Edwards Bakery, a pie-baking company in Georgia, puts Scripture verses on the bottom of its aluminum pie plates. All of these serve as public recognition. Involve your home as well as your office. If I walked into your office, what would I see on your desk, walls, and bookcases? Why not "write them" today?

The most effective teachers use all teaching levels and their classrooms reflect it. Their walls are filled with colorful and stimulating words and pictures—all carefully placed and constructed for maximum indirect teaching.

Therefore, to maximize your teaching and reinforce your message in the minds and lives of your students, make sure you employ all four levels of the instruction process: teaching, talking, personal signs, and public advertisements. Remember, God doesn't look at "teaching" merely as what we do when we enter the classroom. God teaches all the time (Psalm 19) through every direct and indirect means possible.

RETENTION MODEL

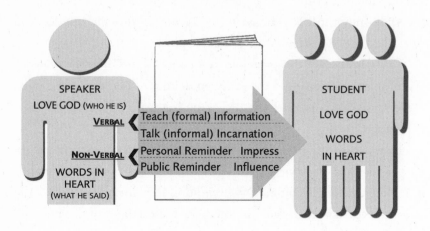

By way of summary, do you see the progression of these four approaches? They move from the interior of one's life to the exterior. From more formal to less formal. The first two levels, "teach" and "talk," comprise the tutor level. They are direct and "verbal." The last two, "personal" and "public reminders," are testimony. They are indirect and "nonverbal." At the tutor level you're transferring truth to others through speaking. At the testimony level you're providing visual means to teach your message. All of these methods help us to pass on our heritage to our students.

The Bible is clear that we are to "pass it on." The truth that we know and love must be communicated in such a way that our children and students know and love the same truth. The heart of our ethics and value systems, as contained in the Scriptures, must be passed on to the next generation. The older generation must transfer it to the younger. And that transference cannot be accomplished merely through good intentions or best wishes. That transference is to be accomplished through everything we say, do, and represent.

RETENTION MAXIMS

The Law of Retention presents revolutionary principles and methods to speed-teach facts to students. When applied, it accomplishes amazing results for those who would bravely move beyond "the way it's always been done." Here are seven principles of Retention that are foundational to speed-teaching.

Maxim 1: Retention of facts by the student is the teacher's responsibility.

Judging from the response of students around the world, it's a rare teacher who causes the student to know the facts. Instead, we see the proverbial "content dump" practiced over and over. Many teachers think, "Since it's not my responsibility to teach you the information, I'll just dump it on you." Students furiously write page after page of notes, because they realize the teacher doesn't own the problem of whether they actually learn the content. Since students copy the information down to learn it later, did the teacher actually teach?

This maxim reminds us that it's our responsibility as teachers to present the lesson in such a way that our students remember it. It should be locked in their minds because we skillfully put it there. Unfortunately, national test scores demonstrate that just isn't happening. The constant decline of SAT scores is not primarily the fault of the students or the parents. The primary responsibility lies with the teachers and, ultimately, with many of the teacher-training institutions.

Until we teachers realize that the success of students is the only real measure of our success; until teachers start becoming student-oriented rather than teacher-oriented; until teachers start doing what's right for the student rather than what's easy for the teacher, learning will continue to decline.

But don't students have any responsibility for their own learning? Yes, they do. It all depends on whom you're addressing. Right now I'm addressing teachers and communicators, and we have 100 percent of the responsibility for our students learning. If we were students, the Law of the Student would state that we have 100 percent of the responsibility for our own learning, regardless of the quality of our teacher. So who's responsible? In this book, our answer must be "the teacher!"

Once the teacher accepts this most foundational of all responsibilities, he will view teaching in a new light. Just imagine how a teacher would change if he evaluated himself not on what he was able to cover during class but on how much the students actually learned during class.

Think outside the box for a moment. Suppose a Spanish teacher said, "Today I'm going to teach you thirty-five Spanish words until you actually know them. I guarantee you'll know at least thirty-three by the time I'm done. You'll be tested on them tomorrow. But don't panic; if you don't get at least thirty-three correct, I'll throw the test out!" And so the teacher goes through all thirty-five words, giving his students a picture for each word and reviewing them until mastery occurs.

Compare that process with the teacher who teaches by saying, "Here's your vocabulary list. There will be a quiz on these words tomorrow."

Maxim 2: Retention of facts is effective only after they are understood.

It amazes me how many times I meet students studying for class and find out they have no idea what they are learning—they just know it's required on the next test. Recently I heard some high school students talking to each other about a math class in which only two of the students understood what was going on—and one of them had hired a tutor to keep up. You should have seen their frustration as they threw up their hands and said, "I don't know how we're going to do it. The teacher just gives us more and more material and none of us knows what's going on."

The teacher thinks it's his job to be a "delivery man." When he's finished covering the course textbook, he's completed his job. It seems to make little difference to him if most of the students have no idea what's going on. Can you imagine the revolution it would cause if he would change his mind about what teaching is?

Retention of information is much more effective when students fully understand the information. Although this maxim may appear obvious, many teachers nonetheless have their students memorize lists of information and dates and names without any corresponding comprehension.

Therefore, teachers must ensure that their students understand the meaning and significance of the facts before memorizing them for the tests. *Understanding must always precede memorization.* Memorizing what you do not understand is like memorizing a random list of numbers. Ever tried to memorize random numbers by the hour? Fun, isn't it?

Maxim 3: Retention increases as the student recognizes the content's relevance.

Notice the second word of this maxim. Retention *increases* as something happens. Students learn faster and deeper according to the degree they feel the material is important and relevant to them in the present or future.

How many times have you sat in class as a student and thought, *What good is any of this?* And when one of your friends had the nerve to raise her hand and ask, the teacher jumped all over her as if she had committed the unpardonable sin. Learning plummets if the student can't see how the information has any practical value. It plummets even further if the teacher can't either!

The first time my son had to give a speech at school, he experienced the normal stage fright and soon came up with a creative idea. "Dad, can

I come down to your office and have you help me make one of those fancy overheads of my speech on President Reagan? The kids will love it, and I need all the help I can get."

We brought some magazine pictures to the darkroom at Walk Thru and I showed Dave our big camera. We put the picture of President Reagan in it, closed it up, turned on the lights, and went into the darkroom and looked through the large camera lens.

"All right, son, look through this hole."

"That's President Reagan, Dad."

"Right. Now, you see these two knobs here that turn like this? This is how you make that picture become large enough for the overhead projector. Dave, you ever heard of percentages?"

"Sure, Dad, we've been studying percentages for months at school."

"Great. Why don't you take your picture back on the table and figure out what percentage we're supposed to turn these knobs to enlarge your picture to an 8x10, and I'll step down the hall and get a couple of Cokes."

The second I walked back into the darkroom I could tell he hadn't figured it out. "Dave, what's the matter?"

"Dad, I can't do it."

"I thought you told me you'd been doing percentages for months?"

"We've been doing it for months, but I guess I don't know how to do it." He was real quiet for a moment, then said, "Dad, I thought percentages were only for school. I didn't know you actually used percentages for anything!"

At that moment, I could have throttled that teacher. No wonder David didn't know it. He saw no relevance to learning percentages except to pass a test. And his teacher hadn't seen it as her responsibility to build the need before teaching the content (see the Law of Need).

When Jenny was younger she was having a tough time learning how to convert from one unit of measurement to another. So Darlene asked Jenny if she wanted to help make a cake.

"Why don't we make two cakes," my wife said. "We'll give one to

Granny, and we'll keep one. Here are the ingredients. I'll be in the other room if you need me."

She left Jenny in the kitchen to figure out for herself what three-fourths of a cup meant if you doubled it. As that little girl went back and forth to her mom, you could see the light go on in her head. Math suddenly had relevance. You needed it to make a cake.

If you as the teacher cannot point out the relevance to your students of the material you are presenting, you can be sure you will develop an apathetic and frustrated class. Make the material live—not just in your mind, but in the hearts and minds of the students. At those times when you cannot come up with anything more than "an educated American needs to know that the Civil War ended in 1865," then make sure you surround that information with enthusiasm. Bring from it lessons about prejudice and unity that make it a living moment in what otherwise could be dead history. Use your God-given creativity to develop a real episode out of the Civil War. Use the date of 1865 four times as the crux of the skit. When you do, that fact will be forever marked in your students' minds.

Relevance develops motivation and concentration. As students enter class they have many things on their minds. The teacher must focus student interest on the subject by demonstrating relevance and then continue to command their attention through content and delivery. Your *content* arouses your students' attention through general interest and its ability to meet their needs. Your *delivery* continues to command attention by entertaining the students and overpowering conflicting attention-getters. As you build the need and relate the relevance of the subject, you can keep that interest and concentration through a varied and creative delivery.

Maxim 4: Retention requires the teacher to focus on the facts that are most important.

Believe it or not, not all facts are created equal. Listen to many teachers, however, and you'd think each piece of information was vitally important.

If you're going to teach people to memorize material, you must take responsibility for separating the important from the unimportant. We need to become "sifters of the information" for our students.

Is this not how God sifted through history when He gave us the Bible? That's why the book of Genesis skips hundreds of years without one verse revealing what happened, then spends chapter after chapter on just one person—Abraham—revealing detail after detail of his life.

God skipped whole centuries and then wrote about mere minutes. Why? As the Divine Teacher, He was sifting the content for us. Look at Exodus, where the four-hundred-year captivity is barely mentioned, but the giving of the Covenant at Mount Sinai spans over twenty chapters and yet covers only a few months!

Likewise, in the four Gospels dozens of chapters detail the last week of Christ's life, yet they don't reveal anything about what happened between Jesus' twelfth birthday and when He turned thirty.

In contrast to the example of the Lord God, many ineffective teachers try to leave everything possible in. Master teachers know what to cut out. Maximum attention must be given to the most important items. If one fact is more important than another, *the more important should receive the greater attention.* If it is three times more important, it may well deserve three times the attention. The more effective the teacher, the more carefully the class time and homework will reflect the relative importance of the many facts and concepts.

In business, this concept of proportion is known as the Pareto Principle, or the 20/80 rule. For example, 80 percent of a company's profit almost always comes from 20 percent of its products. Or 80 percent of the business a company does comes from only 20 percent of its clients. It applies in a church—80 percent of the work is done by 20 percent of the people. Or 20 percent of the people in a church give 80 percent of the funds.

The Pareto Principle can be applied to almost every context. In your work, for instance, you probably spend 80 percent of your effort generating only 20 percent of the results you seek. And only 20 percent of your time is spent on activities that generate 80 percent of your desired results.

I explained this principle to a business owner once on a flight up the East Coast, and he took his financial reports out of his briefcase, checked out his product line, and determined that 84 percent of his products produced only 18 percent of the profit. I encouraged him to immediately raise the price of these products by 20 percent because he wasn't risking much, and as a result would increase his company profit. Second, he identified the 16 percent of his products that gave him 82 percent of his profit, and I advised him to refocus his management time and expertise to expand those products.

Well, fellow teacher, this principle is also true in our classes—20 percent of our content carries with it 80 percent of the real benefit to the student. Therefore, identify those issues and change your priorities today.

Imagine the impact on your teaching when you identify the 80 percent that gives only 20 percent of what you desire. Cut your time on that content in half, and spend the newly available time on the 20 percent of activities that bring 80 percent of the results you want! If the average teacher would just implement this strategy, he would see immediate and encouraging results.

How foolish most of current thinking is regarding this issue. The average student panics before the test as he desperately struggles to identify what he thinks the teacher might ask. As if learning is improved by making the student guess what is important! How can we expect the novice to know what is primary and what is secondary in a subject where we are experts? And how is learning benefited by this hide-and-seek game that most teachers play with their classes? Why not identify the 20 percent of the content that the student should know to master the 80 percent? Just think how helpful it would be if the student were enabled to maximize his study time.

Your task is to identify those facts your students must know in order to say they truly "know" the subject. I call this group of facts the "Irreducible Minimum." *The Irreducible Minimum is the smallest unit of information necessary for a given class to gain acceptable understanding of a given subject.* Without the Irreducible Minimum, a student cannot pass the course; with the Irreducible Minimum, a student can adequately perform and be promoted to the next level of achievement.

This Irreducible Minimum must first be understood by everyone and then mastered by everyone. The teacher should not only identify the Irreducible Minimum for the class, but assume full responsibility to teach it to every student in the class. The teacher has not taught a subject adequately unless every student has mastered its Irreducible Minimum.

Imagine student enthusiasm if the teacher *guaranteed* that students would pass his course if they attended class and paid attention, because in class the teacher would teach everything they needed to know to pass every test. Identify what is foundational. Structure your time to maximize the most important, and then teach it to everyone.

Maxim 5: Retention arranges the facts so they are easy to memorize.

Some teachers gather their content, haul it into class in a big sack, and unload it all at once. I call this a content dump. Other teachers take the next step and put their content in outlines. That is a good start. But although that looks neat, how many of those facts can the average student name one week later? Just outlining the material does not necessarily make it easy for the student to memorize it. All it does is make it easier to transfer from the teacher's notes to the students' notes.

But what would happen if I as the teacher took that same content and repackaged it in a way that would make those facts easy for the student to memorize?

In a sense, you are the teacher computer and all of your class are student computers. Your goal is to take information that's in your memory bank and transfer it as quickly and effectively as possible to their memory banks. In computer terms, to download without loss of data in the transfer.

Let's say that you want your class to know the content of a certain book. Can you take the book, place it on the head of your student, and say, "Input—memorize it"? Obviously that won't work. The mind cannot receive and memorize material unless it's first correctly arranged and formatted.

Why is it that we'll format material to put into a computer, but we won't format material to put into the minds of our students? God, who created your students' minds, designed only a few ways that they can receive and retain information easily. Do you know what they are? Are you using them? In the next chapter, the seven primary methods to reformat material will be revealed.

Obviously, the more difficult something is to memorize, the less the students will memorize. Since it is the ultimate responsibility of the teacher "to cause the student to learn," the teacher will present the material in such a way that it will be relatively easy for the student to memorize it. The teacher will smooth out the corners, throw out the jagged rocks, and "prepare the way" for the minds of his students. He will know the shortcuts through the content. He will have already marked the pitfalls, notched the trees along the way, built bridges over the raging rivers. Campsites will have been located in safe and suitable places.

The effective teacher realizes that his role isn't to organize an annoying and inefficient camping trip, but to lead the students in the most effective and efficient manner to the desired destination—to get from point A to point B quickly and without losing anyone along the way.

Many teachers seem to feel there is great merit in students' struggling to learn the information. But why? Why shouldn't learning be made as easy as possible? Can you name one benefit of hard versus easy learning? If the teacher were truly wise, his real effort should be saved to assist the student to use the information, not merely to learn it.

That's the real test for the Law of Retention—what do you do with those facts. Are you going to serve them 3 eggs, 1/2 cup of butter, 3/4 tablespoon of almond extract, 2 cups flour, 1 sliced apple, etc? Or are you going to present them with a delicious apple cake? Both feature the same ingredients. Both are put together by the teacher and presented to the student. But which one do you think the student will "digest" more quickly? And which will cause him to want to come back for more?

Is it more work to mix the ingredients together and bake it? Undoubtedly. But is an extra thirty minutes of teacher preparation time worth thirty students' performance and attitude? It keeps coming back to the issue of "causing the student to learn." That requires going the extra mile, fleshing out what the Bible calls "love"—doing what the other person needs regardless of how you feel about it at the moment.

Maxim 6: Retention strengthens long-term memory through regular review.

God created man with short-term memory and long-term memory. Effective teaching respects God's divine design, cooperates with it, and doesn't arrogantly force the mind to operate beyond its normal way of operating.

You and I use short-term memory all the time. You use it when your spouse asks you to pick up three things from the store. When a friend shouts across the parking lot to call her tonight and tells you her telephone number, you say it to yourself a couple of times and you've got it. At least you've got it for that night. But can you retrieve it from your memory in a week? God designed short-term memory for the short term.

Have you ever crammed all night before a big test and thought that if someone bumped into you, you'd lose half the facts you'd stored? As a student, I frequently began exams by searching for all those long lists I had just "learned" so I could write them down before I forgot them.

How much do you think was actually learned? If the teacher had unexpectedly given that same final the week before, or a week later, the results would have been a disaster. What would such an experiment demonstrate about how well that teacher managed his students' learning?

You will never cause your students to really "know" unless *you put the material in their long-term memory*. And there's only one way to get that material back there: Review. A vital part of your responsibility is to review and review and review the material with the students until they master it.

The goal of review is to take that Irreducible Minimum and plant it firmly in the long-term memory of your students. Keep reviewing it at different times and in different ways until everyone knows it. For good.

"Covering the material" is not teaching; it is talking and at best will only impact the short-term memory. Teaching occurs when the students know the material—before and after he sits down to study for the test!

Imagine the impact if teachers were evaluated by what their students knew one month after class was over. Wouldn't that revolutionize teaching! Isn't it tragic that we have settled for only the surface results and not the long-term? Tragic because our approach is focused only on the entrance to long-term memory—the short-term. Tragic because it breeds a surface mentality to life—that life is merely the passing of certain milestones, of learning a few lists rather than mastering learning.

Effective teachers identify the Irreducible Minimum and teach it in such a way that 100 percent of the students master it deeply enough to have it lodged in their long-term memory—available to them anytime they need it.

Maxim 7: Retention minimizes time for memorization to maximize time for application.

As you practice the Law of Retention presented in the next chapter, you will become more skilled in speed-teaching. Soon you'll be able to teach twice the material in half the time so effectively that all your students will master the content.

But that only gets you halfway home. Because the real point of teaching is the *use of the material*. If there's no possible use for the information, then why are you teaching it?

We must focus our efforts on equipping our students for life. We must launch from content, information, and knowledge to practice, application, and wisdom. Therefore, format your content so it is easy for your students to understand and memorize. Then don't wait until they know everything; immediately show them how valuable and important and relevant your material is. The more relevant and usable your students believe and discover the material is, the more motivated they will be to learn it, and the more they're going to appreciate you for educating them to succeed in life!

Throughout my graduate education, Dr. Hendricks would comment that "impression without expression leads to depression." Whenever the teacher believes that accumulation of content is the ultimate purpose of the course, his students will slowly lose interest, develop apathy, and eventually become critical and cynical. If the content is not used by the student, eventually it becomes an irritant. As the teacher continues to require the student to learn more and more content without showing how that content is helpful to the student, the student will have to use more and more self-discipline to force himself to pay attention and concentrate.

Master teachers balance their presentations—50 percent content and 50 percent application. Effective teachers not only spend time during class teaching facts but seldom ask their students to memorize facts on their own time. Instead, the teacher assigns students homework on the practical usage for those facts already mastered during class.

The Law of Retention strives to empower teachers to be more effective in teaching that content. So you can teach 500 percent more content in the same time, or 250 percent more content in half the time, or 100 percent of the content in one quarter the time it currently takes. These percentages are real and can be achieved by anyone who becomes minimally proficient in this law. The result should be more time to focus on application of the content.

MEANING

The essence of the Law of Retention is these three words: "Master the minimum." The teacher should enable all students to enjoy maximum mastery of the Irreducible Minimum.

CONCLUSION

Master teachers help students master content. Recently I received a surprising letter about this very philosophy from Donald Campbell, the president of the seminary from which I graduated. In it he told a story about Lewis Sperry Chafer, the founder and first president of the seminary:

> As I celebrated Easter a few weeks ago, I thought back to an unforgettable scene from my days as a student at Dallas Seminary. It was the fall of 1948, and I was studying under Dr. Chafer the biblical doctrine of salvation through Christ's death and resurrection.
>
> I loved his crystal-clear explanations and illustrations of deep theological truths. When he came to a discussion of the finished work of Christ, Dr. Chafer was passionate. It was clear he wanted us to have an unshakable grasp on the doctrines of redemption, reconciliation, and propitiation.

After weeks of compelling lectures, I faced the midterm. Along with other students, I painstakingly filled my exam book from front to back with my best thinking on the subject of salvation.

A few days later, Dr. Chafer walked in the class with the stack of exam books in his hands. There was a sense of excitement in the air as we waited to receive our test results.

But I sensed something was troubling Dr. Chafer.

As he placed the graded papers on the desk in front of him, he solemnly told the class how deeply disappointed he was that we had not adequately understood the meaning of these important theological concepts. In fact, he said his heart was broken.

With that Dr. Chafer ceremoniously dumped the exams into the wastebasket and proceeded to expound again on the finished work of Christ.

Needless to say, we all paid careful attention! In a few days Dr. Chafer gave another test and everyone passed with high marks.

Dr. Chafer was a master teacher as many of his students have testified throughout the years. Once again, a master teacher realized that the failure of his students to learn was ultimately his failure. So what did he do with that incriminating evidence? Tossed it into the garbage can. You see, my friend, teachers are fully in control of where they file their students' papers!

But don't miss his next step. After recognizing his students' poor grades, he "proceeded to expound *again*." He reviewed. He took the responsibility of his students' failure upon his shoulders and retaught until they learned.

But did this master teacher continue to teach until all his students had mastered the lesson? Did he teach to the point he enabled all his students to "master the minimum"? Dr. Campbell attests, "In a few days

Dr. Chafer gave another test and *everyone passed with high marks.*"

Before you turn this page and discover the fascinating secrets of how to teach so that "everyone passes with high marks," will you permit me to ask you a few closing questions? I've learned over the years that unless a person fully buys into this mindset, all the secrets in the world won't help.

As you have read this chapter, you've realized that these are revolutionary concepts and fly in the face of contemporary teaching philosophy. But as the declining test scores reveal, contemporary teaching philosophy doesn't have much to boast about. Of course, the current philosophy would have us believe that low test scores are the results of poor parenting or too much television or the depletion of the ozone layer—certainly not the results of poor teaching.

For the most part, I believe that teachers are hard-working, sacrificial, highly committed people who truly care about their students. Why then the widespread poor achievement in the classroom? There are two underlying causes:

1. The philosophy of the modern teacher is not in line with the principles of Scripture, and therefore
2. the practice of the modern teacher is countereffective in causing the student to efficiently learn the material.

May the Law of Retention sharpen your perspective and equip you to teach so effectively that all your students "Master the Minimum."

DISCUSSION QUESTIONS

How the teacher thinks about teaching controls how the teacher actually teaches. Wrestle with these five questions and challenge your own thoughts about teaching.

1. In nine years of college, graduate, and postgraduate education, I never had a teacher throw a set of papers in the garbage can. But I did endure countless lectures about our lack of competence and poor study habits. Since the definition of the teacher is the one responsible to cause the student to learn, who should have been giving the lecture to whom? If you had given that lecture, what would have been your main points?

2. Since the purpose of grades is to reflect the competence of the student regarding the subject, what is the significance of the curve? Is there a difference in philosophy if you grade in comparison to other students or in comparison to how well the students actually learned the material? Could it be that the philosophy of grading on the curve is precisely the wrong way to approach education? The curve allows the poorest teaching and poorest performance to receive an outstanding grade if everyone around you does worse than you. I remember in one graduate class earning a 36 percent and receiving an A. Do you know why? None of us knew what was going on—including the professor. Or take the 95 percent I received in another college class and yet received a C because of curve requirements. I had it

down cold and yet received a C. Discuss the differences in student learning under each philosophy.

3. Remember cramming? Remember trying to learn the material the night before the final? Had you therefore been truly taught the material? And if you had been given that same test one week later, how would you have done? Is true education to equip you for the day of the exam or for life? Is short-term teaching really teaching? How would you teach differently if you taught for life?

4. One teacher gave six to eight pages of notes per class period. We all called it a lesson in futility and wanted to call the class "speed-writing" or "cramped hand." Toward the end of the semester, one of the students raised his hand and asked, "Do we need to know _____?" What an outburst he received from the teacher—as if he had committed the unpardonable sin. Had he asked a wise or foolish question? Of what value is it to require students to waste their time and learn the irrelevant? Should there ever be any surprises on exams in which the students despair because they thought the teacher would never ask that?

5. All students study for exams the same way. They decide what will probably be on the exam and then find ways to memorize the material. What do you think would happen to the student if the teacher actually taught the material in ways easy to remember and then openly stated the areas where test questions would be selected?

CHAPTER EIGHT

Retention

Method and Maximizers

I t was the day before the final exam. The college students entered class full of enthusiasm and excitement. Today was the final review and they couldn't wait.

Neither could I. Both teacher and students had worked hard all semester, and we all knew we knew. I asked them to stand and in unison work right through the entire semester of Bible survey. Then I sat down and started the timer. Even to this day I can hear them chant, almost sing, with joy:

Bible—66 books
Two parts:
Old Testament and New Testament
Old Testament, 39 books
New Testament, 27 books

Old Testament—three parts:
> *Historical, 17 books*
> *Poetical, 5 books*
> *Prophetical, 17 books*

On and on they went. As these freshmen neared the end of their long review, they began to cheer, clapping and screaming. They had quoted nonstop for twenty-seven minutes—through every important fact (the Irreducible Minimum) I had taught them the entire semester!

The final was six pages long, single-spaced. High grades were earned everywhere. But when the college administrator reviewed the grades, he immediately summoned me to his office: "Bruce, there's no way everyone in your class could earn such high grades."

My heart began to pound, but I had anticipated this moment and was prepared with a response: "May I show you the final exam so you can see if it was too easy?"

For two minutes he was quiet as he read the six pages of questions. Then he said, "You gave this test to freshmen? This is harder than most of my seminary finals. They knew all this?"

"Yes! But do you think I should fail a few?" He laughed. I could breathe again. The grades stuck.

Most important, those students really learned. And they loved it because the course was not a threat but a thrilling experience in speed-learning.

RETENTION METHOD

Lola May said it best: "There are three things to remember teaching school. Number one, know your stuff. Number two, know whom you are stuffing. And number three, stuff them elegantly."

"Stuffing them elegantly" is the theme of this chapter. For the first time in print, I'm going to share some of the fascinating secrets behind the Walk Thru the Bible approach to speed-teaching. This innovated method has been used all over the world, from New York City to the most remote villages in India. Because the Retention Method cooperates with the way God engineered our minds, these methods are fully trans-cultural and immediately effective.

The Retention Method presents the five stages I have found to enable people to speed-teach with startling results. When you begin to understand their flow, you'll then be ready for the seven universal ways to make all material "mind easy" so students can memorize the Irreducible Minimum easily and enjoyably.

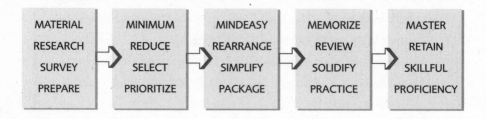

Stage One: Material

First the teacher gathers the "material" from which he will select the facts he wants to teach. This involves "research." At the outset the teacher does a "survey" of the entire subject in order to accumulate as much information as possible to "prepare" the teaching material.

The more painstakingly the ground is prepared, the greater the chance for a garden to grow and flourish. The stronger the foundation, the taller a building can be built. The more deeply the subject material is researched, the better the chance for the lesson to have strong impact.

As I write this chapter, I'm also working on a speech to answer the question, "What does the Bible teach will happen in the Middle East before the Second Coming of Christ?" I have far too much material and only forty minutes to speak. Half of this audience doesn't attend church regularly, and most have never heard of the Abomination of Desolation spoken about by Jesus in Matthew 24. As I prepare this lesson, I work through three steps:

1. Overview the subject
2. Organize the subject
3. Outline the subject

Your purpose in *overview of the subject* is to fly over the content as quickly as possible to get a bird's-eye view. Glance through encyclopedias, handbooks, tables of contents, and flip through pages without pausing to study them in depth. This is the exposure stage where you start formulating in your mind the major sections of material and how they might be arranged for clear presentation.

Next, you must *organize the subject.* Your purpose here is to categorize the content into its major units of thought. Divide in order to conquer. Review some of your better sources and see how they divide the material. Construct a list of possible categories. Don't limit your list by evaluating, just brainstorm. When your overview list is complete, then start evaluating and code each subject area by one of the following:

- "A" next to those sections you believe must be required;
- "B" next to those sections you believe would be very helpful but not required;
- "C" next to those sections you believe might help the students somewhat but are optional;
- "D" next to those sections you believe would be of minimal help;
- "F" next to those sections you are certain would not help and might even confuse the students.

When this is done, list your categories in order of priority. By this point you should start to feel at home with some of the broader concepts.

The last step is to *outline the subject*. Review your categories and construct a logical order or presentation of them. Use your ever-growing understanding of the material to determine whether any of your A's, B's, and C's might need to be altered. When the major categories are completed, you can repeat the above three steps to construct the minor points under each major category.

By the time you have completed the *"material"* stage, you have an initial broad outline of the material.

Stage Two: Minimum

Now it's time to boil down your content to the *"minimum."* You researched it; now *"reduce"* it. You surveyed it; now *"select"* appropriate material and effectively *"prioritize"* it.

This second stage may seem unusual at first, but it's crucial to effective instruction. Initially you may find this step challenging *because we wrongly believe that a greater quantity of content covered is better than a greater quantity of content learned.* When you change your focus to the material that you want to have the student learn, you think about it differently.

When I developed the Walk Thru on the Life of Christ seminar more than twenty years ago, I surveyed every single thing Jesus did—everywhere He went, everything He said, every miracle He performed. There were over three hundred such events. Then I reminded myself, "I have an hour and a half to teach an audience the life of Christ, and many of them don't know much about Him. What does a person have to know to say, 'I understand the life of Christ'?" From my prioritized list—A, B, and C—I selected the most important ones.

This second stage requires that you discard some of the work you completed earlier in the *"material"* stage. But remember—all your content is not equally important. Most of it not only doesn't need to be memorized by your students, some probably doesn't even need to be discussed. At most, it should be skimmed for general awareness.

Average teachers don't discipline themselves at this stage and therefore *talk a lot but teach little*. Great teachers are as skilled at knowing what should be excluded as what should be included. Excellent teachers eliminate average material in order to focus on superior material.

A master sculptor was once asked how he created such magnificent pieces of art out of plain blocks of marble. He replied that all he did was chip away all the marble that didn't belong to what he was making. If he were sculpting a horse, he chipped away everything that didn't look like a horse.

Masterpieces in both marble and in the classroom are created by masters who know that all parts of available material are not equally important.

How do you choose which elements are most important? There are three shapers of material: first, the *audience*; second, the *time* available; and third, the *purpose* of the class.

Let's say the subject is the Life of Christ and you will be teaching three different *audiences*:

1. Sixth-grade girls.
2. Twenty-five-year-old young marrieds.
3. Doctoral students in seminary.

How successful would you be if you took the same approach for all three? Your selection of material is determined by the students you are teaching.

Second, your selection is also controlled by the amount of time you have available to teach. What material would you keep in your lesson plan for the following three constraints of *time*?

1. A twenty-minute meditation.
2. A fifty-minute classroom hour.
3. A thirteen-week curriculum.

Third, the teacher selects material according to the purpose of the class. What are you trying to accomplish with your students? Notice how you would select different content if you were teaching the same book of the Bible but with three different *purposes*:

1. To survey the Life of Christ.
2. To prove that Jesus Christ was the Jewish Messiah.
3. To respond to Jesus Christ in worship.

After you prioritize your material according to the characteristics of the audience, the amount of available time, and the purpose of the class, you need to consider how well your students need to comprehend the material.

Students ask us different forms of this question all the time: "Do we have to know this?" They are actually asking, "How important is this material?" Obviously, the teacher believed the material was important enough to cover, but is it important enough to memorize?

Educators have long recognized that there are many levels of "knowing a subject." For sake of simplicity and utility, three are particularly helpful:

- Surface Awareness: "I have heard of that before, and I think I know a little about it."
- Average Understanding: "I learned that and generally know how it works."
- Thorough Comprehension: "I know all about that—here are the ten key points."

Depending upon how well you want your students to know the information, not only should you teach it differently, but you should also test it differently. If it falls on the most surface level, use multiple choice; if it is on the midlevel, use either true/false or essay (explain what you know); and if it is on the most thorough level, require a list of the complete facts or an intelligent discussion of its main components and their implication.

The Law of Retention insists that the teacher is responsible for the following activities:

1. Selection of the information to be taught.
2. Determination of which level the information should be learned.
3. Communication to the student of not only what should be known, but at what level they should know it.
4. Presentation of the selected information in such a way that the students learn it at the desired level.
5. Examination on the agreed-upon material and based upon the correct level of comprehension as previously announced by the teacher.

Teachers often waste the majority of classroom, homework, and student study time because they are either not focusing on the appropriate material or not teaching it at the correct level. Students waste much valuable time and effort in attempting to figure out what the teacher thinks is important and by studying information which is practically irrelevant to the heart of the course.

Don't do that to your students! Instead, clearly identify those facts and concepts that are required for an acceptable level of comprehension. This Irreducible Minimum must be identified clearly and should be reviewed repeatedly. Everyone should master the Irreducible Minimum or the teacher has not taught at the minimal level of performance. Remember, if a student fails to learn, the teacher has failed to teach!

At the end of the first stage, "*material*," the content of the lesson should be clearly identified and outlined. This usually is the normal ending point of lesson preparation.

By the completion of this second stage, "*minimum*," the content should have been thoroughly reevaluated and reprioritized. Instead of six pages of notes, perhaps you have used the 20/80 rule and cut away the large areas of fat and isolated the meat. You've even marked those facts that everyone must master because they are clearly part of the Irreducible Minimum. You have been ruthless regarding "what my students really need to know" and have the essence clearly identified. You've given more space in your outline to the most important and reviewed tightly the space allocated to the secondary. You admit all facts aren't equal and that wisdom demands planned prioritization in your presentation.

When you compare the "*material*" outline with the new "*minimum*" outline, you are amazed at the difference. You realize that distinguishing the primary from the secondary was vital for establishing an effective outline.

Your "Outline of the Minimum" is the essence of *what* you are going to teach but is not yet organized into the best *way* to present the material. You have the best raw ingredients but how will you package it so it is a joy for your students to learn it?

Stage Three: Mind-Easy

Believe it or not, when you have completed the second stage, "*minimum*," you are already light years ahead of the normal teacher because your effectiveness is far superior. You have isolated the important material from all the available material. Instead of wasting a great amount of time on the irrelevant material, you have cut away everything that isn't a "horse in the marble." Therefore you won't be wasting class time on the chips on the floor. You won't be tempted to cover material which should best be left uncovered.

Now it's time to transition your thinking from material to the minds of your students. The material has been selected; now the correct method must be chosen to efficiently transfer it into their long-term memory.

Unfortunately, only a handful of teachers implement this step. *Too many teachers believe that teaching is the presentation of the facts by the teacher rather than the memorization of the facts by the students!* The moment our philosophy of teaching becomes student-oriented rather than teacher-oriented, we immediately recognize that our current teaching is woefully inadequate.

As the philosophy of *The 7 Laws of the Learner* begins to burn in your heart—and you seek to cause your students to really learn the material—you immediately start searching for better ways to enable them to learn the Irreducible Minimum rather than merely covering the material as usual.

This process is a profound and far-reaching one. It flies in the face of normal educational practice. The vast majority of the teachers I had as a student never carried the responsibility of causing me to learn the material—that was my responsibility!

So what did we all do as students to learn the material? We desperately sought ways that made the material easy to memorize.

This third stage strikes at the heart of that philosophy. Since the teacher is responsible to cause the student to learn, the teacher must identify and employ the most efficient method to teach the material so the students learn during class, not after it.

After searching the dictionary and thesaurus and not finding an appropriate word for this vital process, I have coined the word "*mind-easy*." This is the stage in which you "*rearrange*" your material and "*simplify*" it. You mold and "*package*" until it slips into your students' minds almost effortlessly and at times even spontaneously. You may be wondering, *How can I possibly teach like that?* But as you'll see in a moment, you already know the secret.

Remember the process you used as a student when you became serious about cramming for a test? After trying to figure out what would be on the final exam (an attempt to identify your teacher's list of the Irreducible Minimum), you probably labored to rearrange the material so your mind could remember it. You sought for ways to take the random and unrelatedness out of the information and put what remained in a different order or structure that made sense to you. You connected the facts into a whole so you could recall the parts for the test.

Unless you were privileged to have a photographic memory, that's exactly what you did for years and years in school. Since it worked for you as a student, why not make it work for you as the teacher? *As you teach your content, why not help your students "cram" right while you teach?* Imagine your students' exhilaration as they leave each of your classes already having mastered the content that will be on the next exam.

With that goal in mind, you must apply your creativity to the Irreducible Minimum and refashion it into a form easily retained by human minds. Highly skilled teachers in this mind-easy stage mold their content so it fits two key requirements:

1. Easy to understand.
2. Easy to memorize.

First let's consider the *Degree of Understandability*. My son complained recently about the difficulty of his current math textbook. Last year's book, he lamented, made everything much easier to understand, but this year's text might as well be written in a foreign language.

Similarly, have you ever read an article that confused you more about a subject than when you started—then you discovered a different article that made the same subject crystal clear?

Therefore, the material may either be clear and helpful or confusing and frustrating. All material can be rated on a scale of understandability from simple to difficult.

Such a scale has existed for a long time in rating the difficulty of various books, magazines, and articles. Compare the difficulty in reading *Reader's Digest* (eighth-grade level) to *Harper's* (eleventh-grade level), or compare *People* (seventh-grade level) to *Scientific American* (twelfth-grade level). Even Bible versions can be graded by readability scales—from the International Children's Bible (third-grade level), to the New International Version (seventh-grade level), to the New King James Version (ninth-grade level), to the Revised Standard Version (tenth-grade level), to the New American Standard Bible (eleventh-grade level), to the King James Version (twelfth-grade level).

As a teacher who wants your students to learn all that is possible, simplify your material as much as possible without harming its nature. Regrid it to the appropriate level for your audience. Master teachers take the most difficult of concepts and make them so simple that even children can understand! If you've ever attended a class taught by a master teacher, you probably rarely, if ever, became confused or lost. It's the poor teacher who loses his students. It's the ineffective teacher who confuses her students. Profundity is not complexity; it is simplicity.

Don't allow anyone to tell you that some ideas are just too complicated to make simple; it simply is not true. Some concepts are more difficult to grasp than others, but that does not mean the master teacher cannot develop his lesson in such a skillful manner that the class not only follows and understands, but never knows it is being taught a complex concept!

This brings us to the second part of this stage—the *Degree of Memorability*. The teacher now takes the material that has been made easy to comprehend and delivers it for easy retention. The teacher reformats the material in such a way that it lodges in the student's mind with minimum effort—even subconsciously, when that's possible.

Our minds often learn more rapidly on a subconscious level than by conscious memorization. To illustrate, just watch how a family that moves to a foreign culture learns the language. The younger children play with the other children in the village, while their parents study in an eight-hour-a-day crash course. In the same period of time, the children will outperform their parents every time. As the parents concentrate and memorize the language, their children *learn without even paying attention.*

The Degree of Memorability can be classified on a scale of difficulty. The more difficult it is to memorize the material, the less "memorability" it has. The easier to memorize, the better the learning!

When you develop the content's "memorability," remember that the mind only receives facts it is prepared to receive. It cannot receive facts presented in an unknown language. *You cannot expect the mind to receive facts that have no logical order or relationship.* You cannot expect the mind to receive facts beyond its grasp—that would be like trying to teach calculus to second graders.

What you can expect is that the mind will receive and retain facts that are uniquely prepared for quick and permanent entrance into memory. Remember the musical acrostic "Every Good Boy Does Fine"? How long have you remembered that? What would have happened had you tried to remember those letters—E, G, B, D, F—in that order? Certain arrangements of facts are easier to memorize than others.

Perhaps your mind is racing at this point. You're dreaming of the dramatic impact such a revolutionary approach would have on your students. Your creativity is starting to stretch and you are wondering what are some of the most effective ways to arrange your content to make it mind-easy. Well, after careful study and testing, seven have surfaced and will be revealed later in this chapter under the Retention Maximizers— seven universal methods to make any set of facts mind-easy. But before that, focus your attention on the fourth step in speed-teaching.

Stage Four: Memorize

Up until this stage, class hasn't even begun yet. Stages 1–3 take place before class; they are the private preparation before the public presentation. Your focus has been the managing of the message; now the focus is upon the transference of the truth to your students.

The goal of the Law of Retention is to enable your students to "*memorize*" the material you have identified as essential. You do this by "*review*." This is where you "*solidify*" the material in your students' minds—you "*practice*" over and over again until all your students have it.

The goal is to move the mind-easy content from short-term memory to long-term memory, to keep pushing that information deeper and deeper until your students can recall it without even thinking. They just know it.

Many teachers wrongly believe they must spend all of their time giving out new material or they're wasting their students' time. But that may be precisely the wrong thing to do. For a refreshing perspective, study how much new content Christ taught in the Gospels. You'll see that He reviewed His primary content over and over again, repeating the same concepts in different ways. He'd express something in a direct conversation and then reinforce it by a miracle or a parable. He repeated the same ideas over and over. It's as if He were saying to us, "There are a few things I want the world to know. Here they are. I'm going to keep reteaching them until you know them!"

The current educational malaise in this country demonstrates that most educational institutions are minimally involved in this type of teaching. The truth is, if any teacher is going to assume the responsibility of causing her students to know, it will be a voluntary commitment. The "system" doesn't require it. Such commitment is unusual and often carries with it a high price tag. That high price tag, however, purchases the deep satisfaction of knowing you are positively influencing your students for the rest of their lives. Not only will their performance soar with this type of commitment, so will their outlook and attitude.

A teacher so committed takes the lead in assuring the students that they will learn the Irreducible Minimum if they cooperate. This type of commitment by a teacher is so unusual and appreciated that it soon wins widespread cooperation by the students.

Therefore, do whatever it takes for your students to memorize the facts necessary to pass every quiz and test. And whenever the test scores reflect that they did not know the material, whose fault is it? Do you have to count that quiz if it reflects your lack of performance? *When you realize that the primary role of the teacher is to cause the students to learn, you look at things differently.* What good are poor grades? The point isn't whether the students learn the material on the second quiz or the fifth; it's that your students learn the material.

Grade not on how quickly they learned the material compared with others, but solely on the objective standard. Did you or did you not teach them so they knew?

We must lead our students from total lack of knowledge on a subject to mastery of the Irreducible Minimum and then onward to advanced competency. En route, we must transition our students through a number of stages of comprehension and memorization.

The key to student memorization is review. Review can either be the "mother of all learning" or the "father of all boredom," depending upon the skill of the teacher. The subject of review cannot be adequately treated here, but by way of overview, here are *seven key principles for effective review*:

1. Review is the primary method by which everyone memorizes everything.

2. Review is effective only when the student adequately understands the material.

3. Review should be practiced in the same order and with the same words until the Irreducible Minimum is fully memorized.

4. Review should be most frequent and intense when the facts are first taught.

5. Review should be regularly practiced but spaced less and less frequently as time passes.

6. Review should continue until all the students demonstrate complete mastery of the Irreducible Minimum.

7. Review should be done using a variety of methods.

How do you know when you've reviewed enough? When your class has "memorized the minimum." All that remains in the Retention Method is the fifth stage which purposes to develop the student to fuller proficiency in the subject—from memory to mastery.

Stage Five: Master

During this final step of the Retention Method, you are intent on leading your class from acquiring the information to applying the information. You started this process by discussing the information, leading your students to memorize the information, and now you focus your creativity on how to lead them to the pinnacle of the learning process, Independent Proficiency.

When this stage is complete, the students will have become "masters" of the material. They will "retain" what you have taught them and are "skillful" and "proficient" in their understanding and utilization of the subject.

Mastery has four parts to consider, although they are usually interrelated during the teaching process:

1. Indelible memorization.
2. In-depth comprehension.
3. Intuitive integration.
4. Independent utilization.

Indelible memorization occurs when the students know the content so well that it is forever with them. You cement the content with super review glue so that it sticks—for good. Transferring the content to the students' long-term memory requires regular review. Eventually, however, the facts will be burned into their recallable memory.

What is 5 times 5? What did the citizens dump into the Boston Harbor in 1773? Because of the constant review of the first and the unusual nature of the second, you knew those two facts. In fact, you'll know them forever. When you are dealing with the Irreducible Minimum, you want your students to know the facts forever. Review them so that it is no longer a chore for anyone at any time, anywhere, to give the answer.

In-depth comprehension moves beyond the surface meaning of the facts and ensures that the students fully understand the meaning and significance of those facts. To ensure they comprehend the meaning behind the facts, class discussion and essay work are helpful.

If you know that tea was dumped into the Boston Harbor but don't know why it was dumped and what built up to those events, then that information is of significantly less value to you. After all, how many job applications ever asked you about the Boston Tea Party?

Intuitive integration occurs when the class is able to sense how the facts can be used in areas beyond their immediate context. You will have to lead your students to think on the principle level of the facts and become so at home with them that their intuition is released.

While speaking recently at a Christian education meeting, I ran right into this very step. I was attempting to teach the audience how God the Father taught His audience. I didn't focus upon His content, style, or delivery. As I revealed ten separate examples of God's style, I was able to lead the audience to uncover many observations and principles of God's style.

However, when I asked them to integrate those same principles into how they would teach their next lesson, no one moved. No one spoke. Everyone saw the value of the question and strained to "intuitively integrate" what they had learned, but they were not able. Therefore, I had to back up to the preceding step and deepen their comprehension and give example after example of integration. The lights began to go on all across the auditorium, but for a while it was a challenge for all of us!

I commented to my audience that I sensed they were having a difficult time in "thinking" and that it reflected a poor habit of "meditation" in their lives. After the session, one of the leaders came up to me and said something I'll never forget: "You're right about our inability to think. We stopped meditating years ago. Now we read books for our answers, but we don't just think."

The Scriptures describe this stage as moving from "knowledge" to "wisdom"; it is the true value of knowing a given set of facts. If the students know the facts but cannot use them or apply the principles behind them, then those facts may have been learned in vain. Although you may disagree, I believe that knowing facts for facts' sake is of little value and can be a poor use of time and effort.

Independent utilization is the real goal of all education. When you weren't around and there was no external pressure to do so, did the student use the content you taught him? Did the student learn the material so thoroughly that he couldn't help but use it in his own life?

I call this process "teaching for life change." Your purpose shouldn't be, Did the students learn the material and could they repeat that material on a preannounced day at a preannounced time and place? The real and only valid goal of education is that the student was instructed and trained in such a way that he changed and behaved differently as a result.

As you think through these four steps of the "*master*" stage, realize that you can use class time and homework to develop complete mastery. *As memorization and comprehension of the facts should be a class function, integration and utilization should be the primary focus of homework.*

This may be a radical departure from what you're used to doing, but it will make an incredible difference in the perceived and real value of your teaching. Too many times our teaching sessions are too narrowly limited to a student writing down what we've come up with for our lesson plans. And we celebrate success when that student can write it down once more on another piece of paper we call an exam.

Seldom do we teachers consciously teach for the purpose of lasting life change rather than the short-term accumulation of facts.

Just recently I was helping a young person with some algebra equations. He lamented how glad he would be when the "stupid semester" was over and he wouldn't have to take another algebra class ever again. In the middle of explaining a typical "x" and "y" question, I asked if these equations would ever be used in real life. He exploded with laughter—the thought was utterly ridiculous to him. He was sure this was just one of those things that schools forced on their students.

I began to show him how real-life problems could be solved by the equations. It took a while, but the light began to shine in his eyes. And when it finally did, he suddenly began to want to understand; he saw a glimpse of the value of algebra and intuitively sensed its importance to his life.

But it was too late. The semester was almost over, and he was stretching for a low D.

Why?

Perhaps because his teacher was merely covering Algebra II. Perhaps because his teacher never caused him to learn Algebra II. Perhaps because his teacher never realized that the purpose of Algebra II was to help this young man be more successful in life.

As far as I'm concerned, the only person who failed more than this young student was his teacher.

RETENTION MAXIMIZERS

Speed-teaching enables speed-learning.

No matter how much a student desires to learn the subject quickly and thoroughly in class, the teacher holds the keys to the process.

The speed of learning is determined by how quickly the teacher causes the students to learn. The amount that is learned is determined by how skillfully the teacher prepares the content and then leads the students to learn and master it. The value of learning is determined by how effectively the teacher builds comprehension, integration, and practical application.

This section of the Law of Retention focuses specifically on maximizing the speed with which the teacher causes the student to learn the facts. The seven methods revealed in this section will double, triple, or even quadruple the material you can move from your notes to your students' minds. Or it can cut in half the amount of time you would normally spend teaching the content so that you can double the time on applying the content.

These seven methods are the primary means the teacher uses to make the material memorable or easy for the student to memorize. These methods were not invented by us. Ever since man has existed these principles have been in force. They work every time with every person in every culture simply because they correspond to the ways God made every human. God created man with *universal patterns of thought* and *universal receptors of stimuli.*

The ability to hear and recognize sounds is the basis for music. Wherever man exists, therefore, music communicates. If a teacher uses music to communicate content, he is cooperating with God in the communication process.

Music is one of the classic methods to speed-teach in every culture and at every age. Do you know the most effective way known to space-age, computer-literate America to teach children the ABC's? Right: The "ABC Song." Nothing else compares, even remotely, because it follows the patterns of learning implanted by the Creator.

Before this section has been completed, you will know of six additional *universal patterns* that the Lord God has implanted in all of us. As soon as you read them, they will be immediately self-evident. In fact, you already know them, though you probably don't know that you know them.

God has not only designed patterns of thought in all mankind, He has also placed in us a series of *universal receptors* for all kinds of information. Patterns of thought would be almost useless if new information were not added regularly. We would have to live off our imagination if there were no possible way to receive new, additional material.

Those receptors are often called our "senses." They are the physical ports through which new information is added to our current patterns of thought. If we did not have the sense of hearing, music could not aid our learning. If we did not have the sense of sight, pictures could not aid our learning.

Therefore, as teachers who desire to maximize our students' learning, we must interface with the senses of sight, smell, hearing, taste, or touch. Our experiences in life are the result of those senses and a blending and interaction of them. For example, certain blends of these senses are combined into categories such as musical or dinner play.

We rarely describe the experience in terms of the senses used but rather the results of those senses. A pleasure of sight is beautiful or attractive. A displeasure of sound is an awful noise or racket. A displeasure of smell is a stench or foul odor.

A wise selection or combination of sensory inputs can be incredibly memorable. When consciously used by the teacher, it clearly accelerates the learning process. Those combinations are available to you anytime you choose. They are accelerators that empower you to speed-teach.

Because these combinations of sensory inputs cooperate with the patterns of thought and with the five senses, they are not bound by culture, time, age, or content. I have used them around the world and have found that they enable me to speed-teach in the jungles of Bolivia or the beaches of Brazil, the villages of Alaska or the apartments of New York.

The seven Retention Maximizers are transcultural, transinformational, transgenerational, and interchangeable. They are the standard tools of the speed-teacher:

Maximizer 1: Represent the facts in a picture.

Pictures are incredibly effective as a *sensory lever* into the student's memory. Why do you think we all take pictures and store them in photo albums? Don't we experience a flood of memories when we look at those pictures, even if it's just a glimpse? See the power of retention right in your daily life? One picture brings to your memory scores of accompanying facts. Instantly. Even twenty-five years later.

That's true of everyone, including your students. Just apply what you now know, and your students will remember what you teach in an instant.

Where did we stumble onto this in our research and meditation? From the Master Teacher Himself. Remember when God used a picture for the first known time to stimulate a "flood of memories"? God placed a rainbow in the sky to cause everyone to remember His promise not to send a flood to destroy the world again.

The use of pictures is powerful because it is visual, universal, transcultural, and nonverbal. The link is instant. The link is attached to many sights, sounds, smells, and feelings. I recently saw a picture of President John F. Kennedy's shooting. What a sweep of feelings and a flood of memories it conjured. I could recall instantly where I was, what time of day it was announced to the world, and how remarkably sad and full of grief I felt. One picture, many memories.

If you want your students to have many memories of your content, then develop one picture that links all the content to them. What would you remember if you saw a picture of one glass slipper outside of a fancy coach drawn by two magnificent horses?

That same principle awaits your speed-teaching imagination. Instead of capriciously allowing a picture to stimulate memories, carefully select or draw a picture to stimulate the memories you want your students to recall.

Many teachers help their students remember Bible verses with pictures. Speeches are recalled by various pictures the speaker used to highlight the points of the address. Husbands remember the five or six things to purchase at the store through stacking the items into an imaginary picture.

At Walk Thru the Bible, we even used cartoons to help people remember instantly what is in every book of the Bible. Just remember, when you desire to speed-teach, you can use the tool of pictures—whether real or cartoon, professional or stick figures.

Maximizer 2: Express the facts with a story.

Before the mass production of books and the invention of television, people used stories to pass on facts, values, heritage, and traditions. *Stories were the paper upon which facts were written to the next generation.* Extended families would join together and share story after story of past generations in order to teach and model desired traits of living.

When you look at how God revealed in the Bible His truth to mankind, you're immediately struck with the fact that the majority of the Bible is in the form of stories. God used stories, both real and imaginary, to transfer His maxims to our mind, His content to our consciousness.

Similarly, our stories are tremendously effective as a transfer mechanism for information in preaching, teaching, and normal conversation. Why is it that stories are the most memorable part of the sermons we hear? We forget the three points and even the poem. But we remember the stories.

Could it be that the Lord created the mind of man to receive and recall information the best through stories? He may well have, which would explain why Jesus used stories more than any other form of communication.

Therefore, never underestimate the value of stories and illustrations and parables. Recast your information into a narrative and you may have made it indelible.

Remember the Parable of the Good Samaritan? Or the Prodigal

Son? Or the Sower and the Seeds? Perhaps the next time you teach, you could follow in Christ's footsteps and present your subject through stories. Then you wouldn't be upset if all that your students remembered were your stories—because then they'd have the essence of what you wanted them to learn.

Maximizer 3: Transfer the facts by the alphabet.

This memory link is the easiest and most utilized of all seven. It is the way many students successfully cram the night before an exam. The use of the alphabet is effective because it adds order to disorder and builds a pattern with which the mind can link disjointed pieces of information. The structured use of the alphabet takes away the toil of random or unrelated pieces of information. It answers the question of what comes next in the list I am to remember. The alphabet is the glue of memory. Each letter when recalled immediately alerts the student to the next item on the list.

Under inspiration, the writers of the Old Testament sometimes used the alphabet to facilitate memorization. If you look at Psalm 119 in the original Hebrew, you will notice that the first eight verses all begin with the first letter of the Hebrew alphabet. In fact, Psalm 119 contains twenty-two stanzas of eight verses each, with all verses in a stanza beginning with the same successive letter in the Hebrew alphabet.

The book of Lamentations is composed of five "laments," each containing twenty-two verses, except the third lament which contains sixty-six verses. Except for chapter 5 (the fifth lament), each verse begins with the next letter in the twenty-two-letter Hebrew alphabet.

The early Christians picked up this same idea and used the Greek word for "fish" as a mnemonic device—an alphabetic aid to retention of key facts—and also as a code among early arrest-prone Christians. By drawing the single-stroke oval in the sand, with unmet ends and an eye in the middle, anyone could follow the fish's nose as a directional marker to where the brethren were secretly meeting. Alphabetically, *ichthus* meant:

I	*Iesous*	Jesus
Ch	*Christos*	Christ
Th	*Theo*	God's
U	*Houios*	Son
S	*Soter*	Savior

Modern students and teachers use this same method frequently, for it affords the easiest memory payback per ounce of effort. The most popular approaches to using the alphabet are as follows:

1. *All the same first letter.* Many people remember the outline of the book of Romans with the letter *S:*

   Sin (chapters 1–3)
   Salvation (4–5)
   Sanctification (6–8)
   Sovereignty (9–11)
   Service (12–16)

2. *All the same last letters, which rhyme.* Many students use this method to remember the doctrine of Scripture:

   Inspira*tion*
   Revela*tion*
   Illumina*tion*
   Preserva*tion*

3. *All the first letters follow in some meaningful order.* This is the way Lamentations and Psalm 119 were written. Each verse or set of verses is arranged according to the order of the Hebrew alphabet.

4. *All the first letters form a word.* This is called an acrostic. In *The 7 Laws of the Learner,* each law is based on one of the letters from the word *learner.*

Learner

Expectation

Application

Retention

Need

Equipping

Revival

The most effective way to use the alphabet is through an acrostic, since it leads the learner to self-discover the next fact in the preferred order. To maximize an acrostic, link it to the essence of its subject so that the student can recall it easily. The next time you want your students to remember a list of facts, why not construct a "linked acrostic" to help them?

Maximizer 4: Associate the facts with objects and actions.

Whenever a teacher can associate a fact or concept with a concrete object or action, it's possible to greatly improve student retention and recall. God did not create a flat world but one with three dimensions filled with innumerable objects, and operated on action and reaction.

God used memory objects such as the tabernacle, the ark, Aaron's rod, the tablets of the Ten Commandments, and even the cross as memory pegs for all generations. A pile of twelve stones from the Jordan River were erected in Canaan as a memory device for all generations. Those stones served to remind the people that God stopped the flow of water so that Israel could pass over on dry land when they entered the Promised Land.

God also used actions that were attached to the celebration of the feasts, the Sabbath, and the Passover to capture many lessons. Remember that Christ asked us to celebrate the Lord's Supper "in remembrance of Me." Baptism is another memory-laden action.

In modern-day life, objects are frequently used to trigger memory and carry paragraphs of content. When you see a wedding ring on a person, what do you remember? Or the American flag? Or the Vietnam War Memorial? Or the grand Statue of Liberty?

Actions are also frequently used to bring back memory and truth. When you bow your head to pray (an action), what are you remembering? Or when you pledge allegiance to the flag? What do handshakes mean when an agreement has been completed? The closer the action is to the specific fact to be remembered, the faster it will be recalled.

Maximizer 5: Impress the facts with drama.

Drama is the most intense of all memory links. In real life, a dramatic moment filled with violence, loss, intense passion, or poignancy is usually unforgettable. In fact, moments of intense pain or shock are ones we often have to try to forget. Yet they are burned into our minds so deeply that they continue to reassert themselves into our consciousness. They are so memorable, we cannot forget.

Biblical examples of drama that can be used to help memory are everywhere. How could Jonah ever forget his lesson of obedience learned in the belly of that great fish? Or the handwriting on the wall? Or Daniel in the lion's den? Or the sheet that Peter saw coming down from heaven? Or the raising of Lazarus? Or the feeding of the five thousand? Or the crowing of the rooster with Peter? These are dramas used by the Master Teacher—and they are unforgettable.

Dramas are effective memory tools for only a limited number of pieces of information. Drama is best used to teach one lesson deeply so the audience will never forget. Act out an Old Testament person who brought his sheep to the priest as an atonement for his sin—and then put his hands on the sheep's head as the priest cut the innocent animal's throat in your place. The penalty for sin was never so poignantly taught except in the case of Jesus, our Passover Lamb, dying on the cross for us.

Maximizer 6: Note the facts through music.

The secular world knows the worth of using music to embed its message into the listening audience's memory. Just listen to an hour of popular radio or television and you'll hear numerous musical jingles. They are so effective that we find ourselves singing their catchy phrases throughout the week—all from memory.

Music was God's idea and was used not only to engender worship and adoration, but also to enable memory of the words, will, and ways of the Lord. The whole book of Psalms is the ancient hymnal of the Israelites—revealed by God. The New Testament instructs us to "be filled with the Spirit, speaking to one another in psalms *and hymns and spiritual songs, singing and making melody* in your heart to the Lord" (Ephesians 5:18–19).

The hymns of our faith are sermons put to song. They blend the ideas with sounds and lock them into our memories after we've sung them a few times. Who can't remember "Amazing Grace" or "Jesus Loves Me" or "How Great Thou Art"? The composers of our hymns had a message they wanted us to sing and remember and so they put it to music.

In like fashion, when teachers have a message they want us to remember, they can put it to music as well. The easiest method is to take a well-known tune and put your words to it. Have your class sing it a few times, and they'll have the Irreducible Minimum down before you know it.

Maximizer 7: Summarize the facts with graphs and charts.

Graphs and charts are the memory aids that are most helpful to show relationships, proportions, and flow or direction. They transfer facts into visual representations. When visual-oriented learners have an auditory teacher, they will often complain that they "just can't picture it." They are unconsciously seeking a visual representation.

The descriptions of the temple in Ezekiel 40–48 and the New Jerusalem in Revelation 21–22 are graphic in description. In order to best see what the author means, most students take a piece of paper and draw a chart for clarity.

When I wrote the Bible outlines for the *Open Bible: Expanded Version,* I included a chart for every book of the Bible. Many people have commented on how helpful the charts are to their understanding. The blackboard, overhead transparency, and flip chart are standard formats for display of this memory method. When combined with alliteration and acrostics and color, charts and graphs are an incredible help. Here's the book of Genesis in simple chart form.

FOCUS	1:1	FOUR EVENTS		11:9	11:10	FOUR PEOPLE		50:26
UNITS	CREATION	FALL	FLOOD	NATIONS	ABRAHAM	ISAAC	JACOB	JOSEPH
CHAPTERS	1-2	3-5	6-9	10-11:9	11:10–25:8	25:9-26	27-36	37-50
TOPIC	HUMAN RACE				HEBREW RACE			
	HISTORICAL				BIOGRAPHICAL			
PLACE	FERTILE CRESCENT				CANAAN			EGYPT
TIME	+/-2000 YEARS				+/-200 YEARS			+/-100 YEARS

CONCLUSION

You'll never know when your ability to speed-teach will turn out to be more valuable than you'd ever imagine.

I was sitting before the board of directors of a large, prestigious foundation in order to answer their questions about our request for a very large grant. It was my first time before this board, and I was more than a little anxious.

One of the directors had privately mentioned that not all of the members were excited about my proposal. One member in particular was not supportive, and I wondered how his attitude would surface.

The first three minutes went reasonably well—and then he asked the zinger: "I understand you speed-teach the Bible. I don't believe you can teach me the book of Genesis."

He had every right to question. Good questions were a sign of good stewardship, and the foundation I was sitting before was well known for its careful stewardship.

Yet I felt the fate of the whole proposal was at stake, and I thought my heart was going to explode.

"Yes, sir, I believe I can speed-teach the Bible. In fact, I can teach you the book of Genesis in five minutes."

No one moved. I took off my watch and purposefully laid it on the mahogany table. This was no time to be timid.

Then I took a deep breath, prayed a few million prayers, smiled, and said, "Five minutes. When the five minutes are up, you be the judge if you learned the book of Genesis."

He sort of smiled, but I sensed he was enjoying the moment.

Then for the next five minutes, I forgot everyone else in the room but him. He was all the way across the room, sitting in a high-backed leather chair. I taught and reviewed and questioned him. And then I reviewed and taught some more, all the while keeping an eye on the second hand, steadily tick-ticking away.

At the end of five minutes, I quietly put my watch back on and asked him if he would tell me everything he had learned in the five minutes. He laughed, then proceeded to review everything I had taught him in those five minutes. Perfectly!

Everyone broke into joyful celebration, and I could breathe again. I silently thanked the Lord, and watched the board proceed to vote.

I left with the entire amount I had requested.

Does speed-teaching pay? How about $84,000 a minute? And that's the truth.

The moral of the story? Speed-teach and your students will reward you richly.

DISCUSSION QUESTIONS

1. Step 2 of the Retention Method occurs when the teacher boils down the content to the "minimum." Why do you think so few teachers take this step? What would be the result in the lives of the students between a teacher who believed that a greater quantity of content covered is better than a greater quantity of content learned?

2. Think back to your "cramming" days as a student— you know, memorizing everything for the test the night before. What were the tricks that you and your friends used to memorize quickly? How would your students feel if you employed those same memory aids when you taught them? Do you think their grades would be affected if you regularly practiced this?

3. It is the responsibility of the teacher to transition the content from the short-term memory of the student to the long-term memory. Repetition is the way that material is eventually memorized. List at least twenty different ways you could review any subject with a class. Use your imagination!

4. Review the seven Retention Maximizers which list the top ways to arrange material for speed-teaching and learning. Put them in order, from easiest to most difficult. What are the characteristics of the three

easiest in relation to the three hardest? If there were no limitations of time or money, which would be your favorite to use and why?

5. When the teacher speed-teaches, he enables the student to speed-learn. The only problem is that it takes the teacher more time in preparation to teach the material in less time in the classroom. How would you feel about your teaching career on the day of your retirement if you looked back over your life and had or had not used these principles as you taught? What will have been the right decision for you from your students' perspective?

LAW FIVE

The Law
of Need

CHAPTER NINE

Need

Mindset, Model, and Maxims

Many years ago my wife and I and our two small children lived on a farm in south Georgia, complete with a small pond with a tiny, rickety old dock.

I'll never forget the day we decided to take David and Jenny fishing for the first time. We bought four rods and reels, little $4.97 K-Mart specials. We also bought some red and white bobbers and some brass hooks.

When we got home I told David to "go turn over some rocks and see if you can find some worms." He scampered off and had great fun. Jennifer, who was about five years old, couldn't stand the thought of worms.

In a few minutes we all marched over to the dock and I prepared everyone's rod and reel, putting hooks and bobbers on each one.

"Let's put a worm on," I said.

"Okay, Dad!" David said. And he began sticking a poor worm to death.

Jennifer was aghast. She became alarmed and almost started to cry. "Daddy!" she shouted. "What's David doing?"

"Well, Jenny, he's putting a worm on his hook."

"Oh, Daddy!" she said innocently. "Why? What did the worm do wrong?"

"Nothing, Jenny. You just need to put a worm on your hook."

"Daddy—doesn't God love worms?"

Seminary never prepared me for such a question! "Well, yes, Jenny, He does."

"I'm not doing that to a worm."

"Jenny, you need to put a worm on your hook to catch a fish."

"Daddy, I'm not doing that!"

So she made her way down to the end of the dock carrying her new fishing pole with a red and white bobber and an empty, bright brass hook and plunked her hook and bobber into the water.

David went to the opposite side of the dock and put down his line. Now, no one had been fishing in this pond for a long time, and little sunnies were everywhere. Within seconds David had his first catch. There was a frenzy of excitement. That little fish was flopping and David was jumping up and down. He reeled in his fish, took it off the hook, and put it on the dock. Naturally, Jennifer ran down to see this first catch. She wouldn't touch it, but she was terribly excited.

In the meanwhile, David put on another worm. "Jennifer, you want a worm?" he asked.

"No. I'm not putting a worm on."

David shrugged and threw in his line. Almost immediately he caught another fish. Jennifer looked at her pole, then at his pole. Slowly she moved down the dock and stood right next to her brother. I guess she decided that the fish weren't hungry where she was fishing. He put on another worm, threw in his line, and caught a third fish. And my little girl began to cry.

"Honey, what's the matter?"

"Daddy, David has a lucky fishing pole!"

"Jenny, you're sure that's what it is?"

"Yes!"

So, with a little coaxing from me, David agreed to switch poles. He put a worm on Jenny's unlucky pole, tossed the hook and bobber into the pond, and immediately caught another fish. After a few moments of silence, Jennifer announced, "I'm never gonna fish again."

"Jenny," I said, "you know what the problem is?"

"No."

"Guess what fish love to eat."

I could see her little brain going whirrrrrrrr. Finally she said softly, "You mean fish love to eat *worms*?"

"Yes. So why don't you put a worm on your hook?"

"But Daddy—look how pretty the hook is!" To her, that shiny new hook should be enough to attract and catch fish.

I've often thought about that memorable day, not only because it taught Jennifer about the basics of fishing, but because it so indelibly impressed upon me one of the basics of fishing for men. We stride into class carrying our big black Bibles, walk to the front, and announce, "Turn in your Bibles to Ezekiel chapter 38!" And we think our students can't wait for Ezekiel 38. We imagine all of them racing into the room thinking, *Oh, I hope we talk about Ezekiel 38 today!* We try to catch our students with nothing but a bare hook. No wonder nobody's interested. No wonder we soon question whether it's worth "fishing."

Jenny thought the hook was attractive to her and therefore mistakenly thought it would attract fish. She expected her pond audience to see life from her point of view.

But I have some news for you—fish are not attracted to bare hooks. Nor are learners drawn naturally to bare content. If you want an interested and motivated class, then stop dropping shiny brass hooks into the water. We often become so enamored with the beauty of our content that we forget our students will avoid it unless carefully enticed to it.

"The Parable of the Bare Hook" illustrates one of the primary roots of ineffective teaching: a class structured and conducted to meet the needs of the teacher rather than the learner. You can't force a fish to bite your hook; neither can you force students to learn.

Let's go one step further—who's supposed to bait the hook, the fish or the fisherman? Of course, the fisherman! But we expect our fish either to be motivated by our brass hooks or to put their own bait on our bare hooks.

That's the essence of the Law of Need. As the teacher I am responsible to help my students chase after my content. We call it motivation. If you've ever had a class that doesn't seem to be motivated, perhaps the reason is that you didn't have a worm on the hook.

By the end of this chapter, you're going to understand how Christ baited the hook for His students. You will discover how to bait the hook for any subject you teach so that your class may become so motivated, they may jump right into your boat!

NEED MINDSET

There's a particular physical and emotional reaction only teachers experience. Every teacher has experienced it at least once; others far more.

It starts with a sinking feeling in the pit of your stomach, followed by a weakening of the knees, a reddening of the face, a softening of the voice, a straining for and stammering with words. Panic-stricken, the teacher wants only to dash out of the room, to be free from the classroom walls which seem to be pressing steadily inward.

What is it? It's the "Oh, what's the use?" depression that first takes hold when one student yawns, then another. It grows inexorably when another slips a magazine from in between books and a student you thought was taking copious notes is discovered writing a love letter. It overwhelms when one student gazes dreamy-eyed out the window and still another is reenacting the Stanley Cup hockey finals…with pennies.

You've lost contact. They no longer hear you. You're simply exercising your jaws.

What do you do? Pretend it isn't happening? Assign blame to the spring weather, the low student IQs, the lateness of the hour? Vow to resign and change occupations once and for all? Or do you grab hold of the situation and do something about it?

Now, change the picture for a moment and imagine your students begging to hear what you have to say. Anxious to get class started. Disappointed when the lesson is over. And successfully putting your content to work in their lives.

"Dream on," you say. "You don't understand my students!"

That may be what you're thinking at this moment, but by the end of the Law of Need, you are going to discover some insights that will empower you to revolutionize your teaching. But first, let's consider this "bare hook" issue.

The common mindset about motivating students is that it is the students' problem. If they are apathetic and bored, it's their fault. If they don't want to pay attention, it certainly isn't the teacher's problem!

The Law of Need presents the opposite perspective: The teacher can and should build the need for what is to be taught. In other words, if you are going fishing, then bait the hook! To see how this fleshes out in real life, let's take a look at the Master Teacher, Jesus Christ.

When you study the life of Christ, you cannot miss the fact that Jesus regularly addressed the needs of His hearers. He sought to meet those needs through two different approaches: *First*, when the person's needs were obvious, Jesus immediately sought to meet them. Of all teachers who ever taught, Jesus was the Master Need-Meeter!

Second, when people were out of touch with their needs, Jesus sought to surface their needs and then to meet them. In both instances, Jesus taught in response to His students' needs and not in spite of them. The starting point of the teaching of Jesus was the needs of His class, not His content!

As teachers, we face both situations every day. At times, the needs of our students are very apparent, and we can seek to meet them as soon as possible. If the need is in the life of an individual, we seek to meet his needs through a private conversation or correspondence. When the whole class reflects a common need, we seek to meet that need by inserting appropriate comments into our presentation, slanting our applications in that direction, or simulating discussion along those issues.

On the whole, however, most teachers find themselves in the opposite predicament: They have to teach a subject or lesson that the student has little natural interest in or felt need to know. They are not teaching in response to the students' felt needs but in response to the assigned curriculum. Since that is true, and since that means you are dropping a bare hook into the pond, what kind of students response should you normally expect? Real problems of disinterest, inattention, and lack of motivation should be expected and anticipated in those classroom situations.

Most teachers are distressed and even shocked to discover that their students lack interest and motivation toward their subject or class. But should we be shocked? I believe our feelings are misplaced and cause undue pressure and tension for both the teacher and the students. The vast majority of classes are normally out of touch with the felt need of the students and therefore are always accompanied by frustration, apathy, and lack of motivation.

If you are troubled by these comments, spend a moment and recall your experience as a student. Didn't you find yourself frequently disinterested and wishing you didn't have to endure a given course or lecture? Didn't you ever find yourself saying, "If I didn't have to take this course, I could…" and then proceed to enumerate any number of things that seemed far more worthwhile?

When I was developing these concepts, I spent considerable time interviewing students about their educational experiences. Most students viewed many courses as not only not meeting their needs, but even interfering with their needs. Frequently I heard responses such as

"That course was a total waste of time," or "Totally irrelevant," or "That course will never help me even for one day." I remember asking a class of about twenty-five college students what percentage of their classes they would drop if they had the authority. Their answer: More than half.

This is the heart of the motivational problem in the classroom. Instead of teaching in response to the felt needs of our students, we frequently teach in spite of their needs.

What should we do?

The answer lies in the example of our Master Teacher. He faced this identical problem, and His limitless wisdom provided a most refreshing solution. And the wonder of it is that His approach can be duplicated by anyone who seeks to serve the needs of his or her students.

Jesus' five-step approach is transferable to every teacher; it works in the lives of teachers everywhere around the world who are committed to teach like Christ. When they do, the only people more thrilled than the teachers are their students. Class all of a sudden becomes incredibly important and relevant. It becomes vital to all their needs.

How? The teacher applies the five steps Jesus used to build the need in His students' hearts. The teacher's students respond the same way Jesus' students did, and motivation and excitement flourish. Students become so motivated they seem to pull the lesson right out of the teacher.

If this vision of the classroom strikes a responsive chord with you, then stick with us as we equip you to unleash student motivation through the Law of Need. As we begin, see if you can discern the five stages Jesus led the woman at the well through in John 4:5–30:

> So He came to a city of Samaria which is called Sychar, near the plot of ground that Jacob gave to his son Joseph. Now Jacob's well was there. Jesus therefore, being wearied from His journey, sat thus by the well. It was about the sixth hour. A woman of Samaria came to draw water. (vv. 5–7)

There's the Master's class—one woman who showed up to get some water. She had to come. It was hot, she was thirsty, she needed water. She was totally uninterested in the man resting there.

How similar to our own situation. Our students come because they have to come. And most of them aren't even consciously thirsty! But Jesus takes advantage of the situation. He knew that to teach, you have to cause the listener to learn. Notice that Jesus took it upon Himself to cause His listener to want to learn, to be interested in seeking the lesson.

NEED MODEL

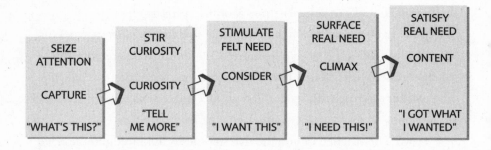

Step 1: Seize Attention

The first thing Christ does is "*seize attention.*" She came to the well absorbed in her own thoughts, intent on her own purpose. Then out of the blue this stranger says, "Give Me a drink."

Although it's hard for us to understand why, His comment truly surprised her. It was unexpected because in that culture a Jewish rabbi would never talk to a Samaritan woman in a public place. The shocking thing isn't that He asked her for water; it's that He spoke to her at all. Jesus' words seized her attention immediately. The teacher knew His actions would spark immediate interest, and that was His purpose.

When you teach, follow this first step and immediately "*capture*" your students' attention. Use a provocative statement, a skit, a joke, a thoughtful question, a loud noise, or an abrupt change in your normal delivery style. Even a poignant moment of silence can seize your students' attention.

Remember, your students enter class with their attention scattered everywhere. It's your job to repossess it. You had it at the end of the last class period (you hope), but since then their attention has been on the loose. To start class, take charge of their attention. Grab it. The moment your class begins, take it away from what is holding it. If you don't have their attention, you can never teach them. Having your students' attention is the first universal requirement of learning.

Attention is a remarkable thing. It is immediately drawn to the most vivid stimulus present. Therefore, to seize your students' attention, all you must do is *overcome the stimulus that is currently holding their attention.*

Because most students enter class under a low level of stimulus most of the time, overpowering that stimulus is usually simple and straightforward. If you find it difficult to get their attention, it's because the current stimulus is stronger. So power yours up!

You "*seize the attention*" of your students and "*capture*" it as they break free from the current source of their attention and wonder, "*What is this?*" You refocus their eyes, their ears, and their minds. For a few short seconds, you have them. But it's impossible to keep their focus for long unless you move to the second of Christ's five stages in building the need.

Step 2: Stir Curiosity

Attention spans are fleeting. We must move to a deeper and more intriguing stimulus that engages more than our students' temporary attention. This second stage "*stirs the curiosity*" so much that it lessens the dependence upon the immediate external stimuli—sight, sound, smell, touch, and taste. Jesus stirs the woman's curiosity in a most instructive manner, until she desires for her teacher to "*Tell me more!*"

Then the woman of Samaria said to Him, "How is it that You, being a Jew, ask a drink from me, a Samaritan woman?" For Jews have no dealings with Samaritans. (v. 9)

Notice how Jesus replies. Does He say something you would expect like, "Well, I'm thirsty and I don't have anything to draw water with"? No, He never even answers her question. He simply continues His need-building process:

Jesus answered and said to her, "If you knew the gift of God, and who it is who says to you, 'Give Me a drink,' you would have asked Him, and He would have given you living water." (v. 10)

Try to put yourself in the woman's place for a moment. Jesus' response must have aroused her curiosity: "What's this gift He's talking about? Where is it? How do I get it? How much is it worth? And who is this man, anyway? Why is He so important? And what in the world is 'living water'?"

Don't miss how Jesus was teaching His student. Don't miss how He baited the hook of her curiosity. In fact, He baited not one, not two, but *three* hooks! Did you see them?

Bait 1: God's Gift   "If you knew the gift of God"
Bait 2: His Identity   "[If you knew] who it is who says to you"
Bait 3: Living Water "He would have given you living water."

Did Jesus know she didn't know the answer to those questions? Was He purposefully engaging her mind to start the thinking process? Could Jesus actually be planning this learning process? If He did, then what implications does His approach have for your approach? The last time you taught, how did you stir your student's curiosity? Or did you just start right into the lesson?

Starting right into the lesson is dropping a bare hook into the pond. Students aren't attracted to bare hooks. Jesus knew that and chose to throw out three different baits. Was this complicated? No, it was just one sentence. Was it time-consuming? No, it took just a matter of seconds. Why three hooks? Since different fish are motivated by different kinds of bait, master teachers often bait more than one hook.

How many of those hooks did she bite? She bit all three, but in reverse order.

> *Bait 3: Living Water*—The woman said to Him, "Sir, You have nothing to draw with, and the well is deep. Where then do You get that living water?" (v. 11).
>
> *Bait 2: His Identity*—"Are You greater than our father Jacob?" (v. 12). In the original Greek, this question expects a negative answer from Jesus. She could not conceive of anyone greater than Jacob.
>
> *Bait 1: God's Gift*—She goes on to mention Jacob's gift: "Who gave us the well, and drank from it himself, as well as his sons and his livestock." Indirectly she was asking, "What is this gift you are talking about giving? Could it be better than the gift of this well that Jacob gave us?"

This is a remarkable example of the way Christ teaches one of His students. He possesses unlimited knowledge, unlimited wisdom, and unlimited love for His student, and yet He takes a very careful and considered approach. He builds her curiosity so she cannot help but seek, even desire, further information.

Now Jesus takes the woman's curiosity and moves her to some deeper issues she can immediately identify with.

Step 3: Stimulate Felt Need

The woman is not yet tuned in to the real lesson that Jesus plans to teach. Knowing that, He continues nurturing her sense of need. It's the teacher's responsibility to bring the students' attention to the agenda of the class. How did Jesus do that? He chose to *"stimulate her felt need"* and led her to *"consider"* the issues much more seriously until she felt, *"I want this!"*

> Jesus answered and said to her, "Whoever drinks of this water will thirst again, but whoever drinks of the water that I shall give him will never thirst. But the water that I shall give him will become in him a fountain of water springing up into everlasting life." (vv. 13–14)

The first two steps are merely preparatory for this third one. The teacher must link student curiosity to issues that easily and quickly touch their felt needs. Jesus knew that water and thirst were foremost in His student's mind, so He started there. *The best starting place for all teaching is the surface felt need of the students.* What they are feeling and thinking is the best launching pad for our lessons.

Jesus knew she would give anything to avoid going out into the heat to draw water every day. His bait of "never thirst again" and "become a fountain of water" made her feel, *"I want this!"*

The closer you become to the students' preexisting needs, the easier it is to stimulate their interest. Master teachers, therefore, are always surveying their students to pick up where they are at that moment. They watch their students' body language and attune their ears to the conversations before and after class. Effective teachers have threaded themselves right into the very fabric of their students' lives and intuitively sense where they are.

Your introduction must skillfully link your lesson right to their existing interest. *You don't have to wonder how to raise their interest, only how to involve their interest.* To see another example of this vital link, watch how Christ followed this exact procedure with Nicodemus in the preceding chapter of John.

What a relief to realize you don't have to build interest—just uncover and cooperate with it. Remember, students always enter the classroom interested in something.

The next step is the most challenging. How do you lead your students to the subject you've prepared?

Step 4: Surface Real Need

It's obvious that Jesus intends to share with the woman the gift of salvation from her sins—but she's a long way from sensing her sin and need for that gift. She didn't come to the well deep in thought about her desperate situation and need for a Savior.

Her teacher was fully aware of this and therefore continued the process of building her need. Jesus is so intent on building her need that He once again doesn't answer her questions about the miracle water He's been discussing. Instead He changes the subject (in her mind, not His!) and says to her, "Go, call your husband, and come here" (v. 16).

What does that have to do with her thirst? Nothing. And yet everything. Jesus wanted her to thirst at a much deeper level, not just the felt need level. Now watch what happens.

> The woman answered and said, "I have no husband."
> Jesus said to her, "You have well said, 'I have no husband,' for you have had five husbands, and the one whom you now have is not your husband; in that you spoke truly." (vv. 17–18)

Jesus didn't condemn her. In fact, He commended her honesty. Then He paused to see if His fish would keep on coming. And she surely did— and threw out some of her own bait! She's motivated to learn more:

"Sir, I perceive that You are a prophet. Our fathers worshiped on this mountain, and you Jews say that in Jerusalem is the place where one ought to worship." (vv. 19–20)

She wants to learn more about worshiping God and indirectly asks Jesus for further content. He had encouraged her questions and now had *"surfaced the real need."* This is the *"climax"* of need building and leads the students to feel, *"I need this!"*

Step 5: Satisfy Real Need

Only when the class is in touch with their real needs should you proceed to *"satisfy their real need"* with the *"content."* With your class so motivated by their real needs, will you struggle with disinterested students? Will you fight with their apathy?

Not a chance! They will be thrilled. "I got it! I finally got what I really wanted!"

The woman said to Him, "I know that Messiah is coming" (who is called Christ). "When He comes, He will tell us all things."

Jesus said to her, "I who speak to you am He." (vv. 25–26)

Jesus withheld the answer until His student asked the appropriate question. Teachers are most effective when they follow this same pattern. Instead of starting our class with our content, we should create student hunger for our content. Unfortunately, most teachers see this need-building stage as an unnecessary step—a waste of valuable class time.

If building the need is unnecessary, then why did our omniscient Master Teacher spend such a large percentage of His class time building His students' need? In this case, *Jesus spent more time building the need than teaching the lesson.* In so doing, He modeled a distinctly different mindset from contemporary teaching and preaching. He considered building the need the first part of the lesson rather than a disposable add-on.

Building the need is the baiting of the hook—the first step for all those who desire to catch fish.

Let's step back for a moment and review what Jesus just did. What was His mindset through the whole process? As we watch the Master Teacher at work, what can we learn about the attitude of heart that is essential to meeting needs and good teaching?

First, notice that Jesus met her "where she was." He was sitting by the well, she approached, and He asked her for a drink. Jesus made contact in a natural way, in a setting familiar to her, with a subject she was already interested in. This reflects the first aspect of the Need Mindset: *It is crucial for the teacher to begin with the students' frame of reference.* To meet their needs, you must initially meet them on their ground.

Second, the Lord took responsibility for getting her attention and discussing her needs. As the conversation progressed, she became an active participant. But Jesus was clearly the responsible agent causing her to learn. With His questions and comments, He saw to it that their meeting was not merely a casual exchange. This is the second ingredient for the Need Mindset: *The teacher must assume responsibility for addressing the students' needs.*

Meeting needs doesn't happen by accident. If Jesus had not felt responsible for seeing that His meeting with the woman ended up addressing some of her needs, she would have left just as needy as when she came. The same is true of our classes. If we don't assume responsibility for addressing our students' needs, they may remain unaddressed.

This brings us to the last and most important ingredient for the Need Mindset. In Jesus' discussion with the woman about her husbands, He could easily have said things about her past that would have crushed her. But He didn't. He dealt with her graciously and gently. That's the third aspect: *Address your students' needs in a gentle and sensitive manner.*

Jesus knew that real needs don't come to the surface easily. When they finally do surface, there is often some tenderness, some emotional ache. It's much like a little boy who runs to his mother after falling and scraping his elbow. He needs the wound cleansed, but as soon as Mom begins to clean the scrape, he pulls away. For her to meet his need, she has to be gentle and sensitive.

Whenever you begin to address the real, heartfelt needs of your class, you shouldn't be surprised to find some sensitive, tender wounds. As a teacher who seeks to meet your students' needs, you must be gentle.

As you become more and more skilled in teaching your students in such a way that their needs are surfaced and then met, the last problem you'll have is student motivation. In fact, every once in a while they may even jump into your boat!

And your best fishing stories won't have to be about the "big one" that got away.

NEED MAXIMS

Maxim 1: Need building is the responsibility of the teacher.

"A great teacher is not simply one who imparts knowledge to his students," said one master teacher, "but one who awakens their interest and makes them eager to pursue knowledge for themselves. He is a spark plug, not a fuel line."

All great teachers understand this secret that they are responsible to awaken student interest before they begin teaching their content. They purposefully plan how to engender eagerness. They inspire and even entice their students. Like Jesus with the woman at the well, they attract their students to something they desire to have. They lead them from one step to the next until they are absorbed in the lesson—thrilled that they are finally getting what they really wanted!

Unfortunately, most students rarely enjoy such teaching. Their teachers enter class and immediately proceed to lecture on the subject of the day with utter disregard for the condition of their students' attention or sense of need.

And then when students are bored or distracted, they must endure their teacher's criticism because they wouldn't pay attention! Finally, when the students' boredom blossoms into disruptive behavior, teachers rise up in anger, lambasting their students with a display of power and authority.

After all, it's the students' responsibility to pay attention, isn't it? Just like it's the responsibility of the fish to bait their own hook. (Picture the fisherman screaming at the unbiting fish while using a baitless hook.)

Will you accept this responsibility of baiting your hook every time you teach? No fish ever baited his own hook—nor will they in the future! The lack of attention in your students is simply their way of telling you, "You need some fresh bait!"

Never again become angry when your students aren't paying attention. Never again misdirect your frustration at them for not biting your subject. Instead, refocus your attention on regaining their attention. Take your focus from the outline and direct it to the student. They need a different tack, a different approach, a new set of stimuli or incentives. A bare hook yields boredom; a baited hook, motivation.

Since God made mankind to feel need in order to pay attention and learn, perhaps we should bury our arrogance and cooperate with Him. And if Jesus taught through the use of need, perhaps we should destroy our independence and follow Him. When we do, not only do we open ourselves to the blessing of God, but we also open ourselves to enjoy the delight of our students.

So take that bare hook, and unlike my young daughter, grab hold of one of those juicy, wiggly worms.

Maxim 2: Need meeting is the teacher's primary calling.

The first maxim dealt with building need before you teach; this second maxim deals with meeting the needs that already exist in your students when you teach. Jesus taught the woman at the well in such a way that she felt the need to seek more and more truth from Him until He led her to meet her real need.

Of all the Need Maxims, this one is the most difficult to communicate—and it is the one most frequently opposed by those who stand behind lecterns and podiums across our land. But I have seen incredible life change occur in innumerable teachers and preachers who have experienced the liberating truth of this maxim.

Listen in on a conversation I had with a pastor at a recent conference:

"My church isn't doing very well. Attendance plateaued more than a year ago and has been going down pretty quickly in the past six months. What do you think is wrong?"

"Perhaps the problem may lie in the church's pastor."

"What? You think I might be the problem? Why, you've never even met me!"

"Well, aren't you the shepherd of the sheep? You've said that your flock's not very healthy—that the sheep are leaving and not having lambs like they used to. When that happens, it inevitably circles back to the shepherd since the condition of the flock is your delegated responsibility. What do you think may be the problem?"

"I don't know. The people just don't want good Bible preaching anymore. TV has wrecked everything. People just want to be entertained, and I'm not going to stoop to becoming an entertainer!"

"What are you preaching on these days?"

"I'm preaching on Galatians and having the time of my life! I'm preaching verse by verse, even word by word. I've always wanted to do this. I'm getting into the Greek. I mean, I'm going deep. I'm plumbing the depths!"

"No kidding? How long have you been preaching on Galatians?"

"Two and a half years, and I'm just starting chapter 2."

"And are you enjoying it?"

"I'm loving it—but attendance is going down."

"I wonder why? Let me ask you another question. What's the big idea of Galatians?"

"The theme is that you're not saved by works."

"Pastor," I probed, "how many of your people think they are saved by works?"

"None that I know of."

"Then why are you spending two years telling them something they already know? Why are you teaching Galatians?"

"Because I've always wanted to preach Galatians!"

Do you see the error in this man's thinking? He tragically thinks that the correct way to determine what to preach or teach is based upon his "wanting to preach Galatians." His focus is upon himself and not upon his students. His focus is upon what he wants and not what they need. He should be awarded the blue ribbon for the "Bare Hook Preacher."

I can't tell you how many times I have had similar discussions across our country. Teachers and preachers feel that their primary calling is to explain the truth. The only fallacy is that the truth does not have any needs! The Bible does not have a need to be preached or taught.

Only people have needs. The calling of the shepherd is to meet the needs of his sheep; the calling of the pastor or teacher is to meet the needs of his class.

If we were to interview this pastor's sheep, we would find that they are leaving for a very good reason. They have given up hope that their shepherd will ever preach to meet their real needs. So they are leaving to find a shepherd who will, while the pastor in his arrogance blames them for not responding correctly to his irrelevant preaching.

How can we dig ourselves into such graves? How can we who teach ever become so mixed up about our purpose?

Let me delve a little deeper for a moment. Let's say someone from your class calls one evening and in a trembling voice begs for help because her marriage is breaking apart. She asks if she and her husband can come over.

You agree and have them come right over. You've been studying the tabernacle all week so you are ready. When they come, you immediately turn to Exodus and begin describing all the parts of the tabernacle—the altar, the laver, the holy of holies. You are so excited to share everything you have learned.

Every once in a while you look up and see their perplexed look. But this is such good stuff. After all, you are explaining the Word of God— and the Word of God is powerful and won't come back null and void. On and on you lecture, sketching each item piece by piece on a nearby pad.

But right in the middle of the best part—when you are explaining the significance of the different colors of the tabernacle coverings—the man jumps to his feet and with neck veins bulging yells, "What on earth are you talking about? How is this supposed to save my marriage?"

He stomps out and his wife looks with utter disbelief at you, then runs sobbing after her husband.

You can't believe it. They left. And you were doing such a good job teaching the Bible! How could they leave when you were sharing so many powerful insights about the tabernacle?

You shake your head. Stupid people. People just don't care about the Bible anymore. People don't want the "meat" anymore. People just want the mush and the milk.

You never see the couple again. Your secretary tells you that the husband has filed for divorce and the wife has started going to another church on the other side of town. But you know about that pastor; he isn't committed to preaching the Word like you are.

This story is ridiculous, isn't it? It's pathetic. It's pathetic because it is repeated week after week in hundreds of pulpits and thousands of classrooms!

Students enter the classroom with their marriages in shambles and their children having severe problems and their finances at the breaking point. And there we stand—poised, prepared. We're ready. "Turn to the book of Exodus, please. I want to share some deep insights about the tabernacle..."

Sound familiar? Believe me, as one who speaks on the subject all around the world to teachers and preachers, it is the norm! We have so twisted our understanding of the calling of those who teach and preach. *We have separated the message from those we are called to minister to.* We think that if we have taught what the Bible teaches, then we have fulfilled our calling.

But the only time we fulfill our calling is when we teach the Bible to the needs of our people. Do you think that the pastor who tried to counsel the couple with severe marital problems with an explanation of the tabernacle fulfilled his calling? Obviously not!

Why is that so very clear in the counseling office but not so clear in the classroom? Fellow teacher and preacher, it *is* clear in the classroom—to the audience, not the communicator. The deception is wide and it is deep. And from my experience, it is emotionally explosive.

Teachers feel it is not their responsibility to meet the needs of their students when they teach. Preachers feel it is not their responsibility to meet the needs of their students when they preach.

Somehow, communicators feel it is their responsibility to teach the content. But what for? And for whom? If our content is to help our audience, then should not our focus always be upon what they need to enable them to live in obedience to the Lord?

Because the Bible is inspired, we think that all parts of it are equally important to our audience. *They are not!* If we say that some parts aren't as important to preach or teach, we somehow think we are also saying the Bible isn't inspired or authoritative or inerrant. No, we aren't.

If you believe otherwise, then I challenge you to be authentic with your own beliefs. Let's be consistent. Let's see if our preconceived notions really hold water. Next week begin a new series and teach or preach the following six verses word by word—taking two or three verses each lesson.

> The descendants of Manasseh: his Syrian concubine bore him Machir the father of Gilead, the father of Asriel. Machir took as his wife the sister of Huppim and Shuppim, whose name was Maachah. The name of Gilead's grandson was Zelophehad, but Zelophehad begot only daughters. (Maachah the wife of Machir bore a son, and she called his name Peresh. The name of his brother was Sheresh, and his sons were Ulam and Rakem. The son of Ulam was Bedan.) These were the descendants of Gilead the son of Machir, the son of Manasseh. His sister Hammoleketh bore Ishhod, Abiezer, and Mahlah. And the sons of Shemida were Ahian, Shechem, Likhi, and Aniam. (1 Chronicles 7:14–19)

Those are only six verses of one chapter—and in the first nine chapters of 1 Chronicles, there are more than four hundred additional verses just like them!

Now let's take our pastor friend who spent the last two years preaching the first chapter of Galatians, an average of some four weeks per verse. Since all the Bible is equally inspired, we should spend an equal amount of time on each verse. The six verses from 1 Chronicles would take twenty-four weeks, or six months of preaching. At that rate, you would still be preaching in 1 Chronicles 1–9 after eight hundred weeks—more than fifteen years!

I hope you find yourself smiling, because the illustration is utterly ridiculous. If anyone preached for fifteen years on those genealogies, even the Spirit of God may have a hard time staying with him.

Why is the truth depicted by this example so easy to accept but the principle under discussion so difficult? Why wouldn't we even consider teaching or preaching these verses for fifteen years? Because they are irrelevant to the real needs people are facing today. Because they wouldn't help our congregation. Because everyone would leave!

That's the whole point.

Since we all readily admit we are selective about what passages we teach—we aren't planning any sermon series from 1 Chronicles 1–9— my encouragement is to be more selective than you already are. *Be consistent with your already existing beliefs that not all the Bible should be taught equally to all people.*

Would you teach Romans 9–11 to five-year-olds? Or Ezekiel 40–48 in the New Believers class? Of course not. They are the wrong parts of the Bible to teach to those audiences.

See how selective you already are? This maxim isn't trying to convince you to be selective; it's trying to help you be even more selective. Since some amount of selectivity is wise, could even more be more wise? Could selecting the right message for this audience at this time help your ministry of teaching?

Just take a moment, like I have, and ask the average person who sits in our churches and schools, "Do you feel most preaching and teaching is relevant to your needs?" Less than 20 percent of those I ask say yes. The other 80 percent feel like we are teaching 1 Chronicles 1–9 to them.

But we teachers blame our students for not paying attention. We preachers blame our congregation for not wanting "good preaching" anymore. In reality, they are screaming for good preaching. They are pleading for preaching that is good—for them! It's what meets their real needs.

Believe it or not, the Bible does not have a need to be taught. Only people have a need to be taught, *and it is their real need that should determine our teaching and preaching calendar.*

If you sense I feel strongly about this, you have sensed correctly. Because I have my ear to the ground across the country, I am aware of the widespread frustration that exists in students.

The teacher is off teaching about something that is useless to life—and doesn't make the link that at that moment he is also useless to his students. The preacher is off preaching about something irrelevant to his congregation—and won't realize that the declining attendance is proof that he's missed the mark so many times, his sheep have left for greener pastures. They were starved and went in search of food.

We must open our eyes, we must open our hearts, we must open our ears to Jesus' command to all who would teach and preach—*"Feed my sheep!"* When you obey that command, the sheep stay and grow and bear lambs. Your class grows. Word gets around that if you are hungry, there's good grazing up the street.

Meeting real needs is the teacher's primary calling. If we would ever fully understand and apply this one principle, our classes would never be the same. They would be relevant. According to those who must listen to us, most of our lessons are irrelevant; they are not fitting, not suitable, not pertinent, and not applicable. They don't fit our students' needs.

Many teachers think, "It's my responsibility to teach the Word, and it's God's responsibility to make it relevant. It's not our worry if the subject we've selected is relevant, it's God's. Just pick any passage and preach it. Just pick any truth and teach it. Somehow, God will fix it."

What is the correct starting point of preaching and teaching? Most would say that the Bible is the starting place—just preach it and it will be relevant. Start with the content and somehow it will help the students. See the order: First, the content; second, the need.

This order is backward! Just preaching the passage and hoping it will meet needs is like the pastor who walks up to the pulpit and lets the Bible fall open to wherever it may, trusting God to speak through him wherever it opens. How many of us would advise that approach?

Is this traditional way of thinking about subject selection correct?

Did Jesus Christ start with His content and then look for someone to listen to Him, or did He start with the needs of His followers and then teach the truth about that need? Almost without exception, Jesus taught in response to the apparent or hidden need of His audience. *Jesus started with their need.*

Did the apostle Paul write the letters of the New Testament merely because he had some interesting things to say? He wanted to teach some doctrine and wrote it in a book? Hardly. Paul wrote letter after letter in response to the needs of a congregation or person(s). *First the need, then the letter; first the problem, then the proclamation.*

Not only did Jesus and Paul start with the needs of their followers; so did the rest of the apostles. Check out Peter or James or John or Luke. They realized that the only reason for a ministry is the needs of their followers.

When they saw a need, that need set their agenda. They never came with an agenda and hoped it would meet a need. They realized that *the most important first step of lesson preparation is the selection of the correct subject.* They never could separate the two. But we certainly seem to try to.

Why can we separate the selection of the subject from the separation of the preparation of the passage? How can we be so determined to adequately prepare our content and yet so inadequately select our content?

Could it be that the incorrect subject perfectly prepared will still be the wrong message for our people? If my patient is dying of a rare kidney disease and I skillfully remove his gall bladder, have I helped him?

God has given us wisdom and discernment so that we can carefully choose the appropriate content for our class. Therefore, select your subject with much care! Select a subject that is suitable, pertinent, fitting, and applicable to your audience—something they would describe as eminently relevant. (The next chapter will show you how to select the subject that will hit home with your audience every time you teach.)

So what is our task, our calling? Need meeting is the teacher's primary calling.

Maxim 3: Need building is the teacher's main method to motivate students.

Classes and churches everywhere struggle with the problem of motivation. How do we smash complacency and blast boredom right out of the classroom? What is the secret of motivation?

The heart of motivation is *providing a need*. The teacher who motivates is the teacher who provides the need. If that need is an appropriate one, then it will automatically incite students to action. When boredom, apathy, and disinterest reign in the classroom, it's the teacher's fault. The teacher has not done her job of "providing the need" to her students.

Is building the need difficult? Does it take a lot of time? In most cases it takes less than two minutes. It took Jesus 116 words with the woman at the well—just over a hundred words to motivate her to seek her Savior.

Copy Christ. Use your words to build the need. Be extravagant, if you wish, and use twice the number He did—it will take you only four minutes.

If you want to catch a fish, bait your hook.

If you want motivated students, build the need.

Maxim 4: Need motivates to the degree it is felt by the student.

This is the second half of the secret of how all master teachers motivate their students. They know that need is primarily felt.

When you seek to serve your students by building their need, remember that *you must touch their feelings*. They must be moved to be motivated. When you provide the need, you must provide it in such a way that the need is felt.

You must build the need from the unconscious to the conscious. You must build and build until that need finally breaks into the consciousness of your students. When you build the need you are bringing it out into the open.

One of the universal laws of all the communication is that the deeper the student feels the need to learn, the more he will be motivated to learn—and ultimately, the more he will learn.

The first step must be to light a fire in the heart of the student. He must want to learn. He must desire to learn. He must feel intense longing to learn.

Those feelings must be aroused by the teacher for the student before the content is actually revealed. Lead the class to chase your content like Jesus did to the woman at the well. Wouldn't it be incredible to be able to create such hunger for learning that your students pull the lesson out of you rather than you trying to push it into them?

Master teachers know how to motivate any audience at any time on any subject. How can they do that? They know the seven universal motivators that are presented in the next chapter, and they use them masterfully. All the time.

How many do you know? Can you list them? Do you know how to use them? Or have you decided that motivating students is something that happens by chance—you just have to wait and see what develops? Have you decided that you just don't have the charisma or personality to motivate your students?

I hope you've not decided either of those, because neither is the truth. The truth is those universal motivators work for everyone, every time. I had a couple of teachers in college and graduate school who used them consistently when they taught. Their classes were full to bursting with students. Every class session they motivated us incredibly.

Some of your students—perhaps those 80 percent who say their classes are incredibly boring—may be hoping, even praying, that you'll discover those universal motivators.

But perhaps you're the exception. Perhaps your students would say the opposite about your class. Then you don't need to read any further.

Leave the universal motivators to be studied on a rainy day. But for those who desire to know how to "incite" their students, I'll outline those motivators in the Need Maximizers.

Maxim 5: Need building always precedes new units of content.

Carl F. H. Henry, one of the greatest living Christian scholars, once said, "I had a good philosophy teacher who refused to give us answers until we literally hurt with the questions." Unless your class is dying for the answer, don't give it to them.

Isn't it interesting that Jesus said, "Follow Me and I will make you fishers of men"? In fly fishing you get thigh deep in a brook or a lake, and you start flicking your line and letting more and more of it out until you've let out about twenty or thirty feet of line. Then you pick a promising spot, maybe one beneath a ledge or a tree, and you just flick the surface with your lure. You don't let the fly sink; you just want to get the attention of the fish.

"What was that?" asks a fish.

"I don't know. It's gone," says another.

"Next time it's mine."

So you lay your fly down, again and again. All the time the fish are saying, "I want that, I want that. It looks so good. I hope it comes back again." Finally one can't resist and bites.

Your class should never know you're building need. They should never say, "He's motivating me for the lesson." The adept fisherman hides the hook. The more adept the teacher is, the more that class is thinking, "Boy, I can't wait to hear that. I really need this."

As you progress through your lesson, be careful to build the need for each unit of content before teaching it. You can lose your students when they sense your content is irrelevant to them.

Jesus did that with the woman at the well. She didn't want to know about salvation; she wanted some water. So what did Jesus say? "Before I give you the answer to your need of salvation, I am going to help you want it."

When's the last time you helped your students want the answer you were going to give them? An ounce of need building is worth a pound of content because *content is useless unless your learners are prepared to receive it.*

I think that's why Paul, inspired by the Holy Spirit, spends three chapters in the book of Romans talking about sin before he moves on to salvation. By the end of those three chapters he has demolished every self-justification for goodness you could come up with. You're begging for relief! Only then does he lay out the solution.

You can use the same principle in witnessing. Unless the person you're talking with senses his need for Christ, there's no reason to explain the solution. He's not ready for it. You have to focus on his need, prove it from Scripture, until he finally faces up to the fact and says something like, "Oh no! I have no hope—I'm going to hell!" At that point you could say, "The Bible teaches that there's a way to avoid that— but I don't suppose you'd be interested in finding out what that is." If you've learned the secret of building the need before giving the goods, that person will be highly motivated to learn the answer!

There are four distinct situations in which you should build the need.

1. *Build the need at the beginning of each new series.* Any time you start a major new unit (quarter, semester, series), care- fully explain the benefits the student will enjoy by attending. The more meaningfully you build the need now, the less you will have to build it later. Clear the pre- sentations of the need "hook" the student for the whole term so that he won't want to miss any part of it.

2. *Build the need at the beginning of each lesson.* Don't take for granted that the student remembers or even attended when the general need-building session was presented.

Usually a student enters class with blurred vision as to the benefits of what he's about to hear. Refocus the student's attention on the value of each lesson in order to ensure maximum learning.

3. *Build the need during class for the next class.* Help the student anticipate the reward for attendance and attention at the next class.

4. *Resurface the need any time you sense interest waning, motivation sagging, or apathy increasing.* Remember, your primary weapon to combat an unmotivated class is your sword of need building!

Maxim 6: Need should be built according to the audience's characteristics and circumstances.

To build need for your content, you must know your audience well. Be aware of your students' personal characteristics and circumstances.

Many factors contribute to selecting the appropriate need to build on. The need-building devices used for three-year-olds, thirteen-year-olds, thirty-year-olds, and sixty-year-olds vary greatly. Age largely determines the appropriate methods available for need building.

In addition, the preexisting interest of a group greatly determines the appropriate methods. Have you ever tried to teach a class where all the students are forced to attend against their will? The teacher must strategize the need building differently than if students attend of their own will or paid to learn something they are desperate to know.

You must get to know your students' characteristics and circumstances. Age is obvious, but what about occupations, social involvement, hobbies, and personality traits?

If you're teaching four-year-olds, do you know how you build needs? "You know, boys and girls," you say, "inside this bag I have the biggest cookies you've ever seen. I'm going to give these big, chewy, chocolate chip cookies away. But not just to anybody. I'm going to tell you a story and to the boys or girls who sit the quietest, I'm going to give a great big cookie. Now, who wants a cookie?"

Should you bribe little kids to pay attention? Absolutely! No doubt about it. With four-year-olds, never motivate with words only unless you have to. Adults can cope with just words, though even then there's some question. Do you care for a cookie?

Maxim 7: Need building may be hindered by factors beyond the teacher's control.

The teacher must be sensitive to internal or external factors that will hinder students' motivation. As much as possible, the teacher should deal with those factors, realizing that occasionally he must yield to them.

Generally, the principles that govern the teaching-learning process are similar to the laws governing nature. For instance, hold a lit match to a piece of paper and it will catch fire. It doesn't take a prophet to predict that if that procedure is duplicated a hundred times, the paper will burn a hundred times.

Similarly, if you build the need appropriately, you can expect your class to respond 100 percent of the time. The motivated class isn't a secret—some teachers have a motivated class every single time. Still, it is true that occasionally you may have followed those basic steps and discovered to your dismay that the paper wouldn't light. There are exceptions to general rules:

Rule: Paper burns 100 percent of the time when lit by a match.
Exception: Wet paper doesn't burn.
Exception: Dry paper doesn't burn without sufficient oxygen.

In teaching, proper need-building activities will result in a corresponding student motivation to learn. But there are a few "wet paper" rules. Let's consider the two basic categories of factors that hinder the need-building process.

External Factors

If your air conditioning is broken and the temperature in the classroom rises to 98 degrees, it may be hard to get your students to concentrate. A crying baby or other distraction may cause you to lose your whole audience.

If you're trying to build need and you keep failing, there may be some exceptions at work. The law still works, but some external factor may be working against you. You'll have to reestablish the need—seize their attention again, and go on from there. Your job is to keep ownership of the students' attention and motivation by building their need for your lesson.

Internal Factors

How can you discern when you have a problem with internal distractions? Notice your students' body language—folded arms, slouched posture, impatient or disgusted looks, low groans, and high-pitched shrieks can all be clues. Negative or reactionary comments are another sign. Those signals indicate your students have an inner conflict between the need you are trying to build and another conviction, perhaps a wrong one.

How effective would you be at building the need in a high school Sunday school class for witnessing at school when the majority of the youth aren't committed to a godly lifestyle and doubt that the Bible is true? Try building the need to sacrifice financially for the missions budget when the people disagree with how the money is being spent.

An internal struggle erupts whenever we try to build the audience's need in an area that conflicts with another established conviction or commitment. This internal struggle may be mild or intense depending on any of three factors:

1. How far apart your area of need building is from their present conviction.
2. How intensely and emotionally you are building the need.
3. How rapidly you transitioned through the five stages of need building that we will discover in the next chapter.

New Christians will skip all those stages when sharing their new-found faith with close friends and family. They try to get their loved ones to commit to Christ before they show He's the answer to the problem of sin. No wonder they experience such violent reactions to their witnessing.

But there are other types of internal hindrances that get your students' insides churning. What if in the early service your beloved pastor of fifteen years resigned unexpectedly and left everyone in shock? Or perhaps you are the senior high Sunday school teacher and the home team lost the championship game at 11:30 on Saturday night—by one point? Maybe a student is distraught because his parents are divorcing, or he's absorbed by a major project for another class.

One of my students in college continually fell asleep. I would pump up my delivery and work hard at building the need for this one young man, but to no avail. Finally I talked to him privately and discovered he had taken a night job because his wife was having a difficult pregnancy and could no longer work. Sometimes you might have to let a student sleep!

What should you do if you follow the standard steps to motivate your students and nothing happens? First, try the obvious: Bring the match closer to the paper and hold it there a little longer. That is, raise the intensity of your delivery and extend your attempt by a few moments. If the situation does not change after that, you've either got "wet paper" or "no oxygen," and you need to find a different strategy.

The underlying cause of the disruption lies somewhere along a universal hierarchy of needs that range from most important to least important. Physical needs—food, water, air—take precedence. Second are safety and security needs—organization, protection, health. Third are social needs, and so on down the line. If the need you're attempting to meet isn't working, there probably is another, higher need at work in your students.

So what do you do? Here are a couple of options:

Don't worry about it. After all, it's their problem. Besides, you need to move ahead and finish covering your material. So just continue teaching without their attention. (If you picked this option, please turn back to chapter 1 of this book and begin reading again.)

If possible, stop and meet the more pressing need, then return to your lesson. If they're asleep, have them stand up and stretch; if they're hot, open the window.

If it's a more serious matter, stop and acknowledge the tension. First, tell your students you sense something unusual is happening in class. Surface the issue either by general discussion or more direct means, such as asking one of your more vocal students to fill you in. Then ask the students' permission to postpone (set aside) their agenda and permit you to accomplish the purposes you have established for the class.

If their need is more of a dramatic nature, consider postponing your lesson and spending the time instead meeting their need. This requires you to weigh the importance of their needs—the one consuming your students, or the one you wanted to address. Ask your students' assistance in making the day's class meaningful in the midst of trying or difficult circumstances.

One time my college students were having a major exam in the next class period and they were all tense. I said, "You really are under pressure of that next class, aren't you? I tell you what—if you give me forty of the next fifty-five minutes, I'll let you study for the last fifteen. Is it a deal?" It worked. So ask permission. Treat your students as adults who have their own needs.

Whenever you feel your class will allow it, return to the need-building stage you left. Relax, slow your pace, deformalize your body language, and reestablish control. Sometimes interruptions can give opportunities to teach a truth more personally and intimately. If you sense the Spirit is using the interruption, minister to your class directly on the subject. Perhaps a few moments in prayer would be the best use of class time.

One time a fellow student had just been killed and the whole class heard about it between classes. We stopped, talked about it, and prayed for the family and friends. We never did get back to the lesson I had planned, but who would have learned it that day anyway?

It's foolish to continue pushing content when a more basic need is controlling your students. "Yes, but I have to finish my lesson!" Why? Lessons don't have needs. People have needs. And the purpose for teaching is to meet your students' needs, whatever they are.

MEANING

The essence of the Law of Need is these three words: "Build the need." The teacher should build the need before teaching the content.

CONCLUSION

The teacher should surface the students' real need before teaching the content.

The Law of Need draws on a basic truth of human nature: We all are motivated by our needs. Since teaching is best accomplished when students are motivated to learn, we'd better make sure their needs are involved or we'll find ourselves dangling a beautiful bare hook in the water.

In many ways, the need-building stage of teaching is similar to the role of advertising in marketing. Ads have one purpose—to entice the consumer to buy the product. The billions of dollars spent in advertising each year indicate it must be having some effect.

It worked on my family. I took a moment to list the drugs in our medicine cabinet, then drove to our nearby drugstore and asked the pharmacist if I could have purchased the same products any cheaper. He laughed and said I could have saved 40 to 50 percent by buying generic versions instead of the name-brand drugs.

This "fish" selected certain national brands over generic versions because I chose to. No one forced me. I bit. I paid 40 percent more because someone knew how to build my sense of need through advertising.

Now there's nothing inherently wrong with trying to motivate another person to do what you want. I did it when I asked my wife to marry me. I do it when pleading with a non-Christian to believe and receive our wonderful Lord Jesus Christ. Since we teach the very Word of God, which is able to save our souls and bring us into the rich inheritance of Christ, how much more should we help others buy into the life of faith than those who sell dog food, frozen yogurt, and hamburgers?

The teacher of a Sunday school class Darlene and I attended recently did a nice job describing the temple in Ezekiel, but I sensed he was not aware of some of the problems in the group. After class I told him what a nice job he'd done and how much we learned. Then I said, "Are you aware of some of the problems in the class?"

"What do you mean?" he asked.

"Well, that couple over there, for example. Their daughter's in the hospital with anorexia and is down to less than a hundred pounds. They haven't solved the problem yet. And this couple over here—he lost his job eight months ago, and they're in the midst of losing their home. And the couple over there—his father just died; his mother has Parkinson's disease and has moved in with them, and they are both at the end of their rope." I went around the room and named the major problem in each couple's home.

"I had no idea the church was filled with problems like that—especially not in my class," he said.

"How did today's class help them?" I asked, and watched his face as the light went on.

"Oh…I doubt it helped very much."

"If one of those couples had come over to your home last evening and told you their problem, would you have gotten out your Bible and taken them to Ezekiel's temple?"

"Of course not," he laughed.

"Why not?"

"Because I would have seen that their problem is dealt with biblically elsewhere, and I'd try to help them with the appropriate Scripture."

"Then why don't you do that when you get up to teach Sunday school?"

Friends, let us today commit ourselves to meeting our students' real needs. This is not a commitment to make lightly. True teaching is sacrificial. Often you'll find yourself having to lay aside your own needs in order to meet the needs of others. But that's what it's all about, isn't it?

May students jam your classroom because they know every week you will feed them food that satisfies—the real meat from the Word of God.

DISCUSSION QUESTIONS

1. What percentage of teachers that you had as a student regularly "built the need" before teaching the content? Why do you think the percentage is so low? What difference would it have made if they had built the need first?

2. Contrast the "felt need" and the "real need" of the students. List five of the felt needs of your students and five of the real ones. Which kind have you dealt with most during the past year and why?

3. Do you think most teachers realize that their primary calling is to meet their students' real needs? If they don't, what do they usually think is their calling? Describe the differences their students would see if they truly taught to meet real needs.

4. Maxim 3 states that the teacher's main method to motivate students is to build the need. Read the story of Jesus and Nicodemus in John 3 and describe how Jesus built his need. Do you think Jesus was aware of building Nicodemus's need? If He was, what implications does that have for the next time you teach?

5. God is the Master of all master teachers. He is so committed to you and me that He promised to "supply all your need according to His riches in glory by Christ Jesus" (Philippians 4:19). Whether we know it or not, God has been actively seeking to meet our needs all of the time. If we interviewed Him about you, what main need would He say He's been teaching you about the past year, and how has He created your need?

CHAPTER TEN

Need

Method and Maximizers

T hese particular trout are very difficult to catch," he said. "They suck in your fly, sense the hook, and immediately spit it out. You have to set the hook in that split second or he's gone. Do you think you can do that?"

"Of course," I replied. After all, hadn't I caught all kinds of fish in lakes, ponds, and the ocean? Trout fishing in the Colorado mountains would be a snap.

The guide continued his instructions. "If you cast over there and let your fly float downstream about twenty or thirty feet, you'll probably get a few bites."

I did as he said. But nothing happened. Within seconds he said, "You missed one." And a moment later, "There, you missed another one."

"What on earth are you talking about?" I hadn't felt or seen anything.

"You don't believe a couple of trout actually bit your hook, do you?" I guess he couldn't miss my look of skepticism.

"Let me have your pole and I'll show you what I mean." On the next cast he caught a big ol' trout right where my fly had been. I couldn't believe my eyes.

Over and over again our trusty guide worked with us. He would encourage us by saying, "It's in the feel of the pole and the fly's movement in the water—you've got to learn to tempt the trout!"

Nonetheless, hours went by without my catching a fish, and I was beginning to lose hope. Then all of a sudden I began to catch those trout, right where we had fished earlier. I could now "feel" the river. Everything he said began to click. What a thrill!

Later that afternoon a young teenager, carrying a large red and yellow tackle box, climbed down the bank where we were fishing. We smiled encouragingly. But then he took out some large lures used to catch bass and even saltwater fish, but certainly not trout. Our guide worked his way up to the young kid and began to instruct him that those lures didn't appeal to trout, but a certain kind of fly did.

That young man told the guide to get lost. He'd fish with his favorite lures and he'd catch the fish just like he did back home.

Soon our guide led us around the bend to a different patch of water that moved much more swiftly. He began to search through his fishing vest for a particular fly. He smiled when he found a couple of them. "These flies are the only ones I know that will catch the trout in this section of the river. I made them last night just for this spot. They're heavy enough to sink into that strong current—and they'll tempt those trout every time."

He was right. We changed flies and immediately started catching larger trout. After a while we returned to where that young man was fishing. He hadn't caught any fish yet and was obviously frustrated.

"Stupid fish!" he exclaimed. "They just aren't biting. I hate fishing."

Our guide was a master fisherman. As the afternoon passed and we paid close attention to his instruction and his example, we slowly became more and more effective trout fishermen. Just as he'd said, it's all in the *right lure* on the end of your string and the *right action* on the pole. The fish are always there and can always be caught—if you know how.

If you'll close your tackle box for a moment and permit me to be your teacher/fishing guide, I'd like to share with you how to be a fisher of men in the classroom. During the Need Method, I'll discuss the way to select the correct *lure* to catch your fish, and then in the Need Maximizers, the optimum *action* on your pole to set that hook.

In reality, however, fishing for men is a lot easier than fishing for trout. Not only are they a lot easier to see, but in almost every case, they won't run away until after the entire hour has been spent trying to catch them!

Master fishers of men that I know seem to catch their whole class, every class session. They have mastered the skill of selecting the correct lure and then guiding the correct action with their pole.

And for those of you who insist it's those "stupid students" who "just won't pay attention"—well, it may be time to put away your lures and close that red and yellow tackle box. The truth is that the fish are hungry. And you just missed one. And another.

NEED METHOD

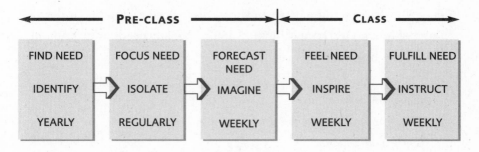

Step 1: Find the Needs

Since our primary responsibility is to meet the students' needs through a tailored presentation of content, the first step is almost too obvious. The teacher must "*find the needs*" of his audience and clearly "*identify*" them, usually in a major way "*yearly.*"

My research, however, shows that the average teacher doesn't know his audience's needs. When asked to list the top ten needs of their class, most teachers are 80 percent off the mark—they only know two out of ten! No wonder classes around the world are so lacking; we are trying to catch our fish with the wrong lure. Our lures are irrelevant and uninteresting to our students.

I wonder—can you list the top ten needs of your class in order of importance? Just think how valuable it would be to have a list of all the major needs in your audience. Never again would you have to wonder if your lesson would be meaningful to your audience.

You can uncover your students' needs in the following three ways: Direct method, indirect method, and need inventory.

1. Direct Methods to Find the Need

It's the rare person who can merely look at an audience and list its needs. One reason is that the American public has become expert at wearing the "I'm fine" mask.

Don't forget those masks. Life isn't usually what it appears to be. Unlike the Lone Ranger, the mask isn't our best friend but our worst enemy. It drives wedges between friends who need each other. It derails those of us who teach into thinking no one has any needs or that no one would like help with their needs.

Don't be fooled by me.
Don't be fooled by the face I wear.
For I wear a mask.

I wear a thousand masks—
Masks that I'm afraid to take off,
And none of them are me.
Pretending is an art
That is second nature to me,
But don't be fooled...
Please don't be fooled.

I give you the impression
That I'm secure.
That all is sunny
And unruffled with me
Within as well as without.
That confidence is my name.
Coolness is my game,
And that I'm in charge
And that I need no one.

But don't believe me.
My surface may seem smooth,
But my surface is my mask,
My ever varying
And ever concealing mask...

Who am I?
Who am I, you may wonder?
I am someone you know very well.
I am every person you will ever meet.

—Anonymous

Years ago I was speaking at a conference for young people. After the second day I said to those in charge, "There are a lot of drugs in this group." They denied it. "Let's see," I said. The next night I preached on drugs and asked the kids to bring up their drugs and pills and dump them out on the stage. We collected quite a pile. The most shocked people in the room were the leaders who didn't have a handle on the real needs of their group. They were teaching subjects that were so far off the mark that it amazed me that even one person paid attention.

The direct method surfaces the facts without an intervening agency or step. Ask your class yourself! Teachers always seem to be amazed at how open the average student is when approached in a personal, nonthreatening manner. You not only hear the answers right from the student's mouth, but you also benefit by sensing how important a given area is by his intensity and emotion. It's not uncommon that the student will unknowingly reveal other needs you could not have imagined. So be aware of the messages between the words.

Listed below are six primary vehicles for searching for your audience's needs. Use those best fitted to your personality, class, and circumstances.

Direct questions. When the situation is casual and relaxed, ask your need-seeking questions directly. Here are a few ideas.

"Betty, I value your wisdom and insight and wonder if you could help me be a more effective teacher by telling me what you think the three biggest problems are that people like you face today."

"John, I'm concerned that our class meet the needs of its members. Could you help me by giving two or three areas in your life that you wish we would address in the future?"

"Mr. Smith, what topics would you like to see taught during next quarter's classes?"

Open-ended questions allow the student to be as personal as he wishes. People will respond to a sincerely asked question, especially when the teacher asks for help. Remove the threat and fear factor. Develop the regular habit of asking good questions and you'll be amazed how soon you have the right answers!

Low-key interviews. This method is less difficult than the first in that you don't ask questions directly or personally, but instead ask about general class needs:

> "Martha, I noticed that our class seems to be feeling pressure lately. What do you think some of the reasons may be?"

> "Frank, your kids are really growing up! How old are they now? What are the struggles kids their age seem to be facing these days?"

> "Mr. and Mrs. Smith, did you happen to see the article on the front page of Sunday's paper reporting that Americans have never had more personal debt than today? How do you think debt is creating hardships for families in their midforties?"

What a natural way to uncover the thoughts and feelings of your class! Low-key interviews can capture significant and practical insights that will give your content timeliness and personal interest.

Anonymous questionnaire. This is a most effective vehicle. A questionnaire can be controlled, involves more people than you could personally talk to, and asks questions on a variety of subjects. The key to its effectiveness hinges on three conditions.

First, the audience must know both the purpose and its ultimate use. Is it for teacher's eyes only, or will the results be announced and discussed? Be aware that the latter purpose may reduce honesty.

Second, the audience must be convinced of the anonymity of the questionnaire. Any hint that they could be found out will tilt the response.

Third, the questions must be carefully constructed so that the responses present a true picture. The questions are as important as the answer.

Frequently I'll distribute blank three-by-five cards with the following open-ended questions and instruct the class to answer anonymously:

- The biggest problem I struggle with at work is…
- Whenever my spouse and I get into arguments, it's usually about…
- My biggest personal disappointment during the past few years was…
- My greatest triumph as a person is…
- When I get angry with God, it's usually because…
- When I get to heaven, my biggest insight about what I should have been doing will be…
- If somebody could give me one good piece of advice about how to raise my kids, it would be about…
- Probably the area of my spiritual life that causes me the most problems is…
- Rate your Christian walk on a scale of 1–10. The one area in my Christian life where I stumble the most is…
- The sin I seem to wrestle with and rarely have victory over is…
- On a scale of 1–10, how honest were you in answering these questions?

Spend a few hours with those cards—they represent a gold mine of need. Quickly you will be able to identify the top ten needs in areas such as your students' work, family, and spiritual growth. Write those top ten needs in the back of your Bible. Aim each class at one of the top three felt needs. Never again will you have to wonder if a lesson will hit the mark.

Remember the pastor who taught the book of Galatians for two years and still was only in chapter 2? Over lunch he asked me what he should do. I told him about the anonymous questionnaire.

"I can't do that on Sunday morning," he said.

"You can if you want," I replied. "If you care about your people enough to know, you can."

"They'll never tell me."

"Yes, they will, if you promise to rip up the cards and throw them away when you're done."

"Okay, so I do the questionnaire. What then?"

"When you preach next Sunday, take a break from Galatians and preach God's answer to problem number one. Call me and let me know what happens."

My friend passed out the questionnaire and called me Sunday afternoon, before he even preached his next sermon.

"Bruce, I did that thing with the questionnaire."

"What happened?"

"*I wept all afternoon. Bruce, I had no idea what was really going on in my congregation. I can't believe how out of touch I've been!*"

"Pastor, have you looked back over your past sermons?"

"It shocked me—I haven't hit one of the top three felt needs in more than a year."

"So what are you going to do about it?"

"I'm going to take the top need, and next Sunday morning and next Sunday night I'm preaching God's answer to that problem."

He called me a week later. "Bruce, in all my years of ministry, I've never ever had a response from my people like this. On my way out, people who rarely shook my hand were hugging me, thanking me. There were tears in their eyes. They were saying, 'Thanks, Pastor. That's exactly what I needed.'"

"Are you going back to Galatians?"

"Not right away!"

Friends, what are you preaching this Sunday? What are you teaching? What percentage of couples in your church are having problems in their marriages? What percentage of parents are overwhelmed and don't know how to rear their children to have Christian values? It's far more than half. If that's true, what are you doing about it? You're not teaching a twenty-week series about Ezekiel's temple, are you?

Interaction with family members. There are two ways to approach this: (1) comments by the student about his family; and (2) comments by the family about the student.

Vague, general, and open-ended questions about a student's family can reveal volumes to the discerning listener. How many needs can you uncover in the life of thirty-year-old Stan?

Q: "Stan! It's great to see you again! Is Judy still treating you like a king now that you've been married ten years?"

A: "Are you kidding? Judy is so wrapped up in selling real estate that she's never around anymore."

Q: "Busy, eh? Well, that second income must be great with the bills we all have to face these days."

A: "Not a chance. We have more bills than ever! Judy had to buy a second car. Can you believe it? I never knew that marriage could be so hard."

Q: "Oh, hello, Mary [Stan's ten-year-old daughter]. I've just been talking to your dad and he tells me your mom's real busy these days. Have you become the cook yet?"

A: "Nope, Dad hired a maid. Now all he does is watch football and eat pizza. Besides, I don't miss my mom much anyway..."

If you know how to read the signs, you may have recognized half a dozen needs reflected in this one-minute conversation—some of them quite serious. The real secret to this method lies in your ability to provide an acceptable, appropriate, and safe environment in which people can reveal their needs.

Personal visits to the student's home or work. The best insights are frequently obtained through a brief, personal visit to a person's home or place of employment. It's the only real way to walk in someone else's shoes. Today's classrooms are so unnatural and structured that students seldom reveal their true selves. We have to look elsewhere for glimpses of reality. Home is where our masks crumble and where needs lie right on the surface. Attitudes, atmosphere, frame of mind, harmony or disharmony, order or disorder, all are apparent to those who care enough to look.

One of the delights of my life was to serve on the board of the Fellowship of Companies for Christ for many years.[1] Composed of more than seven hundred companies from across the country, FCC trained presidents and owners to lead companies with Christian principles and procedures. Over the years I became good friends with quite a few owners of companies, whose corporate annual sales ranged from $25,000 to over $100 million. And whenever we chatted, the subject of local churches always came up.

Although these men were deeply committed Christians and solidly supported their churches, they constantly expressed disappointment that the pastor and Sunday school teacher seldom communicated what the Bible teaches about how to live as a Christian in business. Until FCC began, most of those men had surmised that the Bible didn't speak to the needs of the marketplace!

One memorable evening I probed a little deeper. Why did they think the situation was so prevalent? Immediately one of the men said he thought his pastor didn't even know the problems and challenges his people faced. The others agreed. Then I asked why they thought that was so. "Because the pastor never bothered to ask!" All eight of them said the pastor never visited their companies in all their years of membership to find out.

You can't meet a need if you don't know what is. If you want to know your students, look behind the doors of their homes and offices.

Personal observation. This method focuses upon those clues which are available during all of life. At least five arenas could be noticed:

First, the questions people ask in and after class reflect areas of inner interest and need.

Second, body language speaks so loudly it often can be heard above spoken words. Arms folded, hands over mouth, body slouched, torso leaning aggressively forward—all carry loud messages.

Third, class attendance is probably the most direct indicator of how well you meet the needs of your audience. People's presence or absence clearly denotes what they think of your class. The more helpful the class, the more people will come for help!

Fourth, class discussions reflect needs which require further consideration. Whenever students try to keep the ball rolling on a given subject, you know you've hit oil.

Fifth, after-class activities and conversations mirror the true interests and concerns of your class because they are neither required nor structured.

Those are the major, direct methods of finding the needs of your students. But don't forget some valuable indirect methods you can also use to get a good feel for the relevant issues.

2. Indirect Methods to Find the Need

Unlike the direct approach, which puts you face-to-face with your audience, the indirect approach offers valuable information through other people's research and experience. Although the information will frequently give you solid and dependable insights, it must be evaluated carefully as it does not deal specifically with your class.

Collect information around two basic frameworks: (1) topics that you know most interest your class; and (2) characteristics of the age group of your class members, noting their problems and trends.

There are many available sources for this information, but here are a few of the primary ones:

Books. Standard psychology, child development, and Christian education books usually survey the main characteristics, problems, and interests of all ages and are a ready reference. Regularly browsing the shelves in your Christian and secular bookstores gives a snapshot of the bestselling books, and therefore conveys where the current interests and needs lie. Ask the store manager what trends he's seeing and what types of books people in your class's age bracket are purchasing.

At the time I was writing this book, the top four bestsellers were about money, business, sex, and health. When is the last time you taught on money, business, sex, or health?

A friend of mine who pastors one of our country's largest churches began to notice a recurring theme in his counseling sessions. People were questioning whether they married the right person. So he decided to preach on the subject. "Next week," he announced, "I'm preaching the answer to what happens if you think you married the wrong person." Word got out in the community, and next Sunday he had two thousand *visitors.* (That's right, two thousand!) Do you have a sense that he touched a real need?

Magazines and newspapers. Because the magazine industry is so consumer-oriented and must meet the ever-changing interests of the American public, it frequently presents a panorama of the needs of your targeted audiences. Pay close attention to the types of articles they feature as well as the types of books they review and advertise.

Skim through some magazines like *Today's Christian Woman, Christianity Today, Guideposts,* and *Discipleship Journal.* On the secular side, scan *USA Today, U.S. News & World Report, Time, Newsweek, Reader's*

Digest, Ladies Home Journal, People, and *Good Housekeeping.* Many of these magazines include valuable articles, surveys, and Q&A columns. Remember, people only read what they are interested in. And whether or not you agree with advice columnists, keep a close eye on the subjects they repeat or for which they receive overwhelming responses. They're not the most-read journalists in America by accident.

Want a real eye-opener? Take any well-known magazine and look at the Q&A section. Those are the questions people are really asking. Next Sunday, teach God's answer to those questions. I guarantee you nobody will move.

Research studies and polls. George Gallup and George Barna frequently conduct polls to establish the true feelings and positions of the public on myriad subjects.

Individuals interacting with the public. Doctors, dentists, barbers and beauticians, counselors, psychologists, guidance counselors, police, teachers, principals, and a host of others have their fingers on the public pulse and can be interviewed about the trends they see. I make it a practice to ask such "pulse people" about the problems they see on the rise.

3. Develop a Need Inventory for Your Class

After you complete your initial investigation, organize the information into a usable form: the true diagnosis of your class summarized in order of priority on one piece of paper.

There are as many ways to arrange your findings as there are people. The most basic is to list the top ten needs in priority from top to bottom. Here are a few other formats:

By key need areas. List everything you surfaced under such topics as temptation, sin, problems, fears, anxieties, inadequacies, and disappointments. List the top sins, then the top fears, and so on.

By time references. List the needs according to those your class has faced, is currently facing, and will face. This method encourages some preventive medicine. If your students are high school seniors, teaching about handling college will be right on target.

By the roles we play. Arrange the needs by the different titles we hold, including husband/wife, father/mother, lover, provider, friend, boss, employee, child, parent, grandfather/grandmother, grandson/granddaughter, friend, Christian, teacher, counselor. What are the five largest needs of wives, of employees, and so on?

By the major categories of life. Categorize the needs under such headings as physical, emotional, intellectual, moral, spiritual, and financial.

Whatever the method, find a way to arrange the information so you find it practical and easily usable. This document will be invaluable. Seeing the real needs of your students on a single sheet of paper will direct and motivate your teaching as never before.

Do this at least once a year. It's the foundation upon which this whole law rests. If you don't find the need, you can't do the rest of the steps in the Need Method. You'll continue to use the wrong lures, and no matter how hard you try, you'll not be successful at catching fish.

Step 2: Focus the Need

In this step you look at all the needs you've discovered and "*focus the need*" to "*isolate*" one to deal with in your lesson. This step needs to be done "*regularly*" depending upon the length of the series.

This is a critical step. If you've done your survey right, you will have uncovered many critical needs and hurts. The following quotes are not at all uncommon:

> "My husband refuses to let me participate in any money decisions. I think he may be hiding it in case we get divorced. What should I do?"

> "I'm considering declaring bankruptcy. What does God think about that?"

"There's no passion in our sex life. When my wife and I make love, she seems bored and in a hurry to get it over with. What right would she have to complain if I had an affair?"

"My doctor just told me I have a brain tumor and will soon lose my ability to take care of myself. I don't want to be a burden to my family. If I kill myself, will God forgive me?"

I don't care where you attend church in what part of the country or world—if you do that anonymous survey, you'll uncover needs just like these—tough, heartbreaking, vital needs.

But not all your needs are created equal. Some are more important than others. *Your job is to focus on the most important one first.* Keep it simple. Focus on only one need at a time. How do you choose the correct one? With careful thought and prayer.

While the first step of researching the various needs of your audience is to be done only once or twice a year, this step is needed every time you prepare for a new series. Unlike the first, which takes real time and effort, this step is easy and seldom very long.

The benefits of spending those few moments in focusing on the most important need cannot be overstated. Don't leave it to chance! Why spend your precious time preparing a great lesson on the wrong subject? What good is a beautiful bass lure to catch brook trout? At the end of this step, you will have selected the one primary need you are going to teach to meet during your next class or series.

Step 3: Forecast the Need

Steps 1 and 2 are concerned with how to select the correct lure to catch your students, and steps 4 and 5 effectively equip you to catch your students using that lure.

Just because you were discerning in the *selection of the correct lure* doesn't guarantee that you'll be effective in the *application of your lure.* The first skill has to do with the choice you make; the second, with the ability to use that choice.

Remember how I was initially unable to catch those trout, yet our expert fisherman hooked a fish using my pole and fly in the exact same spot I was fishing? He knew how to "play the river" in such a manner that the fly appealed to the trout. Mine must have looked like a hook trying to look like a fly. Didn't appeal to a single fish.

As a result of Step 2, you have the correct lure in your hand, but do you know what to do with it? Are you able to connect with your class? Or does your fly just float down the river—tasteless and boring to the students?

Step 3 is the vital link between the lure and the learner, between finding the correct need and helping the student feel how important that need is to them.

The best way to complete this step is to become one of your students for a moment and *"forecast what would happen if the need was met."* Use your *"imagination"* and step into their shoes and look at life from their point of view. Why should they desire this particular need to be met in their lives? What are the positive and negative reasons for chasing your lure and having this need fulfilled? Practice this each *"week"* you teach.

The essence of this forecast stage is to write a short list of the positive benefits and negative consequences that would occur in the lives of your students if they enjoyed success or if they suffered failure. Let's say that the need you've selected for your junior high boys' class is "obey your parents," and you wonder how to cause them to be vitally interested in your upcoming series, to deeply desire to attend and to listen.

Start by listing every possible good and bad thing that could result if you "obey your parents" or if you "disobey your parents." These two lists are the specifics you will use in the next step to cause your students to feel the need and desire to learn to obey their parents.

The positive always relates to pleasure and surfaces feelings of "I want..." The negative anticipates pain and surfaces feelings of "I don't want..." The crux of this step is the identification of a number of "want's" or "don't want's" that are immediately felt by your students. Motivation frequently comes from feelings that are based in the hope of pleasure and fear of pain. The more powerful or poignant the reasons are to have this need met, the better chance you will have in the next step to raise your students' feelings and motivation.

Three secrets lie behind effective forecasting. The first is to *survey your experience and imagination* to find possible examples of youth who do or do not obey their parents. Think through all the people you know directly or indirectly who either benefited or suffered as a result of their choices of obeying their parents. Consider the books you've read, the stories you've heard, the television programs you've seen. As you do, your list of the positives and negatives will grow easily and quickly. If you are experiencing difficulty at this point, then open your creativity and unleash your imagination—what are some of the things that could happen to a junior high student who obeys or disobeys his parents?

The second secret to successful forecasting is to employ the *principle of the extremes.* Think of the best that could happen to a junior high student if he obeyed and the worst that could happen if he disobeyed. Take your examples and push them to the extreme in both directions. You'll uncover a multitude of additional examples en route to the farthest limits. And when you identify the extremes, you'll have some great ideas to work with. Feelings are easiest to arouse when the most wonderful or the most terrible are considered. Intense desire comes from intense hope of pleasure or fear of pain.

The third secret to successful forecasting is to *picture the person* in your class who would most likely choose to obey to the fullest and the person who would most likely disobey to the maximum. When you have them selected, imagine yourself in their place when they experience the consequences of their choices. Get in touch with their future.

Forecast yourself as them, and through your imagination, identify and empathize what they'd experience as a result of their choices.

By practicing those three secrets to forecasting, you'll soon be able to think almost immediately of a number of key motivations you can use to arouse your students' feelings in such a way that they desire what you have planned to teach them.

Step 4: Feel the Need

You are finally ready to lead your students to *"feel their need"* for what you have selected to teach them. The first three stages are all preparatory and converge on this climactic moment. You now have prepared yourself and are ready to drop the lure in the water and begin to fish. How you work this bait in the classroom will determine whether or not your students chase the bait as the woman at the well did in response to Jesus' effective fishing (John 4). The key to step four is to *"inspire"* them emotionally as you build the need *"weekly."*

Never forget that it was because of Jesus' skill as the Master Fisherman that the woman sought the solution to her need. Likewise, the skill by which you work the lure in the classroom determines the interest and attention of the students.

A disinterested student is the result of an unskilled teacher. A bored student is also the result of an unskilled teacher. Whenever I hear a teacher complain about her "stupid and unmotivated students," I always know she put the wrong lure in the water or didn't use ample skill with that lure.

Never will I forget the day Glenn Alsworth flew his biplane onto the lake to pick up my son Dave and me from fishing in a remote Alaskan lake. We had fished all day and had lost most of our lures. Our extra pole had become jammed and we couldn't reel the line. We had a few big ones to show for our efforts but hadn't caught anything for the last two hours. Glenn said he had a few moments to spare, picked up the broken rod and reel, spotted a lure that had lost all of its feathers and had only a bare hook showing, and joined us in the water. I smiled to myself because I appreciated Glenn's gesture of kindness to give us a few more moments of fishing.

But then I noticed he was fishing in earnest. He held that pole as if it grew right out of his arm, and in the twenty minutes before we flew out, he caught his limit—on a bare hook, with a broken rod and reel, and with fish that "wouldn't bite."

How? He was a master fisherman. He knew how to make even that bare hook look incredibly alive to those shrewd fish who had all too successfully avoided our colorful lures for most of the day.

Can you catch your class on a bare hook? *You can if you know how.* If you know how to effectively work your lure, they will chase even the barest of hooks.

As a public speaker, I've been to many conventions in my life, and I've watched teachers chase students away time after time with perfect lures. And then I've seen master teachers come along with an assigned topic (which often was completely off target for the audience—the wrong lure) and through deft skill, lead the audience to desperately seek the message they had prepared. Before they even began their main points, the audience had decided that this message was going to be the one they needed most.

This fourth step isn't intellectual as much as emotional. Not fact but feeling. Not a transfer of information but a calling forth of interest. Emotion is the primary motivator. Therefore, emotion must be your primary context during this stage.

Consider the relationship between *"need"* and *"learning."* If the felt need is low, how much learning do you think will ordinarily take place? Not much. If your students identify strongly with the need, however, a great deal of motivation to learn will be present. Your students will pull it out of you. They will become like the woman at the well, full of the right questions all leading you to the next point in your outline. In the Need Maximizers, I'll identify the seven ways to help your audience really feel the need.

Step 5: Fulfill the Need

Now we've reached the goal you have been driving for. It's time to help your students *implement* the solution to their need through your content and applications. This last step is to "*fulfill the need*" you have been surfacing and "*instruct*" them on the content as you teach them each "*week*."

Have you ever sent away for something thinking it would be wonderful, only to be gravely disappointed when you opened the package? You probably felt cheated. That can also occur in the classroom. As you become adept at building the need, make sure you live up to the expectations you build. Don't overpromise; don't underdeliver.

Whenever you overpromise, you move from appropriate motivation to manipulation. Your promise must be realistic and appropriate, and your delivery must cause the students to think, *That was great!* If you err, it is better to do so on the side of underpromising—then you can deliver more than they expected, not less.

The flip side is when you underdeliver. It is possible to build realistic and correct need but then fail to deliver the goods. Usually this occurs because the teacher didn't adequately prepare the lesson.

Both of these situations demotivate students. Every teacher occasionally fails in one or both areas. But regular overpromising or underdelivering breeds apathy, lethargy, inattention, sarcasm, and lack of respect. Remember the parable of the child who cried wolf too many times? "Wolves" eat up student motivation.

It is important to link carefully the lesson you are presenting to the need you surfaced earlier. While it's obvious to you how the lesson relates, is it obvious to your students? They are all that matters. Therefore, sprinkle "relating sentences" all through your lesson.

"Do you see how…?"

"Remember at the beginning we told you that...?"

"See how this relates to...?"

"Isn't it great that you know the...?"

The master teacher creates a web of almost imperceptible threads of relationship throughout the lesson. Students don't recognize it while it's happening, but during the wrap-up they feel a high degree of satisfaction.

Fulfill what you promised. Then add some unexpected ice cream and a cherry. But never again serve it if their mouths aren't watering for it!

NEED MAXIMIZERS

The purpose of these Need Maximizers is to equip you with seven ways you can "Build the Need" in any audience, anytime. You can use them at the beginning of class, at the end of class, even in the middle of class if you sense your students lack interest.

Initially, they may not feel natural to you. In time, however, they'll become second nature. Effective teachers use these seven maximizers almost unconsciously—one or more of them every time they build a need. These maximizers help a person feel the need regardless of where he lives, what subject he's being taught, or how old he is. Remember, these are used to move the audience emotionally to want what you have chosen to teach.

Maximizer 1: Describe the need in a factual presentation.

This is the principle of *information*. Often a factual presentation—through statistics, quotes, or descriptions—can reveal the need in graphic ways. The number of teenage pregnancies in the U.S. last year, the number of bankruptcies filed, the number of teenagers drinking alcohol, the number of divorces in a period of time, and similar statistics can have a powerful effect on an audience. *USA Today* is a good source of statistics such as these.

I use this maximizer when I teach about "The Seven Trends Among Youth Today." Statistics concerning sex, drinking, drug abuse, and suicide among today's teens are shocking. Listing fact after fact is effective because it makes us upset about the world of teenagers and builds in us the need to find an answer.

Maximizer 2: Express the need through storytelling.

This is the principle of identification. I've used this maximizer throughout the book. Each law features one primary story that illustrates the law at work.

When you tell a story, the listener should sense, "That's the way I feel, too." Most people will never remember your outline or main points, but they'll have it down cold if you tell them a story.

D. L. Moody was a master at this—his sermons were filled with stories, mixed with content. Howard Hendricks, Charles Swindoll, James Dobson, and so many others are masters at using stories to build the need.

The closer the story is to your students' life experiences and the more empathetically you describe it, the more you will raise the need. Before long, your students will be saying to themselves, "That's how I feel" and therefore "I need to pay close attention."

You can make up a story, such as Jesus did repeatedly in the parables, or tell an actual one. Whatever you do, the point should be audience identification: "I don't want to be like that" or "I want to be like that."

This story from *Time* magazine (April 11, 1983) could illustrate the illusions of the "good life":

Phil and Rita's life shimmered like an advertisement. Indeed, to an outsider it seemed less a life than a perfect lifestyle: tree-lined California suburban street, tasteful $150,000 home (with piano), two sunny youngsters—Phil, 37, was a $30,000-a-year microchip sales engineer in Silicon Valley; Rita, 34, was a $20,000-a-year bookkeeper.

Like their smart, attractive Northern California friends, Phil and Rita played tennis and ate interesting foods and knew about wine and, starting four years ago, sniffed cocaine. And more coke. And then more. That is why several times last year Phil stood quivering and feverish in the living room, his loaded pistol pointed toward imaginary enemies he knew were lurking in the garage. Rita, emaciated like her husband, had her own bogeyman-strangers with X-ray vision outside the draped bedroom window—and she hid from them in the closet.

The couple's paranoia was fleetingly sliced away, of course, as soon as they got high: they "free-based," breathing a distilled cocaine vapor, Phil alone all night with his glass water pipe and thimbleful of coke, Rita in another room with hers. In the mornings, Phil and Rita got back together, down on all fours, scratching and picking at the carpet for any stray grains of cocaine. This is the good life? This is hip?[2]

Here's an example of using a make-believe story to build the need:

Have you ever felt like Freddy the frog—stuck in a hole, unable to get out of the muck of your life and hop freely around?

Freddy the frog was in a real mess. There he was, hopping along and minding his own business when—plop!—he landed right in the middle of a huge pothole. Try as he might, he couldn't get out—it was just too deep. "I know!" he thought to himself. "I'll call for my friends." And with that he croaked as loudly as he could.

Just as his throat was getting tired from croaking, he heard two of his frog friends croak back. Finally they found him. "What's the matter, Freddy?"

"I'm stuck in this pothole and I can't get out!" Freddy explained from the bottom of the pothole.

"Come on, you can do it! Try again, Freddy!" his frog friends coaxed and cajoled him, but Freddy couldn't muster enough strength to jump out. They left him to his fate.

The next day the two frog friends saw Freddy jumping toward them. "Hey, isn't that Freddy?" one asked. "It sure is!" the other answered. "How in the world did he get out?"

Freddy bounced to his friends. "Hi, guys!"

"Freddy, what happened? We thought you couldn't get out!" one of his frog friends exclaimed.

"I couldn't," Freddy replied, "until a truck came along and I had to!"

Good stories not only move your audience emotionally, they stay with your students long after they have forgotten your outline.

Maximizer 3: Sensitize to the need through drama.

This is the principle of involvement. People love intrigue, good versus evil, and conflict resolution. Drama can capture that need-building intrigue through a monologue, dialogue, or interview; a spontaneous skit; or a planned drama. You can involve others through advance planning or do it all by yourself.

Drama differs from storytelling because you don't tell it, you act it out. You become the people in the story. You can play different roles either from a biblical or modern point of view. Become Judas, Pilate, Elijah, the temple pillars when Christ whipped the moneychangers, the donkey Mary rode to Bethlehem, the tree that wasn't cut down for

Noah's ark but left for shade while people watched Noah work. Forget you are a twentieth-century person and pick up the robes of yester-year. Here's an example:

You know, we argued all the way down from Galilee, down to the Holy City, because we knew this was the week the Messiah was going to set up His kingdom. We argued half the time about who was going to sit on the right and who on the left, and which of us was going to die if a revolution came up. We knew Jesus would resurrect us for the kingdom.

And then when He started to wash feet, I got so frustrated. I didn't want to wash feet; I wanted to fight. That's servant's stuff to wash feet! But me—I'm going to be sitting at His right hand someday. And then when Jesus came around to me, I didn't want Him to wash my feet. I was embarrassed.

Then He said to me, "If you don't let Me wash your feet, it's all over between us. You have no part of Me." I almost fell off my seat. Man, I gave up my fishing, I gave up everything to follow Him! And just because I won't let Him wash my feet, He's telling me it's all over? I couldn't believe it. So I told Jesus to wash all of me, if He was going to be that way about it. And then He told us somebody was going to betray Him. And everybody started looking at me!

You could easily go on with Peter's monologue and play out his feelings as he saw Jesus arrested and as he denied the Lord three times.

Here's another example—the Parable of the Prodigal Son. Instead of reading it and teaching it, why not become the prodigal son yourself?

I couldn't believe what was happening to me. I got $24,500 from my dad—my whole inheritance!—when I started nine months and three days ago. I had the time of my life. Let me tell you, I ate prime rib, I bought expensive suits, and I just made friends everywhere. It was a blast. But now...I have exactly $7.23 to my name.

You can involve a person in your class or audience and continue the story:

You know, Tom, when I first came here about six months ago, I had all kinds of money. I bought you those shoes—I spent all kinds of money on you, remember? Well, Tom, now I need a little help. I'm running low on cash, and you know what my dad would say if I came back home with my tail between my legs? He'd never let me forget it.

You can even become the oak tree outside the prodigal's home:

Suddenly I saw a figure in the distance, through my branches. It looked like him, but it couldn't be, could it? I remember when he used to climb on my limbs. We had such fun together. But look at him now. He's aged beyond his years. He's walking slowly; he seems fearful. Is he afraid of his father's reaction? He doesn't know that his father sat out here for days, looking for him in the horizon, weeping, weeping. I thought that I would become a weeping willow!

Maximizer 4: Increase the need through your delivery.

This is the principle of intensity. How you say something can often have more impact than what you say. The intensity, body language, tone of voice, range of gestures, eye contact, and speed of speaking are effective builders of emotion. Anger, fear, trust, acceptance, love, hope, and insecurity are all feelings easily developed through delivery. Even moments of silence can increase attention and need. Vary your delivery for greater effectiveness and be sensitive to appropriate intensities.

Well-chosen, handcrafted words that arouse feeling can be extremely powerful. Read the Lord's Prayer. Or the Twenty-third Psalm. Or the Gettysburg Address. Read out loud this portion of one of President Reagan's State of the Union addresses and notice how you feel as you read his descriptions:

> We honor the giants of our history not by going back but forward to the dreams their visions foresaw. My fellow citizens, this nation is poised for greatness. The time has come to proceed toward a great new challenge—a Second American *Revolution* of hope and opportunity; a *revolution* carrying us to new heights of progress by pushing back frontiers of knowledge and space; a *revolution* of spirit that taps the soul of America enabling us to summon greater strength than we have ever known; and a *revolution* that carries beyond our shores the golden promise of human freedom in a world at peace. Let us begin by challenging conventional wisdom: There are *no* constraints on the human mind, *no* walls around the human spirit, *no* barriers to our prayers except those we ourselves erect. We stand on the *threshold* of a great ability to produce *more*, do *more*, be *more*. Our economy is not getting older and weaker, it's getting younger and stronger; it doesn't need rest and supervision, it needs new challenge and greater freedom. And that word—*freedom*—is the key to the Second American Revolution we mean to bring about.

Delivery can make even the most unimportant issues seem important. Imagine a slick, robust, strong-lunged huckster speaking to you over late-night TV:

> Imagine if you will a comprehensive device that finally will allow you to organize your life with the utmost efficiency. That's right!

When you put this item to work, you'll enjoy a sense of stability, order, and peace of mind that you never thought possible. In mere seconds you'll experience the settled confidence that comes when everything is in its proper place.

And not only is this attractive item from the ultimate organizational system, you can also use it as an attractive book-mark—you'll never lose your place again! Open it to its full size and you'll have a smart-looking, reusable place mat—the perfect thing if you have a messy family! If you have kids or grandkids, they'll love expressing their creativity by coloring on this sturdy item. Plus, it makes a great sign for advertising your garage sales, selling your car—whatever you want to say, write it right on here and millions of potential viewers will see it. You can even use it to draw straight lines!

Imagine the camaraderie you'll experience as you join millions of fellow owners. You can even form neighborhood clubs and share your experiences and ideas for other uses of this amazing tool! It comes in a beautiful warm cream color—fits in any decor. It's precision crafted, too. You'll marvel at the die-cut craftsmanship exhibited in each one.

How much would you be willing to pay for this item with a million and one uses? Five hundred dollars? One hundred dollars? Fifty dollars? Well, order before midnight and we'll send you one postpaid for only $10! That's right! Ten dollars. But this is a limited-time offer. Order a dozen and save—pay only $119.95! Yes, imagine the comfort, the confidence, stability, fulfillment, and just plain fun that will flood your life when you receive your very own...manila folder!

Vary your tone and pace. Change intensities. Get loud when that's appropriate, and whisper when that would be most effective. Think through your delivery ahead of time for maximum impact.

Maximizer 5: Raise the need through music.

This is the principle of *inspiration*. A vocal solo, choral number, or instrumental piece, even if it's recorded, can raise the need for your message. Choose something your students can identify with—it may be "Just as I Am" or "Chariots of Fire," the theme from "Rocky" or "We Shall Behold Him." Tie it closely to the need you want to build.

This is one of the reasons we sing hymns in churches or have a solo before the sermon. Music helps prepare our hearts. Needs are involved with our emotions. You feel needs; you don't think needs or will needs. Music can get to those needs much faster than most other means at our disposal.

And don't use music merely to build need before you speak or while you speak. Use it after you speak as well. Give your audience time to think about what they've heard by playing some music that's appropriate to the mood and the message. It will have a dramatic impact.

Maximizer 6: Exhibit the need with a diagram.

This is the principle of *imagination*. It's amazing what a small diagram can communicate. The blackboard or overheard can truly be a parateacher with you. A circle can represent a person, an arrow personal growth. A diagram of the tabernacle can demonstrate man's need for holiness in approaching God. The creative possibilities are endless.

Some of us can't teach without a chalkboard or flip chart. Allow the blackboard to become a moving picture of the concepts you are discussing. Draw arrows, exclamation points, stick figures. Don't be concerned with how beautiful something appears—be concerned with communicating.

Although this may sound odd, the use of graphics can be very emotional. You can talk to a blackboard in a way that you can't talk to the audience. You can beat on the blackboard. You can use colors. It's easy for people to identify with diagrams. They can cut right to the core of what you're trying to communicate. Imagine the following class episode:

> Let's say this circle is you. The arrow is temptation that comes along and hits you, but bounces off. You just aren't going to yield to that temptation. Then Satan throws another temptation. And it bounces off, too. You continue to say no, but you're relying on your own power, not God's.
>
> Finally one of those arrows of temptation hits you during a weak moment, and it sinks in, leaving a little wedge right in the surface of your life. The next time it comes it won't be as easy to say no. These arrows keep hitting you at that temptation spot, and before long, the wedge has weakened your protection. It keeps growing and growing, a spot getting bigger and blacker.
>
> Then you are tempted in another area of life, and since you are weakened, you succumb to it without even realizing what's happening. And then another sin. Before long you have these blackened areas of sin all through your life, eating away at you.
>
> Well, before this class is over, you'll know how the Bible teaches that you can enjoy victory the next time that temptation shows up. You'll have the power to say "no."

See how effective that can be? A circle with some arrows and black spots can hold each one of us in suspense, building strong need.

Maximizer 7: Symbolize the need with a picture.

This is the principle of *illustration*. A drawing, photograph, painting, video, or other picture can build need dramatically. Photos of starving children are used repeatedly in advertising to raise funds for starving people overseas. Why? Because they work.

How do you feel when you walk through a magnificent forest? Or sit on a rock next to a bubbling stream? Or sit watching the ocean surf pound the beach? Or gaze at a setting sun on a spring evening? God's creation can certainly move us, can't it?

Why do you suppose movies are so popular? They dramatically stir people's emotions through strong visual impact. Look through a magazine and you'll notice how the pictures are used to move you emotionally and cause you to read an article. People desire visual stimulation.

How much visual stimulation did you use in your recent classes?

Recently I spoke at a banquet. At the end a man presented a slide show of magnificent pictures from nature, accompanied by praise music. It was so wonderful. There wasn't a dry eye in the house. We were so filled with praise. That production confirmed and deepened the message of the evening in a way few other media could have. Why? It combined two of the most powerful need-builders: music and pictures. The more need-builders you can combine, the more effective your presentations will be.

CONCLUSION

At the beginning of this Law of Need, we studied the remarkable story of the woman at the well (John 4). Throughout the story we noticed how carefully and purposefully Jesus Christ built her need and how intensely she then sought for the answer to that need. She moved from disinterest to intense interest. She sought for what He desired her to seek.

Although some would shrink back from that picture of Jesus, they cannot argue with the clarity of the biblical text: Jesus knowingly and purposefully selected the "bait" and worked the "rod and reel" in such a way that His "fish" chased the "lure."

Jesus was the Master Teacher not only because He had the *message* she needed, not only because He had the *motive* for her complete good, but also because He had the correct *method* that appealed to her.

No one today argues with Christ's message.

No one today argues with Christ's motive.

Are you still arguing with Christ's method?

Do you still feel it is improper to purposefully arrange your content for your students—like Christ did—so that they are incredibly motivated to learn the lesson? Do you still feel that it is improper to lead your students from disinterest to felt need to real need—like Christ did?

Would you rather leave this step of building the need to chance? Or do you think that just entering your class and "depending upon the Holy Spirit" and hoping that somehow, something will happen to make your students motivated is the better way? Is confusion the way of the Lord? Is lack of forethought and preparation the way of the Lord's servant? Should we not study how Jesus walked so we can then walk in His footsteps?

Why is it some churches and some classes are brimming with excitement, spiritual vitality, and numerical growth, and others know only boredom, spiritual lethargy, and declining attendance? Although numerous answers could be given about the source of the problem, I suggest that inevitably two characteristics exist about the teacher:

First, the teacher has the false concept that he or she isn't responsible to meet the needs of the students in his class—that somehow and in some way, God is. Certainly the teacher could not be responsible, through careful research, to select the appropriate topic to meet the main needs of his students' lives, could he?

Second, the teacher has the false concept that he isn't responsible to present the lesson in such a way that his students become interested and motivated in that subject—that somehow and in some way, God is. Maybe the students should just come to class brimming with motivation. In any case, it certainly is not through his careful preparation that his students are moved to know and experience the truth being taught.

In both instances, the teacher has abandoned his rightful assignment as a teacher. He has delegated to the Lord what the Lord has assigned to him. He is actively thwarting the very will of the Lord who is committed to train him to be a "fisher of men." Do you think that Christ chose that word picture by accident?

And do you still walk into your class with any old lure, never having wrestled with whether that lure is appropriate for your fish?

And do you still walk into your class expecting them to automatically desire your content, blaming them or the system or the time of the day for their disinterest and widespread boredom?

May these two chapters on the Law of Need open your eyes to all that Christ may have meant when He said to His followers, "Follow Me, and I will make you fishers of men."

Before we leave this vital concept, let's conclude that remarkable story from John 4. What did that woman at the well do after Jesus led her to Himself? She practiced on her class what He had practiced on her!

> The woman then left her waterpot, went her way into the city, and said to the men, "Come, see a Man who told me all things that I ever did. Could this be the Christ?" (John 4:28–29)

Now, *look beneath the message to uncover her method*. First she got their attention with, "Come, see a Man who told me all things that I ever did." Remember, this woman was the city prostitute and was addressing the men of the city. Talk about immediate attention!

Then she moved to the second step—she *captured their curiosity* with, "Could this be the Christ?"

Because of the way she carefully approached her class, she enjoyed incredible success. The Bible records that the men "went out of the city and came to Him" (v. 30). Now don't miss it. The men of the city closed shop in the middle of the workday. They willingly lost business...all because of two sentences one woman spoke.

The woman at the well became the teacher of the city through introducing the Savior of the world. Because of the way she built the need, the city sought Jesus.

See how vitally important it was for her to build the need? If the need is built effectively, whole cities come looking for Jesus.

So remember the next time you reach to open your classroom door, it's up to you. Here comes your "woman at the well"!

DISCUSSION QUESTIONS

1. Make a list of what you think are your class's top ten needs. List them in order of importance. Then distribute an anonymous questionnaire and see how well you actually knew your class. (Remember, the average teacher gets less than three correct.) What did you learn?

2. From your questionnaire, what is the number one need in your class? What are the causes that developed it into number one? List the possible results of having this unmet need in a person's life—in their family life, job, recreation, friendships, and so on. How would the members of your class feel about you and your class if they were enabled to enjoy full victory in that area?

3. Take a few moments and do a little detective work. Go to your nearby secular bookstore and browse

through the best-selling books. Make a list of the top five needs being written about. Then look at the most popular magazines in the rack and list the top five needs discussed in them. Combine these two lists into one. What do you think would happen if you taught on those top five needs during the next five Sunday school classes? One more thing—list the last five subjects you taught on. How many of them scratched where people really itched?

4. You just experienced a massive heart attack and died. Because you accepted Christ's substitutionary death for your sins, the angels welcome you through heaven's gate. You are free from all selfishness and also see life on earth from God's perspective. What a difference—your perspective is dramatically altered. From God's perspective, what are the five greatest needs in the church today? If you made them your teaching agenda for the next year, what are the possible outcomes?

5. If you were able to see yourself completely as God sees you, what would be your top five needs? Since you have the Scriptures and the Spirit, could your needs be the next six months' subjects for your personal devotions? How would you feel about life if those needs were met? Why not take the Lord at His Word and seek His wisdom!

LAW SIX

The Law
of Equipping

Chapter Eleven

Equipping

Mindset, Model, and Maxims

I'd been steeling myself for three weeks and couldn't avoid it another day—I had to fire one of the team members of Walk Thru the Bible. I'd never had to fire anyone before, and I worked for weeks to build up the courage. I even wrote out my speech and practiced it. I was so anxious that before the day finally arrived, I had fired my dog, my kids, and my mother-in-law.

I felt terribly guilty—the employee was such a great guy. "Well, it's his fault, not mine," I tried to convince myself. "If he was more conscientious and was doing his job, I wouldn't have to fire him at all." So I forged ahead.

The appointed day arrived, and I called this young man into my office. After nervously discussing the weather, twisting an eraser off a pencil, and asking a few dumb questions about his wife and kids (he was single—I knew that), I took a deep breath and started into my speech.

Somehow firing in practice isn't anything like firing a living, breathing person. It took only a split second to realize he had no idea what was coming. Meanwhile, my well-practiced words got stuck in my throat. In desperation, I blurted out, "So, how do you feel you're doing here at Walk Thru?" I figured I'd let him describe his obvious work record and thereby convict himself. Then I would simply agree and...I was beginning to think this was true managerial genius.

But to my shock and dismay, the young man immediately leaned forward in his chair and with a gleam in his eye replied, "Great!"

That doesn't sound like the answer of a man about to hang himself, I thought. "Oh, really? Tell me about your work," I sputtered.

For the next twenty minutes he listed all the exciting things he was doing at the ministry. His enthusiasm became so great that he even rose from his chair and paced back and forth. He could barely contain his excitement.

As he reached the conclusion (I almost thought he was going to give an invitation), I found myself deeply moved. What an inspiring list of accomplishments this young man had achieved. What an employee! Without thinking I leaped to my feet, extended my hand, and offered him a raise.

"Bruce, you did what?" I asked myself later. That's right, I gave him a raise. But what about all those problems he had? It suddenly dawned on me that he was not the problem. His boss was. The young man was doing tremendous work. Unfortunately, his activities were 180 degrees off the mark of what I thought he should have been doing.

Because I had never given him a job description, he had the unenviable task of trying to guess what his boss wanted him to do. I had violated one of the most basic principles of all organizational theory and practice by not clearly communicating what I expected an employee to accomplish. And to think I was going to hold him accountable for my failure! What a memorable lesson. We mutually agreed upon specific items I wanted him to achieve in his position, and he went on to become a truly outstanding employee.

A job description is an extremely important document, isn't it? It defines in clear and objective terms what the leader expects the follower to achieve. The leader is responsible to define those expectations clearly, and the follower is responsible to fulfill those expectations to the best of his ability. My story would have been decidedly different had this young man's job description been clear and he had willfully and regularly disregarded those instructions.

The primary issues in this chapter are: (1) What is the biblical job description for the Christian teacher? And (2) is the average teacher fulfilling those responsibilities or rebelling against them?

EQUIPPING MINDSET

Someday each of us individually will stand before the Lord for our Final Performance Appraisal. As 1 Corinthians 3 and 2 Corinthians 5 clearly teach, God is going to hold us accountable for what we have done with our lives.

What will happen when God asks you, "Tell Me, how you think you did on earth?" I wonder if at the end of our recounting the Lord will say to many of us, "That's very interesting. I can see all those things are important to you. *But what about the things I asked you to accomplish for Me?*" Would you know what the Lord was referring to at that crucial moment? Do you know what the Lord has written in "the divine job description for teachers"?

Unlike the young man who experienced the trauma of having done the wrong things and then readjusting his work to meet his boss's goals, when you and I face the Lord on that day, it will be our final appraisal, not just a midcourse correction. When our day comes, it won't be possible to return and readjust our lives to come in line with the Lord's commands. It will be too late.

Since we are absolutely assured of this upcoming evaluation and because it would be an eternally tragic act to achieve goals that are ours but not the Lord's, do you know where to find His "Divine Job Description for Teachers"? If you don't, you could be aiming at precisely the wrong goals as a Christian teacher.

This reminds me of a golf tournament Walk Thru the Bible used to sponsor for its employees every year. None of us played much golf, but during our annual planning retreat, we would dust off the clubs and compete. Dale Houchin, WTB's print shop manager, and I had performed neck and neck for the past few years, and we'd been razzing each other all winter about the upcoming tournament.

When the tournament began, I found myself in the foursome just in front of Dale and received no little amount of verbal abuse as I strained to keep the ball in the fairways. Finally we came to a hole where you couldn't see the green because it was over a hill. The first shot usually put you in a position where you could see just the top of the flag over the hill and would have to shoot "blind" down to the hidden green in the valley below.

Well, my first shot was a strong one—directly into the woods on the right. More verbal abuse from Dale. (Company presidents don't get much respect.) As our foursome finished out the hole, I could distinctly hear Dale from over the hill berating my rather "generous" score on that hole.

I was just about to put the flag back into the cup when it hit me…Dale couldn't see the green. Perhaps the Lord had provided a way of escape for the "righteous." With clear resolve, I took the flag and planted it firmly into the largest sand trap I could find, far away from the green.

I yelled over the hill that Dale was going to have to hit the green to beat me. Our foursome retreated into the woods to watch the antics we knew were coming. Dale's shot crested the hill perfectly—clearly his best shot of the day. He knew it and was shouting, "Look at that, Mr. President, it's on the green. I just know it! Once more the print shop is going to beat the corner office!"

Such carnal comments.

His ball landed two or three feet in front of that misplaced flag and buried itself. I would have given almost anything to have captured Dale's expression as he came over the hill and saw the misplaced flag and his ball right in the middle of the Sand Sea!

What was the problem with Dale's shot? His expertise? His intensity? His desire to do well? Not at all. Score him high on all counts. Dale had hit that ball right to the target. *But it was the wrong target.* His hard work had turned out to be worthless because he was aiming at the wrong goal.

As we have been discussing since the opening chapter, most teachers think their primary responsibility is to "cover the content" or "explain the outline" to the students. When those teachers crest the "final hill," I wonder if they will discover their lives have been aimed at the sand trap rather than the green. Then it will be too late, won't it? But it's not too late for you to make some midcourse corrections if you discover through this chapter you've been off course.

Before we discuss that vital Biblical Job Description for Teachers, it may be profitable for you to list what you think the main points of that job description are.

The community of Christian teachers can be viewed as the "faculty" of God's church, with God as our "Principal." There must be certain things He expects us to be doing in this "enterprise" of His, but what are they? How do we know we will receive a positive evaluation from God regarding our work for Him?

Jesus Christ alerts us to the incredible importance of this final appraisal when He teaches us in Matthew 25 that all life is a manner of stewardship to Him. In the Parable of the Talents, the master rewarded only those servants who used his resources in the manner he expected. They were strongly complimented and received wonderful positions of leadership. The third servant, however, received severe rebuke and discipline for misusing the master's resources.

The issue isn't whether or not we are doing a good thing; the issue is, are we doing the Lord's thing? The Law of Equipping is written to reveal the Lord's Job Description for Teachers; the following chapter will train you how to teach in light of God's eternal agenda.

So where in the Bible would you look for God's Job Description for Teachers? The most complete and definite passage is Ephesians 4:11–12. Read it carefully to get the big picture, and then we'll immerse ourselves in its rich insights:

> And [Christ] Himself gave some to be apostles, some prophets, some evangelists, and some pastors and teachers, for the equipping of the saints for the work of ministry, for the edifying of the body of Christ.

Within this passage is found the clear job description for those called to teach in the body of Christ. From this passage, three main principles surface immediately.

Principle 1: The primary <u>purpose</u> of teachers is to equip.

Here's the bottom line. The Bible reveals that teachers are given by God primarily to equip and not merely to explain.

Pick a class—any class. Sit in that class and you'll find, nine times out of ten, that the focus of the hour will be on explaining what the Bible or content means.

The tragedy, repeated thousands of times weekly in our finest churches and schools, is that while the class may be interesting, informative, educational, and often entertaining, it is not consistent with the job description God gave for His teachers. A student in a class or pew can be informed, educated, and entertained and still not be equipped.

Christ gave teachers to equip the saints for the work of ministry. To equip means to furnish with whatever is needed for any purpose or undertaking. The idea from the original Greek word, *katartizo*, is to prepare, make ready, complete, or restore. It's used in Matthew 4:21 for mending nets to prepare for fishing.

In Ephesians 4:11, equipping means making ready for service and ministry. The apostle Paul is helping realize that the primary task of the teacher is to prepare the student to do something. Our focus must move past knowledge to the use of that knowledge in the person's life.

Principle 2: The primary <u>audience</u> of teachers is Christians.

God not only makes it clear what we are to do; He also makes it clear to whom we are to do it: "For the equipping of the *saints*...for the edifying of the body of Christ" (v. 12). The activity is equipping and the audience is the Christians.

One of the most frequent complaints I hear from lay people who attend Bible-believing churches is, "Why does my pastor/teacher present evangelistic sermons/lessons to the unchurched people week after week? We've heard the gospel time after time, and we're starving for some solid food from the Word."

In utter disregard for God's agenda, many teachers have decided that the primary audience for their lessons should be the unsaved. Tragically, preachers and teachers are speaking to the wrong group week after week; they haven't equipped the Christians to do the work of the ministry during the week and so they try to do it for them on Sunday.

Principle 3: The primary <u>result</u> of equipping is Christians doing the work of the ministry and edifying the body of Christ.

How do you know if your teaching is having the correct result? The saints are doing the work to the degree that *"every part does its share, [and] causes growth of the body for the edifying of itself in love"* (v. 16).

GOD'S JOB DESCRIPTION
FOR ALL TEACHERS

What then is the Lord going to be looking for when He evaluates us as teachers? Consider some startling core issues that God has revealed will probably be on our final exam.

1. *The nature of the ministry that our students are involved in ("work of ministry").* We tend to have a completely different mindset than God about our teaching. His emphasis is always on what our students do; our emphasis is upon what we, the teachers, do. His emphasis is upon the work of ministry our students are engaged in; our emphasis is upon the course outline and notes we are engaged in. The first question God may ask us will most likely focus upon the specific work of ministry that our students are doing as a result of our class.

2. *The percentage of our class who are personally ministering ("every part").* Notice again the contrast in mindset. God's emphasis is always upon the full participation of all members; our emphasis is upon the 20 percent who seem to be the "faithful." Somehow we have compromised and allowed 80 percent nonparticipation. God's standard is "every part," and therefore we will be evaluated on that basis.

3. *The degree to which our students are doing the work of ministry according to their capacity ("its share").* What a striking mindset the Lord presents in this and other key New Testament passages—that He has given to each believer not only a unique personality but also sovereignly bestowed a spiritual gift for the purpose of ministry. All too often we think that as long as a person is "at least doing something for God," we have accomplished our duty and fulfilled our

commission. The Lord is not looking for us to settle for ten-talent people doing two-talent works of service! Nor is He pleased when His children are misplaced outside the area in which He has sovereignly gifted them.

4. *The quality and quantity of the work done by our students ("effective working").* When God finished His work of creation, He stepped back and evaluated it and exclaimed, "It is good!" God is a God of excellence, and all His works are excellent. He expects us, as commissioned officers in His teaching army, to continually train and upgrade the performance of our students. How different our mindset is from the mindset of God. Too few classes have an objective standard of performance beyond some testing of the content. Not only is the Lord concerned that our students are working, but He is concerned that they are effectively working. To have effective workers, we must be effective teachers.

5. *The percentage of growth in our class ("cause growth of the body").* Whenever we take the Lord at His Word and do His work in His way, we can be sure to see the results He has promised. As every person actively uses His spiritual gifts in effective ministry, the Lord promises it will "cause growth of the body." Such a class cannot help but grow! Unlike God's mindset and promises, however, our mindset is that effective teaching will not necessarily result in class growth. Ephesians says effective teaching "causes growth of the body," which should not be limited to merely spiritual growth. For a biblical model, note the explosive growth of the church in the early chapters of Acts.

6. *Constant, normal, and spontaneous mutual ministry between class members ("edify itself in love").* The mindset of most teachers is that they are the ones almost single-handedly responsible to minister to their students. In contrast, the Lord expects

our equipping to be so thorough and complete that it enables our students to minister to each other as if they were the teacher or minister. God is concerned that Christians not just meet together, but actually meet so that mutual edification takes place. He desires each member of His church to become more and more self-initiating so that when they see or hear of any need, they immediately respond out of a sense of ownership and responsibility.

As you can see, the mindset of the typical Christian teacher is often significantly different from the Lord's commission to His teachers. Probably the most basic difference between how we think and how God wants us to think is one of perspective. As teachers, we tend to focus upon what we do, especially during the class period. The Lord strongly directs us to focus upon what our students do, especially between classes!

May this Law of Equipping prepare you for the Final Performance Appraisal with your Ultimate Supervisor. May you hear Him say, "Well done, good and faithful teacher...."

EQUIPPING MODEL

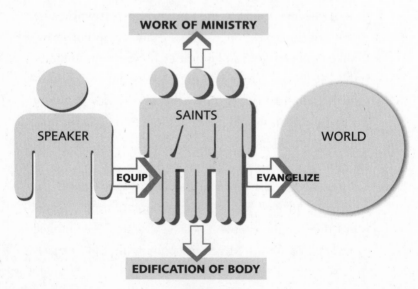

In order to understand Ephesians 4:11–12 more clearly, let's study this chart, which flows from left to right.

The first figure represents the *"speaker"* or teacher, and the Bible makes two intriguing observations about him in this verse. First, the Bible states that God *"gave some...teachers,"* which means that teachers are a gift from the Lord to the church. What a remarkable revelation—the Lord views you and me as a gift to the people we teach! We aren't put in our classroom by accident but by the grand design of the Creator Himself.

Second, *God is the source of teachers*. God doesn't want any confusion regarding where this gift comes from. Therefore, the next time you open your classroom door and wonder if you are the right person to teach the class, remember the Lord God has sovereignly selected you to be His teacher of that class on that day. So enter with confidence in the power and the calling of the Lord.

The middle or second box represents the *"saints"* (the biblical term for those who know Jesus Christ as their Savior) who are the recipients of the gift called "teachers." God gave His gift to Christians, not to non-Christians. Although we are all commissioned to go into the world, those of us who are called to teach are commissioned by God to work primarily in the sphere of the saints.

The third and final box represents the *"world,"* which includes everyone not in the category of saints. Therefore, the world represents the unsaved, or unsaints.

The delegated responsibility of the teachers is to *"equip"*; the delegated responsibility of all saints, including teachers, is to *"evangelize."*

What is immediately apparent is that the typical teacher conducts himself in a number of unbiblical ways. First, too frequently in the local church, the Christian teacher focuses on the wrong audience. This chart reflects the Bible's emphasis on the teacher not going directly to the world. If the teacher does that, he has to abandon his primary audience, thus disobeying the responsibility God has given him.

Second, many teachers have a tendency not to equip for godly character or effective service, but merely to cover a set of notes. Biblical teaching focuses upon the outflow of the students' lives, not just the input of the teacher's notes.

Third, most teachers focus upon content rather than character as the goals of the Christian teacher. In the vast majority of churches, Christian schools, and Christian colleges, character and integrity aren't the subject of even one course. It is the rare Christian educational institution that seeks to uncover the character of its students, even though Ephesians 4:13 clearly states one of God's objectives for Christian teachers is to teach "till we all [become]…a perfect (mature) man, to the measure of the stature of the fullness of Christ." Why do we so seldom teach for character and even more seldom test our students' character? Christ expects character to be objectively observable by others and to be carefully tested (1 Timothy and Titus).

The two remaining arrows pointing up and down from the *"saints"* reflect two specific things teachers are to equip their students to do. The top arrow, *"work of ministry,"* captures the first result of the teacher's equipping efforts. The bottom arrow, *"edification of the body,"* captures the second result of equipping.

In a sense, *"equipping"* is the key to God's plan of "building His church." It outlines the flow of His main strategy—from God's gift of "teachers" all the way through the presentation of Himself as the "Gift."

The deciding factor on the whole chart is whether or not we who are the Lord's designated teachers will do the most important job—equip the saints. If we don't equip the saints, then the saints cannot do what they have been commissioned to do; they cannot do the *"work of ministry"* nor *"edify the body"* nor *"evangelize the world."*

Do you sense how far some of us may have strayed from God's strategy? So many of us lament that the teaching ministry is too difficult. It may be so difficult because we will not submit ourselves to the clear directives of the Lord.

Tragically, some of us are committed to doing the ministry our way, aren't we? We still think all that matters is *what we do* instead of *what they do*.

It reminds me of the old *Road Runner* cartoons we used to watch when our children were young. Time after time, Wile E. Coyote would chase the Road Runner (beep, beep!), and time after time he would *almost* catch him. But every ingenious effort would be foiled, and he would always experience failure and pain. I can't imagine the number of times he fell over that cliff and crashed on the canyon floor in a puff of dust.

No matter how hard Coyote ran, he always bit the dust. No matter how carefully he read the wrong signs, he always bit the dust. No matter how carefully he arranged his bomb or balanced the boulder on the top of the mountain, he always bit the dust. No matter how close he got to his target, he always bit the dust.

The amount of effort isn't enough, is it? The amount of preparation isn't enough. Nothing is enough if you are ultimately going to bite the dust.

When we face the Lord, He isn't going to ask if we tried or if we prepared. He's not concerned that we expend our effort in doing something; He's concerned that we expend our effort in doing what He has asked us to accomplish.

There's only one thing worse than not knowing what your Boss wants you to do—it's knowing what He wants you to do, but doing your own thing anyway.

God said, equip the saints so that they do the work of ministry and edify the body. Perhaps it's time to fulfill our job description in light of our coming Performance Appraisal.

EQUIPPING MAXIMS

If the Teacher's Job Description from Ephesians 4:11–16 caused you to seriously reconsider what you are doing in the classroom, then you are poised at the threshold of an explosive breakthrough in your teaching.

Perhaps one of the major reasons we don't experience the desired results in our teaching is that we focus on the wrong things. *Doing the wrong thing the right way—even with the right motives—is still doing the wrong thing!* God's interest goes beyond our motives to our actual performance. God is looking for us to do what He has instructed and to accomplish the performance objectives He has outlined.

How does your class measure up to the Lord's objectives, according to Ephesians 4:11–16? Consider the following questions. Let them alert you to how your Performance Review as a teacher might have gone had the Lord called you home today.

1. Do my students actually do a lot of the "work of the ministry"?
2. How close to 100 percent of my students are involved in meaningful ministry on a regular basis?
3. What percentage of my students' capacity for ministry is being reached as they work? Are they serving Christ with all their heart, soul, and mind?
4. Has your students' service for the Lord become substantially more effective because of your equipping? Give a couple of specifics.
5. How much growth (numerical and spiritual) did your class achieve in the past year?
6. How many ministry activities that are spontaneous and unsponsored by the church normally occur between the members of the class each week?
7. How many people did your students lead to the Lord during the past twelve months?

Sobering, isn't it?

Do you know why it is so sobering to so many of us? Because we haven't been asking the right questions. We've been lulled to sleep by a false sense of confidence. Somehow we have allowed ourselves to stray so far from the real objectives of the Lord that when we seriously consider them even for a moment, we find our mouths dry and our palms damp.

Consider for a moment the striking contrast between God's list of objectives and the typical teacher's focus. Here's a more normal list:

1. Have I prepared my content?
2. Did I arrive on time?
3. Did most of my class attend?
4. Were there some good questions or discussion?
5. Did I cover my content?
6. Did I finish the lesson on time?
7. Did most students seem to like the class?

Imagine the incredible revolution that would explode in the classroom when the teacher purposefully seeks to achieve God's objectives! Here are a few differences that could develop immediately:

1. The focus would move from what the teacher did to what the students did.
2. The focus would move from the lesson that was taught in class to the ministry that was achieved after class.
3. The focus would move from "covering the content" to helping the students do the "work of service."
4. The focus would move from the ministry of the teacher to the ministry of the students.
5. The focus would move from how many attended class to how many served between classes.
6. The focus would move from the theoretical to the practical—what "works" rather than what "sounds good."
7. The focus would move from "content for church" to "material for the marketplace"—majoring on how

Christianity makes a difference in one's job, neighborhood, club, and so on.

We have strayed so far!

One of the meaningful rewards of traveling and ministering across
our country is that I meet teachers and pastors who actually practice
Ephesians 4:11. Let me describe a church three hours from Atlanta
where I once spent a weekend ministering.

Everyone is ministering in that church. Enthusiasm is everywhere.
Both the church and the Sunday school are bulging at the seams. The
biggest problem is where to put everyone. The focus is always on the
people and not on the leadership. The leadership serves the people
and is forever equipping more and more people for ministry. The
leadership is forever "bragging" on the people's ministry and service
and sacrifice. Laypeople are running everything. Everybody's doing
two or three different things for the Lord and loving it. People feel
stimulated. They feel their contribution means something. People feel
appreciated. People feel fulfilled. They feel challenged. They know
they have been called to minister. They know what to do, and do it all
the time.

One year after I visited that church, we celebrated the fiftieth birthday of one of Walk Thru the Bible's senior vice presidents. One of the
other vice presidents had just come back from ministering at the same
church. Do you know what he said over ice cream and cake? "What an
incredible church! *Everybody is involved.* I felt the electricity everywhere.
Those people love their church!"

Why? Because that church had decided to do it God's way. And
because they were pleasing the Lord, His mighty arm of blessing was
moving powerfully in their midst. Do you know who was the most
thrilled with that church? Not the pastor, not the staff, not the deacons, not the laymen, not even the local community. I believe the most
thrilled person was the Lord God. *His dream was coming true.* A church

had actually decided to *try His plan* and discovered what incredible results occur for all who do it His way!

So my fellow teacher, as Joshua of old asked his students, why not "choose this day whom you shall serve"?

If you are sick and tired of mediocre results, of boring classes, of uninvolved and apathetic students, of rampant lack of participation, never again point your finger at anyone but the teacher. Do it God's way and you will experience the miraculous rewards of His blessing.

Obey God. Equip His saints. And enjoy His blessing!

Maxim 1: Equipping is the responsibility of the teacher.

As you spend the next few moments considering these maxims, you are going to notice repeatedly how God focuses on "equipping for service" while we tend to focus on "speaking for understanding."

I am struck by how intensely God feels and constantly acts regarding equipping. For instance, in the Law of Application we studied 2 Timothy 3:16–17 and discovered the following major principles:

The Word of God was a gift from God
("All Scripture was given by God")

with a primary audience of the Christian
("that the man of God")

for the purpose of edification
("may be complete" or perfect or mature)

and for the purpose of equipping
("and thoroughly equipped")

for the result of good work
("for every good work").

In the Law of Equipping, we have considered Ephesians 4:11–16 and discovered among other things the following major principles. Compare them with the ones above—you may observe an amazing set of similarities!

The teacher of God (you) is a gift from God
("And He Himself gave some pastors and teachers")

with a primary audience of the Christian
("for the saints and the body of Christ")

for the purpose of edification
("for the edifying of the body of Christ")

and for the purpose of equipping
("for the equipping of saints for the work")

for the result of good works
("for the work of ministry").

Amazing, isn't it? Both the Bible and the teacher:

- are a gift from God.
- are for the Christian community.
- are for the purpose of edification and equipping.
- are for the results of good works.

Of all the purposes God could have chosen, edification and equipping are the two He chose. The first focuses on the character and the second on the conduct of the Christian. Therefore, let us not lose sight that equipping is one of the Lord's two main purposes for His most significant gifts.

The tragic truth, however, is that those who have been called to equip not only rarely equip but also frequently misuse the other equipping agent (the Bible) as a book to be studied for knowledge rather than a Book to be practiced.

Haven't you always found it a bit fascinating that Jesus said, "If you love Me, you will keep My commandments"? Because from what I've heard in many Christian classrooms, I might have thought He said, "If you love Me, you will know My commandments." (After sitting in American public classrooms, it appears we think He said, "If you love Me, then please don't post My commandments.")

Maxim 2: Equipping occurs best when the teacher assumes the biblical role.

God didn't stutter or mumble when He said He gave teachers to the church to equip members for the works of service and for edifying each other. The result God desires is that 100 percent of our students be fully serving Him through good works. He gave the teacher to help them do more ministry better.

If you randomly observed one hundred teachers every week for one year to determine what they are seeking to accomplish, what would you conclude? Would it not appear that they were teaching students to prepare them for the final exam of a thousand multiple-choice and true/false questions? But how would you feel about that preparation if you could open the file cabinet in heaven and inspect God's Final Exam? You'd find God doesn't seek "answers" to questions but "actions of service." He seeks fruit, not facts; disciples, not data.

God has already printed that Final Exam and alerted us teachers to prepare our students for His questions, not for those that won't be on the test. Now I fully agree that knowing content is extremely important—but not nearly as important as obedient actions. *Content is always to be the servant of conduct!* Whenever we enthrone information at the expense of acts of service, we have the wrong king ruling.

Therefore, what role should we assume to best achieve God's purposes? Since our central thrust must be to "equip" or "train" or "enable," we must become the coach. Coaches help their teams play effectively.

Coaches work on improving each team member. Coaches guide the team to work together to accomplish designated goals.

Does the coach teach information? Of course—lots of it. But only so the players can better play the game. Does the coach teach information so that the students can repeat the information on a quiz? No! Quizzes don't change anything, nor do they capture the depth of the students' actual use of the information. The real issue isn't whether the players know the plays, but that they perform the plays correctly.

Some teachers, I fear, think they are the star player rather than the coach. These teachers "suit up" for the big game each week and go to the "stadium" (their classroom or sanctuary) where their students gather to watch what new plays have been devised during the week.

The teacher runs to the center of the field, calls the play, snaps the ball, takes the snap, passes the ball, runs downfield and catches his own pass, blocks those imaginary defensive backs, and sprints across the goal line. Touchdown! The "crowds" are cheering—great class! The material was great—but tragically, no one in the stands played ball.

Does this sound familiar? Friend, get off the field! Rip off your jersey. Take off your cleats and start wrapping the ankles of your players. Coaches don't exist to play the game but rather to equip the *players* to play the game.

God wants your whole team out on the field playing their hearts out. No one should sit on the bench except for exhaustion (physical rest) or fouling out (gross sin). God's rules do not limit the number of players on the field. The coach should be the only one left on the sidelines—cheering!

Maxim 3: Equipping is best evaluated by what the student does after class.

When I played college basketball and soccer, no one seemed very interested in our practice games. There were no crowds, no popcorn stands, no cheerleaders. Yet we were the same players who on Tuesday nights and Saturday afternoons would play before full stands. Somehow people knew the difference between practice and the real game. Not only did the fans know, but so did the players. Even when the scrimmages were close and the "skins" barely won over the "shirts," the moment of glory was short-lived. We all knew it was just practice—and practice didn't count. It was only preparation for the real game.

Just the opposite happens in the church or classroom. *Everyone comes to practice and no one pays attention to the real game.* The real game is played in the marketplace, not in the classroom. The real game isn't won during the weekly quizzes but in the daily ebb and flow of life. But we keep score of the practice sessions instead of the real game.

Let's get practical for a moment and see if we can validate what I am saying. How do we evaluate how a basketball team is doing? The final score is the most critical—it determines whether you won or lost the game. Lesser "scores" include the field-goal and free-throw percentages, the number of assists, the number of rebounds, the number of turnovers, and the number of fouls. But the statistics are never as important as the final score.

But how do we keep score at church? Pastors-teachers share the score in the same way all across the world. Every time I speak at a pastors' conference, I hear their scores discussed during coffee breaks:

"What's your total membership?"

"What's your annual budget?"

"How many people are on staff?"

"How is your building program doing?"

"How many baptisms this past year?"

On the surface, these seem like reasonable and understandable goals. *But do any of them reflect the correct score?* How many of them reflect whether the pastors-teachers have equipped the saints? How many of them alert you to the real score that God is keeping in His eternal scorebook?

How many of the questions reflect whether the saints are doing the work? Does attendance demonstrate effective equipping, or could that be caused by a great preacher of a new gym? Does the number of staff indicate that they are doing the work of the ministry or that they are equipping many laymen to do the work of the ministry? Are the baptisms the result of the pastor's Sunday morning service or the result of your students leading people to the Lord?

Get the point? What kind of information *should* be gathered and recorded to monitor the work of ministry done by the students? Here are a few suggestions.

Tests of the effectiveness of the teacher in equipping his students for an effective work of evangelism:

- What percentage of your students shared the gospel with another person during the past week?
- What percentage of your students led a person to Christ over the past twelve months?
- What percentage of new converts attending church during the past twelve months are the result primarily of lay evangelistic efforts rather that the pastor's preaching or other staff involvement?
- What percentage of last year's new members are involved in a formal evangelism training class?
- What percentage of new converts came through ministry in the neighborhood or workplace rather than through the church?

Tests of the effectiveness of the teacher in equipping his students or an effective work of discipling one another:

- What percentage of your students are involved in a regularly scheduled meeting with other laypeople for the purpose of spiritual accountability and growth—not including scheduled church functions?
- How many different discipling courses or tracks has the pastor taught to provide a tool for the laypeople to disciple others?

- What percentage of your students are involved in teaching a Bible study/discipleship group outside the confines of an officially sponsored church function?
- What percentage of your students during the past twelve months have taken a teacher-training class of at least six hours to equip them to teach more effectively?
- What percentage of the lay Bible study groups have spawned another group during the past twelve months?

Tests of the effectiveness of the teacher in equipping his students for spiritual vitality:

- What percentage of your students have regular (at least five times a week) personal devotions?
- What percentage of your students have regular (at least three times a week) family devotions?
- What percentage of your students have regular ministry in which they serve the Lord at least once a week?
- What percentage of your students tithe?
- What percentage of your students would rate their spiritual life and growth as 7 or above on a scale of 1–10?

I think you can see the dramatic difference that would occur if we started keeping track of the right scores! These scores refocus the attention of the teachers from what they do (lead practice) to what the players do (play the real game).

Maxim 4: Equipping should impact both character and conduct.

We are called to equip people not only to "do the ministry" but also to "be a minister." We must never allow ourselves to forget that all *work for the Lord* essentially comes out of our *walk with the Lord*. Our conduct is the result of our character. Who we are determines what we do.

Therefore, equipping must influence both actions and attitudes. Didn't the Lord demonstrate this when He listed His requirements for church leadership? Nearly all of His requirements are character qualities rather that skill abilities. If a person is "blameless...temperate, sober-minded, of good behavior, hospitable...not given to wine, not violent, not greedy for money, but gentle, not quarrelsome, not covetous" (1 Timothy 3:2–3), then that person's conduct and ministry will be fully acceptable. His walk will validate his talk and his life will "overspeak" his words.

If we are committed to equipping others, then our daily activities will be focused upon those identical goals. Out of curiosity, I reviewed my personal journal for the last couple of weeks to determine which type of equipping I have been involved in recently. Was I spending more time seeking to equip people in their character or their conduct?

I identified seventeen different interactions with people, either at work, church, or home, where I was attempting to equip someone in character or conduct. Here's what the first ten interactions (dealing with thirteen different people) looked like, broken down by what I was dealing with in the person's life:

PERSONS INVOLVED	EQUIPPING CHARACTER	EQUIPPING CONDUCT
Person 1	100 percent	0 percent
Persons 2–3	20	80
Person 4	20	80
Persons 2–6	50	50
Persons 7–11	50	50
Person 1	0	100
Person 12	50	50
Person 4	60	40
Person 13	0	100
Person 1	0	100
Total	35 percent	65 percent

Then I studied the ten interactions previous to those and the averages were flip-flopped: Total time equipping character was 71 percent and equipping conduct 29 percent.

Obviously, your percentages and mine for a normal week depend upon the needs of our students and our desire and determination to equip them. Take a few moments and think about the last few people you were involved with and see if you were actively equipping them. If so, did you spend more time with their character or their conduct? My hope is that your interactions have focus and purpose with eternal value.

Maxim 5: Equipping should focus more intensely on the most committed.

One of the most crucial characteristics of effective equippers is that they carefully select the people they are going to equip. Isn't it interesting that the Lord knew the apostles for a period of time *before* He selected them? The Lord called the people He selected and purposefully focused His intense equipping on those few.

Effective leaders purposefully focus their resources on the most strategic goals of their organization. Effective equippers focus their resources on the most faithful candidates who demonstrate the most promise for long-term and meaningful ministry for the Lord.

Ineffective equippers squander their most precious resource—their available equipping time. They become reactive rather than proactive. Instead of seeking others that they have selected, they allow other people's agendas to become theirs.

Why didn't Christ spend an equal amount of His equipping time with each person? Why did He spend some time with the seventy, more with the twelve, and still more with the three? He knew He had to steward His time and energies to maximize the growth of the kingdom. We must do likewise.

We cannot equip everyone in the classroom, but we should follow

Christ's example and equip a few of our students at a deeper level. When you determine the inner circle you are going to equip, select carefully. Test their resolve. Being under your equipping should have a substantial price tag that tests their commitment and desire to be equipped.

One of the most effective equippers I have ever known practiced this principle regularly. If you wanted him to discipline you, he would meet with you initially to discuss the possibilities and then say, "I'll meet you at 5:30 in the morning at Denny's. Have these three verses memorized by the time you come." The person's reaction reflected his level of commitment of the equipping progress.

Isn't it remarkable that when Christ selected the twelve He was going to equip, He prayed all night? Jesus knew the selection progress was extremely important. And do you remember how He tested their commitment to Him? He asked them to abandon their "fishing nets" and "tax table" and follow Him. Jesus tested their resolve! Have you tested your students' resolve lately?

Paul captures the heart of this maxim when he writes to his student Timothy: "And the things that you have heard from me among many witnesses, commit these to faithful men who will be able to teach others also" (2 Timothy 2:2). Paul knew the equipping process is God's living link to pass the ministry from one generation to the next.

Therefore, don't focus your time on the unfaithful. You are not only being foolish, you are being disobedient. Carefully select the most faithful, and make them the most equipped.

Maxim 6: Equipping requires knowledge, skill, and long-term commitment.

Equipping is one of the hardest things you'll ever do. We tend to underestimate it every time.

We think it will be easier than it is.

We think it will be faster than it is.

We think it will be shorter than it is.

We think it will be finished when it isn't.

But it is one of the most strategic ways you'll ever invest your life. There are so few equippers these days because it's harder than everyone expects it to be. It is harder than I ever expected. And because of that unrealistic expectation, early on I was disappointed a lot.

When Walk Thru the Bible was just getting off the ground in the early 1970s, I experienced all kinds of fears and doubts about its future. During that time, Dr. Howard Hendricks flew to town, and I took him out to lunch and asked him, "Prof, what do you think about Walk Thru the Bible?"

"It's good, Bruce," he said.

"No, Prof, I mean what do you really think?"

He smiled and said, "Well, it's obviously being blessed by the Lord, so be encouraged."

Unfortunately I wasn't, so I asked him a third time, "No, tell me the truth, Prof. What do you think about the future of Walk Thru the Bible?" I wanted someone to assure me that my fragile dream would work.

He noticed that I had stopped eating and must have sensed I needed a deeper answer. What he said next is one of the most important pieces of advice I've ever received about the nature of the equipping process. "Bruce, the real issue isn't what Walk Thru the Bible is doing today, or next year, or even ten years from now. The real test is what Walk Thru the Bible will be doing in fifteen, twenty, and even twenty-five years from now.

"Right now you can do it all by yourself, but the real test will come if the Lord blesses your ministry so much that you can't do it all by yourself. Then you'll really be tested! Can you equip others to expand the ministry far beyond your abilities? Yes, Bruce, the truth about Walk Thru the Bible will not be known until many years from now when the fruit of your labors will start to ripen. It will reveal either that you learned how to equip or that you didn't learn. That's the secret to Walk Thru the Bible's ultimate success."

He hit the nail right on the head, didn't he? It's the long-term perspective that the Lord wants from us, not the short-term. He wants our commitment to equip not just for the sprint, but for life's marathon.

I'll never forget the moment I glimpsed another man's marathon. We were packed into a huge auditorium for a major national Christian convention, and I was sitting toward the back next to one of our nation's greatest Christian educators. He was a legend in the Christian community and had mentored many men and women with whom I have served. Each of them always spoke of this man with deepest respect and affection.

As we listened to the plenary speaker, however, it quickly became obvious that he had mastered the art of boredom. After a while, this elder statesman sighed and pulled out a small wad of three-by-five cards from his inside jacket pocket. They were dog-eared and tattered, but from the way he handled them, it was obvious that something very special was written on them. My curiosity got the best of me and I glanced down at them. Each card had three or four names with six or seven points beneath each name. Slowly he reviewed each card and then turned to the next card.

After the session we talked over coffee. I told him I had noticed his cards and asked if he was reviewing notes for a quiz. He smiled and said, "That's a list of every graduate who received his advanced degree under my leadership. I have been praying for them by name every day and have kept in touch with many of them throughout these many years. They're my fingers and my mouth and my feet. I have equipped them and now they are equipping others around the world for the cause of Christ. Besides my family, these men and women are the most significant achievement in my life."

Sounds a little like the apostle Paul! What a commitment to long-term prayer and correspondence.

The founder of Chick-fil-A, Truett Cathy, saw some unique foliage during a tour of Malaysia. From his guide he learned it was an unusual type of bamboo with an extraordinary growth pattern. You plant the seed in a mound of dirt, and water and fertilize it. Nothing happens the whole year. The second year you water and fertilize it, and nothing happens. The third year you water and fertilize it, but nothing happens again. In the fourth year you again water and fertilize it, and nothing happens. Finally, in the fifth year you water and fertilize it, and within ninety days, it grows ninety feet!

We must guard against "instantitis" in our equipping. Sometimes it takes years of constant watering and fertilizing before we see growth. Equipping is a long-term commitment. Maybe the one you are considering giving up on needs only one more year of watering—so don't give up!

Maxim 7: The ultimate goal of equipping is independent equippers.

One Sunday morning I ran into one of the most outstanding teachers in the church that we attend. He looked like he was carrying a big sack of overripe discouragement. "What seems to be the matter?" I asked him, hoping to be of some encouragement.

"Another couple just quit my class this morning," he said. "My class is a revolving door. After twelve to eighteen months my students leave and I have to start all over again. I don't know what the problem is, but I'm thinking of quitting."

It didn't sound too good, but I took a chance and explored a little further. "Do you have any idea why they might be leaving? Is your content missing the mark?"

"No, I think my subject is right on target. The class members grow like weeds and then leave. Just this year I've lost six great couples that I've really been working with. They've quit my class to become teachers of their own classes."

I couldn't believe what I was hearing. What an exciting problem he had! Quickly I shared how the Lord felt about his ongoing "problem"—that my friend was undoubtedly an extremely effective teacher because he was equipping his students to teach others! Perhaps someday we'll all know enough to celebrate the right victories.

Independent equippers are those who have mastered a ministry skill, who are actively using it, who enlist others with similar gifts and interests, who train them to become proficient, and who send them out with ongoing guidance to do the same.

Can you capture the power inherent in the Lord's Method of Multiplication? He doesn't want us to just train people; He also wants us to train people to become trainers who will eventually train others to become trainers.

People come into our classes needing guidance and oversight. Our task is to continue developing them in light of their spiritual gifts to become active "workers in ministry" to the point that they reproduce themselves.

This cycle perfectly duplicates God's cycle of life for all of us, doesn't it? From birth, to maturity, to marriage, to reproduction, to training children until they're independent, to nurturing through grandparenting. Ultimately, the Lord wants the godly line to grow and exert more and more influence through physical and spiritual multiplication.

As you and I mature in our lives and teaching skills, we should become more aware of and committed to this reproductive process. Our most crucial responsibility is to pass our batons to the next generation with effectiveness. If we pass the baton to runners who are "sterile" and do not have the commitment to reproduce, then the whole process has been severely hindered.

The sobering reality underlying this process is that all it takes to drop the baton is for one generation of teachers to be content-focused rather that equipping-focused. Whatever we do, we mustn't drop the baton the Lord has entrusted to us. So run, my friend, knowing that your race is but one lap, and the quality and quantity of runners to whom you pass your baton will determine the eternal impact of your personal race.

MEANING

The essence of the Law of Equipping is these three words: "Equip for service." The teacher should train students for a life of service and edification.

CONCLUSION

It was late at night after an intense three-day meeting with Peter Drucker, the management guru. Thirty of us had participated in the by-invitation-only sessions, and we were all leaders of major Christian organizations or pastors of churches with national influence. It was an exciting, stretching time. But the most memorable moment for me occurred unexpectedly through a relatively young man whose church had enjoyed almost unbelievable growth through evangelism and discipleship. I asked him to share some of the lessons he had learned.

"At first, it almost killed me. In fact, I was seriously considering quitting the ministry." I nodded because I understood. He continued, "I couldn't keep up with the rapidly growing church demands, and it was starting to rip my life apart. I pleaded with God for some relief, or, I told Him, it was all over.

"The next morning in the middle of my personal devotions, I stumbled onto Ephesians 4:11–16. I already knew these verses and had preached on them many times. But like a bolt of lightning sent from heaven, God helped me really see what they were teaching—I think for the very first time.

"I knew it was my job to equip the saints for the work of the ministry and the edification of the body, and I thought I was doing that. But the

Lord showed me that I wasn't even close. I became so convicted by this that I got on my knees and committed to the Lord *that I would do exactly what the Bible said and trust Him for the results*. If the church failed, so what, because I was going to quit anyway.

."Well, I told my deacons what the Lord had made clear we were doing wrong and asked them if they would join with me in this commitment to complete obedience. Every one of them was excited about the idea. Later that week, we made a list of all the faithful people we knew in the church who met the requirements of leadership in Timothy and Titus. We identified 147 men and women.

"We met with each of them individually—or, if they were married, as couples—and told them of the commission the Lord had given us to equip them as ministers. We asked them to pray about joining us in a yearlong intensive training process to equip them to be ordained as lay ministers. I couldn't believe it, but all of them said yes. It shocked me and it shocked our leadership team. *The people were waiting to be asked and equipped.*

"The next twelve months were intense and exciting, and before we knew it, the big Sunday arrived. There I was, in front of the congregation, and across the front and both sides of the auditorium were 147 godly, committed, and now-equipped men and women. I had them all kneel, and that morning ordained them as lay ministers in the church. Then I preached about the heart of God as it relates to all of us doing the work of ministry, and I told these 147 that I was giving them the ministry at that moment. Never again should they wonder if they are called or are supposed to meet a need; they were to act as I should act, as a minister fully committed to meeting the needs of their people."

"What an incredible story," I told him. "What an inspiration! But did it actually work? What happened to your burnout and the overwhelming workload?"

"You won't believe it," he said. "I didn't either—at first, anyway. Usually on Monday morning, the church telephone rings off the hook with counseling needs and all kinds of emergencies. You know what happened? No one called on Monday. I thought my sermon had bombed and that I had offended the congregation. In addition, that morning one of our key leaders had been in a terrible accident, but because of other emergencies, I was unable to visit him until after dinner that evening.

"I rushed to the hospital and went to the intensive care desk to get permission to visit my good friend. The nurse said that no one could visit intensive care except the immediate family or the pastor. Then she asked me who I wanted to see. I told her the man's name and then told her I was his pastor.

"She jumped right out of her seat and said, 'Oh, no, you're not! Don't try and tell me you are his pastor, too!' I asked her what she was talking about. She said, 'You're the eighth person this afternoon who has come in here saying that they were his pastor!'

"Then it hit me! We didn't have eight pastors, we had only two. That is, until Sunday morning—because now we had 147! Eight of them responded—and we never called them from the office.

"Bruce, that is the secret to the explosion that has hit our church. My workload has been cut by 90 percent, and the ministry going on by the church members and among the church members has exploded by over 1000 percent."

Earlier in this chapter I promised that when we get our teaching in line with the Lord, He supernaturally blesses our efforts. That story is living proof, isn't it?

Would you like that kind of thrill when you teach? Would you like to see the utter joy and celebration when your students discover that they can "do the work of ministry" and find through it incredible fulfillment and satisfaction? Then why not commit yourself to this revolutionary approach to teaching—that you, as God's divinely appointed instructor, will begin equipping the students He has entrusted to you?

In every direction we look, the work is left undone. But in almost every classroom you visit the workers are left unequipped. So commit yourself to the commission of the Lord: He Himself gave teachers "for the equipping of the saints for the work of ministry, for the edifying of the body of Christ" (Ephesians 4:12).

DISCUSSION QUESTIONS

1. Our study of Ephesians 4 revealed a number of key principles on equipping: (1) The primary purpose of the teacher is to equip; (2) the primary audience teachers equip is Christians; and (3) the primary result of equipped Christians is that they are doing the work of ministry and edifying the body of Christ. Evaluate your own teaching ministry in the light of these principles. Ask yourself, how true are these principles in my teaching? What needs to change in order for it to be true? How should I accomplish that change?

2. Do you agree that the majority of teaching focuses on content rather than character and conduct? Why do you think character has become such a low priority in recent years? What will be the eventual result? How much of your last two classes contributed to developing a godly character?

3. What do you think would happen if local churches began to record equipping results, such as those outlined under Equipping Maxim 3, for each Sunday

school class and morning worship service? What causes us to stray so far from the Lord's clear directives, and how do we suffer because of it?

4. Limited time and opportunity require that we carefully invest our lives. Paul said to pass the truth on to faithful ones. Therefore, spend your time equipping those who already prove to be the kind of people discussed in 1 Timothy and Titus. (It's important to have one or two special people, of course, who need some close attention in building them to that level.) Maximize your efforts by choosing your team carefully. List the top three to five people you should be equipping for the Lord. Start with your family. Will you take the first steps today? Then schedule some time with each one to discuss your desire to equip them.

CHAPTER TWELVE

Equipping

Method and Maximizers

I t's Sunday morning. The choir just completed its special number, and the director of Christian education comes in at the side door and whispers to the pastor. Then he strides to the pulpit with a glazed look in his eyes. Suddenly you feel anxious—you've seen this before. Everyone around you stiffens. Eyes stare at the floor. Faces bury themselves in the bulletins.

The CE director starts with a nice little speech about how wonderful it is to serve the Lord as a Sunday school teacher and that teachers are strategic to the life of the church. Eyes are now rolling to the ceiling. Everybody knows what's coming next. Every word is producing more and more guilt until he finally says it: "We need you! And I promise we'll train you. We'll prepare you! But if we don't get six volunteers right now, we can't go on with the service. So until six hands are raised, the pastor cannot preach the sermon. Now, who's going to raise their hands this morning?"

Slowly you slide you hands under your legs to ensure safety. Only three hands are raised and the tension could be cut with a knife. Suddenly, you wife's elbow slams into your ribs, and in a painful reflex your arm shoots to the sky.

"*I see that hand. Thank you, brother!* We have a wonderful group of junior high boys waiting for an inspirational teacher like you."

You look around to see who he's talking about, and then it hits you—you've been had! Your heart is racing. Your palms are sweating. You're ticked at your wife. That's the last time you'll forget her birthday!

Then some relief pours into your heart. He did say you'll receive training. Boy, do you need that! Probably a semester of coaching. Maybe it won't be too bad after all.

Your wife nudges you again—but you know better than to move that hand. Out of a dazed stupor you hear, "We need you right now. *Today.* Please meet me in the hallway." The other five volunteers are heading out the side door. Everyone is breathing again and the pastor is smiling.

You're the last of the six to hit the hallway. There's a swirl of activity as the CE director tosses the Sunday school quarterly in your direction. As he gallops off into the sunset, you hear him say, "Thank you, thank you very much. And may God bless you!"

As you turn down the corner you notice two chairs crashing out the doorway. An eraser hits the opposite wall. It's your classroom.

Sound familiar? Somehow—though I'm sure this has never happened in your church!—I think you know exactly what I mean.

What is this church's secret formula for training? *Exhortation plus guilt plus the Sunday school quarterly equals training.*

I wonder what we'd discover if we could be a fly on the wall of that poor junior high teacher's room right now. How does he feel? And how do his students feel? More important, how would Christ evaluate the church's "equipping of the saints for the work of ministry" in that situation? How would it stand up to His priorities for us?

If you want a vivid answer to these questions, then observe Christ's own priorities when He ministered here on earth. Did He merely throw a quarterly in the direction of a person He manipulated? Hardly! Instead, Christ invested three intense years equipping and training His "faculty" to teach and minister. If Christ modeled such a deep level of commitment to training, then how should we evaluate the aforementioned all-too-typical training fiasco?

No wonder that on anonymous questionnaires, 80 to 90 percent of the students respond that their classes are boring and irrelevant. No wonder teachers are experiencing burnout. They feel so ill-equipped! You can hold your breath for only so long.

Somehow in the church we've fallen prey to the idea that training is a low priority. But outside the boundaries of the church, in the marketplace, the exact opposite is true. Whenever you find companies with superior performance, you find companies with superior training. Conversely, whenever you find companies with poor product quality and inferior customer service, the employees receive minimal or no training. Poor companies and poor teachers are bred in the womb of poor training.

It continues to amaze me how the world stumbles on the secrets of success outlined in the Scriptures, while we who have the Word of God don't believe these secrets enough to practice them. Christ devoted the heart of His ministry to equipping His men. God commissioned the heart of our ministry to equipping our students and teachers.

So what should we do?

My good friend Ron Blue, a well-known Christian financial counselor, often says you can tell a person's priorities just by looking at his checkbook and datebook. No matter what a person may say about his priorities, his money and time always reveal the truth.

To find out the real commitment to training in an organization, school, or church, look at the time, money, and human resources it invests in training its people.

I have studied various church budgets to find the amount of money spent on teacher and leadership training. Most churches do not even have a budget category for training. Those that do typically spend less than *one-tenth of 1 percent* on training. What does this say about our priorities?

Training greatly multiplies results for the long term. Often young people ask me whether I recommend attending college or graduate school. I often give them this illustration.

Let's say your life is represented by a seemingly endless field. Your responsibility is to clear the field, plow it, plant it, and harvest it for the rest of your life. The challenge is to harvest the right crops (fruit that lasts forever) in the largest amounts possible (hundred-fold harvest). You have a number of options:

- First, quit before high school, and you'll have a hoe to work your field—but you can start immediately.
- Second, quit after high school and you'll have a dozen hand tools.
- Third, stop after college, and you'll have a Rototiller with an unlimited amount of gas.
- Fourth, stop after graduate school, and you'll have a diesel tractor with a number of implements.
- Fifth, don't ever stop, even after graduate school. Keep learning, and you'll gradually gather a whole series of tractors, combines, irrigation systems—everything you could possibly imagine and need for your field.

Now, if you stop before you finish high school, you'll be able to get quite a few rows planted and harvested by the time another person can finish college. For a while it will look like you have done the wise thing. But give that Rototiller or tractor one year in action, and then watch the results.

Do you see the unbelievable difference that equipping can make in the life of a person and what they can do with the gifts God has entrusted to them? Whenever we pay careful attention and devote key resources to equipping the saints for the work of ministry, we greatly multiply their lifelong fruitfulness for the kingdom of Christ.

Although Christ gives all of us gifts—and although He gives gifted men and women to the church as teachers, pastors, and so on—He allows us to decide how diligently we will use those gifts. As you remember from the Parable of the Talents, the Lord judges all of us on the basis of what we did with what He gave us.

Equipping isn't an option. It isn't even a suggestion. It is a command. So obey it. Go against the trend. Throw down your hoe and turn on the tractor.

EQUIPPING METHOD

At Walk Thru the Bible, I regularly encouraged our leadership team with this motto:

If you want a perfect product, then perfect the underlying process.

If you want effective teachers (perfect product), you must develop and manage an effective and ongoing teacher-training curriculum (perfect the process).

The five steps of the Equipping Method are universal and work for any person in any place with any students and for any skill. They are equally effective no matter if you are training a person to play tennis, ride a horse, preach a sermon, witness in the community, or run a household budget. This process works between teacher and student, parent and child, boss and employee—in virtually any relationship.

You are undoubtedly already using some or all of these steps, but bringing them all to your attention will enable you in the future to sense

exactly what needs to be done and in what order. Often when the training process is not working well, it's either because a major step has been left out or because a step has been presented in the wrong order.

Step 1: Instruct

The first step in teaching a skill is to "*instruct*" the students with the basic fact and information regarding the skill. The teacher is to "*educate*" the students and "*prepare*" them with the required foundational truths upon which the skill is based.

A number of summers ago, my daughter Jennifer and I spent a couple of weeks in Colorado while I taught a college course. At one of the meals, we met the son of one of the married students in my class. He was a tennis instructor who sparked Jennifer's interest, and he eventually invited her to take some free tennis lessons.

A few hours later she came bounding into the condo. It was obvious she had had a wonderful time, but she didn't look like she had played much tennis. "How did it go?" I queried.

"Great! But we didn't play much tennis because he spent a lot of time teaching me the rules and strategy of the game. Dad, I never knew there was so much to tennis! Now that I finally understand, I think I'm ready to learn how to play the game."

That young man already had a major step up on most of his peers. Not only did he recognize a real catch in my wonderful daughter, but he also recognized that instructing is the first stage of any skill acquisition.

By the end of this first step, your students should feel relaxed about how the skill you're equipping them with works. Up to this point, you should stay in the factual presentation stage.

Step 2: Illustrate

The second step of teaching a skill is to "*illustrate*" to the students what the skill actually looks like when it's being used. "*Expose*" them to the use of the information of the first step as the skill is practiced. Give them an actual "*preview*" so that the words of the first step become a living picture in this step. You should move them from "I understand" to "I see."

Tragically, the vast majority of all equipping never leaves the first step of "telling." Most teachers think they've trained a person to do something when the person knows the theory behind the skill.

But do you actually know how to play tennis just because you know the distinction between a forehand and a backhand?

We must not allow ourselves to define equipping as merely the ability to repeat information from memory. Knowing how to do something in our mind is not the same as doing it in real life. Yet in my more than nine years of college and graduate education, less than 5 percent of my teachers even attempted this second step!

Many years ago I took a course in "*witnessing*," which lasted more than three months. The only tests the teacher gave were to see if we could recall his notes. Not once did we see the professor attempt to demonstrate what "witnessing" looked like in real life. In that teacher's mind, equipping was equal to knowing rather than doing! Training was limited to information. Many of the students were no more skilled at witnessing after the final exam than they were at the start of the class. Neither did they practice it any more frequently. Yet some students earned an A in a course where the teacher was supposed to teach a skill which they never saw demonstrated or practiced personally.

Tragic, isn't it?

Step 3: Involve

The third step of teaching a skill is to "*involve*" students in actually doing the skill themselves. At this point the students need to "*experience*" the skill firsthand. Lead them in a "*practicum*" so that you move them from "I understand" and "I see" to the "I'm doing it" stage.

Until this step, the students remain passive. In the first step they hear about the skill, and in the second they watch the skill. Now they practice the skill themselves.

This is when the ideal becomes real. School knowledge transitions to street knowledge. As the teacher, your responsibility is to practice the skill with them as a player-coach. Be close to them, always encouraging their every effort.

Years ago when I served as a youth pastor in northern New Jersey, I challenged a dozen of my best young people to an advanced level of discipleship and Christian service. One of our young women had a real flair for art, and I was trying to train her to use flip charts to present the gospel on the Long Island beaches.

After explaining to her how it worked (Step 1: Instruct) and demonstrating it myself in a youth group meeting and on the beaches (Step 2: Illustrate), I encouraged her to participate in the process. She drew the sketches on the flip chart as I did the talking (Step 3: Involve).

The next day I encouraged her to do the talking while I did the drawing. We went to a "safe" part of the beach at her suggestion, but by the end of the day, she was doing it all. I was standing on the side-lines, silently cheering as she dynamically presented the good news of Christ to upwards of 125 children and adults at a time.

This middle step, then, is the important pivot or hinge of the equipping method. It greatly determines the degree of success your students will ultimately enjoy. *Therefore, more than with any other step, you must pay careful attention to the progress and emotional stability of your students during the practice stage.* If they experience a disaster full of embarrassment and disappointment, you can be sure your equipping won't be very effective. But if you can insure that they enjoy a wonderful learning experience, that they feel good about themselves and their achievements, then the remainder of the process will be a pleasure.

Make sure your students succeed! Don't count the score at this stage, just cheer the process. Normal students are full of insecurity and anxiety, so affirm everything they do. Guarantee the success of this step by taking all risk of failure and embarrassment out of the picture. Never throw students into the deep end to sink or swim. They should leave this third step loving the process and wanting more!

Step 4: Improve

The fourth step of teaching a skill is to "*improve*" the students' newly obtained skills. At this point the students need to develop and become more "*efficient*" as they "*perform*" the skill over and over again. You should move them from "I understand" and "I see" and "I'm doing it" to the "I'm getting much better" stage.

The process of improvement is an unending one for all who wish to be champions, so this step could be viewed as never being completed. The acquisition of a skill beckons all of us to grow from the novice to the intermediate to the expert to the champion. At Walk Thru the Bible, we called this "the Relentless Pursuit of Excellence."

As equippers, we wanted to bring out the highest and best in the natural talents and gifts of our students—to cause our students to blossom to their fullest potential. Of course, the needs of our students varied. Some needed to be pushed out of the nest while others needed to be held in the nest until they developed a few more feathers. As teachers, you and I must be aware of the needs of each student and risk their momentary displeasure if we have to hold them back or push them forward before they think they are ready.

A number of years ago I was training a young man to share his faith in Christ. He had watched me witness to a number of people. Little by little I was throwing him the ball, but he'd always throw it back at me within the first thirty seconds—out of fear of failure or potential embarrassment. He was afraid the person might ask him some of the more difficult questions: "What about the people in Africa who have never heard about Jesus?" or "Where do dinosaurs and cavemen come into the Bible?" or "Who was Cain's wife?"

We had role-played how to handle each of those questions, plus the remaining "dirty dozen," until I was satisfied that he knew the biblical answers. But he kept hitting that wall of fear. Finally, we were witnessing together to an entire family, and I saw that same glazed look in his eyes. This time I knew he needed to be nudged out of the nest and made to fly on his own.

I waited until someone asked one of the hard questions. The family's seventeen-year-old son, who had an obvious chip on his shoulder, asked about the people in Africa. I said, "That's a great question, and my friend Mike has a great answer. But right now, could you please direct me to the bathroom?" I didn't look at Mike. Before he could even breathe, I was down that hall and had the door tightly closed behind me. I knew he could fly—but he wouldn't unless there was no way of escape. Luckily there were a couple of magazines to read as I timed my "leave of absence" for fifteen minutes.

As I walked back into the den, Mike was now sitting on the edge of his seat. He was well into the presentation of the gospel and everyone was spellbound; even the seventeen-year-old's chip lay on the floor. Mike was soaring and enjoying every second.

The goal in this fourth stage is to develop students to the point of competence so that without our guidance or even presence they can fully perform the skill with excellence.

When we equip someone, we train him to the level of competence. It's refreshing to discover teachers who understand and practice this principle. One of my fellow seminary classmates had an unusual way of testing his students for that level of competence and achievement. Upon graduation he went back to his home country of Indonesia and started a seminary. The final requirement for graduation was to start a church from scratch and develop it to self-sustaining stability. Only when the student's new church had trained and installed committed elders/deacons who were leading and growing the church could that diploma touch the student's hand.

Since the goal of true education is to train a person to the point of competent and independent use of that skill, this step is absolutely crucial. Ephesians 4:11–16 doesn't present us with the challenge to equip the saints to "know" about the work, but to equip the saints to "do" the work. Therefore, shouldn't we validate our equipping not merely on the basis of factual answers on tests, but also on the basis of our students' specific achievements?

Do you see how powerful such training for competence is? Can you imagine how faculty would restructure their classes if they knew the real issue was the use of knowledge rather than its accumulation? All their students would quickly know if the content works because they would try it the very next week!

Further development must include equipping in advanced skills as well as the accompanying strategies necessary to become an outstanding user of the skills. The more advanced our students become, the more we must help them refine their techniques and advance their personal style.

Advanced information should not be shared in the first step (Instruct) because information is valuable only when the person has matured to the level where it can actually be used. As the person advances, continue sharing more and more information and techniques and strategies to encourage him ever onward and upward.

Recently I saw this improving part of the process firsthand when I met with the best of Walk Thru the Bible's Old and New Testament seminar instructors for a four-day training conference. My purpose was to train them to teach the *7 Laws of the Learner* conference to churches, colleges, and conferences around the world.

Before this equipping began, each instructor had already heard me teach the course in person at least twice, listened to the audio tapes a couple of times, read the 560-page training manual, and taught the course twice in small practice sessions. As we sat around the table, I sensed these men were highly prepared. They came as master teachers in their own right.

After an extended time of prayer, I decided to explain the underlying philosophy behind how I had structured each of the Seven Laws of the Learner to maximize lasting life change in the listeners. After an hour of instruction, I noticed that they had become very quiet. Too quiet. I thought I had lost them somewhere in the process, so I asked them what was the matter.

One of our most senior faculty members answered, "I had no idea all that was going on beneath the surface! Now I understand why this material has such a revolutionary impact when I teach it. The reason we are so quiet is because we are all blown away by what you have told us. But I'll tell you one thing, what you've shared will really improve my teaching from now on." Effective equipping continually provides deeper understanding of the content to the learners, no matter how advanced they may be.

A few weeks after that in-depth training, I team-taught the 7 *Laws* with one of those instructors. When the conference was completed and we were celebrating the Lord's blessing over a nice dinner, he asked me for some straightforward suggestions for improvement.

For every presentation he gave that weekend, I had written six to eight pages of evaluation, so I wasn't at a loss for affirmations or suggestions. Overall, he'd done an outstanding job. However, one weakness of his was his tendency to cover information in such a way that the audience missed the "aha!" of discovering it for themselves. He presented the correct material but lessened its potential for lasting life change because the audience received the answers before they had mentally asked the questions.

During the next hour I carefully explained some of the secrets of building further dynamic into his teaching (Step 1: Instruction), showed him how it looked and felt using the two different methods on him— the one he had used and the way he could have done it (Step 2: Illustrate)—and worked on a couple of real-life examples together (Step 3: Involve). As I saw him grasp the finer points of this advanced teaching technique, I also saw the fire glow in his eyes. The next time he taught, I saw the fire glow in his audience (Step 4: Improve). Effective equipping continuously provides advanced techniques to the learner, no matter how advanced he or she may be.

Step 5: Inspire

The final step of teaching a skill is to *"inspire"* students to continue using their skill. Over time, your influence becomes much more indirect and your role will be to *"encourage"* a lifestyle of not only using the skill but also *"passing it on"* to others.

You should move your students from "I understand," "I see," "I'm doing it," and "I'm getting much better" to the "I'll keep it going" stage.

Teachers who train at this stage are the real equippers—the champions of the cause. They have the vision to pass it on. They skillfully guide their students from being spectators to becoming learners to becoming teachers and eventually becoming equippers of other teachers. They understand there is far more power in reproducing oneself than just doing it yourself. They do anything and everything to continue the ongoing development of their students. They won't let their students go when they threaten to quit. They continue to nurture and encourage and cajole and do whatever it takes to coach a team to the top.

Does it come naturally to think this way, to coach others to do the work rather than do the work yourself? No, it doesn't! I've had to learn and relearn this lesson numerous times in my career, but one of the most powerful was during the early days of Walk Thru the Bible.

When I first started teaching Walk Thru the Bible seminars in Dallas in the early 1970s, many of my closest friends told me that no one could teach the seminars like I could. Whatever I did, they said, don't let anyone else teach it because they will ruin it.

Other friends were just as sure the opposite was true: "You must train others to teach the seminars. You can't and shouldn't do it all yourself."

For months I wrestled with this decision. One weekend I became so anxious about it that I stopped everything and contacted a dozen of my closest friends and mentors, hoping to get a clear and unanimous recommendation. When the calls were completed, six had voted "train others" and six had voted "teach the seminar yourself."

The frustration continued to escalate, and later that weekend I felt it was going to rip me apart. Finally I walked down into our basement and began to pray that the Lord would guide me to His answer. I called one of my favorite professors and told him of my plight. I asked him what he thought I should do. I'll never forget what he said, nor the way he said it: "I can't believe that you don't know the biblical answer to your question." (Oh boy, he was my Bible professor—there went my grade!) "What does 2 Timothy 2:2 say? It directly answers your question—train 'faithful men who will be able to teach others also.' Therefore, if you want God's fullest blessing on your life and ministry, you had better start practicing 2 Timothy 2:2. Start equipping others immediately!"

This direct and very biblical advice turned out to be a crucial turning point in my life and ministry. That evening, *the doctrine of equipping became my conviction of equipping.* I finally believed what the Bible said—to the point of obeying it.

But I have to admit that planning to do it and actually doing it were two very different things. The first time I watched one of my friends teach the Walk Thru the Old Testament seminar, everything in me was screaming, "No! Don't do it that way. Do it like me!" It would have been a lot easier and better (at that point, anyway) to do it myself. But because of the undeniable clarity of 2 Timothy 2:2, and later Ephesians 4:11–16, I disregarded my feelings and deepened my resolve to do it God's way, not mine. I chose to obey the Lord and trust the results to Him.

As the years passed, God graciously began to change my heart. Slowly and painfully what brought fulfillment changed from "what I did" to "what others did." At first, I enjoyed being the "star quarterback"; a decade later I enjoyed far more "coaching from the sidelines."

I often found myself nodding with pleasure, buttons straining, as I watched one of our instructors teach. More often than not, I'd smile as I walked away, thinking, *That's better than I could have done!*

It's a delight to realize that my students have outdistanced their teacher. Isn't that the whole point of equipping—to help our students run faster than we can, run farther than we can, run smarter than we can, and run with more resolve than we do?

The optimum aim of equipping is to train students who outperform their coach.

May your heart respond with deep commitment to "train the faithful to teach others also." May you enable others who look to you for leadership to stand on your shoulders. May the fire that burns in your heart kindle the coals of others who follow you.

Do this and you will realize you are expending your life in ways that will far outlive you—and make an impact that will last forever. Then perhaps a century from now, when we watch from glory our "spiritual great-grandchildren" bear fruit that lasts forever, some of them will say, "It all started back a hundred years ago when [your name] equipped my great-grandfather in the faith."

EQUIPPING MAXIMIZERS

The disciples were equipped by Christ to minister effectively using the same five-step process:

Step 1: Instruct—they listened to Him teach the multitudes publicly and themselves privately.

Step 2: Illustrate—they watched Him minister in various settings and to different audiences, from sympathetic to hostile, as He demonstrated His content in all parts of life.

Step 3: Involve—they ministered with Him throughout Judah, Galilee, and Jerusalem, and eventually He also sent them out to minister without His direct presence.

Step 4: Improve—when they came back to report their activities, Jesus was waiting for them and immediately involved Himself in their further training and equipping.

Step 5: Inspire—Jesus personally visited them numerous times after His resurrection and later sent the Holy Spirit to train and comfort them until their life on earth was completed. Jesus sent His disciples into all the world but promised He would never leave them nor forsake them.

Jesus didn't give the disciples a Sunday school quarterly and a class and tell them to go teach. No, *He assumed responsibility for equipping them for the ministry.* When He said, "*I will make you fishers of men*," He declared He was the one in charge of the equipping process. Note carefully: Christ didn't say, "I will teach you" (activity) but "I will make you" (result). He didn't just pick up a fishing pole and pass it to His disciples; He invested His life in teaching and training and equipping them to fish for men.

Jesus Christ placed a great deal of importance on equipping. He knew that how parents equip their children greatly influences the children's entire lives. He knew that how churches equip their members greatly influences the health of their church. He knew that ultimately we are shaped by the equipping process—*either for good or for evil.*

Ultimately, the five steps in the Equipping Method can be used to train anyone to do anything. For instance, a growing number of parents effectively equip their children against alcoholism, sexual abuse, drug abuse, and dysfunctional relationships. With rare exceptions, we carry for the rest of our lives the imprint of the hands that have equipped us.

The seven Equipping Maximizers listed below reveal further insights on how to deepen your impact upon others for good. May your "fingerprints" leave a mark of godliness and maturity everywhere you go.

Maximizer 1: Train your students until they are successful, independent users of the skill.

The semester was three-quarters over when the student next to me whispered, "I just hate this class. When it's over, I'm never going to look at this Hebrew Old Testament again. At least I'm getting an A—that'll look good on my report card!"

Did that student benefit from the skill he had learned?

Or consider this reality. The study of Greek was required in seminary, as you'd expect, since it's the original language of the New Testament. Each student had to take six semesters of Greek, and New Testament majors had to take many additional courses. Three solid years of studying Greek. In our fourth year, four seniors were talking about the level of competence we had or had not gained. I asked my three friends to tell me their opinion. If a hundred of our fellow seniors who had just successfully completed the extensive Greek curriculum opened the Greek New Testament at random, how many could successfully read and translate one paragraph?

The response was laughter. "Maybe three. Five, tops." In other words, my fellow seniors assured me that 95 to 97 percent of the seniors couldn't read Greek after three years of being "equipped."

Now, I have a question for you. Do these two examples surprise you? Or are they all too common in almost everyone's experience?

The first maxim focuses our attention on the clear goal of equipping: the teacher must equip until the student independently uses the skill in real life. In the first instance, the student won't use the skill in Hebrew because of his *negative attitude*. In the second, the students won't use their skills in Greek because of their *inadequate ability*.

Consider, then, the value of those courses. Did the "equipping" result in positive and lasting results? In the first case, the teacher failed to develop positive sentiments in the emotions of the student; so regardless of the level of the skill, *the student would not use the skill*. In this case the teacher overemphasized the "factual" and underemphasized the "feeling."

We have failed greatly when students despair of the course ever ending and leave less inclined toward the subject than when they started. Many times I have entered a new class extremely motivated to master the subject, but within the first month languished under the process. The teacher killed the heart by beating over the head.

The second teacher failed to develop adequate competence in the students, so regardless of their desire, *they could not use the skill*. In this case, the teacher underemphasized the "mastery" and may have overemphasized the "motivation." We have failed just as greatly when the student likes the course but is unable to use the skill when he leaves.

Since the student's conviction and capability determine the student's ultimate success, those two factors should also determine the teacher's success.

Some classes build on one another, so a student can't be expected to know and use Greek after one semester. But isn't it realistic to expect that he would have that skill by the time he graduates from seminary? If, upon graduation, the students can't read the Greek New Testament, the teacher probably has failed to teach them. On the other hand, if the students hate the subject, the teacher has failed just as soundly. In either case, the students are the losers.

Maximizer 2: Reproduce yourself by focusing on students' skill, not your style.

Duplicating style builds shallow saints.

As teachers, our responsibility is to train students to become effective users of a skill within the boundaries of their personalities and temperaments. We are arrogant when we either directly or indirectly imply that our way is the inspired way. Instead, our efforts must be focused upon guiding students to produce the desired results regardless of the style they select.

God Himself focuses upon results rather than style. Just observe the New Testament books for a moment. It is indisputably clear that "God breathed/inspired" the Scriptures; yet when you read the first chapter of James and compare it to the first chapter of Romans or Revelation, you immediately are struck by how differently those books communicate. James writes short, punchy, and direct sentences. Paul writes Romans with complex sentences and extended logic. John writes Revelation using highly descriptive and emotional passages.

How can this be if the same God inspired all the books of the Bible? Shouldn't they all be written in the same style? No, God chooses to achieve His goal of revelation without altering or overpowering an author's personality or temperament. Since that is God's modus operandi, should it not also be ours?

Jesus demonstrated that same commitment through His purposeful selection of the twelve disciples. He almost reveled in their diversity—fiery Peter, practical James, intellectual Thomas, organizing Matthew, sensitive John. Why do we not see Him molding them into one style and approach? Because Christ is also the sovereign source of personality, and He plans to use each individual temperament for His wonderful purposes.

Therefore, never allow your students to copy your delivery or method or gestures. Constantly give honor and dignity to them and their glorious diversity.

Maximizer 3: Alter equipping according to your students' characteristics and circumstances.

The successful use of skills depends not only on the students' knowledge, practice, and experience, but also upon their innate abilities. Every student has a different IQ, educational background, and social background, as well as different innate physical abilities.

Therefore, when we equip our students, we must alter our course objectives and lesson plans according to our students' characteristics and circumstances. Even the best equipping in the world cannot bring some students to the level of desired competence. I am one of those students—in certain areas.

I can still remember when my high school class was preparing for graduation and practicing the song "You'll Never Walk Alone." We were in one of those climactic musical moments ("Walk on, walk on…") and along with everyone else, I was singing at the top of my lungs.

Suddenly the choir director rapped on the podium with his baton and shook his head vigorously. It was obvious he wasn't pleased. "You," he said, looking directly at me, "you in the third row—do me a favor. Please just move your mouth, but don't sing out loud."

No matter how hard the choir director tried to "equip" me to sing, he wasn't successful. He couldn't be successful because in God's good humor, He had given me the gift of "making a joyful noise" and expected me to use it discreetly around others.

Recently my wife and I were with a good friend who is an outstanding sixth-grade teacher. She teaches in a very rough neighborhood, and I asked her if she had noticed any trends in the students over the past five years. She sighed and said that three years ago she had four students who had severe behavioral disorders; this year it was over half the class. During the past semester, the father of one of her students was shot and killed because of drugs. Many of her students were regularly abused. The majority lived in a single-parent home. Some suffered from malnutrition. One twelve-year-old boy kept taking a paper home to be signed by his mother and kept bringing it back unsigned. Our teacher friend finally confronted him on the third day, and he blurted out, "I don't have a father, and my mother left three days ago. We haven't seen or heard from her, so I don't have anyone to sign my paper. I don't know when she's coming back."

With deep disappointment and sadness she said, "We can't teach anything near the same amount of material we did only three years ago. The students cannot cope with it. Sometimes we have to cut our teaching objectives by two-thirds."

Ensure, therefore, that as you strive to equip your students, you take into account their individual and class-wide needs and characteristics.

Maximizer 4: Increase students' motivation by relationship, retribution, and reward.

A universal truth about all equipping is that the more students desire to learn the skill, the quicker and better they will learn it. Therefore, in addition to using the five-step Equipping Method, this maximizer is critical in optimizing your students' progress. *Increase their motivation!*

The purpose of using motivation with your students is to "incite them" to pursue the skill with greater determination and enthusiasm. The three main inciters to action are:

1. Our relationship with another person or entity.
2. Our fear of retribution or pain.
3. Our hope of reward, pleasure, or benefit.

All three inciters are universal and work with every audience if used with sensitivity, though not all are equally effective with all audiences and situations.

For instance, when you see those blue flashing lights behind you on the freeway, how do you think that officer of the law is going to motivate you to stop speeding in the future? Is he going to say, "If you really cared for me, if you truly loved me and my family, you'd stop speeding"? Or "If you stop speeding right now, I'll enter your name in the sweepstakes drawing for a trip to Hawaii"? Or will he use the motive of fear and pain to encourage behavioral change?

Effective teachers use all three as they teach. Obviously, grades can be either a reward or retribution, depending upon the level of performance. Do grades motivate? Yes! And they should. High school students are frequently motivated by the hope of not having to take the final exam if their grade point is high enough at the end of the semester. Athletes often are motivated by fear of punishment and strive to keep their grades above a certain level to continue competing.

Recently my wife and I attended our son and daughter's high school play, which was written and directed by their favorite teacher. You should have seen the outpouring of effort and sacrifice during the two months preceding that play. When the play was over, the loudest applause came from the student actors for their director—they cheered and screamed and gave him gifts and hugged him and carried him on their shoulders and showered love on him for over an hour.

What motivated those students to such incredible levels of performance and hard work? Without a doubt it was the love and respect they had for their teacher.

Evaluate the past three or four classes you taught. How frequently did you consciously assist your students to learn through fanning the flames of desire to learn? How often did you use reward, retribution, and relationship? Effective teachers cause their students to learn at a higher rate through the use of appropriate motivation.

If you want an absolutely incredible insight regarding motivation, study how God motivates mankind to choose to believe and act in the ways He desires. You'll find that these three universal motivators are universal because God put them in every normal human being. If you study the Scriptures carefully, you'll also see God using all three to motivate us to action. For instance:

What is the *retribution* for those who reject Christ? Eternal suffering in hell.

What is the *reward* for those who accept Christ? Eternal pleasure in heaven.

What did Christ say that the *relationship* of loving Him should cause us to do? Keep His commandments.

I have studied thoroughly every major biblical passage where either God the Father, God the Son, or God the Spirit encourages a person(s) to act in a certain manner. Without a doubt, God uses all three of these motivators regularly.

Since He does, and since He never compromises to use carnal means to accomplish perfect ends, shouldn't we also follow His patterns? Indeed, I believe the most effective teachers are the most like God in motivating their students through their use of relationship, retribution, and reward.

Remember, it's not our responsibility just to equip them to use the skill but also to motivate them to desire to use the skill. May your students tell their friends that your class is the most motivating one they've ever had.

Maximizer 5: Nail down the basics before developing advanced skills.

The stronger the foundation, the higher the building may be constructed upon it. Likewise, the more firmly our students have mastered the basics and underlying skills, the more readily and successfully they will be able to learn and use advanced skills.

If you have older children, you've probably had the experience of seeing them move into more advanced material before they adequately understood the preceding material. It's like trying to do a division problem without knowing the multiplication tables. It's not only impossible, but it develops more and more frustration and failure in the students.

I ran into the reality of the failure of some high school English teachers during my first week of teaching college. At least 40 percent of the students were unable to write an acceptable college-level paper. Frequently, grammar was a disaster, spelling a joke, and mature thought processes of logical progression in another galaxy.

When I received those first papers, I was so astounded that I brought them to a lunch table where some of my fellow, seasoned professors were gathered. They laughed and looked at one another with knowing glances. "Welcome, Bruce, to the reality of college teaching!"

As we teach, we must follow the general guideline of ensuring that our students master the required minimum before moving on to advanced skills and techniques. One high school math teacher I know requires all of his students to master perfectly the multiplication tables from one to thirteen. Each month every student takes the same random test of the 169 multiplication questions, and it must be completed in one minute less each time. If you miss even one, you have to come after school every day and retake it again and again until you get all the problems correct in the allotted time. What a wise teacher! He ensures that all of his students achieve the minimal level of competence in that area.

Too many teachers allow their lesson plans rather than the learning rate of their students to set the pace of the class. If we aren't on guard, we can easily fall prey to the concept that covering the material is the point rather that ensuring all students master the material.

Maximizer 6: Encourage students more frequently during early training.

Whenever people contemplate learning a new skill, they normally experience some degree of anxiety and fear. A little internal tension is a good thing, but frequently our students are riddled with overwhelming fear of failure and embarrassment. Strong feelings of fear and anxiety seriously blunt the impact of our teaching.

Therefore, actively lessen your students' fear and heighten their courage. Courage and fear are opposites—when courage grows, fear declines; when fear grows, courage declines.

Give the "gift of courage" regularly.

Isn't it interesting that even such a great leader as Joshua battled severe fear and doubt? Over and over again God told him, "Do not be afraid, nor be dismayed." God also provided numerous ways for Joshua to take courage. Note these five ways to encourage your class, taken from only a few verses of Joshua:

1. *Promise your presence.* Give your students courage by reminding them that you are going to be right with them throughout the training process. Whenever we are afraid, it's often because we feel we'll be alone and vulnerable. Therefore, we are greatly comforted when someone we have great confidence in promises to be right at our side.

"Do not be afraid, nor be dismayed, for the LORD your God is with you wherever you go." (1:9)

"As I was with Moses, so I will be with you. I will not leave you nor forsake you." (1:5)

2. *Promise their success.* Give them courage by ensuring them they will succeed as they try their hardest (remember Christ's words, "I will make you fishers of men"). Whenever we are afraid, it's often because all we can imagine is that we won't be able to do it. Early in learning a skill, we vastly underestimate our chances of success. Therefore, we are greatly strengthened when the leader takes the responsibility for making sure we will succeed.

"Now therefore, arise, go over this Jordan, you and all this people, to *the land which I am giving to them*" (1:2).

"Every place that the sole of your foot will tread upon *I have given you*" (1:3).

"From the wilderness and this Lebanon as far as the great river, the River Euphrates, all the land of the Hittites, and to the Great Sea toward the going down of the sun, *shall be your territory.*" (1:4)

"For to this people you shall divide as an inheritance the land *which I swore to their fathers to give them.*" (1:6)

3. *Promise victory over the hardest parts.* Give your students courage by promising that they will be able to succeed even over the most difficult part of your course. Whenever we are afraid, it is often because we cannot picture ourselves experiencing victory over a certain part of the skill or class—something appears insurmountable. Therefore, we receive solid support when the teacher identifies those areas he knows breed the most fear and relaxes us by promising success as we work with him to master the material.

"No man shall be able to stand before you all the days of your life." (1:5)

Thus God promised victory over the giants in the land, the fortified high country, and the powerful walled cities.

4. *Promise success if they do their part.* Give your students courage by assuring them that they will succeed as they follow your leadership and complete their responsibilities. Learning is a two-way street, and we build confidence by sharing our expectations and requirements, especially if they are within the reach of all students.

"Only be strong and very courageous, that you may observe to do according to all the law...do not turn from it to the right

hand or to the left, that you may prosper wherever you go."
(1:7)

5. *Promise their competence will ensure their success.* Give them courage
by showing that their success will be assured because of the competence
they will soon have. Whenever we are anxious, it is often because we do
not see the long-range benefit that will result from our study and labors.
We all find comfort and confidence by seeing that we will be a better
and more competent individual as we learn and use the skills being
taught. Therefore, picture your students enjoying success in their future
because their current efforts will wonderfully pay off.

"This Book of the Law shall not depart from your mouth, but
you shall meditate in it day and night, that you may observe to do
according to all that is written in it. *For then you will make your
way prosperous, and then you will have good success.*" (1:8)

*Remember, the greater the students' fear, the greater your need to bestow
courage.* As we all have the greatest fear at the beginning, we must share
courage most frequently during the opening sessions of learning a new
skill. Further, whenever any of your students perform well at any level
in the early stages of a skill acquisition, give public affirmation.

Maximizer 7: Reaffirm students' value independent of their level of performance.

When Christ revealed to the disciples that the poor widow's mite was a
far greater gift than the sizable donations of the wealthy, He freed us
from the bondage of comparison. He refocused our attention, reminding us that performance should be appraised not only on the basis of
what a person did, but also what a person did in relation to what he
could have done.

Such a theological perspective about people's performance can wonderfully empower our equipping. If we limit our approval to those who demonstrate an outstanding level of achievement, then we are like the Pharisees who only congratulate the wealthy and devalue the widow's mite.

Christlike equipping considers the whole truth of a person's innate, God-given abilities and seeks opportunities to encourage students in at least five areas of performance:

1. *Amount of effort.* How hard the student is trying reflects his desire to succeed and should be noticed and affirmed.
2. *Degree of improvement.* One benchmark for everyone is improvement over previous performance.
3. *Demonstration of team spirit and morale.* Unity and mutual support is a critical ingredient for maximum equipping. Class members who encourage and assist others should be highly affirmed.
4. *Extra credit and unrequired practice.* Be alert for students who "run extra laps" after practice, who complete optional extras, and who seek to go beyond the externally established requirements.
5. *Outstanding performance.* This is the most obvious and most frequent basis for affirmation. Effective equipping must recognize excellence and exceptional performance.

I once counseled a junior high boy who had concluded he was a terrible failure because of his not-so-good math grades. Listen in on our conversation:

"No matter how much I study or how hard I try, I never get above a D or C. Other kids in my class don't even study and they always get As."

"So," I asked, "how do you feel about that?"

"I'm a failure…it's just not fair. I'm going to stop trying. I mean, why try so hard just for a C anyway?"

This young man needed to "renew his mind" on the basis of how God thought about the issue. So I drew a box and said, "This box represents you. Now, who's in charge of how smart you are in math?"

He was unsure for a moment, but since he knew what the Bible taught, he finally said, "God, I guess."

"Okay. Now, how hard have you tried in class? Have you given a 100 percent effort? A 50 percent effort? What?"

"I try hard. Probably 95 percent—not all the time but most of the time."

"Then draw an arrow almost to the top—to the 95 percent level in your box." He did, and then I wrote a "C-" above the box to indicate his math grade. "Now, let's think about your friend who gets an A without trying hard. How much smarter do you think he is than you?"

"He's really smart—probably twice as smart as me."

So, next to the box that represented this young man, I drew a larger box which pictured his smarter classmate. Since this boy was getting an A, I put an A on the top. Then I asked, "How hard is your friend trying? Do you think he is doing his best?"

The boy laughed. "Not only is he not trying hard, but he makes fun of us who are having a difficult time. I know he's smart, but I don't think he tries more than 50 percent. Mostly he goofs off."

I drew a line across the middle of the second box and marked it "50 percent." "Now you can see the two different grades," I explained. "Those around us see the grades because they are on the outside, but guess what God also sees? He sees what people are doing with the talents He has given them. God sees the inside and would have given your smarter friend 50 percent—an F—because he only did half of what he could have done, and perhaps gives you a 95 percent—an A—because of what you did with what He gave you!"

You should have seen the boy's eyes light up when he realized the "Two Grades of Life." He quickly announced that he was going to keep working to get As on God's report card.

Jesus presented us with a far greater illustration of this perspective about our performance—especially in comparison to others—in Matthew 25. A few insights from this great passage should help us be alert to reaffirm our students in light of their God-given abilities:

God gave each of us different talents. "And to one he [representing Jesus Christ] gave five talents, to another two, to another one, to each according to his own ability" (25:15).

God tests our performance. "After a long time the lord of those servants came and settled accounts with them" (25:19).

God rewards based upon ability, not quantity. The first person returned to the Lord five talents and the second returned only two talents. The first servant produced 150 percent more than the second. But observe how Christ rewarded (graded) His two students:

FIVE-TALENT PERFORMANCE:

"Well done, good and faithful servant; you were faithful over a few things, I will make you ruler over many things. Enter into the joy of your lord." (25:21)

TWO-TALENT PERFORMANCE:

"Well done, good and faithful servant; you have been faithful over a few things, I will make you ruler over many things. Enter into the joy of your lord." (25:23)

Did you see the vast difference?

Shocking, isn't it? There isn't even one! Christ saw that although the first servant vastly outperformed the second in quantity, they both doubled what they had been given. To the human eye, their achievements were radically different; but to the Lord's eye, they were identical.

Because Christ would say "well done" to a two-talent as well as a five-talent achievement, we must also affirm each student's performance without comparison to the performance of another.

CONCLUSION

What can be the eventual impact of a life of equipping? Let me answer that by sharing just one small insight into the life of one of the greatest equippers I have ever known, Dr. Howard Hendricks.

Dr. Hendricks has taught many thousands of men and women to do the work of ministry. Each of those individuals has his own story, but because I happen to know mine best, I want to describe the impact he had on me and Walk Thru the Bible.

His equipping influenced me before I started Walk Thru in the 1970s. Many of his perspectives helped shape the organization to become what it is today.

During the first months, I taught all the seminars myself. But soon the requests far outreached our capacity, and I started training some of my friends from graduate school. Eventually it became apparent that Art VanderVeen was not only an outstanding seminar instructor but also would be a very competent dean of faculty. Over the early years he trained many instructors, including another excellent communicator, John Hoover. As the years passed, John continued developing his leadership and eventually was promoted to vice president of our international efforts and began taking the ministry around the world.

His first step of "planting the WTB vision" on foreign soil was in Australia when he recruited and trained Gary Coleman (not the actor). As the Australian ministry matured under leadership, Gary took his own missionary trip and started WTB in the Philippines and trained a number of key leaders, including Paul Newman (not that actor, either).

Paul quickly rose to leadership in that country and eventually began training additional Filipino instructors, including Ben Yngaio. Under Paul's guidance, Ben later trained three additional WTB instructors located throughout the Philippines.

One of those three instructors was teaching his first Walk Thru the Old Testament seminar and led twenty people to the Lord. One of those twenty went home after the seminar and led his wife and two daughters to the Lord that evening.

Look at that incredible string of equipping!

Howard Hendricks
Bruce Wilkinson
Art VanderVeen
John Hoover
Gary Coleman
Paul Newman
Ben Yngaio
Filipino pastor
Father
Wife and children become Christians

Ten generations of equipping. I sketched that on a sheet of paper and showed it to my wife, Darlene. "Look at what this one man, Howard Hendricks, has done for all of eternity! Not only this chain, but equally exciting stories branch off in every direction from every person on the list."

She smiled and said, "I wonder if that's the whole story. You see, Dr. Hendricks didn't start that equipping ball rolling by himself. Remember the story he told us about when he was in sixth grade growing up in a broken home in Philadelphia?"

Dr. Hendrick had told us that one day he and his friends were play-ing marbles, and a kind, older man walked over and stood next to them encouraging their game. Soon he was on his knees playing beside them. As the weeks passed, they came to know him as Walt and that he worked at the nearby factory.

After a number of days playing marbles with these sixth-grade boys, Walt invited them to attend his Sunday school class. They didn't know he had a class and asked him to tell them about it.

"Well," he said, "I don't have one yet, but maybe you guys could help me start my own class."

That's how Howard Hendricks and his buddies started to attend church...because of Walt. In fact, every member of Walt's Sunday school class came to know Christ, and eleven of them went into full-time Christian work!

You see, my friend, behind all those tens of thousands who have been influenced by that well-known equipper, Dr. Howard G. Hendricks, stands an obscure sixth-grade Sunday school teacher who remained faithful to his calling.

Can you imagine what will happen when Walt enters Glory and sees the masses that have been influenced because he taught that Sunday school class? He never could have known. But he will know. And he'll celebrate for eternity.

Never again underestimate the eternal impact of your teaching. Never allow yourself to say, "This class isn't going to make much of a difference." Don't ever think, "I've done my share; I think I'll take the next five years off." Sitting in next week's class may be the next Howard Hendricks whose equipping ministry will influence an international ministry that will touch millions for the cause of Christ.

The next time you walk in the door of your class, take a firm hold on your torch and deepen the resolve in your heart—and light the fire of those who await you!

DISCUSSION QUESTIONS

1. Master equippers know that the secret to effective development of their students' skills often is centered in identifying the root of their difficulties. Consider someone you are currently teaching who seems bogged down in his development. Is he bogged down because he doesn't understand the basics, because he never saw them correctly modeled, because he has never been coached through the initial hurdles of technique, or because he is locked into a poor or negative attitude? After diagnosing his problem, list as many alternatives as you can to help him overcome his problem and progress further.

2. Think again through the five steps of the Equipping Method—Instruct, Illustrate, Involve, Improve, Inspire. Which teacher modeled this process best for you during your student days? Discuss the impact you experienced.

3. Motivation to learn a skill is a key to success. Consider again the motivations of relationship, retribution, and reward as outlined under Maximizer 4. How would you define each of these motivations in your own words? As a student, which of these motivations spurred you on the most? Why? Now, as a teacher, which do you use the most and the least? How could you use all three during the subject you are now teaching? Think about your own teaching situation. How are you trying to equip your students? In what

specific ways could you use those three motivations to encourage them in their progress?

4. Who is the one student in your class who is the most discouraged because of his limited ability? Consider the five ways under Maximizer 7 to reaffirm this student and come up with a simple plan to help him respond correctly to those limitations. Try your best ideas and discuss what happened.

5. Who is the one person who has equipped you the most for life? What has he or she done and how has it affected you? Now switch roles for a moment. Of all the people you have equipped in your life, who would think they had benefited the most? How could you multiply the impact of your life even further?

LAW SEVEN

The Law
of Revival

CHAPTER THIRTEEN

Revival

Mindset, Model, and Maxims

When my good friend called and asked me to speak for his church's Valentine banquet, it took me less than a second to decline. My gifts are in teaching rather than entertaining, so I gave him the names of some friends I knew would be excellent in this setting.

A week later he called again and told me he really felt I was the perfect person and that he hadn't called anyone else. I declined again and encouraged him to find another speaker.

I couldn't believe it when he called me for the third time a week later. "Just do it for me as your friend," he begged.

"What a dirty trick," I told him. But if it was that important, I said, I would do it for him.

I worked hard on the talk. The banquet went nicely and the presentation seemed well-received. I told some jokes and a few romantic stories, recited a couple of appropriate poems—in short, delivered your typical banquet speech.

Afterward my friend and his wife invited us to a nearby restaurant for pie and ice cream. As I was finishing the last few bites of my favorite, blueberry pie, I asked him how he felt about my speech. He became quiet and started looking at his plate. I noticed he was rolling one of the cherries with his fork—my first clue that my speech had not hit the mark.

The silence was deafening. Finally I asked, "Weren't the stories any good?"

"Oh, the stories were fine." He kept rolling the cherry.

"The jokes must have been a disaster, right?"

"Nope, they were pretty good, I guess."

"Well, then what's the matter?"

He sighed, put down his fork, and looked me right in the eyes. "Bruce, as you and Darlene know, my wife and I have been coming to this liberal church for six years. For six years we've been trying to receive permission for an evangelical to come speak at our church and the pastoral staff has always said no. Finally, when I told them you were willing to come, they surprised us and said yes."

I started rolling my blueberries.

"And after six years of praying for an opportunity like this, you spoke for forty minutes to a roomful of people who didn't know Jesus Christ—and you never gave the gospel!"

Like the thrust of a double-edged sword, those words stabbed me in the heart. For the first time in my life I didn't finish my blueberry pie à la mode. I thanked my friend for his sobering words and stumbled in a daze to my car. The Holy Spirit powerfully reminded me all the way home that the Lord didn't call me to recite poems and jokes, but to beckon men and women to a life of commitment and consecration to Christ.

God continued His refining work in my life for the next few months, right up to the time of Walk Thru the Bible's annual faculty conference. Our faculty flew in from across the country for a week of in-depth training, and one evening I revealed how the Lord had convicted me.

As we spoke with each other, the presence and conviction of the Lord swept our gathering. Soon we fell to our knees as many confessed their need for revival. Many tears of repentance were shed as commitments to Christ were renewed.

The year of ministry just ended had seen about 370 people come to Christ. As we prayed, the men began to plead with the Lord to use us greatly for ministry. Someone prayed for more people in our seminars to come to know Christ. Others joined in the prayer. Then the man kneeling on my left asked for a spiritual harvest ten times greater during the next year—instead of an average of one person a day coming to know Christ, that God would enable us to lead an average of ten.

The first month after this revival, more than 400 people came to know Christ! When that year came to a close, the Lord enabled 3,700 people to know Him through the ministry.

To me this is an incredible illustration of the overwhelming results that can occur when we are revived and renewed. The seminar was the same, the faculty was the same, and the general audience was the same. The only difference was that our hearts—the hearts of the teachers—had been revived.

REVIVAL MINDSET

What do you think of when you hear the word *revival*? Most think of great crusades or weeklong evangelistic meetings or the sawdust trails of bygone eras. In the New Testament, *revival* is a translation of the compound word *anazao*, which translated literally means "again—to live." It is used of the physical resurrection of Lazarus, Jesus Christ, and our future bodily resurrection.

Spiritual revival is the bringing back to full life a Christian who has been spiritually alive but has slipped back into sin and rebellion. In this law, revival refers to the process of bringing back to full life a Christian who has fallen into sin and is living in disobedience to the Lord.

The classic picture of this process is seen in Christ's parable about the prodigal son who left his father's house in rebellion, lived in disobedience and sin, finally came to his senses, repented, and was restored to full harmony with his loving father.

Many teachers believe revival is a topic far removed from the experience of the normal classroom. When asked how he teaches for revival, the average teacher stands startled because such a thought has never crossed his mind. Revival is for preachers. Or, to many others, revival just isn't for the twentieth century.

Besides, who among us is capable of leading a revival? We haven't been trained, nor do we feel spiritually adequate for such a task. Bring revival to my students—are you kidding?

It's time to look at a key Scripture passage and determine whether we are living in obedience to the teachings of the Bible. If my hunch is correct, for the seventh time in a row we will discover how dramatically we have strayed from the way that brings blessing.

REVIVAL MODEL

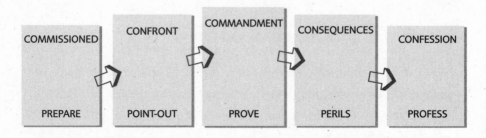

The Law of Revival is graphically pictured in the Old Testament story of Nathan confronting David regarding his sin with Bathsheba (2 Samuel 12:1–15). Follow along as we discover five steps Nathan pursued to bring his student to repentance.

Step 1: Commissioned (2 Samuel 12:1a)

"Then the LORD sent Nathan to David." Note that it was the Lord who sent the teacher (Nathan) to the student (David). God could have spoken to David directly or used an entire angelic host, but He sovereignly chose to speak through a person. God desires to accomplish His perfect work through imperfect people like you and me.

The first step is to be *"commissioned,"* to be given authority to carry out a particular task or duty, or to be granted certain powers. This is where you *"prepare"* yourself to go to a person in need of revival.

When Nathan stepped before David, he had full assurance he was doing the will of God. The deeper we feel that same assurance, the surer we'll be during the intense process of revival. The problem is that many teachers do not have that sense of personal responsibility to call their students to revival. Invariably they think God has commissioned others (pastors or evangelists) to that task, but certainly not them.

How would you carry out your teaching duties if you heard a direct and unmistakable word from God to call your wayward students back to the Lord? Would you not find conviction and courage from that commission? The next time you taught them, would you not have God's clear agenda before you?

Later in this chapter, under the first maxim, we will explore three key commissioning passages that relate to your call to bring revival to your class. Whether or not you are aware of it, your nickname in the heavenlies is "Nathan," and all of your students are called "David."

Step 2: Confront (2 Samuel 12:1b-9)

As Nathan began class, he had a clear perspective of where he needed to go and how best to get there. The commission of God is to bring wayward sheep back into the fold. Therefore, the first step of all spiritual restoration is to lead the sheep to recognize their problem—that through willful disobedience they have strayed from the fold and are living in opposition to the will of God.

To *"confront"* means to come face-to-face with; to stand in front of; to bring together for comparison or examination. Originally the word came from the Latin *confrontare,* meaning to have a common border. It eventually came to mean bringing agreement through pointing out the boundary that has been overrun.

When the commissioned teacher begins actively to pursue the wayward student, he must first help him come face-to-face with his disobedience. The teacher leads the student to look in a mirror, thereby facing his real problem. The student must see himself and what he has done.

Nathan helped David to see himself with such shocking clarity that the king's sense of conviction was overpowering. To do this, the prophet led David through three discoveries:

1. *Confront through telling a parable (2 Samuel 12:1–6).* What a powerful story Nathan constructed for his student! There's no more effective teaching than leading your class to make a strong and emotional judgment in the very area of their own sin without even knowing it. I call that "Doing a Nathan." Read the story and sense all the emotion Nathan built into it and see how it perfectly pictured David:

There were two men in one city, one rich and the other poor. The rich man had exceedingly many flocks and herds. But the poor man had nothing, except one little ewe lamb which he had bought and nourished; and it grew up together with him and with is children. It ate of his own food and drank from his own cup and lay in his bosom; and it was like a daughter to him.

And a traveler came to the rich man, who refused to take from his own flock and from his own herd to prepare one for the wayfaring man who had come to him; but he took the poor man's lamb and prepared it for the man who had come to him.

Then David's anger was greatly aroused against the man, and he said to Nathan, "As the LORD lives, the man who has done this shall surely die! And he shall restore fourfold for the lamb, because he did this thing and because he had no pity."

Nathan's student prejudged himself and prepared himself for the next dramatic revelation.

2. *Confront through describing the nature of God (2 Samuel 12:7–8).* How utterly direct Nathan was with his student as he told him, "You are the man!" With his parable, Nathan prepared David for everything that followed as he sought to break the king's heart on the rocks of repentance. But first the prophet confronts David with the nature of the God he had betrayed:

> "Thus says the LORD God of Israel: 'I anointed you king over Israel, and I delivered you from the hand of Saul. I gave you your master's house and your master's wives into your keeping, and gave you the house of Israel and Judah. And if that had been too little, I also would have given you much more!'"

What incredibly wonderful things God had given to this man David. When strung together one after another, they forced David to look into the eyes of the very One who had bestowed upon him all those wonderful gifts—and also the One against whom he had done all those terrible things.

Why was Nathan leading his student through this step? Because David needed to remember the kind of God he had sinned against. As David sinned repeatedly and willfully, he had turned his back to God, attempting to forget God's goodness and loyal love.

Whenever any of us continues in sin, we inevitably alter the nature of God in our minds. We remake Him by our own thoughts into a God who no longer deserves our loyalty and obedience. God eventually becomes evil in our sight as we revert to the Garden of Eden and believe Satan's lie that God's motives are to withhold good things from us.

Nathan knew the deceitfulness of even David's heart, so he forcefully confronted him with seven statements of the truth about God—each one carefully sharpened to pierce that wicked heart and open it to the light of God's Spirit. Can you imagine the power of the final knockout punch, "and if that had been too little, I also would have given you much more!" The jarring realization of the limitless goodness of God that he had spurned must have rocked David to the soles of his feet.

3. *Confront through listing specific sins (2 Samuel 12:9–10).* Observe how direct Nathan is as he enumerates each act of disobedience:

1. "Why have you despised the commandment of the LORD, to do evil in His sight?
2. You have killed Uriah the Hittite with the sword;
3. You have taken his wife to be your wife, and
4. [You] have killed him with the sword of the people of Ammon.
5. You have despised Me, and have taken the wife of Uriah the Hittite to be your wife.
6. You did it secretly (v. 12).
7. You have given great occasion to the enemies of the LORD to blaspheme" (v. 14).

What a list of sins! Nathan knew that in order to be effective, confrontation must be direct, specific, and true. He didn't beat around the bush—he marched right through it.

Confrontation is not easy for anyone, but the Lord admonishes all of us to "speak the truth in love." Somehow in the process of speaking the truth directly to the sinning Christian, the Holy Spirit is liberated to convict with even greater clarity and power. Having another person list our sins out loud in our presence is a strong incentive to repent.

There are two valuable secrets to follow when you confront Christians. First, always use the biblical word for the sin they have committed. Say adultery, not affair; say homosexual acts, not gay lifestyle; say lie, not fib. The use of the biblical term instead of the euphemism further clarifies and convicts.

Second, do not move beyond this step of confrontation unless the person openly admits his sin. Frequently after confronting a person I will ask him to list out loud the sins he has committed. If he cannot or will not, then I continue to help him see his acts as God does; otherwise, full repentance does not occur. The person must openly admit his guilt and sin to himself, to you, and eventually to God. If the person is unable to confess his sins to you when you are confronting him, he probably cannot confess them to God.

David readily admitted his guilt after his confrontation with Nathan: "I have sinned against the LORD" (v. 13).

A few years ago while preaching at a well-known Bible college during Spiritual Life Week, I called for repentance for existing sins. At the end of that sermon I began listing specific sin after specific sin and describing it so there would be no confusion.

"Some of you committed fornication or adultery this past summer," I said, "or are currently involved in an immoral relationship. Some of you have cheated on your tests or copied term papers from your friends. Some have gone to stores and stolen things you wanted. Others are involved in homosexual or lesbian relationships." You could have heard a pin drop.

Then I encouraged the students: "You need to repent of those sins and you need to start right now. If you are guilty of any of these sins or others like them and are willing to confess them to the Lord and through His power be set free, then stand up."

That large auditorium was so quiet I heard my heart pounding. Then all at once, with a noise like thunder, hundreds of courageous students rose to their feet all across the chapel. Many were in tears, some were sobbing, some had fallen to their knees.

As you can imagine, my counseling load went through the roof as student after student sought help. I'll never forget what one outstanding student blurted out through his tears: "I'm a senior and for all my years at Bible college, no one had ever challenged me to get my deep, dark sins right—until today. Thanks for telling the truth."

Perhaps the greatest hindrance to honest confrontation is the "fear of man" rather than the "fear of God." We are afraid of the pain we will suffer by speaking the truth. We are afraid of the rejection we may face as we speak the truth. Can we not love our students enough that we endure the pain for their good?

Step 3: Commandments (2 Samuel 12:9a)

The foundation of all Christian confrontation must be the Bible. We should confront people when we are sure they have broken a clear *"commandment"* of Scripture.

It is because a student has chosen to step across God's boundaries that he needs to repent. It is our responsibility to demonstrate the exact border the student has overstepped. Nathan made clear that David was breaking the Lord's commandments.

Without the Bible, there are no absolutes. But with the Bible we can all know whether an act is a sin or not. The Bible establishes those "common boundaries" by specific commandments and principles that govern all of us equally. Because these standards are written down so all can see, we are able to be sure whether a person's behavior is really sin in God's eyes. Nathan called David's actions "evil in [God's] sight" because those commandments were broken: "Why have you despised the *commandment* of the LORD, to do evil in His sight?" (2 Samuel 12:9).

Nathan raised an interesting question when he inquired why David despised the commandment of the Lord. When the Christian chooses to disobey, he looks down on God's commandments with contempt. Indeed, he has decided his will is above the will of God. Nathan knew that David despised the commandment because no one is able to hold to two conflicting positions at the same time. Any time we act, one receives our regard and the other our contempt.

Jesus identified this truth about conflicting values when He taught, "No one can serve two masters; for either he will hate the one and love the other, or else he will be *loyal* to the one and *despise* the other" (Matthew 6:24).

Nathan showed David that the root of his rebellion was not only that he "despised the commandment of the LORD" (2 Samuel 12:9) but that he despised *the Lord* (v. 10). Let us never permit our students to think that sin is merely disobedience to the Bible and nothing more. Sin is ultimately an act of rebellion against God Himself.

Revival, then, must include the sinner's repentance from breaking the will of God as well as the heart of God. These are the two parts of this step—first demonstrate the person has broken the commandment of God; then show that he has broken the heart of God. *Guilt* is experienced at the breaking of the law and *grief* through the breaking of the relationship.

I once spent an intense hour on the phone with a friend who was being unfaithful to her husband. After the first ten minutes I began to ask her if she was committing adultery. She changed the subject time after time, but I always brought her back to the question. My wife, Darlene, was in the room with me and was fervently praying as she heard the conversation. When it was over, I asked her how many times she heard me ask our friend, "Are you an adulterous married woman?" and she told me at least twenty.

Why was I so persistent? Because if she couldn't admit she had committed adultery, there was no hope of her restoration. Finally she admitted that was true. (Completion of step two: Confrontation.) Then I transitioned to this step, commandment, and asked her what God thought about her behavior. With a voice quivering with emotion she blurted, "God understands. In fact, I believe God brought this new man into my life because God loves me and knows I've been unhappy for a long time."

Sound familiar? All of us who live in sin for any extended period rationalize our behavior so much that good becomes evil and evil becomes good. No matter what I asked her, she belligerently argued that God not only understood her adultery, but it was His will for her. After all, God wanted her to be happy.

Finally, I asked her if she had ever heard of the Ten Commandments. She laughed and said, "Of course."

"Well," I asked, "could you please complete the seventh commandment, which says, 'You shall not commit—'?"

When she wouldn't answer, I asked, "When you break a direct commandment of God, what does God call it?" Silence. "It begins with the letter *s* and ends with *n*." No matter how hard she tried to escape the reality of her actions, I kept bringing her back to the broken commandment.

Finally, when she said, "God calls my adultery 'sin,'" I knew the Lord was at work in her heart. But still she wouldn't repent. What should I do next?

Step 4: Consequences (2 Samuel 12:10-14)

The goal of this process, whether used by Nathan or us, is to "restore" the person who is "overtaken in any trespass." For David, the climax was his confession—"I have sinned." Any time our student expresses a genuine confession, this process has been wonderfully short-circuited and there is no reason to continue it.

Sometimes as you lead someone through these powerful steps, the person falls under such great conviction that he confesses in the opening stage when you first confront him. Others repent during the commandment stage. If, however, the person will admit openly to his actions and name them as sins, but still won't turn back to Christ, then this fourth step must be used to lead him to genuine restoration. It breaks through many a hard and stubborn heart. Pay close attention, because it may enable you to literally save a person's life.

After years of ministry, I am convinced that many Christians are overtaken by sin and then *needlessly* remain in it and eventually fall into severe problems (such as abuse, alcoholism, and occult involvements) that can last for years, even for generations. I use the word *needlessly* because had someone in the Christian community gone to that person to restore them, *many would have been restored!*

When a person disobeys God he underestimates two things: (1) the seriousness of his behavior, and (2) the negative *"consequences"* of that behavior to himself, to others, and to the Lord.

As confrontation helps the person see his past and present sinful acts, so consequences help the person see the present and future harmful results. Nathan pointed down the corridor of time and helped David to see everything the king wanted to remain hidden:

1. "Now therefore, the sword shall never depart from your house;
2. Behold I will raise up adversity against you from your own house; and
3. I will take your wives before your eyes and
4. [I will] give them to your neighbor, and
5. He shall lie with your wives in the sight of this sun.
6. I will do this thing before all Israel, before the sun.
7. The child also who is born to you shall surely die."

Can you imagine the anguish David must have felt as these tragic consequences were listed one after the other? Each one must have crushed his spirit and broken his heart. Not only were they the most terrible results he could have imagined, but there was the stark realization that each tragedy would happen solely because of his sin. How could he blame anyone else? The sobering reality of "It's my fault and no one else's" must have echoed throughout the rest of his life.

The confrontation, the commandments, and now the consequences scaled the rocky crags of David's rebellious heart and made room for repentance. Revival entered the picture, and, as James said, a life was saved.

> Brethren, if anyone among you wanders from the truth, and someone turns him back, let him know that he who turns a sinner from the error of his way will save a soul from death and cover a multitude of sins. (James 5:19–20)

Nathan used five categories of consequences which are universally applicable to all of us who must use this last step to lead our students to repentance.

1. *Consequences to ourselves.* Put yourself in David's shoes for a moment, then read Nathan's list one more time and try to sympathize with how David must have felt. God's discipline was directly aimed at David.

2. *Consequences to our immediate family.* Not only would David suffer for his sins, but so also would his children, wives, and even his grandchildren. God's discipline of David reached out to those he loved.

3. *Consequences to the Christian community.* Although Nathan's words give only a slight clue to the disastrous impact of David's sin throughout Israel and Judah, the rest of 2 Samuel and 1 Kings through 2 Chronicles paints a sad story indeed. Many Jews died and suffered because of David's sin.

4. *Consequences to the non-Christian community.* Because Israel had been commissioned to be a blessing to the whole world, the unbelieving community would suffer because of the sins of Israel's great leader. You can imagine the anguish David must have felt—this man who loved God deeply and longed to build a temple so God's name could be praised among the nations—in giving great occasion for the enemies of God

not merely to reject him but also to blaspheme him. Just how many unbelieving individuals were driven even further from the Lord because of David's sin no one can fathom, nor the eternal consequences this caused in their lives.

5. *Consequences to the Lord God.* When children do something tragically wrong, it's often the parents who suffer the most deeply. I wonder if the person who experiences the most pain when we sin is the Lord Himself. For such a noble son as David—a man after God's own heart—to willfully choose sin in the most terrible of ways (murder and adultery) must have brought unimaginable grief to the Holy One of Israel. As Christ wept over the hardness and rebellion of Jerusalem, He may have also wept over His fallen servant, King David. Surely God grieves when those who are made in His image shake their fist at Him in anger and rage.

Each of these five consequences are immediately applicable when we are striving to help a rebellious son or daughter abandon sin, repent, and return home. Although we aren't Nathan and haven't been given a divine revelation of the actual consequences for our students, yet we can use our sanctified imaginations and project the normal consequences of our students' sins.

An effective consequence has six characteristics. It should be *personal, specific, realistic, visual, painful, and affect many people that the sinning person cares deeply about.* Nathan's consequences reflected every one of these characteristics. Ultimately, an effective presentation of consequences presents enough pain to enough different people that it produces deep fear of severe and lasting suffering, which ultimately outweighs the temporary pleasures that sin produces.

As teacher, your primary goal is to prove repentance is the most logical step for the sinning student. Until this point the benefits of sin seem to outweigh the benefits of obedience; that's why he is still sinning. All of us sin because sin's anticipated pleasure seems more real at the time than the potential harm and discipline we may experience from it.

Therefore, consequences must aim at readjusting the person's fantasy to biblical reality. As a person continues to choose to sin, he focuses on the anticipated pleasure and avoids the thought of anticipated pain. The more equal those two areas of pleasure and pain seem in the person's mind, the more he will wrestle with the temptation. When the negative consequences finally overpower the potential pleasure, the person will inevitably repent.

Consequences are simply the negative reasons why a person should not commit a sin. In the book of Proverbs, you can read many consequences which repeatedly picture how foolish it is to choose evil. The greater the feeling of anticipated pain, the less power that temptation exerts.

Nathan's presentation of consequences so overwhelmed David that he immediately broke and confessed his sin. As you become skilled in using consequences in your public teaching and private counseling, you will see scores of people respond in genuine repentance. They will change their minds because the pain of sin far outweighs the pleasure of sin. The Bible defines that as repentance.

Step 5: Confession (2 Samuel 12:13)

When Nathan heard David say, "I have sinned against the LORD," he knew he and his student had touched the finish line. Rebellion had been broken and revival was on the way. (See Psalm 51 for the full confession of David before the Lord.)

To "*confess*" usually means "to thoroughly make known to others one's error or wrongdoing." Confession is the first step on the positive side of revival and represents the hinge swinging between rebellion and revival. Later in the Revival Method we will discuss the actions that will help us lead our students to full restoration.

May your students flourish as you lead them to revival as often as they need it, using Nathan's five steps of commission, confrontation, commandment, consequences, and confession.

REVIVAL MAXIMS

The end of learning is to repair the ruins of our first parents
by coming to know God aright, out of that knowledge to love Him,
to imitate Him, to be like Him.

JOHN MILTON

Maxim 1: Revival is spiritual restoration and is the spiritual teacher's responsibility.

Of all the maxims in this book, this one has caused me the most difficulty. For almost two weeks I wrestled with this principle night after night as I studied. I kept discovering that my preconceived notions about revival contradicted the Bible.

To say I had a hardened mindset would be an understatement. My first writing of this maxim, before searching the Scriptures, produced something like this: "Revival is a sovereign act of God and not the responsibility of man except to be prayed for by the Christian."

If you reread the maxims in this book, you will find that they all put the responsibility squarely on the shoulders of the teacher. But I knew that revival couldn't be my responsibility because it is a sovereign act of God—or so I had been taught. Then, after I wrote that revival isn't our responsibility, I began to wonder—could this be another cloud of confusion lying between us and the truth? Could we have unwittingly abandoned our responsibility?

Buried beneath mountains of human logic was this disturbing question: If God desires revival to occur (and of course He does) and we are praying for it (and many of us are), than why does He not do what both of us desire? Everything I knew about God kept smashing against this immovable wall. There were vast inconsistencies I couldn't unravel.

Finally, during my second week of struggle, I began to make progress by asking: "What are the clearest passages in all the Bible on revival?" Why not let the Scriptures speak for themselves!

First Key Passage: 2 Chronicles 7:14

"If My people who are called by My name will humble themselves, and pray and seek My face, and turn from their wicked ways, then I will hear from heaven, and will forgive their sin and heal their land."

Standing at the very front of that thirty-nine-word revelation towered a small but mighty two-letter word, *If*. It immediately alerted me that all that followed was a *condition to be fulfilled*. Twenty-four words later, the other half of this verbal marriage appeared in the word *then*, reflecting the *promised result* that would occur if the condition was fulfilled.

First I studied the second half, the promise, in order to discover the results of fulfilling the first half:

"Then I will	God's promise to do something
hear from heaven,	God's first promise
and will *forgive* their sin	God's second promise
and *heal* their land"	God's third promise

Then I focused on the condition(s). What did God state were the *requirements* to be fulfilled for Him to send revival?

"If My people who are	The people who can fulfill
called by My name	the conditions
will *humble* themselves	the first condition
and *pray*	the second condition
and *seek* My face	the third condition
and *turn* from their	the fourth condition
wicked ways"	

There it was, in black and white—*a clear and indisputable revelation directly from God that revival was fully dependent on us and not Him!* He clearly promised that He would send revival if we fulfilled His conditions. We weren't doing what He requested in order for revival to flood our lives.

How wrong I had been! God was true to His character and was not withholding revival because of some deep dark secret. Instead, God was ready to send revival when we would do what He required. If we fulfilled those four conditions, would God fulfill those three promises of revival? Indeed He would!

Then I sought to find a way to pass the blame for not experiencing revival. It couldn't be all my fault, could it? Obviously these four conditions are not possible—or else I would enjoy revival more frequently in my life. So I examined those four conditions to prove to myself that revival couldn't be my responsibility.

1. *Could I "humble myself"?* Yes, I decided, I could fall to my knees and genuinely humble myself if I so chose. After all, the New Testament commands us to "humble ourselves," so how could I argue that it was impossible for me to obey?

2. *Could I "pray"?* Yes, I could pray at any time.

3. *Could I "seek God's face"?* Yes, I could seek His face early in the morning and late at night. His face is ever before those who desire to find Him.

At this point I felt the weight of responsibility falling heavily upon my heart. But when my eyes returned to read the final condition, I finally felt completely responsible if I truly desired revival.

4. *Could I "turn from my wicked ways"?* Yes, the known sin in my life could be confessed and forsaken.

But how could turning from my wicked ways be a condition of revival? I had always thought acts of repentance and obedience were the *results* of revival, not the *conditions* for it. I had incorrectly thought that when God finally decided, in His sovereignty, to send revival, then I'd finally have the power to overcome my sins. So ultimately, then, who was I blaming for my wicked ways? In my confusion, who did I feel was responsible for not sending revival and solving all my problems? God!

I sought for a way to escape full responsibility for my action—and found none. If I wanted God to hear, forgive, and heal, then I must first turn from my wicked ways.

Could revival be that clear? Could revival be within the grasp of any of us who choose to obey God's conditions? Yes, 2 Chronicles 7:14 forever answers the question of who is responsible to act so that revival can and will occur.

But I sensed that this was only the tip of this iceberg. Second Chronicles 7:14 was referring primarily to national revival, but what about personal revival? Further, what is my responsibility, if any, for my students when I sense they need spiritual restoration? I kept searching in the Scriptures.

Second Key Passage: Galatians 6:1

Galatians 6:1 adds further insight about this troubling confusion regarding responsibility and revival.

> *Brethren,*
> *if a man is overtaken*
> *in any trespass,*
> *you who are spiritual*
> *restore such a one*
> *in a spirit of gentleness,*
> *considering yourself*
> *lest you also be tempted.*

Only two conditions are required for us to step forward. First, we must be aware that another person is overtaken by sin. Second, that at the time we go to that person there is no major known sin present in our life hindering the work of the Spirit in and through us.

The next four words, "restore such a one," state the specific result we are instructed to achieve. In the original Greek, *restore* is in the imperative and is therefore a command to be obeyed, not a suggestion to be considered.

What a refreshing contrast this is to the way we tend to read this verse. We act like God merely said pray for the person, or even visit the person. This verse commands us to accept the responsibility of not only praying and of going, but—note clearly what God said we are responsible to do—*of restoring!* We have the responsibility to repair and restore a person from the damage wrought by sin.

The message is clear. Get involved, take ownership, get moving! This verse focuses on the desired *results* and leaves the process up to our creativity and personality under the direction of the Holy Spirit. In a sense, God has delegated to us—with a clear command—the responsibility to restore the sinning Christian under the guidance and power of the Holy Spirit.

Third Key Passage: Ephesians 4:11–12

Even though God's will about revival was becoming clearer, I found one more issue yet unresolved. Did God reveal in the Bible any specific instructions for teachers regarding revival? I continued my search of the Scriptures and began a word study of the Greek word for *restore*, hoping to discover it linked somewhere to the teacher. I stumbled across the same word in the passage where God revealed His job description for teachers (Ephesians 4:11–12, which we studied in the Law of Equipping). I could hardly believe it!

And He Himself gave some to be apostles...and some pastors and teachers, for the equipping of the saints for the work of ministry.

The word *equipping* is the identical root word as *restore* in Galatians 6:1! Clearly, then, the reason God gave you and me as teachers to His church was for restoration and revival.

Have you ever viewed revival as the heart of your calling? Have you ever understood that God wants you and me to reclaim His prodigals wherever they may be and in whatever state they may have fallen?

Can you imagine the impact that would occur across God's church if even the smallest percentage of Christ's teachers would shoulder this divinely bestowed responsibility? Never again would we be able to teach only for content; now we would teach for the very hearts of our students!

> Brethren, if anyone among you wanders from the truth, and someone [teacher] turns him back, let him know that he who turns a sinner from the error of his way will save a soul from death and cover a multitude of sins. (James 5:19–20)

Maxim 2: Revival is possible only for those who have first experienced the second birth.

Evangelism centers around bringing the unsaved community to Christ; revival centers around bringing the disobedient, saved community back to Christ. The first is called *conversion* or *rebirth*; the second *consecration* or *revival*. The first coming to Christ graces the believer with eternal life; the latter comings grace the believer with a life of enduring fellowship.

We greatly err when we strive to produce revival in our students without assurance they have already received Christ and become "children of God, to those who believe in His name" (John 1:12). Many teachers assume that their students already are Christians because they come from a good family, or appear to be Christians, or attend Christian institutions.

Would it not be wise, therefore, to present the plan of salvation at appropriate moments during our teaching? Some teachers take this responsibility so seriously that they visit their students individually to determine their spiritual condition and present the gospel.

Remember, though, when you teach or counsel or preach for revival to a class of unconverted students, it is like preaching to a roomful of corpses. Until they have met Jesus Christ, the Bible says they are still "dead in their trespasses and sins" and therefore cannot be "re"-vived until they are first "vived."

Maxim 3: Revival is not a completed event but a continuing experience.

Revival is not an event or meeting we attend but rather an ongoing experience that can continue until we eventually meet the Lord. *True revival isn't held annually but sought continuously.*

Revival must not be so narrowly defined as to include only those severe cases of a believer straying far from the Lord. In its broadest sense, revival occurs whenever a Christian repents of his sin, no matter how slight, and fully returns to the Lord. Therefore when you and I obey 1 John 1:9—"If we confess our sins, He is faithful and just to forgive us our sins and to cleanse us from all unrighteousness"—we have moved toward biblical revival.

Our students sometimes find themselves trapped by their sin ("overtaken in any trespass") and quietly cry out for someone—some Good Samaritan—to pull them out of their despair and guide them back to the place called "home."

Because each of our students fluctuates in and out of fellowship, we must always watch for the telltale signs of spiritual need. It is their spiritual need that we are called to meet. Therefore, always be ready to teach for revival.

Maxim 4: Revival can occur in the life of an individual, group, or nation.

Revival is not limited by geography or number or age. The biblical records as well as church history demonstrate that revival can occur in an individual, a family, a small class or group, a church, a town, a region, or a whole nation.

Revivals have begun at all times of the day, in all parts of the Christian world, and have sprung out of almost every denomination and nondenominational group imaginable.

Revivals have been launched through the power of the Holy Spirit by preachers, evangelists, teachers, educators, businessmen, laymen, young people, and missionaries.

Some revivals have begun seemingly instantaneously while others have grown slowly over the years before they finally broke through. Some revivals have lasted less than a day, whereas others have lasted months and even years.

Revivals seem to flourish in certain times and almost hibernate in others. They seem also to occur in great numbers around either a certain person or a certain place.

Revivals have had varied impact. Some have dramatically altered entire countries for generations, while others have altered only the lives of a small number of individuals for seemingly short times.

What is the point of all this variety and diversity? Namely, that whenever, wherever, and by whomever the conditions of biblical revival are fulfilled, there God's power, presence of cleansing ("I will forgive their sins"), and restoration ("and heal their land") will be. God sends revival to anyone that meets His universal conditions—including you and me, my friend.

Therefore, pray for revival, prepare for revival, plead for revival in every context of your life. There are no boundaries to the omnipotent power of the Spirit of God working in the hearts of His children who choose to meet His requirements. May a spirit of revival accompany you wherever the Lord beckons you.

Maxim 5: Revival always requires true repentance and the forsaking of known sin.

A person needs revival for only one reason: personal sin. If Christians did not sin, either by omission or commission, there would be no need for revival. To think that we can lead our students to experiencing revival without confronting sin directly and openly is to misunderstand the nature of biblical revival.

In its broadest terms, revival has two distinct phases: first the student removes himself from his sin (negative), and then he returns to the Savior (positive). The way to Christ is always through cleansing and forgiveness. We are unable to experience revival and fellowship with Christ unless we first meet Christ at the cross and have our sins "washed away" by His precious blood.

Unless our students first come to grips with how serious their sin is to themselves, others, and the Lord, they'll never find the inner resolve to stop it in the future. Never, therefore, attempt to lead your students to commit to stop a sin in the future if they haven't first appropriately repented of their past participation in that sin.

At the end of a Saturday night talk at a college conference for Ivy League students, I invited those who felt enslaved to sin to see me after the meeting. A young woman came up to me, and it didn't take much discernment to realize she was under deep conviction. We pulled up a couple of chairs and started what turned out to be a wrenching three-hour personal revival.

The first hour brought her to deep repentance over her sin. The second hour was an intense battle to bring her to the firm resolve to end her sin in the future. But when I asked her to call the other person involved and end it, the blood drained from her face. Finally she said, "I'll do it next week, I promise."

I knew that unless the call was made that very night, she would not be free. Through trembling lips and sweating hands she pleaded—she couldn't call and end it. Fear bound her. But as we prayed, the peace of God flooded her heart, and she agreed to call if I would stand by her and tell her what to say.

Together we walked to the corner of the busy hotel hallway and dialed the long-distance number. It was already past midnight but she knew there was a party still going on. Finally the person came to the phone and she stiffened. I prayed and told her what to say. As she told the other person her decision, she began to sob. She soon collapsed against the wall. She seemed to feel the roots of sin as they were wrenched loose and then broke free. It was deep and painful surgery.

Next we called her mother and father on the other side of the country. Tears of anguish were replaced by tears of joy as they heard firsthand that their desperate prayers had finally been answered.

Before we parted, I made her promise immediately to find her four best friends, who were also with her at the conference, and tell them what she had just done. "Ask them to pray out loud for you right now," I instructed. "Then I want to see the five of you together after breakfast to plan our strategy for your enduring victory."

The next morning I saw them coming, singing at the tops of their lungs—not five but eight—still in tears, but now tears of joy and forgiveness and resolve. I knew then that her friends would carry her over the next set of troubled waters.

Your role of restoring your student is never complete until his behavior aligns with full obedience. Just like a surgeon who has opened the patient to cut out the cancer and finds more than he expected, so the inability to commit to obey in the future clearly proves additional surgery is needed. Neither the surgeon nor the teacher can merely ignore that discovery and just sew the patient back up. Although the large cancerous mass may have been removed, the remaining cancer will soon spread and become even larger than the first if left unattended. Therefore, continue the surgery until everything has been cleansed and your student has truly been set free!

Maxim 6: Revival always results in seeking and serving Christ with renewed fervency.

When significant sin is soundly defeated in a believer, genuine "fruits of repentance" will become evident. Private and internal change leads to public and eternal change.

I took a breath from writing this chapter and weeded a small flower garden next to our house which had been neglected during our recent travels. The weeds were over a foot tall and robbed all the sunshine from the flowers below. As I pulled up a huge pile of weeds, I discovered that my plants underneath were small, mushy, and deformed. What was my anticipation when all the weeds were out and the sunshine was able to touch their starved leaves? That they can and would now flourish and grow.

Similarly, sin chokes out the joyful heart and quenches acts of service. During those times, you must look carefully to find the buried plants. But if the person is truly a child of Christ, spiritual life is always present, if only barely. As those plants are freed from weeds and released to the life-giving sun and rain, they will flourish once again.

These are three telltale signs of renewal you should expect to see in your students. First, there should be a heart of sincere gratitude toward the Lord. Second, a new fervency in seeking Christ should be formed. Third, the student should develop a tremendous heart to serve the Lord. The wise teacher will look for and encourage these reactions as validating signs of the reality of revival.

Maxim 7: Revival reestablishes life's proper priorities.

True biblical revival is a deep and strategic process that ultimately realigns the believer with his God, himself, and his world.

Of all relationships, the relationship a person has with God is the most important and pervasive. Therefore, when its condition is improved, so are all other vital relationships. Stories abound of husbands and wives reuniting because they returned to God. Numerous prodigal sons and daughters have returned home from their lives of rebellion because they also got right with God.

During an extended period of sin, the believer moves from trying to please God to trying to please self. Conflict accelerates and eventually selfishness reigns. When revival occurs, however, and God is enthroned as the Master, He quickly begins to restore order and harmony.

Unfortunately, too many of us teach as though external behavior is the key to growth. We constantly exhort our students to make external improvements while their hearts are opposed to the Lord. Such efforts discourage the teacher and defeat the student. We must work from the inside out. First with God, then self, and finally with others.

Many years ago when I taught at Multnomah School of the Bible, I had the privilege of regularly meeting with Dr. John Mitchell. At that time he was in his early eighties and had a daily radio program, taught almost a full college load, and spoke regularly at weekend conferences. His grasp of the Scriptures and walk with God were unparalleled. I remember his prayers the most. Time after time I think he forgot I was in the room as he visited his loving Father. I felt I was holding onto his mantle as he charioted us to the throne room.

One day I asked him if he would consider doing me a big favor. I told him how God was blessing Walk Thru the Bible and asked if he would invest the time to teach me the Bible the way he knew it. Then

I would teach it to our teachers, who in turn would teach people around the world.

After a couple he moments of silence he surprised me with his answer: "No, Bruce, I won't."

I thought I had offended him. I stammered, "What's the matter? Was my request inappropriate?"

He smiled and said, "I'm not going to teach you the Bible because that's not what you need. But I'll tell you what I will do—I'll continue meeting with you each week and help you fall more in love with the Savior. Because when you do, my friend, everything else will turn out just fine."

He had it right, didn't he? He had discovered that the central priority is always the heart.

Always remember Proverbs 4:23 as you teach your students to love Jesus Christ even more:

> Keep your heart with all diligence,
> For out of it spring the issues of life.

MEANING

The essence of the Law of Revival is these three words: "Revive the heart." The teacher should encourage an ongoing personal revival in students' lives.

CONCLUSION

Over the years that I have taught this biblical truth, many people have reported how deeply they were touched by the Law of Revival. Their hearts were awakened to the truth that God has called them to a ministry of revival—both in and out of the classroom.

I had just finished teaching a 7 *Laws of the Learner* conference in the Midwest. People were filing out past me, expressing their appreciation. In the middle of the line one middle-aged woman looked me directly in the eyes and asked intensely, "Would it be all right if I hugged you? I must hug you."

She caught me off guard, but I smiled as the people behind her waited, and said, "Sure, I'd be honored."

Her hug was strong and I felt her tremble as she released me. As she backed up a step she said, "You must know why that hug was so important to me." Tears began to flow down her cheeks. She forgot there were hundreds of people milling around us and continued, "My uncle abused and raped me repeatedly when I was a little girl, and I've never been able to forgive him. But as we knelt during the Law of Revival, I was finally able to forgive him."

I sensed there was more coming as her lips quivered. Her voice broke repeatedly as she spoke. "As I forgave him, a bright heat started burning through my chest and spread throughout my body. I thought I was having a heart attack, so I asked God what was happening to me. He said, 'You have just forgiven your uncle and now I am able to forgive you. I'm burning away all the bitterness and anger that has settled throughout your body.'"

Her countenance suddenly changed, and she smiled as radiant a smile as I've ever seen. She grabbed my hand, leaned over, and whispered, "I haven't been able all these years to touch another man. I hated men. As I walked toward you in this line, I knew that if I could hug you, I had really been healed."

And then she hugged me again and walked away exclaiming, "I'm finally free! Praise God, I'm free!"

Everything was worth it at that moment, wasn't it? The challenge was made to her for repentance and revival. She reached out and experienced a miracle that shattered the chains that bound her. The power of the cross to forgive was the same power that cleansed her and set her free from the tomb of rape and abuse.

Whenever we talk about the responsibility of going to a person or class or church that needs revival, we are flooded with feelings of fear and inadequacy. Who among us will ever be adequate in our own strength to help another person rediscover the Lord? I know I'm not.

The wonderful news is that God doesn't expect any of us to be adequate. He desires us to rely on Him and His complete adequacy. When we do, that same God who sent Nathan to bring back David will also empower us to bring back another David—if we will just open our heart to His leadership. Since God has commissioned you, will He not also empower you?

Revival is my favorite law. Perhaps it's also the Lord's favorite— because He's the One who yearns the deepest for His wayward children. As you bring your Davids back home, look up that holy hill and you will see the Lord running toward you—arms outstretched, already celebrating the return of His wayward child.

Your David will thank you for the rest of his life, and so will your God—for the rest of eternity.

DISCUSSION QUESTIONS

1. Reread the story Nathan told David. Why do you think it was so successful in making the point? List as many specific similarities as you can between the story and David. Has anyone ever "done a Nathan" on you? If so, describe what happened. What are the secrets of "doing a Nathan" effectively?

2. Think back over your Christian life to the time you experienced your most significant revival. How did it start and what were the results in your life? Do you wish you could experience that same vibrant relationship with Christ again? Now that you understand that revival can be yours anytime you really desire it, what hinders you from it right now?

3. Of all the people you have known, which Christian friend cared most for the condition of your spiritual life over the years? Has anyone ever obeyed Galatians 6:1 and come to you seeking your restoration? Describe how the encounter worked and how you feel about what happened. What lessons did you learn?

4. If revival were to come to your church, it would follow the repentance and restoration from past and present sin. From God's point of view, what are the major churchwide sins that need to be confessed and set straight before He is free to send revival? Read Nehemiah 1 and kneel before the Lord and repent on behalf of your church.

Chapter Fourteen

Revival

Method and Maximizers

It was the middle of the night when I received a call from a friend across the country. He apologized for calling past midnight, but he was really upset. Another friend in his church had called him that afternoon to relay the terrible news about a leading elder who had just been arrested for drunk driving—again.

My friend had immediately left his office and gone to the jail, where the elder spilled the whole story. Not only was he in jail for drunk driving, but he had been a secret alcoholic for a number of years. Besides that, he was under huge financial pressure for running up his credit card bill over $30,000. His wife was threatening to leave him, claiming that their relationship had been dead for years.

"But the worst thing is that this leader doesn't care," my friend told me. "His heart is hard and he wants nothing to do with God. What should I do? Almost everyone wants to throw him out of the church and let him rot in jail because he hid everything all this time."

Ultimately my friend asked how the elders could bring their co-laborer back to the Lord and restore his life and ministry. What I told him is outlined in the next few pages.

Do you know how to help a Christian who has strayed from Christ? Do you know how to lead your disobedient children or family or friends back to obedience? The Revival Method is a revolutionary approach from Scripture that any parent, pastor, teacher, or friend can use to help another Christian restore her life. I have used these five steps numerous times and have seen scores of people rediscover the joy of walking in harmony with the Lord.

And, by the way, it worked for my friend. He called back a few weeks later with the exciting news that the elder was on the road to recovery. The church had rallied around him as a fellow Christian who desperately needed their help and support.

REVIVAL METHOD

A study of the revivals in the Scriptures shows that they all follow the same basic steps, with only some minor differences. Each step strategically builds upon the previous one and should not be hurried through nor skipped. Remember, you are not concerned with immediate results as much as lasting results. If the person or class is unable, for any reason, to wholeheartedly accept and act upon a step, then do not proceed to the next. Continue reinforcing and encouraging the appropriate action of that present step.

Remember, too, that when something as spiritual and delicate as revival is analyzed, we face the real possibility of killing the very specimen we are trying to dissect. May we always remember the wonder of God's grace and mercy in allowing a wayward believer to return to the fold—let alone the wonder of using another wayward believer to show the way home.

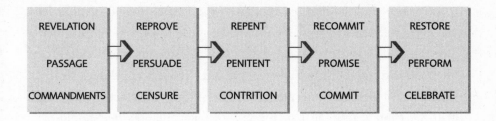

Step 1: Revelation

People need revival simply because they have disobeyed the Lord. We need to begin, then, with the certainty that the person has indeed sinned. Recognize the difference between someone doing something you disapprove of and someone doing a thing that God forbids. We aren't the voice of God on whether something is right or wrong; the Bible is.

If the Bible says it's sin, it is sin. It's not just your opinion; it is the "*revelation*" from God. For instance, God said, "You shall not steal." If a person has stolen, he has sinned. He has broken not only the law of the land; he has broken the law of heaven. Show the person the specific "*passage*" in the Bible and the "*commandment*" or principle that has been broken.

Therefore, if you know a person has broken the commands of Scripture, then God has made you responsible to go to that person in love and restore him. When you go, you are simply obeying God. You are not delivering your own opinion—you are carrying God's divine revelation.

The first step necessary to lead a believer back to the Lord is to bring him face-to-face with the Bible's teaching on his condition. Until the believer sees that his condition results from his direct disobedience, the problem will never be clear and therefore cannot be resolved.

Imagine a sick patient visiting his doctor. "Doc, I don't know what the problem is. I just don't feel good anymore." Then imagine that the doctor immediately prescribes medicine and exhorts his patient to "get your act together." That patient would be at a loss because the doctor never diagnosed the problem. In a similar matter, too many teachers never face the real problem but continue trying to fix symptoms.

The root problem behind the need for revival is the believer's disobedience to the Lord. The teacher must identify and expose the key Scriptures that present God's standards in such a way that the student is forced to face the facts directly. The teacher must present the biblical passages clearly and without personal interpretation. The student must see for himself that the Bible teaches that such behavior is sin. The teacher should hit that nail repeatedly during his teaching until there is consensus by the student(s).

In this first step, the teacher is not reproving or exhorting the student for his sin, only exposing him to what the Bible teaches about it. Be careful to make clear that you are trying to identify only what the Bible states about the issue, not what the teacher or the students might think about the behavior.

Keep the presentation straightforward and unemotional. Avoid any subjective or emotional comments. Either the Bible commands a specific behavior or it doesn't. If it does, be sure you don't apologize or soft-pedal it. You may not be comfortable at this stage, but your role is to present only what the Bible says.

The teacher should drive toward consensus on a statement such as, "Can we together agree on the basis of the passages we have studied that the Bible teaches X is sin?" Do not go beyond this step until all debate is finished. Continue to focus the students' attention on the text, not on their personal behavior.

Step 2: Reprove

When your students agree that the Bible says that a certain behavior is sin, then you must get them to *personally* agree that their behavior is sin. *This step is the crucial bridge between the revelation of God and the repentance of the student.*

This step concentrates the students' attention upon specific sins they have committed. By the end of this step the students should not be saying, "Yes, the Bible teaches that this is sin" (Step 1), but instead, "Yes, I have disobeyed God and therefore sinned in His sight."

Up to this point, three influences already could be *"reproving"* a student. These three "Reproving Agents" include his own conscience, the Spirit of God dwelling in him, and the Bible. All three, however, can be ignored. He can rationalize his actions to his conscience, suppress the Spirit by rejecting His conviction, and silence the Scriptures by avoiding them.

In such a case the Lord has one remaining Reproving Agent. Believe it or not, the Bible teaches that God has commissioned you and me to be this final Reproving Agent. All four agents provide the safety net God has placed beneath His children. Go and seek to *"persuade"* the erring brother while loving him but *"censuring"* his behavior.

To reprove or rebuke someone is to sharply criticize or reprimand them. The element of confrontation is clearly present. It's unfortunate that reproof or rebuke has gone out of vogue in our schools, churches, and businesses. Our society has decided that things are no longer black and white, just various shades of gray. Since everything is gray, then what I do is none of your business. Our society aggressively opposes those who try to uphold God's standards in a public, reproving way.

It's because parents aren't rebuking their children and holding them responsible for appropriate behavior that children run wild. It's because teachers won't rebuke their students and hold them responsible that we have classrooms filled with chaos. It's because pastors and leaders are not rebuking their congregations and holding them accountable to biblical behavior that we have churches that look no different from the world.

Biblical reproof is concerned not only with *what* is said, but *how*. The *what* of reproof is communicated in the confrontation; the *how* of reproof is the style and tone in which the confrontation is delivered. Numerous verses in the Bible instruct us to be gentle and guided by love.

The Lord's discipline is always intended to bring about obedience and growth. At times the Lord must exercise powerful discipline as outlined briefly in 1 Corinthians 11:29–32, where Paul reminds us that he who takes the Lord's Supper in an unworthy manner brings "judgment to himself... For this reason many are *weak* and *sick* among you, and many *sleep* [are dead]. For if we would judge ourselves, we would not be judged. *But when we are judged* [as those in this passage are weak and sick and already dead], *we are chastened by the Lord.*"

Not too long ago I was reproving a married person because he would not stop his adulterous affair. I was finally forced to use the strong consequences of God's discipline and told the person that some people had suffered severely because they would not repent and stop their sin. After giving example after example, the person became uncomfortable and said, "Stop, you are making me afraid!"

"Afraid of what?" I asked.

"Afraid that God may get me if I don't stop my affair."

"You had better be afraid," I said, "because if you think God is going to sit by and let you destroy two Christian families and wreak havoc on all the children and their future lives and marriages, you don't know the level of God's commitment to protect you from your sin. In fact, it's because you don't understand the 'fear of the Lord' that you are acting so foolishly."

If you want a couple of solid illustrations of this, read Paul's rebukes in 1 Corinthians. Some of them are gentle and some are direct and forceful. Or read how John the Baptist reproves the multitudes. Or recall the forceful rebukes of Jesus to the religious leaders of His day. Or reread the books of Numbers and Deuteronomy and observe how God confronts and admonishes the people. There is no doubt about it—the Lord preaches and practices the principle of rebuking. So should we!

What would have happened to me if my parents hadn't loved me enough to rebuke me? I can't imagine. I'm also thankful that throughout my life, many of God's people have obeyed their commission to rebuke me, some gently and some soundly, on issues of conduct, attitude, and occasionally on matters of character. How I thank God for their obedience and love!

In like manner, your children, friends, spouse, family members, and students will rise and thank you for your love in speaking the truth when they stray and need a word of rebuke.

I love the words of Paul to his fellow teacher Timothy, and by application to all of us who serve the Lord:

> I charge you therefore [note the commission] before God and the Lord Jesus Christ, who will judge the living and the dead at His appearing and His kingdom: Preach the word! Be ready in season and out of season. Convince, *rebuke*, exhort, with all long-suffering and teaching. (2 Timothy 4:1–2)

Do you have a heart to be fully obedient to the Lord? Do you love Him? Then honor His command to rebuke.

Those of us who struggle with the pain associated with reproving another person must not miss the phrase "with all longsuffering." Even Paul knew of the pain that frequently accompanies rebuke. So don't be surprised at the thought of suffering when you obey the Lord—just deepen your commitment to stay at it no matter what, and live up to the description of "longsuffering."

Step 3: Repent

This step is the turning point in the life of the person you are trying to help. Everything to this point is building to repentance; everything that follows it is determined by whether he "*repents.*" *Revival hinges on repentance.* Seek to lead the person to become "*penitent*" and experience genuine "*contrition.*"

The basic New Testament word for repentance is the Greek word *metanoeo*, which means to change one's mind or perception. The Bible uses the concept of repentance in three primary ways:

1. To express remorse for an inappropriate act or attitude.
2. To express a change of heart when a non-Christian sees his eternal need, realizes that Christ's sacrifice alone is sufficient payment for his sins, and therefore changes his mind and chooses to believe and receive the Lord Jesus Christ as his Redeemer.
3. To express a change of heart when a Christian changes his mind and therefore his behavior regarding acts of personal disobedience.

This section of the Law of Revival focuses upon the third category of repentance. In order to explain this hinge step in leading a person to revival, I would like to broaden the technical meaning of repentance to include three related concepts.

1. Repentance must include conviction.

At the heart of conviction lies the root word *convince*, which means to conquer something a person believes or thinks by replacing it with something different. At the heart of revival must be repentance, the changing of one's mind. The mind is changed—convinced—because another thought or belief thoroughly conquered the existing one. The foundation of repentance always takes place in the person's mind.

Behind every sinful action lies a causative sinful thought that must be conquered by the correct biblical thought. When we are leading a person to repentance we must first deal with the thought life. We must identify the incorrect thoughts behind her disobedience and overthrow them with the correct biblical thoughts.

When you aspire to convince a person that his sin is unwise, you must oppose and overthrow the *rationalizations* that control his thoughts. To rationalize means "to make something irrational appear rational or reasonable; to justify one's behavior or weaknesses especially to one's self; to find plausible but untrue reasons for conduct." Ultimately, rationalizations are the internal conditions needing repentance.

All sin stems from false thoughts which are misconceptions about the nature of God or the will of God. Adultery is committed because the person has *convinced* himself that immorality will bring more happiness and pleasure than the fidelity God has commanded. Therefore, God must have lied and His ways are not the best.

Rationalizations grow stronger the longer they are left unchallenged. Soon those lies form an alliance and together fight against the truth whenever it attempts to overthrow them. The person slowly changes his mind from thinking God's ways are the best to thinking that God's ways are not the best. You could say that the Christian is experiencing a negative repentance—his thoughts are being overthrown in the wrong direction.

Ultimately the rationalizations become very strong and exert a powerful hold on the Christian's mind and therefore upon his behavior. The Bible calls these areas of mental defeat *strongholds*.

Strongholds are powerful citadels ruthlessly ruling over the previous landlords of that part of the mind. Their purpose is to enlarge their kingdom through deceit and manipulation. As these strongholds grow in their power and in scope, they ultimately force the person to submit to their power and enslave him. Instead of being a slave of Christ, he becomes a slave of the enemy.

In areas surrounding major sins, you can be sure there is not only one stronghold but a whole series of fortresses strategically placed at every gate of the person's mind. Every time the person comes out of the darkness trying to find the light, the strongholds gather their armies and attempt to soundly whip the Christian.

Whenever a Christian who has been married for some time seriously considers divorce, at least half a dozen major strongholds of unresolved anger, unforgivingness, grudges, and bitterness have been constructed. If you have ever tried to overthrow the unsound mind of a person determined to divorce, you have met these forces head-on. You find yourself engaged in hand-to-hand combat with the many rationalizations and strongholds and fortresses.

It is then we must remember that prayer is our greatest weapon. We must call for the cavalry from just over the hill!

For though we walk in the flesh,
we do not war according to the flesh.
For the weapons of our warfare are not carnal [of the flesh]
but mighty in God
for pulling down strongholds,
casting down arguments
and every high thing
that exalts itself against the knowledge of God,
bringing every thought into captivity
to the obedience of Christ.
(2 Corinthians 10:3–5)

Strongholds are to be "pulled down" because they exalt themselves against the very "knowledge of God." Strongholds strain to become the god of the person by overthrowing the commandments of God.

Notice too that we are to "cast down arguments" which also war "against the knowledge of God." An argument is "a reason or reasons offered for or against something; a discourse intended to persuade or to convince." Don't miss the clear direction from God's Word that *we are involved with defeating the argument through convincing the person of the truth.* What sets us free? The truth!

We must never forget it: Our thoughts are held captive either by the Lord or by the enemy. When thoughts are set free from the enemy's fortresses, you have won. The person has biblically repented!

The result is a change in behavior. *When repentance occurs in the mind, revival will occur in the life.* This vital link controls almost every part of our lives. Whatever owns our thoughts controls our behavior. Belief determines behavior.

2. Repentance must include contrition.

Unfortunately in some Christian circles, repentance is limited to its most narrow definition: changing one's mind. Although the Greek word for repentance does mean to change one's mind, it also carries many other shades of meaning.

Contrition is another component to biblical repentance. To be contrite means to feel "deeply and humbly sorry for one's sins; to be remorseful." Contrition describes one's emotions or feelings. When a person deeply repents and changes his mind about a major sin or act of disobedience, his emotions also undergo a change. Contrition accompanies or follows conviction. *Contrition is a hinge emotion in revival as it allows the person to transition from hardness of heart to tenderness of heart.* Contrition is God's "Heart Tenderizer" because it breaks up the crusty old heart hardened by coldness and indifference. As tears wash down the person's face, the heart is cleansed and renewed.

We must never allow ourselves to limit revival merely to the change of mind. It must also include the cleansing of the emotions. Without the cleansing of emotions the person who has experienced a change of mind may not feel forgiven even though he knows he is forgiven.

Many times in counseling I will discover a Christian who has sinned greatly and has confessed it before the Lord and abandoned that sin, but who still lives in defeat because he does not feel forgiven. Often this reflects the lack of genuine and thorough contrition. Thorough contrition allows the Christian to become aware of the pain he has caused others, as well as to completely forgive himself for his sin. As confession to the Lord ensures forgiveness from the Lord, contrition encourages us to forgive ourselves.

Time after time in the Bible, contrition accompanies revival. When the mind changes (conviction) then the heart breaks (contrition). Consider the revival in 2 Chronicles 34:27 where the Lord describes what King Josiah did as he repented:

"Because your heart was tender, and
you humbled yourself before God
when you heard His words
against this place and against it inhabitants,
and you humbled yourself before Me,
and you tore your clothes
and wept before Me,
I also have heard you,"
says the LORD.

Or consider the great revival in Nehemiah 8–9 when the people of God heard the Word of God, realized their great sin, and repented with sackcloth and ashes amidst great weeping and sorrow.

Do you think contrition is important to God? Do you think God cares if we become contrite as long as we "change our minds" about the sin? We have a clear answer to that question in David's prayer of confession:

For I acknowledge my transgressions,
And my sin is always before me.
Against You, You only, have I sinned.
And done this evil in Your sight—

For You do not desire sacrifice,
or else I would give it;
You do not delight in burnt offering.

The sacrifices of God are a broken spirit,
A broken and a contrite heart—
These, O God, You will not despise.
(Psalm 51:3–4, 16–17)

Finally, contrition must be appropriate to the nature of the sin committed. An act of impatience spoken in a fleeting moment is not nearly as serious as stealing from the nearby department store, which is not as serious as committing adultery with a coworker, which is not as serious as murder.

This crucial relationship between the depth of sin and the depth of sorrow is overlooked by many of us as we labor to lead others to revival. The deeper and longer and more willful and more hurtful the sin, the more we must assist the person in feeling deep and wrenching sorrow and anguish.

There is a barrier in all of us between what we think and what we feel. To some this is almost nonexistent and they feel pain appropriately and easily. But others, for whatever reason, have constructed a wall protecting their emotions from pain. We must love them enough to find the door in that wall and release their pent-up guilt and remorse.

3. Repentance must include confession.

Revival cannot remain private. Not only must the Christian confess his sin to the Lord, but he should also acknowledge it to you and any others directly impacted by his acts of disobedience.

The biblical term *confess* comes from a compound Greek word *homologeo*, which means to "speak the same thing" or agree with another person. When a criminal confesses, it means the criminal has agreed with the authorities that he committed the crime.

Why is confession so important? Because this is where the Christian humbles himself and assumes full responsibility for his actions and openly recognizes that he must seek forgiveness and restoration from God and others. Until this point, repentance is only internal and private. Repentance without confession treats the sin as if it were merely an island unto itself rather than an act that offends both heaven and earth.

A search of Scriptures makes it plain that confession is not optional. Not only is it crucial as it relates to our salvation (Matthew 3:5–6;

10:32–33; Romans 10:9–10; Philippians 2:9–11; 1 John 4:2–3), but it has a crucial role to play regarding our sin (Leviticus 5:5–6; 16:21; 26:40–42; Psalm 32:5; 1 John 1:9) and those we hurt through our sin (Matthew 5:23–24; James 5:16). It's sobering to realize that the Bible commands us, under certain conditions, to confess our sins to one another in a similar way as to the Lord.

When a person nears the point of confessing his sin to the Lord, I usually ask him to tell me the specific sins he has committed. Frequently the person will try to give a sweeping statement like, "I sinned a lot and God knows all about it." Try to keep a person at this point until he confesses each sin specifically.

The reason this is difficult for some is because either they have not fully acknowledged to themselves that they really committed those sins, or they are afraid you will lose respect for them if they admit their specific sins. Discern which issue is causing the concern and confront it openly and honestly.

Remember, you are not a judge but a friend and a fellow sinner saved by grace. Occasionally the Lord may bring you a person who has fallen into deep and desperate sin. When the person is able to confess that sin to you, he is in a most vulnerable position. He needs your greatest tenderness and understanding. Obviously, we must hold such issues in the strictest of confidence.

When the person confesses his sins and you have shared the weight of his burdens, consider helping the person to forgive himself by telling him that you forgive him. Look him right in the eyes and say, "I'm sorry that you sinned in these ways, but I want you to know that I also forgive you. Never wonder after you leave this place whether you can look me in the eyes. You can—because all of us are forgiven only through the blood of Jesus Christ." Your acceptance will encourage him to believe that God can forgive him.

After you have expressed your forgiveness, ask the person to confess once again his sin—this time to the Lord. By having him confess his sins first to you, you not only ensure that he is being honest, but you also prepare him to accept and receive the Lord's forgiveness.

We must always lead a person to process his sin appropriately so he can be healed thoroughly. Note the logical progression of repentance:

First: *Conviction* where the *mind* is *changed*.

Second: *Contrition* where the *emotions* feel *remorse*.

Third: *Confession* where the *will* acknowledges *responsibility*.

First the mind must change, then the emotions must feel, and finally the will must act.

Step 4: Recommit

It is time to quickly turn your student's focus from the past to the future. Don't allow yourself to think that you are finished. Remember, the commandment is to restore the one overcome in any trespass. What a thrill when one of our family, friends, or students repents—but the real challenge is to make sure the victory endures.

The longer the person has been practicing the sin, the more resolve he must have to rely upon the power and presence of the Holy Spirit. The ultimate purpose of *"recommitment"* is to strengthen the person so that he will continue to obey. In order to maximize his resolve, three steps should be followed so that he will *"promise"* himself and the Lord that he will honor his *"commitment"* to obey.

1. Recommitment must include confirmation.

This is the crucial question: "How committed are you to stopping this sin that you have just repented of?" If you hear, "I'm not going to give into that temptation ever again—by the power of the Lord who lives within me," or something similar, then commend and greatly encourage your student. If, however, you hear, "I'm not sure about the next time, but I know I'm sorry for the past," then roll up your sleeves, because your task is not completed. Identify whether the person isn't committed to living obediently or whether he does not honestly think he can obey even though he sincerely desires to.

Remember, without confirmation regarding what your student plans to do the next time the temptation arises, he will be greatly weakened. His allegiance is not strengthened by firm resolve. What happens now greatly influences who dominates his future. The only way to ultimate freedom is through freely choosing to submit to the will of the Lord.

Remind the person of God's promises contained in 1 Corinthians 10:13:

> *No temptation has overtaken you*
> *except such as is common to man;*
> *but God is faithful,*
> *who will not allow you to be tempted*
> *beyond what you are able,*
> *but with the temptation*
> *will also make the way of escape,*
> *that you may be able to bear it.*

2. Recommitment may include covenant.

How do we strengthen a person's resolve to stand against the temptation? Do you remember what Joshua did when he wanted to help his students walk in obedience when he wasn't there to guide them? He led the nation to establish a covenant with the Lord: "And the people said to Joshua, 'The LORD our God we will serve, and His voice we will obey!' So Joshua *made a covenant* with the people that day" (Joshua 24:24–25).

Why a covenant? Because it was the most serious commitment possible between man and God. Joshua knew his people needed such a commitment to help them over the rocks of temptation that lay ahead. It's encouraging that further in the same chapter the Bible says, "Israel served the LORD all the days of Joshua, and all the days of the elders who outlived Joshua" (v. 31).

Throughout this Law of Revival we have referred to revivals that occurred in the Bible. From these and other revivals, it's apparent that "making a covenant" or "taking an oath" was the normal step after repentance of major sins. The act of repentance broke the allegiance to disobedience, and recommitment reestablished the allegiance to obedience.

When a person has expressed his recommitment toward the future, you have seen the person make a giant step toward restoration! Because of this, we should consider leading our students to make a commitment of obedience to the Lord and even to you when necessary.

3. Recommitment should include consecration.

By now you should have sensed that I am presenting a complete set of steps you could use. In real life, only parts of them are used.

When a person breaks free from a major sin, he is flooded with appreciation to you and the Lord. Many are overwhelmed by the goodness of God's forgiveness; others are overcome with a sense of freedom and release. At this point you can greatly enhance and enrich your student's spiritual life. She has gathered a great deal of positive momentum. If the situation permits, help your friend enjoy some wonderful additional benefits that will help her tremendously.

This is an excellent time to *challenge your student's consecration to Christ.* As our enemy uses our weakest moments to tempt us to sin, we must use our strongest moments to "tempt" others to deeper godliness. Let me suggest three areas for growth which I call the "Challenges to Consecration":

Challenge your students to further obedience in the specific areas that tempt them. Nehemiah 10 notes that the people's commitments were specific and focused on those areas where they faced the greatest temptation— including intermarriage with nonbelievers, commerce on the Sabbath, celebrating the Sabbath Year, and issues surrounding interest and lending.

Consider focusing your students' attention on those "universal" temptations for people of their age and circumstances. If you are aware of any specific temptations for the individual, challenge those.

Challenge your students to a deeper walk with the Lord through seeking Him in their devotions and prayer life. In the revival under King Asa (2 Chronicles 15), the people began to "seek the LORD God of their fathers *with all their heart* and with all their soul" (v. 12). When your students have broken free from their sin, challenge them to make their spiritual life a higher priority. Encourage them in personal devotions, personal prayer, and involvement in a meaningful Bible study and fellowship group.

Challenge your students to a more complete obedience to the will of God in all areas in life. In the revival under Josiah (2 Chronicles 34), the king covenanted "to follow the LORD, and to keep His commandments and His testimonies and His statutes with all his heart and all his soul" (v. 31). In the revival recorded in Nehemiah 10, the people committed "to observe and do *all the commandments* of the LORD our Lord, and His ordinances and His statutes" (v. 29).

During these precious moments when your student is more open to the Lord, invite him to dedicate himself more fully to the Lord. The New Testament has a name for this process—discipleship. When we try to foster more spiritual growth in our students, we are helping them to obey the call of Christ.

Step 5: Restore

Finally, the finish line is in sight! Remember, God's commandment to all of us is to "*restore*" the person who is overtaken in any trespass. Everything to this point is preparation for that. There are three broad areas to consider under this step, all seeking to ensure your student "*performs*" his promises so you can "*celebrate*" together.

1. Restoration may include compensation.

Compensation may be necessary if the sin in view was against any other person(s). Jesus is clear that before full restoration with the Lord is possible, the offended party must be fully reconciled:

> Therefore if you bring your gift to the altar, and there remember that your brother has something against you, leave your gift there before the altar, and go your way. First be reconciled to your brother, and then come and offer your gift. (Matthew 5:23–24)

Ask your student to go to the person(s) he has wronged and do whatever is necessary to be reconciled. Even if he is the innocent party and has been wronged by another, he must go to the person and seek reconciliation.

One night after I taught in Atlanta, a young man came up and told me he needed to talk. Privately he confessed, "I lie all the time. I lie to my wife, my parents, by boss, my friends—and I even try to lie to God. I lie when there is no reason to lie. I'm really afraid, now, because I can't stop lying."

We talked about his sin, and I led him through the stages of repentance where many a tear was shed. In the recommitment stage I asked, "Are you willing to do whatever it takes to have a clear conscience between God and man and to find release from this bondage of lying?"

"Yes," he promised, "I'll do anything. I need help." We shook hands on his commitment.

He wanted to know how long it would take to get his life back in order. "It won't take long—less than a month," I said, "but you are going to have to pay a heavy price and humble yourself repeatedly."

The first thing I told him was to go home, take a pad of paper, and list every person he could remember to whom he had lied. Then he was to call me the next morning and tell me how many people were on his list.

When he called the next morning, I could tell by the tone of his voice that he was struggling to face the scope of lying. "I have twenty-six people on my list," he said, "and there may be more."

"Good. Next I want you to put each of those names on the top of a new page. On each one, make a list of every lie you can remember telling to that person. Then tomorrow night after work, I would like you to come and show me your list."

What a test of his resolve! The next night we met at Denny's for a hamburger and reviewed his long list of lies. He was sobered and despaired of finding victory. I reaffirmed him and told him I respected him for his courage and that God would bless his efforts. Then I asked him to arrange those lists in order, from the most difficult to handle to the least.

"Now you have your biggest test," I said. "You must go to each of those people and confess your lies. Ask for forgiveness and see if you can do anything to make it up to them."

"What?" he blurted. "You've got to be kidding! I can't go back to those people. Why, the first person I put on my list is my boss—I lie to him all the time, and if he knew it, he would fire me. I've lied on my time sheet many times and have taken pay for time I really didn't work. Besides that, he tells me to lie to customers when they want to know where their order is and it hasn't shipped yet."

My friend was at the crossroads. He had already repented and recommitted himself, but unless he would complete the process of restoration, he would never find freedom.

"I know this may cost you your job—in fact, you may end up owing your boss money for the pay you took falsely. But you must make a hard choice right now and decide whether you are going to obey the Lord and do His will or not. Obedience is never easy, but it is the right thing to do. God will be with you, and even if you do lose your job, He will keep His promise to supply your needs.

Choose to obey God and trust Him with the consequences!"

After a real struggle he agreed to see his boss the next morning. It was nearly lunchtime before he called. "I can't believe it!" he said. "I confessed all my lies to my boss. I told him about lying on my time sheet and about lying to the customers for him. I told him I was a Christian and knew that I shouldn't lie, but I had and I was sorry. I told him that I would pay him back for the time I had stolen, but that I wasn't going to lie *to him* anymore. And even if he told me to, I wasn't going to lie *for him* to a customer ever again. If the inventory wasn't shipped, I wouldn't say it was on its way."

Wow, I thought, *what a courageous young man!* "So what happened?"

"We talked for more than two hours and he accepted my apologies. Then he shocked me by saying my confession convicted him of his lying, and he apologized to me and told me he would never ask me to lie again. He told me not to worry about the pay thing—we'd just figure it as history. And he told me he wanted me to continue working and respected me for my honesty. Can you believe it? He thanked a big liar like me for my honesty!"

Over the course of the next two weeks he called or went to visit everyone on his list. He called in every couple of days for the first week, but we both soon knew he was committed to finishing the task. A couple of weeks later he showed me his notebook, which had a line crossed through every single lie. And then he made the most important statement of the whole experience: "Ever since I started confessing these sins to all these people, I have stopped lying. I am now so committed to telling the truth that I don't think anyone or anything could get me to lie again!"

That was it. My young friend was sprinting across the finish line. He had been restored, and in the process, God had healed him. Just like James promised!

Make sure you help your students compensate for the errors of their sins. Restoration must always include making things right with everyone wronged.

2. Restoration must include cleansing.

Unlike *compensation*, which takes care of those our sin has hurt, *cleansing* takes care of our own lives. The first is public and the second is personal. The first deals with making right our relationships because of the *past* things we have done, while the second deals with taking away all things in the *present* that could tempt us to sin.

Two approaches to cleansing stand out in biblical revivals. First, people take away things that are evil or tempting. Second, they add things that ensure obedience.

So often we unknowingly allow "Temptation Triggers" to dwell in our lives, yet we're confused about why we continue to fall prey to so many temptations. On the opposite end, we do not consciously arrange and install "Commitment Cultivators" that constantly encourage us to become "holy as He is holy."

A Temptation Trigger is anything that lures a person in the direction of sin. It initiates temptations. Triggers may include the person's friends, the places where they spend their time, the events they attend, or the things they watch or listen to. We should help the student identify the triggers in his life and eradicate them, or at least minimize them as much as possible. The more these triggers are removed, the less external temptation the person will have to stand against.

A Commitment Cultivator is anything which stimulates a person in the direction of further obedience and dedication to the Lord. Cultivators incline us to commitment to Christ. They include the same main categories that exist for the Triggers—people, places, things, events, activities, habits, and memories.

During the cleansing stage, try to help the student identify those things that would strongly incline him to continue his walk with the Lord. The more these Cultivators are present, the more the student is likely to progress in his spiritual life.

Biblical revivals always featured Commitment Cultivators: they rebuilt the temple, revitalized the priesthood, reinstituted the temple offerings, strengthened the priests and the Levites, sent teachers to preach and explain the Bible throughout the land, and reestablished the annual practice of the feasts and celebrations. See how obvious it is when we take a moment to notice it?

Our lives are greatly influenced, if not controlled, by the systems we live under. The Bible teaches us that there is a "world system" under Satan's control which is orchestrated to destroy all that is Christian. His system is everywhere and has infiltrated every part of life. The ripping down of the Temptation Triggers greatly reduces the ever-present pull of temptation.

God also has a system through which He is accomplishing His perfect will. Unlike Satan's system, however, God's system normally requires purposeful action. The Scriptures, the Spirit, and the saints are the normal threads woven throughout God's system. The more the Christian is studying the Scriptures, in tune with and submissive to the Spirit, and in regular fellowship and accountability with other saints, the more his system will protect and enhance his development and growth.

Therefore, during this season of *cleansing*, help reorganize your student's life so it is best inclined to grow and flourish.

3. Restoration should include celebration.

Jesus revealed an amazing thing about celebration in the heavenlies when He said, "I say to you, there is joy in the presence of the angels of God over one sinner who repents" (Luke 15:10).

He revealed even more about how God feels when one of His children repents and comes home in the Parable of the Prodigal Son:

"But the father said to his servants, 'Bring out the best robe and put it on him, and put a ring on his hand and sandals on his feet. And bring the fatted calf here and kill it, *and let us eat and be merry;* for this my son was dead and is alive again; he was lost and is found.' *And they began to be merry.*" (Luke 15:22–24)

The Lord knows how to have a happy ending! When a Christian comes back to the Lord from a season of major rebellion, we should have a party. But do we? Never in my life can I remember anyone celebrating with a real party the revival and restoration of a fellow Christian. How far we have strayed from the model of biblical celebration!

Just think of what a celebration would do for the people involved:

Wouldn't it put a final period on this painful process, letting everyone know it's finished?

Wouldn't it make public that repentance and restoration has been completed?

Wouldn't it provide an opportunity for a demonstration of public affection and forgiveness to the forgiven parties?

Wouldn't it end gossip, since everything would be out in the open for all to see?

Wouldn't it allow the victory of restoration to be shared by the whole concerned community, either through direct involvement or through word of mouth?

Wouldn't it greatly strengthen the resolve of the person who had come back, since so many people were involved in his restoration—indeed, wouldn't it be a strong part of his Commitment Cultivators system?

Wouldn't it announce to the world that the church really does care for its wounded?

Wouldn't it give hope to those who are secretly living in sin and who need the courage that it is worth it to come back to the Father?

When the process is complete, find an appropriate way to celebrate, whether it be private or public, an encouraging word or a complete party...or maybe just a joyful testimony in church or Sunday school. Somehow, someway, lead the restored believer to the table of blessing prepared for all God's children who return home.

REVIVAL MAXIMIZERS

Revival is the inrush of God's Spirit
into a body which threatens to become a corpse.

D. M. PATTON

Waiting for general revival is no excuse
for not enjoying personal revival.

STEPHEN OLFORD

The best way to revive the church
is to build a fire in the pulpit.
D. L. MOODY

Revival is a major topic of Scripture and could easily have taken a whole book rather than a couple of chapters to discuss. Now that we have a general sense of how revival could look if it were done in the ideal situation, we must always remember that life isn't lived in a textbook but out there, in the marketplace.

As you begin implementing the five steps of revival there are a number of additional insights and practical suggestions that may further assist you as you "restore those overtaken in a trespass."

Maximizer 1: Realize that revival is needed by most Christians most of the time.

We had just finished praying together and were walking to the huge auditorium for the evening service. I asked this popular preacher a question that has forever altered the way I prepare to minister to a Christian audience: "In your opinion, what percentage of the average evangelical church members are out of fellowship with the Lord on any given Sunday?"

"I've never thought about that," he said as we reached the door to the sanctuary. "I expect it may be 15 percent. Maybe as high as 25 percent."

He must have continued chewing on that question because in the middle of the first hymn, he leaned over and whispered, "Well, what percentage do you think it is?"

"I think it's much higher—closer to 60 percent, and perhaps as high as 75 percent."

He reacted with genuine surprise. "Impossible! Not in a good church! Why, what percentage of the people in the auditorium tonight do you think are out of fellowship?"

If I told him the truth he'd be upset, and if I didn't tell the truth the Lord would be upset. So I just said, "I'm not sure," because that was the truth. During the last stanza, I leaned over and said, "Why don't you ask them and find out?"

That was a bit beyond his comfort zone, but I could see he was intrigued by the question. Before I stood to preach he said, "Why don't you ask them? You're the guest speaker."

So I began my message by asking the congregation: "Your pastor and I were having an interesting discussion about what percentage of the people attending evangelical churches tonight all across the land are out of fellowship with the Lord. We couldn't decide so we decided to ask you. Would you vote on the percentage you think are out of fellowship by raising your hands? All those who think less than 10 percent are out of fellowship? Twenty percent? Thirty percent?" When we were finished voting, the average was 75 percent!

"Now let's get serious," I continued. "What about this great congregation? What about the person on your left and on your right—what percentage of them do you think are out of fellowship?" We voted once again. This time it was almost unanimous—70 percent were considered to be living in some known sin at that moment and were therefore out of fellowship with the Lord.

I've repeated that test in various churches around the country and found that although the average fluctuates, it seems to be somewhere between 50 and 80 percent.

If that's true—and you can test it for yourself—then what percentage of the students in your class will be in need of revival the very next time you teach? That's right, 50 to 80 percent!

Since the Christian's relationship to the Lord is the single most important factor in all of life, and since the decided majority are out of fellowship at any given moment, shouldn't we place revival right at the top of our class's "need list"? Surely we must make revival one of our top priorities when we teach.

Maximizer 2: Earnestly seek revival through intense and persistent private and public prayer.

In every recorded revival that I have studied, I have found that private and public prayers were offered specifically for revival for some time before revival actually began. It seems that the Lord lays it on the hearts of the members of His faithful remnant to pray for revival.

Sometimes these prayer cells meet together during Wednesday night prayer meetings. Sometimes you discover that the nearby Bible college is wet with the tears of a few students who have secretly banded together to pray down the mighty Spirit of God. Perhaps most frequently, you find the most intense and persistent prayer warriors to be the older women—many widowed or shut-ins—who quietly send their prayers into the throne room of glory, pleading for the Lord to move His mighty arm in our behalf.

Why is prayer so important in revival? Undoubtedly because God listed it as one of the four requirements that must be fulfilled before He will grant revival (2 Chronicles 7:14). Since prayer is a prerequisite to revival, if we want to lead our students to experience revival, we must first pray for revival in our own lives and then in the lives of our students.

Not only must we pray for revival, but we should also encourage our students to join with us. Consider making this area of prayer a regular and meaningful part of opening or closing moments of class. As James 5:16 states, "The effective, fervent prayer of a righteous man avails much."

Maximizer 3: Vary your delivery according to your students' spiritual response.

If you have raised children, then you immediately realize the necessity of differing your approach to disciplining and restoring your children when they have disobeyed. Some just need an intense look, others a sharp word, and still others a well-placed "stroke of encouragement" on their "seat of understanding." Some respond well to constructive criticism and others languish and wilt under it. Some respond to great challenges and others need small and secure steps. Whatever your students or children need to return from their disobedience—whether they have disobeyed God or man—we must carefully observe their behavior and select the correct style for that person and situation.

We also need to vary our classroom method. Although the lecture method is used most frequently in trying to bring revival to others, various other methods have proven effective:

- Break the class into small groups that pray for each other's need for revival. Have each person pray for the person seated on his right.
- Use a panel of four or five students who openly discuss the main sins of their age group and what hinders them to experiencing revival.
- Put on a skit where one student is an angel arguing with a "fallen angel" about why revival is so strategic and how each is going to help or hinder "Joe Christian" this next week.
- Have a conversation with the "apostle Paul" and one of

the class members about how to have victory over the sins that plague their spiritual life.

Whatever we do, we must find meaningful and effective ways of assisting our students to repent of their sins and then enjoy revival in their hearts.

Maximizer 4: Instruct your students in the knowledge and practice of spiritual disciplines.

Revival has two facets: It liberates your students from the bondage of sin, and it empowers them to stay out of sin and remain in fellowship. This maximizer focuses on training our students to remain in fellowship.

The knowledge and practice of spiritual disciplines is out of vogue. Few Christians know what spiritual disciplines are, let alone practice them. We are living in an era when externals and how-to's set the agenda. Everyone wants a quick fix rather than the ultimate fix.

I'll never forget learning about the absolute necessity of nurturing the inner man. I was a youth pastor, and the ministry was more challenging than I ever expected. I found myself almost daily recognizing my need for more training. What I really wanted, however, was something deeper—the secrets of the spiritual life—those deep truths that would liberate me to live on a deeper level with the Lord. So my wife and I sold what little we had, packed up a little U-Haul, and began our pilgrimage to seminary, where I was sure those "deep and hidden secrets" of the spiritual life could be found.

It was the first day of seminary and the first chapel was beginning. On my left knee was the Hebrew Old Testament and on my right was the Greek New Testament. My finger was poised on the "record" button of my trusty tape recorder—I didn't want to miss anything. I uncapped my fountain pen and flipped open my new pad. I was ready.

A senior was sitting next to me. He looked me over, slowly shook his head, and smiled. "Freshman, eh?" he said. I wondered how he knew.

The president of the seminary stood to speak. He had already written more than twenty books on theology and prophecy. His graying hair and six-foot-six frame commanded all of our attention. "Today," he said, "marks the first day of this seminary year. Because of this, I am going to speak on the subject most important to all of us: The Secrets of the Spiritual Life."

My heart nearly stopped, and I quickly double-checked to make certain my recorder was working properly. He was actually going to tell me the secrets, and it was only my first day!

"There are three primary secrets of the spiritual life which will influence us more than anything else," he began. (I couldn't believe it— here it came!) "They are: first, read your Bible every day; second, walk by means of the Spirit; and third, pray without ceasing!"

I don't think I heard another word out of that chapel.

Those were the secrets of the spiritual life? I couldn't believe it. I had known about those "secrets" for a long time. What I wanted were the *real* secrets—the "deep" ones.

Many years have passed since that memorable day, and I have come to one resounding conclusion: Dr. Walvoord was absolutely right. Not only are they the secrets for Dr. Walvoord, but they are equally the secrets for you and me and every Christian that ever will sit before you when you teach. Therefore, we must train our students to learn how to walk with God more meaningfully and regularly. Because when we do, they'll spend more time in a state of revival rather than needing a revival.

Maximizer 5: Verbalize the final call for revival clearly and expectantly.

Whether we are calling one or one thousand to repentance and revival, we must invite them clearly and with a sense of expectancy and urgency.

Can you remember the last time you went through a time of personal revival and renewal? If you can picture that experience in your mind, you can undoubtedly sense the feelings of fear and discomfort and anxiety you faced at the thought of that process. When we face our need for revival and repentance, our emotions can become a real hindrance. Many who reach the moment of repentance lose courage because of the fear that sweeps their soul.

Because of the desperate struggle our students face, you and I must invite them to return to the Lord with great courage and unwavering resolve. Our courage must lend immediate strength. Our confidence in the Lord must carry them through their Red Sea.

Fifteen hundred men had gathered in a forest for a spiritual retreat. I felt encouraged to preach for deep commitment to the Lord during the weekend. By Saturday night, I had already done extensive counseling and knew that immorality had sunk its vicious teeth into many of these men's lives. They were unable to respond to the Lord with commitment unless they were first cleansed.

When men get together with other men in the woods, you can really speak the truth openly. I preached on immorality and led them through Nathan's process of "confrontation" and "commandments" and "consequences," then called for them to act—to repent and humble themselves and turn from their wicked ways.

The presence of the Lord was strong, and I felt that public confession was necessary: "I'm going to ask you to do a very difficult thing tonight. If you are involved in an adulterous relationship, then I want you to stand and come forward in an act of public repentance. If you cannot find the courage to humble yourself before the rest of these men who deeply care for you, you'll never have the courage to call that other woman and put an end to your adulterous affair."

I led us in a quiet prayer and then continued. "No head will be bowed because the eyes of heaven are upon this place. You need to repent. You need to humble yourself. You need to end your adultery. If that is your commitment, then stand and come down here in an act of humility before the Lord, shake my hand and then go out to that pay telephone right behind this meeting place and call that other woman and end it. Tell her you have sinned against the Lord, against her, against your wife, and against your children. Ask her forgiveness and tell her you won't see her again. The go out into these magnificent woods and fall on your face and seek the Lord's forgiveness for your adultery and disobedience."

There was no music. No choir. No stained-glass windows. No one had their eyes closed. And no one moved.

My heart started pounding in my chest, and I thought the whole auditorium would hear it. I thought, *What on earth am I doing—asking men to come forward publicly and confess their adulterous relationship? What a foolish thought. No one will come.*

And in the midst of my fear, I cried out to God for the conviction of the Holy Spirit to sweep across the audience and break the spirit of pride and rebellion. I released myself into His hands, relinquished my fear, and recommitted myself to preach the truth regardless of the response. My heart soon slowed. I wondered if I should close in prayer, but sensed I should wait.

Suddenly the wooden bleachers shook as a giant of a man in the second to the top row almost leaped to his feet. He strode right down the center aisle and finally stopped six inches in front of my face. I thought he was going to punch me.

I will never forget his words: "I have been having an affair—no, like you said, I've been committing adultery—for seven years. I'm a trucker. And I'm a Christian. You're the first man who has ever preached honestly about adultery and then asked me to stop. I came down here to tell you I'm stopping." Then he stepped forward and gave me a man's hug that put my back into shape. Then he turned and started out toward those telephones. Holding up a quarter he said, "She's not going to believe it, but by God's help, it's all over."

That broke the ice. Many men began to file forward—tears streaming down their faces. Others knelt right where they were. The glorious return of the wayward sons was once again in process. Much later, when I looked out my cabin window for the last time around one in the morning, there was still a line of men waiting for those pay phones.

God may never ask you to call fifteen hundred men to repentance, but He has called you to call for the repentance and revival of those men and women and boys and girls who sit before you week after week in your class. They may not be involved in adultery, but they are involved in disobedience of some kind. Whatever it is—they need to make their own "telephone calls" and then find a quiet spot to kneel in the forest.

Maximizer 6: Anticipate revival to be accompanied by intense spiritual warfare.

By its very nature, revival is directly opposed to the work of our enemy, Satan. Because both the Lord and His archenemy desire the same territory—the hearts and souls of people—the teacher should anticipate and be prepared for strong resistance to efforts to bring revival.

Don't fall prey to the false concept that just because we are on the Lord's side, the battle will be easy or easily won. In fact, the longer the enemy has control of an area, the more difficult the process will be. The forces that oppose us will have constructed minefields, strung barbed wire, built booby traps, and even dug in large cannons in the surrounding hills. All waiting for our approach.

Therefore, don't ever conclude that just because you are experiencing internal pressure or external trouble that the Lord isn't with you! Such thoughts stem from misinterpreting the nature of the ministry God has called us to. If you are not knowledgeable about this area, then visit a good Christian bookstore and start a reading program on Satan, strongholds, and spiritual warfare.

Maximizer 7: Lay yourself before the Lord as a clean vessel committed to revival.

The only thing that remains as we complete the Revival Maximizers is not the how of revival but the Who of revival. Now that you understand biblical revival, the only question to be answered is whether you will choose to be the person you need to be for God to work His wonderful revival through.

The choice is yours. Will you remain as merely a teacher or will you become a mighty vessel in the Master's hand? Don't allow yourself to settle for mere *transference of information* when you have been called to join in the *transformation of individuals*.

Now that you have been exposed to the ministry of revival, the only requirement that stands between you and that kind of supernatural ministry is for you to stand before God cleansed and committed to teaching God's truth God's way.

Take a moment as you come to the end of this teaching pilgrimage we have been sharing together and examine yourself instead of your students. If you try to call revival from your students when your heart is bound by sin, your words will stick in your throat. Your mouth will become as dry as a desert. Instead of your words bringing life and softening the hearts of your students, they may well harden their hearts.

On the other hand, there is nothing more powerful than the teacher in the midst of personal revival himself. He ministers out of the overflow of his life, and his students are swept along with him. Often when he ministers the class becomes quiet and pens are stilled because the students feel the movement of the Spirit in their midst.

If you need to kneel and confess to the Lord, then take courage, my friend. Follow in the steps of saints throughout the ages and humble yourself and repent! Confess your sins and claim the promised forgiveness.

CONCLUSION

Whenever revival is openly discussed, I almost want to take off my shoes, for the bush is burning and I sense we are standing on holy ground.

Whatever applications we may make, whatever needs we may address, whatever content we may teach, the crown of all of it is found when we take the heart of the student and place it in the hand of the Lord. How precious are those teachers whose hearts join with the heart of the Lord to "seek and restore those who have strayed."

Why not pause right where you are and make sure your heart is prepared for this ministry of revival? I hope that in reading these two chapters on revival, your heart was warmed, your resolve strengthened, and your skills sharpened. Take one last quiet moment to meditate on the "matters of the heart"—to make sure that your heart is right before the Lord, that He is free to move in you and free to speak through you, that no sin hinders His mighty arm, that no unwillingness blocks His powerful message.

Take then, Lord, a burning coal from off the altar before Your throne, as You did for Isaiah of old, and with it cleanse our lips—and our hearts.

Also I heard the voice of the Lord, saying: "Whom shall I send, and who will go for Us?" Then I said, *"Here am I! Send me."* (Isaiah 6:8)

Will you go, my friend? Will you speak for the Lord? Will you teach whatever He has commanded? Will you do your part to fulfill the Great Commission? Remember the words of Christ when He commissioned you and me:

"All authority has been given to Me in heaven and on earth. Go therefore and make disciples of all the nations, baptizing them in the name of the Father and of the Son and of the Holy Spirit,

teaching them to observe all things that I have commanded you; and lo,
I am with you always, even to the end of the age." Amen.
(Matthew 28:18–20)

Now that you understand revival, the Lord may very well test your
obedience to Him by sending right to your doorstep someone who has
a desperate need to be restored to the Lord.

I sincerely hope that when the moment arrives, you will not flee nor
allow yourself to remain silent. Instead, you will take courage, rely upon
the Lord, and shepherd that sheep caught in the thicket...the one the
Lord sent your way.

DISCUSSION QUESTIONS

1. Think of some Christian friends and family members whose lives were severely marred by their rebellion against what the Bible clearly teaches. How many of them do you think were approached by concerned believers seeking to restore them? What do you think would happen if we would take seriously our call to "restore such a one"?

2. Rationalizations are powerful hindrances to personal revival. When we live in disobedience to the Lord for any period of time, we naturally try to justify ourselves in our own sight. What are the normal rationalizations Christians make regarding God, their sin, and themselves? For instance, "God loves me and understands why I am doing this," or "No one is perfect and neither am I. My problems are just normal and things will work out in time."

3. Do you agree with the maximizer that says, "Revival is needed by most Christians most of the time"? What percentage of those who attend your church do you think may be out of fellowship at this moment? Why do you think this percentage is so high? What might be the three top reasons or sins that would cause this to be true? Since Galatians 6:1 commands us to restore people who are "overtaken," how could you obey this verse as a Sunday school teacher?

4. Take an objective view of your life for a moment. What are the primary Temptation Triggers and Commitment Cultivators presently in your life? If the apostle Paul wrote a letter to you today advising you on how to live more victoriously through deleting triggers and adding Cultivators, what would he say? If you followed his advice, how could your life be different?

5. Think back on your life to significant seasons of spiritual growth and revival. Select the time you were closest to Christ and describe how you felt and what you experienced. What do you think brought about that period of growth? What did you do during that time that was different? Was your life more or less fulfilling than it is now? To experience one of those special seasons of your life now, what would you have to do? Make a concrete plan and try it!

Epilogue

If *The 7 Laws of the Learner* accomplished its purpose in your life, then you now view teaching in a different light than when you began. After listening to me for a few hundred pages, you probably also have gotten to look into my heart a few times. The only downside for an author is that the communication is so one-way. Numerous times during the months that I labored to write what was on my heart and mind, I found myself wishing that I could just look you in the eye and make sure that I was communicating.

I'll know if I've communicated, however, by your life. The degree your communication improves will be the true test of the effectiveness of this pen and ink. If one of your students ever comes up to you and asks what wonderful thing got into you—then you and I will celebrate the moment together. And the writing of this book will have been worth all the effort.

Perhaps you are wondering what you can do to make sure these principles take full root in your life. Here are a couple of suggestions:

- Skim the same law for seven days in a row—glance
  through every page especially noting those charts and

sentences in bold print. Make sure you understand the "big idea" in the first half of the law and the "method" in the second. Try to memorize those five steps. Since there are seven laws, you would be spending forty-nine days of review. Time invested in such a way will surely produce good fruit in your life.

- Order the audio CD version of this series from Walk Thru the Bible Ministries (www.walkthru.org) and listen to it once a week for a couple of weeks straight. You'll be utterly amazed by how much you get from each session. (There's just something about reading it and then hearing it...) Much of the content in the audio series is different from what's in this book, so it will offer further insight and instruction.

- Encourage your church or school to invest in the 7 *Laws of the Learner* video series and suggest that they consider making it required viewing for all new teachers. Can you imagine the positive influences these concepts would have with the teachers?

- Sponsor a church- or school-wide seminar for *The 7 Laws of the Learner.* Many churches and schools have found it to be a very significant event in the church calendar, especially to begin the school year in September or January.

- The sister training course to this one is called *The 7 Laws of the Teacher* and features Dr. Howard G. Hendricks. If you enjoyed these principles, you will find these additional laws very stimulating and challenging. There is a textbook, audio series, and video series for your convenience.

- The next course in the Applied Principles of Learning (APL) series produced by Walk Thru the Bible after *The 7 Laws of the Learner* and *The 7 Laws of the Teacher* is

Teaching with Style and deals with the subjects of style, delivery, and creativity. If you would like to continue on in your pursuit of excellence in communication, then I would highly recommend Teaching with Style.

These, then, are the next steps that you would take to further your equipping as a teacher and communicator. Until I have the choice opportunity of meeting you in person, may the grace of the Lord enable you to teach with excellence!

Notes

Chapter 1

1. *Christianity Today,* April 10, 1981, 47.
2. *U.S. News & World Report,* September 8, 1980, 48.
3. Anthony Campolo, *Who Switched the Price Tags?* (Waco, TX: Word Books, 1986), 69–72.

Chapter 10

1. As of March 31, 2002, the Fellowship of Companies for Christ International, Inc., is under the management of Crown Financial Ministries.
2. Kurt Anderson, "Crashing on Cocaine," *Time,* April 11, 1983.

What happens when ordinary people start experiencing miracles— every day?

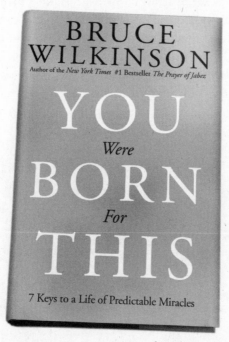

Most people believe that if God still works miracles, He only works through a select group of people—not them! The truth is, you were created to help people in need experience personal miracles. You were created to cooperate with God to accomplish His work by His power.

In *You Were Born for This*, you will discover that all God needs for a miracle mission is a willing servant. No special credentials required.

Looking for your purpose? Come discover what you were born for!

Find Bruce Wilkinson online

YouWereBornForThis.com • **twitter** • **facebook**

Secrets of the Vine

In this powerful follow-up to his bestseller *The Prayer of Jabez,* Bruce Wilkinson explores John 15 to show you how to make maximum impact for God. He demonstrates how Jesus is the Vine of life, discusses four levels of "fruit bearing" (doing the good work of God), and reveals three life-changing truths that will lead you to new joy and effectiveness in His kingdom. *Secrets of the Vine* will open your eyes to the Lord's hand in your life and uncover surprising insights that will point you toward a new path of consequence for God's glory.

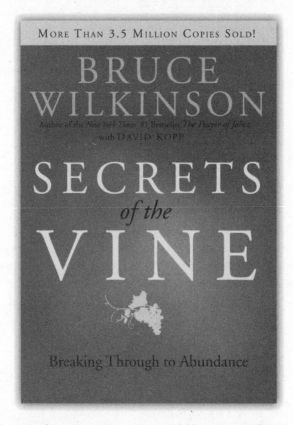

MORE THAN 3.5 MILLION COPIES SOLD!

BRUCE WILKINSON

Author of the *New York Times* #1 Bestseller *The Prayer of Jabez*

with DAVID KOPP

SECRETS *of the* VINE

Breaking Through to Abundance

Additional information and resources available at BruceWilkinson.com.

Discover How One Simple Prayer
Can Change Your Life

If you're ready to live life beyond limits and reach for the extraordinary, join Bruce Wilkinson as he explains how one simple daily prayer can help you leave the past behind—and break through to the extravagantly blessed life you were meant to live.

Since it was first released ten years ago, *The Prayer of Jabez* has impacted the lives of millions of people from virtually every walk of life.

Now you can discover how the remarkable prayer of a little-known Bible hero can release God's favor, power, and protection in your life today.

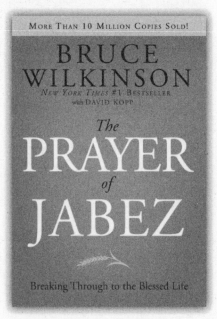

Additional information and resources available at BruceWilkinson.com.

A Life God Rewards

In this book, you'll discover that God's Son, Jesus, revealed a direct link between what you do today and what you will experience after you die. Astoundingly, the majority of spiritual seekers around the world—including millions who follow Jesus—seem to have missed what He said. Could you be one? If so, your picture of the future is missing about a billion stars. Author Bruce Wilkinson shows you what Jesus said about God's plan to reward you in eternity for what you do for Him today. What you'll discover will unlock the mystery of God's power, plan, and will for your life. And you'll begin to live with the unshakable certainty that what you do today matters...forever!

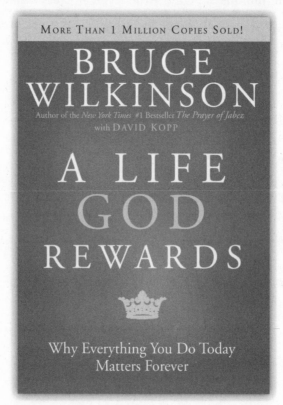

MORE THAN 1 MILLION COPIES SOLD!

BRUCE
WILKINSON

Author of the *New York Times* #1 Bestseller *The Prayer of Jabez*
with DAVID KOPP

A LIFE
GOD
REWARDS

Why Everything You Do Today
Matters Forever

Additional information and resources available at BruceWilkinson.com.

The Dream Giver

Your life dream is the key to God's greatest glory and your greatest fulfillment. There's no limit to what He can accomplish if you whole-heartedly pursue your created purpose! Let Bruce Wilkinson show you how to rise above the ordinary, conquer your fears, and overcome the obstacles that keep you from living your Big Dream.

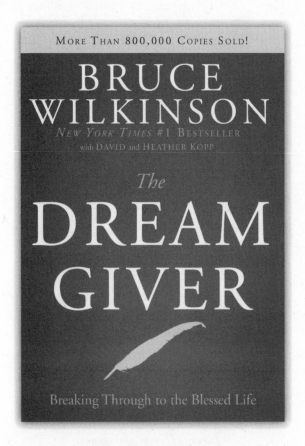

An Indispensible Tool
for Every Teacher!

THIS BOOK CONTAINS one hundred articles that provide insight, inspiration, and instruction for those who communicate God's truth at school, church, home, or in the workplace.

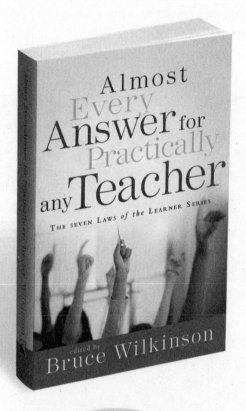

100 Articles handpicked by bestselling author Bruce Wilkinson